Iaido Sword

Iaido Sword

Kamimoto-Ha Techniques of Muso Shinden Ryu

Richard W. Babin, BS, M.D.

Paladin Press • Boulder, Colorado

Iaido Sword: Kamimoto-Ha Techniques of Muso Shinden Ryu
by Richard W. Babin, BS, M.D.

ISBN 1-58160-377-0
Printed in the United States of America

Published by Paladin Press, a division of
Paladin Enterprises, Inc.
Gunbarrel Tech Center
7077 Winchester Circle
Boulder, Colorado 80301 USA
+1.303.443.7250

Direct inquiries and/or orders to the above address.

Cover art by Debi Farmer, a bugeisha from New York City.

Visit our Web site at www.paladin-press.com

TABLE OF CONTENTS

DEDICATION

On December 7, 1941, forces of the Japanese Imperial Navy attacked Pearl Harbor, striking fear into the hearts of West Coast residents. On February 24, 1942, President Franklin D. Roosevelt signed executive order 9066 putting Japanese Americans in internment camps for the duration of the war. This act resulted in confiscation of their personal property, separation of their families, and catastrophic suffering. Their children, however, were allowed to leave the camps to fight and die in Europe, while their parents continued to be humiliated at home.

This handbook is dedicated to the memory of the members of the Delta Ginsha Haiku Kai. First incarcerated in the Stockton (California) Assembly Center (the Fairgrounds) and later moved to concentration camps in Jerome and Rohwer, Arkansas, they continued to express strength and hope through their poetry.

It is also dedicated to my parents, Max and Thelma Babin of San Francisco, who by personal example taught me to seek out and enjoy the unique wisdom and beauty of other people and other cultures.

Autumn foliage
California has now become
A far country
—Yajin Nakao, 1943
(May Sky: There is Always Tomorrow)

加州を偲ぶ

今は遠き国となり樹々紅葉す

ACKNOWLEDGEMENTS

A cut is a block and a block is a cut.
—Harry Dach

If you are going to have someone tell you how to live,
be certain they know more about living than you do.
—Glenn Morris, Martial Arts Madness

I am indebted to my sensei, Harry Dach of Memphis, Tennessee, who not only introduced me to the art of iaido but provided much of the information and spirit contained in this book not only for me but for all the swordsmen pictured in it. Retired U.S. Marine, Vietnam veteran, electronics teacher, herbalist, graphic artist, bugeisha and dreamer, Dach Sensei carries in his heart the precepts of bushido. His 10 years of training from Nakagaki Takashi Sensei of Yamaguchi prefecture, himself the first three-time All-Japan Kendo Federation iaido champion, lead to a Godan in iaido awarded in Japan. He also developed high-level skills in kendo, judo, kenjutsu and the use of the sai. On the untimely death of Nakahama Sensei, his kendo master, he undertook a *musha shugyo* in his honor, walking the width of Japan and practicing in the dojos he encountered along the way. Dach Sensei provides a model of a tested warrior for his students and peers alike.

I am further grateful for the hours of supervision of John Aquadro Sensei, whose dedication to excellence is infectious and whose modesty belies a skill far greater than the arbitrary rank he holds. He is the swordsman in most of the photos in Sections 3 and 4 of this book. His efforts on my behalf are responsible for much of whatever skill I might demonstrate in this art. Likewise the constructive criticism, advice, and fellowship of the students both senior and junior I have had the honor of studying with contributed greatly to my growth both technically and as a bugeisha. In particular, Russell Davis, of Covington, Tennessee, the primary swordsman of Section 2 of this book, has been a good friend and an inspiration. He proofread this manuscript for two of its reincarnations and has aided and abetted my efforts at both writing and sword restoration. Others serving as models in this text include Craig Joe (*suwari waza*), Don Crittenden (*Omori*), Brook Crihfield (*seitei*), Mark Chevalier (*Eishin*), Gary Chase, and Shawn Hanley.

Special thanks are due Thomas Hooper Sensei, rokudan and master of Ken Zen Dojo in New York City who graciously reviewed this manuscript and offered critical suggestions in both context and grammar. The crisp, spirited, and precise technique of his, and of his students, has been a personal inspiration. The generous and knowledgeable instruction provided by Hooper Sensei and the other sensei and shimpan of five years of AUSKF annual iaido summer camps is also tightly entwined throughout these pages. Thank you for sharing your insight and your talents so unselfishly in the pursuit of excellence. The understanding and encouragement of Yamaguchi Tadeshi Sensei, Murakami Ichiro Sensei, and Konno Tetsuhiku Sensei, teachers and swordsmen of great authority, and in the latter case, sword polisher and appraiser as well, have often made the difference in my personal quest.

Other information in this book refers to sources when known. All opinions are those of the author alone and do not necessarily represent those of any organization, dojo, or other individual. Any errors in either history or technique are the lone responsibility of the author and his incomplete knowledge of this fascinating and intricate art.

Richard W. Babin
Covington, Tennessee
July 2002

FOREWORD

At times, because of one man's evil, thousands of people suffer. So you kill that one man in order to let the thousands live. Here, truly, the blade that deals death could be the sword that gives life.
— *Munenori Yagyu,* The Sword and the Mind

We cannot deny what we are. Let Mongaku say what he will about the universe and the impermanence of all things. Life is short and the warrior's honor is everything.
—*Eiji Yoshikawa,* The Heike Story

OK, so why are we here? Most of us do not have samurai ancestors, and have probably never lived in or near an Asian culture. Most of us haven't, won't, and don't ever want to have to defend ourselves with a sword. Most of us are actually too busy to make time to learn any of this in the first place. So what ticks?

I've heard it said that *iaidoka* are able to practice a purer martial art for the very reason that it is not subject to the judgment of the gurus as "practical" or, even worse, "realistic." There is some truth in that, but it is not so esoteric. While the trappings of a given discipline may vary greatly from another, there are many features, usually not overt, that they share. Thus balance, timing, awareness, power, intent, spirit, and fighting distance are very similar among all martial arts. In arts that are technique rich, such as karate or aikido, these deeper factors may be obscured to a student by the demands of the technique.

Iaido is unique in that, to a great extent, all extraneous technique has been stripped from the art. It has been pared to the lowest common denominator. For this reason, it is an ideal vehicle for a martial artist to individually bring out each of these basic factors from within himself, examine them and perfect them. In this regard it is much like taiji. Furthermore, many of the strikes, blocks, and throws of the various Japanese arts were derived from the sword arts or for the empty-hand defense against a blade. Thus a study of a sword art can provide great insight into the reasons why certain techniques are included in an art's curriculum. For these reasons a study of iaido can enrich the practice of most other fighting arts. The techniques of any martial art are subservient to the mind-set of the practitioner. Iaido also offers much to an individual who does not consider himself a warrior. Just as Musashi's *Book of Five Rings* has been adopted as a guide to survival in the business world, so iaido can be used by an individual to study and perfect a variety of personal qualities. Martial arts training and, in particular, the study of iaido, gives you confidence and courage, a philosophy of survival, an understanding of your abilities and limits and, maybe, better physical and mental reflexes as a result of the practice.

I suspect many of us are currently drawn to oriental martial arts because we perceive the value system of our society as somehow wanting. Certainly the equalizer of the Old West and the protector of our freedom for the past 200 years, the firearm, has been maligned to the point that many of us are embarrassed to publicly express faith in our Second Amendment rights any more. My generation at least, grew up with the ethics of the Western movie: the rugged individualist who acted on his beliefs, the outcast who put himself apart from the herd but was willing to respond to its distress, the hero a little on the fringes—John Wayne, Shane, Tom Mix, Doc Holliday, Paladin, and Matt Dillon. Somehow the images don't work for us any more. Something ominous has disillusioned us. Fortunately, we can still adopt heroes of the same ilk who are yet to be tarnished by our culture's cynicism. We can identify with Toshiro Mifune in *Yojimbo* or, in my case, *Red Beard*. We can be the 48th Ronin. We can protect our cub and our society like Itto Ogami. And we can adopt the strength of the sword, that awesome and mysterious power of both the East and the West, as a symbol of our unique resolve as an individual who stands apart from the mass of our rude, selfish, and insensitive brothers and sisters.

Most practitioners of martial arts in our society cannot spend the time necessary to progress as Japanese *budoka* of old. Not only does that slow our overall development because of less practice time, but it also introduces more errors because of weeklong gaps in supervision. The overwhelming motivation in creating this workbook was to provide a document to help jolt the memory of fellow students of muso shinden ryu iaido who, like me, forget much of the detail and frequently the basics between weekly classes. Practicing between classes, even without the supervision of at least a fellow student, is still very desirable. It bears the risk, however, of allowing more bad habits to be incorporated into "muscle memory" due to deficient "brain memory." This book attempts to directly combat that problem.

It is absolutely true that you cannot learn iaido from books or tapes; every book or tape on martial art techniques carefully and rightfully points this out. A knowledgeable, dedicated sensei and constant hard training are the two absolutely essential elements of successfully studying any *budo*. That does not, however, invalidate the ancillary benefit of a written record to consult regarding specific points of technique during individual practice. Likewise written descriptions can facilitate quiet contemplation of the techniques learned at the last class and stimulate insight into their true form and significance.

In an attempt to document the technical aspects of iaido, it was virtually impossible for me, an iaidoka who loves the art, to suppress the urge to try to share with the reader some of the insights into Japanese culture and history I have accumulated along the way. To me, they are an integral part of the art and help to create a tapestry of great beauty. Thus this workbook has grown into something more than just a book of techniques. An effort was made, however, to keep this a practical and affordable manual to be used over and over: something useful to keep in the gym bag, not just left in a bookcase after one superficial scan of its pages.

There is a modicum of religion in this book because Japanese culture is inseparable from it. It is offered for two reasons only: first, some understanding of Buddhism and Shinto is necessary to understand Japanese history, and second, iaido is at least heavily influenced by, and perhaps completely, a Zen activity. There is nothing in the study or practice of the art, however, that need be at odds with the personal beliefs of the Western budoka. Iaido may challenge and ultimately strengthen your personal religious beliefs, but it will not replace them with something foreign. It will, with your effort, add something very human and maybe spiritual to your life and philosophy. It is not necessary to study Zen to do iaido well, but it helps. If you do iaido well, you don't need to study Zen, just live your iaido.

The bottom line is if you are going to play iaido, you are going to have to come to grips with life and death. To that end, the techniques of one school versus another school have no significance. We are all brothers and sisters in this *musha shugyo,* and what unites us is attitude. I am sure that many budoka of all ages and schools will find much here to disagree with. I take no issue with their understanding of this art and offer this material in the spirit of open dialogue, not dogma. If you find any value in these pages it is yours to keep, but please also pass it along to someone else it might help.

An original motivation for me to record the techniques of our dojo was to save them from as much inadvertent change as possible. Fortunately, our dojo has had the benefit of numerous published documents, movies, and videotapes of our sensei of the past that seem to validate our claim to legitimacy. What has proven amazing, however, is that people see what they want to see in these visual aids. Also, the more I have had the benefit of exposure to other ryu-ha, the more I have seen the weaknesses in their and, by projection, our transmission. I can only assume that other transmissions are no more or less accurate than ours and that no one has a claim of absolute authenticity. For these reasons, I have tried to indicate without bias when other traditions with which I am familiar differ from ours.

Section One
History

Another arrow whined; as Yoshihira ducked, Shigemori quickly drew his sword. Steel flashed white against steel; stirrups grated against one another. Whirling, dodging, feinting, and charging in a spectacle of brilliant horsemanship, pursued and pursuing, the two youths rode furiously seven times and then eight round the cherry and orange trees. Their swords grazed, slashed at the air, and seemed to clash in a shower of sparks.

—Eiji Yoshikawa, The Heike Story

It should be known that both "the sword" and "the pen" are instruments for the ruler to use in his affairs. However, at the beginning of a dynasty, so long as its people are occupied in establishing power, the need for "the sword" is greater.

—Ibn Kaldoun, Muqaddimah

INTRODUCTION

The temple bell echoes the impermanence of all things. The colors of the flowers testify to the truth that those who flourish must decay. Pride lasts but a little while, like a dream on a spring night. Before long the mighty are cast down, and they are as dust before the wind.

—Tales of the Heike

From the earliest days of feudal Japan, warriors sought out instruction in inspired martial techniques. Early on, this could not be done in any kind of formal fashion, but survivors of battles could be approached for instruction in their particular methods, which were in no way standardized or even necessarily organized but had at least passed an initial "trial by fire." This process matured as techniques were formalized until samurai eventually studied entire martial art systems involving unarmed techniques and a variety of weapons and other tools, afoot, on horseback, and ub swimming. These methods provided a large lexicon upon which the professional warrior could draw, no matter how a battle progressed.

Individual Japanese budo reached its zenith during the Warring States period, the *sengoku jidai,* when each feudal domain sought to exert the greatest influence in the archipelago. After the Tokugawa shogunate pacified the empire (1615 A.D.), samurai adapted to their new roles by beginning to study skills not overtly martial, such as the tea ceremony, calligraphy, poetry, and the strategy game of *go*, as well as the increasing administrative requirements of the martial-political government, the *bakufu*. With the greatly reduced need for fighting men, many warriors were forced to teach martial skills to others outside their particular school, or even social class, in order to earn a living. Less and less time was available to pursue excellence in all facets of warfare. This all resulted in the curriculum of the original schools being broken up into smaller packages of common techniques, *jutsu,* easier to grasp and teach to students with less and less time to devote to martial concerns. These techniques, including the two sword arts, *kenjutsu* and *iaijutsu,* gradually became entities in themselves developing individual followers who might or might not study other techniques. Toward the end of the Edo period, the military had become so weak and budo so diluted that the nation could not seriously attempt to defend itself from the sudden thrust of the West in the person of Commodore Matthew Perry and his "black ships."

Following the Meiji Restoration in 1868, when the shogunate collapsed and the emperor was restored to power, the samurai lost their status and their right to wear swords. Martial arts were discouraged, and the proponents of the jutsu were forced to change the basic purpose of their techniques for their individual and their art's survival. Falling back on Buddhist principles, the jutsu were refined and distilled into simplified representative *kata* with which the practitioner could strive for personal excellence, introspection, and perhaps enlightenment. This process did not put something in the jutsu that was not there before but simply emphasized the inner or hidden side (*ura*) of the art as opposed to the outer or overt (*omote*). Thus the jutsu that did not disappear were transformed into "ways" or *do* and have grown over the last century into the arts we practice today. They are the direct descendents of techniques born of the efforts of centuries of samurai who literally gave their lives to validate them.

Iaido is the art of drawing and cutting one or more opponents, tossing blood off the blade, and returning it to the scabbard or *saya*. Unlike the battlefield techniques exhibited by *kendo* in which the sword is already drawn, iaido does not start from any formal stance, or *kamae,* because the attack is not immediately anticipated. Thus the iaidoka must (as did the samurai) continuously be in a heightened state of awareness or *zanshin*. This is completely analogous to the "combat mind-set" or "condition yellow" described in self-defense and combat handgun literature (Cooper, 1988). This sense of alertness not only applies to the possible offensive actions of others. Care must be taken when wearing the sword that it is not subject to being grabbed, immobilized, or simply dropped out of the saya. On the other hand it must always be immediately serviceable. This is again analogous to the handling of modern combat weapons.

Iaido is a distillation of earlier sword-handling techniques, kenjutsu, *iaijutsu* and *battojutsu*. The essences of those techniques were woven into kata, which preserve their original spirit while adding an economy of motion not inherent in practical *bujutsu*. Iaido kata are closely related to, but are not strictly, practical sword applications. Their goal is to attack and slay the enemy within rather than the one without. One goal of iaido is for the sword to become an extension of the body and mind of the practitioner who then can use it in an entirely natural "without thought" manner, *mushin*. The ultimate goal of the art, as with other budo, is as a tool for discovering one's self in a typical Zen Buddhist manner of blending the physical, mental and spiritual. This is exemplified by the phrase *ki ken tai ichi*—breath, sword, mind, one. Since there is no chance of attaining perfection in this life, iaido is an unending endeavor. The joy is in the journey, for there is no final destination. Respect is another tool used for this self-discovery. Indeed technique, *heiho*, and ritual etiquette, *reiho*, cannot easily be separated in iaido. Respect shown to the spirit of the dojo, the sensei and his lineage, and to fellow students is a basic part of the discovery process and precedes and ends any iaido demonstration or teaching session. Iaido is considered a traditional budo by the Japanese. Because of this, iaido includes respect for the generations of *bugeisha* who bled in the development of its techniques, the iaidoka who fabricated these techniques into an art, and the culture that spawned it.

There are many schools or streams (*ryu-ha*) of iaido depending on the traditions and techniques being preserved. The two most commonly encountered in the West are *Muso Shinden ryu* and *Jikiden Eishin ryu*. These are closely related, splitting from the same tradition around 200 years ago. From that point until the present they took a more or less parallel course with each other. Many kata are shared with varying differences in technique and emphasis and their names may be entirely different. There are several excellent books available describing the techniques of the Jikiden Eishin ryu. This handbook concerns itself with muso shinden ryu (true, spirit-inspired pathway) as practiced by Kamimoto Eiichi sensei. This pathway is divided into levels of complexity. The beginning techniques, or *shoden,* are composed of defenses starting from the formal kneeling position, *seiza*, and are named *Omori ryu* techniques. The second level, or *chuden*, is from *Eishin ryu* techniques and starts from the semi-sitting position called *tatehiza*. The last group, *okuden* (hidden) techniques, starts from both tatehiza and the standing position, *tachi*. Many of these advanced techniques revolve around very specific situations such as kneeling in a doorway, sliding under a stairway, or cutting someone from an elevated balcony.

During the 1960s, a perceived lack of insight by *kenshi* and the desire for competition among iaidoka led to the "invention" of a basic set of kata by the All-Japan Kendo Federation (Zen Nihon Kendo Renmei, ZNKR), one of the governing bodies in Japan. Termed *seitei* (representative) these were taken from the typical moves of a variety of schools. Originally seven, these 12 kata are not part of any one school's tradition but are meant to provide a standard by which members of different schools can compare their talents. They have undergone relatively minor changes over the intervening 30 years. However, in an endeavor whose ideal—if not absolute goal—is perfection, even minor differences are major issues. Attempts are now being made by the All-United States Kendo Federation (AUSKF) to standardize these techniques in the United States. It seems likely that there will always be changes creeping into these artificial kata but since they are contrived anyway, this does not represent a break with the past sacrifices of generations of warriors. In many schools of iaido, the seitei have become the de facto beginning techniques taught to students. In AUSKF promotional testing, all *kyu* (student) ranks and the first level of *dan* (black belt) ranks concern the seitei kata exclusively. The seitei were never intended to influence the traditional techniques *(koryu)* of any school or individual. Indeed the only standards for koryu are any remaining records and the surviving sensei of that particular stream.

The preceding is not to suggest that the adoption of the seitei set is either universally accepted or somehow "better" or "worse" than not using the seitei set. A second governing body in Japan, the All-Japan Iaido Federation (Zen Nihon Iaido Renmei, ZNIR) was not involved with nor ever accepted the seitei *waza* (technique) and has its own basic set called *toho*. Thus, not only are there various ryu of iaido, there are ryu going by the same name that either follow the ZNKR and include seitei or follow the ZNIR and do not.

This handbook concerns itself with a ryu that originated in Tokyo and matured in Yamaguchi Prefecture that follows the muso shinden tradition and has within its lineage one of the members of the ZNKR committee that founded the seitei kata.

HISTORY OF JAPAN

In my view, the bearing of swords is a custom that characterized our Land of Jimmu even in the ancient era of the Gods. It is intimately bound up with the origins of our nation, it enhances the dignity of the Imperial Throne, solemnizes the rites of the Gods, banishes the spirits of evil, puts down disorders. The sword, therefore, not only maintains the tranquility of the nation but also guards the safety of the individual citizen. Indeed, the one thing essential to this martial nation that reveres the Gods, the one thing never to be put aside even for an instant, is the sword.

—*Yukio Mishima,* Runaway Horses

Iai-do is a unique blend of the ethics of Confucianism, the introspective methods of Zen, the naturalness of philosophical Taoism toned by the severity of bushido.

—*Warner and Draeger,* Swordsmanship Techniques and Practice

In order to get a true feeling for the written history of Japan the Western reader must realize that the indigenous religion of Japan, Shinto, is an animistic one. It recognizes local spirits or *kami*, in animate and inanimate objects within the local environment who interface with the affairs of man. It is similar in that respect to the beliefs of the indigenous tribes of the Americas. While any natural object can or does have an associated spirit, the most auspicious are those associated with the more spectacular natural phenomena such as waterfalls, hot springs, lakes, or mountains. However, personal homes, ponds, and rocks also have their kami. This belief leads to a relationship of a Japanese individual to his surroundings that is of much greater depth than what the average American might consider, even one living near or visiting a beautiful or challenging natural area. In many ways Shinto is more an expression of "Japanese-ness" than an organized theology. It does not have prophets, a formal text, or even much of a philosophy but concerns itself with ritual. In Japan the land itself functions as a collection of natural as well as man-made shrines to the kami.

Another extremely important influence on day-to-day activities throughout Japanese history is the spirits of the deceased members of the family or clan. Aged persons are venerated in the East, and the natural extension of that concept is the continued influence of their memory and how it affects the decisions made by the living. Ancestors return to visit the living in Japanese villages during the annual *Bon* festival, celebrated on August 15. Shrines in the home honor family relatives in the same manner that the shrines in Nikko, for example, honor Tokugawa Ieyasu. Throughout much of Japanese history Buddhism and Shinto were nurtured by the courts of the emperor and of the shogun, respectively. There remained a large gap between these formal teachings and the beliefs of the common classes of Japanese. It was not until the Meiji restoration that any kind of resolution of this gap occurred.

So far much of this may not seem to be closely related to Japanese history. However, from long before the beginning of recorded history, the Japanese considered their emperors the descendents of the sun goddess Amateratsu through her son, the first human Japanese emperor, Jimmu. Japan was/is the land of the Gods and the Japanese, their chosen people. The history of Japan as compiled by the Japanese can be looked at in a similar fashion as the Bible's presentation of the Old Testament history of Judea. Both are purportedly the historical records of a warrior state, written piecemeal by themselves at some time after the events portrayed and compiled using the values of a later age. They pursue the justification of the actions of their major players—emperors, *daimyo*, generals, shogun, priests, and poets—in terms of both divinity and human frailty as filtered through their moral and ethical beliefs. There, of course, the similarity ends, for Japanese historical records are devoid of commandments or overt moral imperatives. Most reflect the dynamic interplay

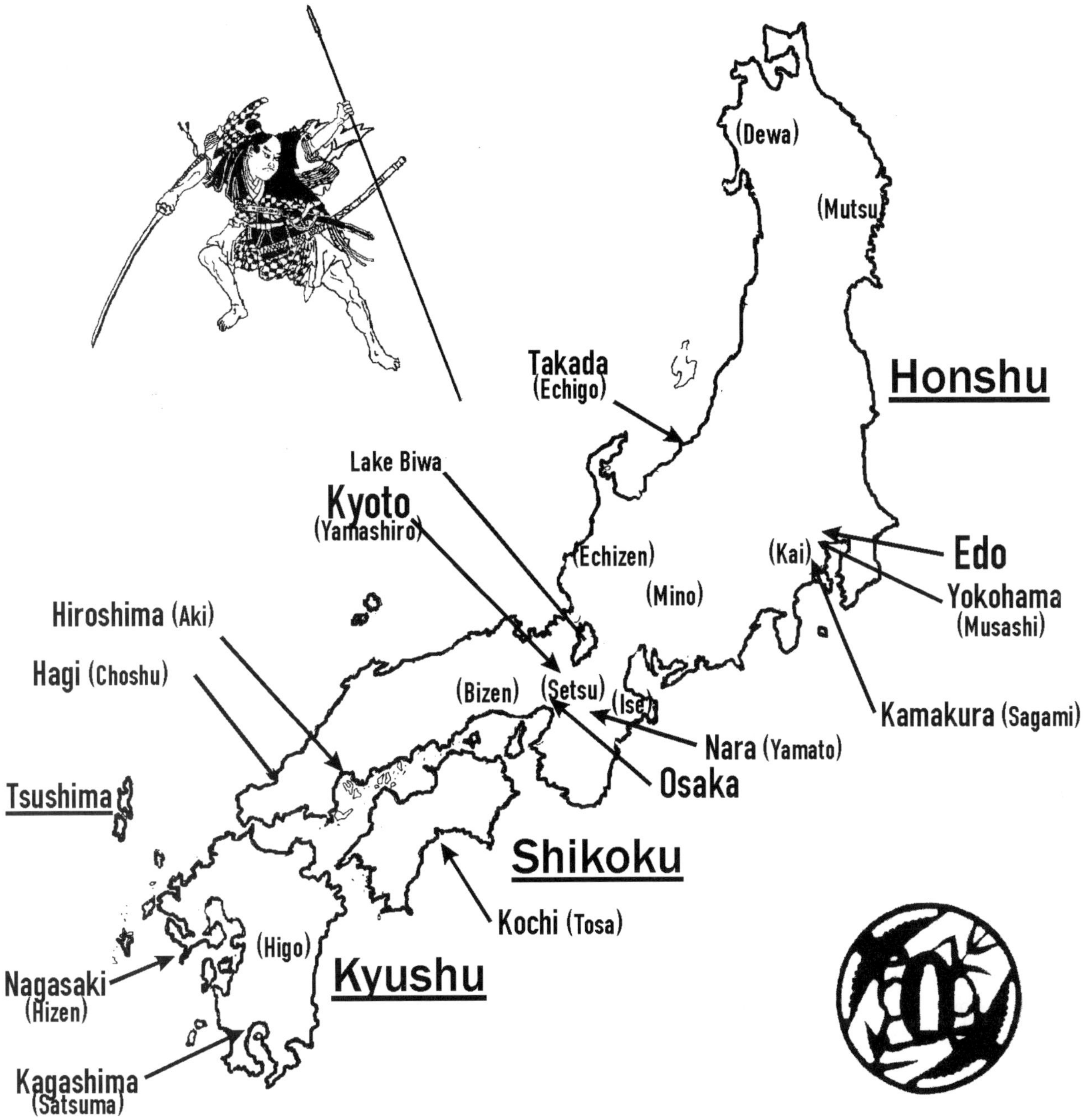

Figure 1: Map of the southernmost islands of Japan (underlined). Locations of cities are noted by the arrows and old domains are given in parentheses. Note that these names are neither contemporary nor necessarily coincident.

between historical figures and the dominant natural world that served as their stage.

During the period between about 600-700 A.D. Buddhism exploded in Japan. Common belief attributes the spread of Buddhism from India to China by Daruma, the semilegendary prince turned teacher of the faith. He also is credited with introducing boxing to the Shaolin monastery and therefore is considered the father of all Asian martial arts. Buddhist influence first came to Japan via Korea and, later, directly from China. The Japanese court in Nara at that time was bringing Chinese culture to Japan on a big scale as a means of organizing itself and society for the first time for a semblance of a nation. The social philosophy of Confucius, the worldview of Taoism, and the morality of Buddhism found symbiosis with the native Shinto beliefs of the Japanese. The most influential in budo were the concepts of Zen Buddhism introduced by two sects, Rinzai by Eisai and Soto by Dogen. Each stressed living for the moment, emptying the mind by means of meditation, acting without excessive intellectualizing, considering death a natural part of life, and accepting fate as an article of cause and effect (karma). These are obviously very practical concepts for a man prepared to die at a moment's notice for the needs of his liege lord.

The imperial court in Kyoto during the Heian period expressed all that the Japanese found worthy in Chinese culture, philosophy, art, literature, and administration. Unfortunately, no matter how well the Chinese model of government might have worked in China, it was ill suited to the Japanese. Over time, through political intrigue and treachery, a warrior clan, the Fujiwara, serving as regents to the emperor, usurped the real power—control over the land and the crops and taxes it produced. In turn, rural landholding clans at a distance from the capital withheld taxes, raised large effective armies, and drained the power of the Fujiwara. Foremost among these were the Taira and Minamoto clans who vied for position through a host of battles, the last of which was finally won by the Minamoto. They moved the effective capitol to Kamakura and the first military governor's court (shogunate) was established. With the eventual collapse of the Kamakura court, military power returned to Kyoto in the form of the Ashikaga shoguns. From that point until the eventual dominance of the Tokugawa clan, the country was immersed in endless fighting between feudal lords (daimyo) who ruled family-organized domains (*ryogoku*). These domains, of which there were some 250, were nominally answerable to the central imperial and shogunal authority; however, they became progressively independent. They were much stronger than states or prefectures as we know them and had the potential for as much autonomy as a country, including foreign and economic policy, de facto taxation, and separate armies and navies. In fact, up until the Meiji Restoration these feudal domains were called *kuni* in Japanese, which means "country." Japan itself was referred to as *tenka*, "all under heaven." One of the earliest actions of the Meiji government was to rename the domains *han*, from the Chinese, in an attempt to redefine and weaken the role of the *kuni*.

This period of power plays among the daimyo of the most powerful domains between the Kamakura and the Edo periods is called the Warring States period. It was then, due to the hierarchical family organization of the samurai culture and its emphasis on loyalty to the titular head of the household, that the concepts of *bushido* matured. It is during this period of continuous warfare that the martial arts achieved their highest level of development. Many of the tales and legends portrayed in samurai movies (*chambara* and *jidaigeki*) and in noh and kabuki theater took place during this period. It is also during this period of relative isolation and decentralization that Japanese life, art, and culture developed the distinct characteristics we recognize today: for example, the standard unit of floor space, the standard cut of clothes, and handicrafts and manufactures. Toward the end of this period while the three or four most powerful daimyo were vying for dominance, a relatively low-ranking samurai gained control over the imperial capital, Kyoto, and eventually unified most of the clans by force of arms.

During the Tokugawa shogunate and its enforced peace *(tenka taihei)*, organized military power and individual warrior talent gradually diminished in strength. The Tokugawa clan initially had great authority both militarily and economically by its force of arms and through the ryogoku led by relatives and vassals loyal to them. On the other hand, increasing dissatisfaction among the disenfranchised rogue warriors (ronin) lead to several unsuccessful coupe attempts during and following the rule of the third Tokugawa shogun, Iemitsu.

The relative weakness of both Shinto and Buddhism during this time left an ethical vacuum, which was filled in part by the adoption of principles expounded by the neo-Confucionists who indirectly influenced the *bakufu*. The state economy was based on the service commitment of each member of society to the next highest level. As time went by, many individual domains continued to develop great local authority and economic strength. Eventually, some domains with no particular loyalty to the Tokugawa clan began to undermine and covet the clan's absolute authority.

Originally active in the exporting of mined products, the Tokugawa bakufu gradually reduced such activities, degrading foreign trade to simply gathering information and maintaining political and ritual relationships. As late as the 19th century there was little concept of "national wealth" in terms of the entire Japanese archipelago. Such a concept would only emerge as the West dragged the fledgling Japanese nation kicking and screaming into the modern world. Individual domains, on the other hand, began to develop strong illicit economies based on local manufacture and agricultural trade with the mainland. They also developed their own manner of dealing with the imperial court. Thus the seeds were sown for a growing discontent with the Tokugawa bakufu and the gradual improvement in the fortunes of the merchant classes. (Most of these independently minded domains were in the southern end of the nation and included Tosa, Satsuma, and Choshu.)

When the West so audaciously imposed itself on Japan in the person of Commodore Perry, there was no hope of forcibly preventing the "opening" of the country. The Tokugawa power stemmed from control of protocol and the allegiance of daimyo, not from direct control of the land or commerce. Out of the frustration of Western involvement grew a violent anti-bakufu movement of imperial loyalists based in Tosa, Choshu, and Satsuma. Interestingly, the French failed to see the handwriting on the wall and continued to support the shogunate, while the British recognized the southern kuni as the potential new leaders of the nation. Had the imperial loyalists not prevailed, there probably would have been a southern shogunate.

Many leaders of these "men of high purpose," or *shishi*, pro-imperialist samurai, were noted teachers of swordsmanship in Tosa and included Takechi Hanpeita and Sakamoto Ryoma (Hillsborough, 1999). Both of these men, and most of their followers, were from the lower class of samurai who, with the exception those of Choshu, were generally opposed by their own daimyo. The strict rules imposed on the residents of Tosa by the ruling Yamanouchi clan prohibited them from leaving their villages or the island of Shikoku. Many were forced to flee Tosa and become ronin, an act that the Yamanouchi had made a capital offense. Many of the leaders of this movement wished to oust the Western forces, but realized to do so they would have to adopt Western technology first. That meant leaving Japan open to the Europeans long enough to buy, steal, and copy their technology.

The Tokugawa hegemony eventually crumbled under this pressure, and the emperor was brought back to power. The fact that the imperial court had not had any practical political experience for 700 years was not a minor problem. The new government was faced with a poorly defined sense of nationalism, a head of state whose lifestyle and history were essentially unknown to the vast number of common citizens, an economy based on local agriculture and trading crafts between domains, a national religion that was almost defunct, and a conflict between the ancient history of the people and the country's need to emerge as a power in the modern industrial world.

The emperor and his advisors went about virtually reinventing a Japanese polity (*kokutai*) as a unified imperial state—rewriting Japanese history, creating "ancient" ceremonies and myths, and establishing a new Shinto to further their aims (Fujitana, 1998). In the process, what had originally been complete dedication to the feudal clan leader by members of the warrior class was transmuted into a blind allegiance by all classes to the emperor.

Unfortunately for the bugeisha, this turn of events quickly resulted in loss of their social and economic power. The samurai lost their topknots, swords, and social status. They were replaced and repressed by a national army of professional soldiers recruited for the most part from the lower classes. Forced into commerce to survive, a role they were eminently unsuited for, many lost all their personal wealth and honor. The abortive if flamboyant attempt of the Satsuma samurai to reinstate the shogunate (with themselves at its head) in 1877 was the last example of warfare using swords in Japan. It conjures up the image of waves of sword-welding samurai falling under a hail of bullets from repeating rifles fired by conscripts. In the meantime the sweeping tide of nationalism in all social levels resulted in the concept that "what was Japanese belonged to the Gods so it had to be correct by definition." Once the samurai became irrelevant in modern Japanese society, he at once became the mythic hero, somewhat analogous to the Native American and his cowboy nemesis in the United States.

From almost the time of the fall of the Tokugawa bakufu there were calls for a constitution. Finally in 1890 the Meiji constitution became a reality, influenced strongly by the Prussian monarchy. The emperor was the only one who could amend the constitution and had supreme power over the established cabinet and legislative body (the Diet). The military was directly under his control and he retained the sole right to sign treaties. Completion of the construction of the Imperial Palace in Tokyo was timed to just precede the presentation of the constitution and the establishment of the Diet and followed a prolonged, agonizing discussion of the relative place of the ancient capital (Kyoto) and modern (Tokyo).

Following Japanese triumphs in the Sino- and Russo-Japanese wars, in which Japan gained solid hegemony in Korea and Manchuria, it emerged into the 20th century as the manufacturing giant of Asia. The politics of the first three decades of the 1900s were a confusion of ultraright, socialist, and communist parties with cabinets rising and falling with rapidity. The militarist-ultranationalists eventually prevailed, resulting in military excursions into Manchuria, China, and eventually the Rape of Nanking (Nanjing). The dream of a greater Asia dominated by the Japanese nation ended in their defeat in the Pacific War. Occupation resulted in a new constitution, essentially pacifist, with a representative congress and a constitutional monarch who renounced his previous status as a deity.

OUTLINE OF JAPANESE HISTORY

Asuka breezes that once curled back the palace maiden's sleeves,
Seeing now the court so far
They blow quite purposelessly.
—Man'yoshu: 51

The outline below is a very Western way of looking at Japanese martial history. While it is useful for putting the events of Japanese martial arts development in some perspective, it should be realized that this is not a Japanese perspective.

Mythic Age

- The Japanese islands coalesce from water dripping from the coral spear, wielded by Izanagi, father of the gods. He and his wife Izanami bring forth the other gods, including the sun goddess, Amateratsu. At some point she presents the emperor of paleo-Japan with a mirror. This is one of the three great treasures of the empire, believed to be enshrined at Ise Grand Shrine.

Jomon Period (10,000 B.C. – 300 B.C.)

- As the neolithic period begins, the Stone Age hunter-gatherers coalesce into small communities, primarily in eastern Japan, where they can put food and drink in storage vessels.
- The earliest earthenware pottery known to exist anywhere in the world is a Jomon vase found in Fukui prefecture that has been dated at 10,000 B.C. This pottery is decorated with a characteristic rope pattern.
- Unlike the rest of Asia, the neolithic peoples of Japan did not develop an agrarian society for another 8,000 years, probably because game, wild fruits, and shellfish were so plentiful.
- The earliest examples of the use of lacquerware, fragments of combs, and vessels date from the end of this period.

Yayoi Period (300 B.C. – 400 A.D.)

- The Bronze Age is ushered in around 200 B.C. by exposure to the early metal cultures of Han China via the Korean peninsula.
- This appears to have followed the settlement of western Japan by a physically larger group of peoples who introduced rice farming including waterway construction and storehouses. Unlike the Jomon culture the Yayoi pottery was fashioned on a potter's wheel.
- Bronze is replaced with iron for edged weapons and ritual objects, most likely again by Chinese influence via the Korean peninsula.

Protohistoric Age (100 – 400 A.D.)

- The age of ancient clans and the first social classes begins.
- According to the Kokiji and Nihon Shoki, Prince Yamato uses a "cloud-cluster" sword to sweep burning grass asunder. The sword is renamed "grass mowing sword" (*kusinagi*) and becomes another of the three treasured regal symbols of the empire: sword, mirror, and jewel. While part of the mythic history, this is described as occurring during this historical age.
- The first known Chinese record of Japanese culture is written during the Wei dynasty (before 292 A.D.) in which it is recorded that the Chinese emperor gave bronze mirrors to the embassy of Queen Himiko of Yamatai.
- The Japanese clans push the Japanese aboriginal tribes, Ainu, farther and farther northward as

they spread across the inland sea to the fertile Kinai Plain in southern Honshu.
- The Japanese establish a colony, or at least a permanent military base, on the southern tip of the Korean Peninsula (Mimana) by 359 A.D. Their Korean ally against the Kingdom of Silla, the Kingdom of Poikche, sends learned men and books as thanks for the Japanese support, which introduces Chinese script to Japan.

Kofun Period (400 – 600)
- Local and central political leaders are buried in large key-shaped mounds (*kofun*), primarily in the western and middle parts of Japan. The largest were some 400 meters across and signify concentration of power in discrete parts of Japan and the early establishment of rudimentary "states."
- Harnesses and armor recovered from these mounds closely resemble those from the same time period in Korea, suggesting the conquest of Japan by mounted Korean warriors.
- The emperor becomes the "protector of the faith" but not necessarily the political leader. That power seems to be held by and contested among a collection of clan (*uji*) leaders serving as advisors to the court.
- The kingdom of Silla finally drives the Japanese from their Korean base in 567.

Asuka Period (592 – 710)
- Named for the district in Nara that served as the capital.
- The court compounds changes with the accession of each emperor, sometimes several times during the reign of the same emperor.
- Buddhism is introduced and recommended by the Poikche court. The Japanese recognize the advanced organization of Korean government and use Buddhism as a means of social and court reform.
- Mound building disappears as the Buddhist practice of cremation is adopted.
- The Chinese calendar is adopted.
- The order of succession of the emperor continues to occupy the energies of members of the high court.
- The Great Reform (Taiho codes) of 646 is initiated, disallowing private ownership of land by making it the property of the emperor, distributing its use based on family size and establishing equitable taxation and local government following the Confucian model of the Tang dynasty in China. This is the model that will continue to be eroded by the landowner clans of the countryside for the next several centuries.

Nara Period (710 – 794)
- The first permanent capital is established in Nara.
- The government continues to be restructured on the Chinese model.
- Literature and collections of earlier poems flourish, as does appreciation of Chinese literature. The development of the *katakana* writing system allows the expression of Japanese language, and a true Japanese literary tradition.
- Buddhist monasteries, most of which are urban, grow in political and economic strength in part because of tax and land dispensations.
- Horyuji, presently the oldest existent wooden building, is built in honor of Prince Shotoku.
- The Great Buddha (*daibutsu*) is cast from bronze, the domestic copper and tin deposits for which having recently been discovered.
- Upon his death, the household goods of Emperor Shomu (724 – 749) and Queen Komyo are collected and preserved to this day in the Shosoin Imperial Repository at Todaiji in Nara.

Heian Period (794 – 1156)
- The capitol is moved to Kyoto by the 50th emperor, Kammu (737 – 806).
- It is at this time in Yamato domain that Japanese sword making is said to have started with Amakuni, who was the first to sign some of his swords. He bridged the gap between the continental-style straight, double-edged blades and the curved, single-edged tachi. His most famous blade,

Kogarasu-maru (Little Crow) is a hybrid of the two styles. His was the founder of the Senjuin school.

- Court nobles dominate the social-intellectual scene and fine arts flourish. While still influenced by the Chinese techniques, the Japanese arts continue to develop into recognizably distinct schools.
- Temple lands, now usually on mountaintops or slopes, become larger and militant warrior monks, *sohei,* train to defend their property and power and, not infrequently, to protest imperial decrees. In later years these monks were generally armed by blades of the Senjuin smiths.
- The Old Bizen School of sword making is begun around 950 near the town of Osafune, probably because of an ample supply of iron and sand and a secure source of flowing water. This is the only domain to have an unbroken line of succession of smiths from its founding until the current day.
- The clan leaders of independent households on the frontier of the Japanese culture ignore the edicts of the court in Kyoto and overtaxed farmers look to them for relief from central authority.
- Imperial power declines as the Fujiwara clan, acting as regents, consolidates its power, chiefly by shrewd management and marrying their daughters to emperors.
- The rapid retiring of emperors with their cloistering and the subsequent appointment of child emperors needing adult advisors, *sessho,* leads to power scrambles, court intrigues, deceit, and assassinations.
- The Taira (Heike) and Minamoto (Genji) clans grow in influence and begin to struggle with each other and the Fujiwara for dominance.

Rokuhara Period (1156 – 1185)

- The Taira clan gains control of the court from the Fujiwara.
- The struggle between Fujiwara Yorinaga who represented autocratic regents and submissive emperors, and Emperor Go-Shirakawa supported by Taira and Minamoto clans proves to be the first step in the long process of developing a feudal state. Imperial power over land and taxes gradually loses to the strength of developing aristocratic manors (*shoen*).
- Both the Hogen and Heiji Wars increase Taira power and temporarily weaken the Minamoto.
- The Taira are finally defeated in the Gempei War (1180 – 1185) by the Minamoto clan wherein Nasu no Yoichi gains fame at the battle of Dannoura by knocking a fan from the mast of a Taira ship with a single arrow shot while mounted on a swimming horse. This is one of the few battles of Japanese history wherein an entire army was nearly exterminated, in this case primarily by drowning.

Kamakura Period (1185-1333)

- Minamoto Yoritomo, one of the best known individual warriors in the Gempei War and Minamoto clan leader, becomes shogun (military dictator). He exiles and persecutes his half-brother Yoshitsune, who in 1189 perishes by his own hands.
- Yoritomo moves the capital to Kamakura in 1185, leaving an emasculated emperor in Kyoto. He sets up a legal system based on the equitable management of land claims and at least temporarily unites the warrior clans. After his death there is the usual power struggle.
- The early Kamakura period is generally considered the time in which the *nihonto* came into being in tachi form. Earlier swords are considered *jokoto.* Near the end of this period, the Sagami (*soshu*) school of sword making came under the influence of Masamune, arguably the most important sword smith since Amakuni.
- During this period, sword polishers emerge as craftsmen separate from the smiths.
- The Hojo clan eventually takes over power from Miyamoto Yoshimasa (1204) and Hojo Tokimasa becomes regent. The Hojo are the relatives of Yoritomo's conniving wife, Masaka, and are not from warrior

stock; however, they prove to be decent administrators.

- The first (1274) and second (1281) Mongol invasions lead by Kublai Khan are repulsed by the spirited Japanese. Traditional individualistic Japanese battle techniques need be scrapped for a unified defense against massed invaders, revamping basic Japanese strategy. Had Yoritomo not had the opportunity to support and nurture the warrior class, these invasions might easily have resulted in the end of an independent Japan. The Mongol invasion also influenced sword shape and weight, favoring a heavier and broader blade. It is in this time frame that samurai begin to wear the pair of swords, *daisho*.
- Repelling the second invasion is aided by the "divine wind" or kamikaze, a sudden, unexpected typhoon, which scatters the Mongol ships drowning many of the would-be invaders. The Japanese repel the Mongols but there is no booty or treasury with which to reward the many loyal retainers and their vassals. Everyone makes claims against the bakufu, including the monasteries for praying for divine intervention. The Hojo's position of power is weakened further as they attempt to increase taxes to try to maintain a prolonged defensive war footing.
- Questions of succession continue to split the imperial and warrior families, and for a while emperors are chosen from alternating branches of the family (senior and junior branches), which maintain separate courts.
- Emperor Go-Daigo is inaugurated in 1318. He ends the practice of cloistering emperors and attempts to overthrow the shogunate by uniting the northern and southern courts and reestablishing the control by the court of land stewardship. This venture, called the Kemmu Restoration, is essentially unsuccessful in reducing significantly the power and influence of the major military clans and eventually leads to the Nambokucho Wars in which supporters of the two branches of the imperial family fight for dominance.

Ashikaga Period (1336 – 1392)

- Emperor Go-Daigo is driven into exile at Yoshino and his successor, from the rival senior branch of the imperial family, is protected in Kyoto by the Ashikaga clan, which gradually assumes power. From his exile on one of the Oki Islands, Go-Daigo becomes patron of the art of sword making, and brings about a cross-pollination of the various existing styles.
- The bakufu forces—including Ashikaga Takauji and his brother Tadayoshi—are supported by the emperor in Kyoto. They fight many intense battles with forces loyal to Go-Daigo, lead by Kusunoki Masashige, defending heavily fortified positions in the steep forested slopes of Mount Hiei and Kasagi and later, the strongholds of Akasaka and Chihaya.
- This extensive mountain fighting spurs the replacement of the boxy cavalry armor (*yoroi*) with a more streamlined wrap-around version (*do-maru*).
- Masashige falls at the decisive battle at Minatogawa (1336) when his ally Nitta Yoshisada begins an ill-conceived retreat. While sealing the eventual fate of the loyalists, Yoshisada's threat persists in the northern domains until 1338 when he falls at Somayama.
- The emperor of the senior line in Kyoto finally names Ashikaga Takauji shogun in 1338.
- Under Ashikaga patronage, Iizasa Choisai Lenao starts the first formal school of swordsmanship after spiritual experiences at the Katori Grand Shrine where a deity of great importance to budo, Futsunushi no kami, is enshrined. It is named the Tenshin Shoden Katori Shinto-ryu.

Muromachi Period (1392 – 1573)

- In 1367 Ashikaga appoints loyal vassals to serve as constables in the provinces under his control.
- Small wars and uprisings gradually increase and there is civil strife as the clans struggle for power.
- In 1408 Ashikaga Yoshimitsu, builder of the

"Golden Pavilion" in Kyoto dies, marking the start of the rapid decline of the shogunate.

- Ten years of civil war called the Onin War (1467 – 1477) begins the rise of large-scale pitched battles using foot soldiers (*ashigaru*) as well as mounted troops and heralds the beginning of the Age of Warring States. Fought primarily in and around Kyoto, the war weakens the "home provinces" allowing the more isolated western domains and as well as those in Kyushu to grow in stature.
- Armour becomes simpler and less restrictive as the sword (*katana*) and spear (*yari*) come into their own as personal weapons of choice for war on the ground, supplanting the bow.
- The Mino school of sword making, begun around 1340 in Shizuyama, comes into its own a century later, and that part centered on Seki becomes synonymous with practical, sensible, and reliable blades.
- Several comprehensive schools of budo are started during this time frame. Takenouchi ryu is begun in 1532 in Okayama, Tatsumi ryu is founded around 1550 in Chiba, and both Hozoin ryu and Toda-ha Buro ryu are developed a decade later.
- Firearms are introduced by the Portuguese in 1543 at Tanegeshima and the Japanese rapidly become proficient in their manufacture.
- Tsukahara Bokuden (1490 – 1571) completes the first recorded musha shugyo. He is eventually invited to teach kenjutsu to the Ashikaga shogun.
- The growth of sea trade with the Arabs, China, Korea, Indonesia, and the Philippines, as well as nearly continuous piracy, increases the wealth of those domains with port cities.
- Nagao Kagetora convinces the constable of Kanto, Uesugi Norimasa, to accept his protection and make him family, then usurps his power and becomes constable himself assuming the name Uesugi Kenshin.
- There is growth in the popularity of Christianity introduced by the Portuguese and Spanish.
- The struggle between the Uesugi of Echigo Province and the Takeda clan of Kai Province results in five separate battles beginning in 1553. Takeda Shingen is instrumental in using orchestrated mass spear charges and famous for never fighting in his own province. His tactics finally fail when he is routed at Hachimanbara in (1561) by a surprise cavalry charge by Uesugi Kenshin. This defeat undoes Shingen's famous chief of staff, Yamamoto Kansuke, and almost kills Shingen.
- In 1565 Takeda finally takes the Uesugi castle at Minowa and kills the only remaining heir to the Uesugi clan.
- Defenders shoot Takeda Shingen during the siege of Noda Castle (1574), opening the way for Oda Nobunaga to begin strengthening his position.

Momoyama Period (1568 – 1600)

- Oda Nobunaga initiates a ruthless campaign of unification in 1568 by force of arms. He occupies Kyoto and eliminates competition in consolidating Japan under one leader by taking the head of Yoshimoto Imagawa at the Battle of Okehazama (1560).
- In the Battle of Nagashima in 1574, Nobunaga slaughters 20,000 men, women, and children of the Ikko sect who supported Amida Buddhism and had amassed great public influence against his unification policies.
- In 1575, Nobunaga breaks a furious charge of Takeda cavalry with massed harquebusiers from the ranks of the *ashigaru*, thus forever changing the place of the sword in Japanese warfare.
- Nobunaga is murdered in 1582 by Akechi Mitsuhide, who is shogun for 13 days until killed by Toyotomi Hideyoshi at Yamazaki.
- Hideyoshi, risen from the peasant class is quick to establish an inflexible class system to keep anyone else from doing what he has.
- Miyamoto Musashi is born around 1584.
- "Taiko's sword hunt" is begun by Hideyoshi

in 1588 to disarm the general population and prevent revolution.
- Hideyoshi invades Korea twice but is monumentally unsuccessful.
- Yagyu Muneyoshi and Munenori meet Tokugawa Ieyasu, then Hideyoshi's top aide, who becomes Munenori's student.
- The year 1595 marks the end of the old (Koto) era of blades. Subsequent blades are termed new (Shinto). During this period the katana displaces the tachi.
- Hideyoshi appoints the Honami family as official sword appraisers.
- Hideyoshi names his son Hideyori his successor before dying in 1598.
- Tokugawa Ieyasu destroys troops loyal to Hideyori including the Takeda clan at the Battle of Sekigihara in 1600.

Edo (Tokugawa) Period (1600 – 1867)
- Ieyasu establishes his shogunate in Edo (Tokyo) and claims direct ownership (*tenryo*) of about one-quarter of the land mass of the archipelago, including the rich Kanto Plain, most silver and gold mines and the major cities of Edo (government), Kyoto (tradition), Osaka (commerce), and the port of Nagasaki (foreign trade).
- William Adams, English pilot to a Dutch trading company and a few survivors reach Japan after an ill-fated trading voyage (1600). Adams eventually becomes an advisor and confidant of Ieyasu.
- Musashi Miyamoto begins a musha shugyo in which he is successful in 60 individual sword fights, including one with Sasaki Kojiro on Funejima (Ganryu Island) in 1612.
- Ieyasu awards trading privileges to the English and Dutch
- Ieyasu destroys Hideyori's stronghold in Osaka Castle in 1615 ensuring Tokugawa suzerainty.
- Ieyasu consolidates his power by awarding his followers the lands of those who fought against him and closes the country to Europeans except in the trading center of Nagasaki, which subsequently becomes a center for the study of Western culture.
- The Spanish are expelled 1624; the Portuguese follow in 1638.
- The system of alternate attendance is started by the shogun in 1635 whereby all daimyos must live half their time with their families in the capital, a ploy that keeps them too busy and too poor to get into much mischief.
- During the reign of the third Tokugawa shogun, Iemitsu (following 1645), dissatisfaction on the part of ronin and their supporters eventually results in several aborted coup attempts. These were handled with remarkable restraint on the part of the bakufu. Hundreds of Christian converts were not shown the same courtesy.
- Yamaga Soko reformulates bushido and publishes it in 1685.
- Popular culture flourishes. The period, called "Genroku," between 1688 and 1704 is considered the apogee of the art of the common Japanese, whose wealth and stature had gradually increased under the Tokugawa surizainship. Separate from styles of the couriers, this period produced the woodcuts, poetry, literature, and music of contemporary life and of the *ukiyo-e*—the fugitive society or "floating world" made up of actors, singers, dancers, and geisha.
- The incident of the 47 Ronin occurs when their liege lord of Ako is forced into *seppuku* (1701 – 1703).
- The year 1781 ends the period of Shinto swords and subsequent blades are termed "new new swords" (*shinshinto)*. Under the same influences of peace and artistic license that brought about the Genroku, the temper-line *(hamon*) of these shinshinto becomes increasingly flamboyant. Some smiths returned to the styles of earlier ages, attempting to recreate the products of the "golden ages" of the late Kamakura and Nambokucho times.
- Commodore Perry bypasses Nagasaki and his fleet enters Uraga Bay in 1853 making U.S. demands directly to the shogun. He returns in one year and concludes the Treaty of Kanagawa, gaining the exclusive

access to the ports of Shimoda and Hakodate. This unprecedented ultimatum and its resulting turmoil become an excuse for a growing displeasure with the Tokugawa bakufu policies in general.

- Anti-bakufu forces, primarily of Satsuma and Choshu, march on Kyoto and are opposed by bakufu forces from the northeast led by those of Aizu in the Boshin War. They clash at Toba-Fushima, and the bakufu forces are soundly defeated and driven toward Osaka.
- The last Tokugawa shogun is persuaded to resign without widespread bloodshed as a result of a plan submitted by the Tosa daimyo.

Meiji Period (1868 – 1914)

- Power returns to the emperor, whose court functions gradually move from Kyoto to Tokyo. He immediately sets off on a series of "processes" throughout the new nation to introduce himself and a new Western-styled nationalism to his subjects.
- The Yasukuni Shrine is established in Tokyo by imperial decree to honor the dead of the struggle for restoration. It eventually enshrines all Japanese war dead up through the Pacific War.
- Samurai lose their topknots and soon thereafter the Hito-rei edict (1876) bans the wearing of swords. Traditional sword making comes to a screeching halt. This marks the end of the era of shinshinto blades. Forged blades made after this event are designated *gendaito* (modern).
- Food riots and general unrest lead to the creation of all sorts of political parties. The Satsuma-Choshu clique dominates the government.
- Considerations of the invasion of Korea lead to the dissolution of many of the legislative bodies in Japan.
- The national army puts down Satsuma rebellion (1877).
- The Meiji constitution is ratified in 1890. It leaves the emperor with veto power over the legislators, sole right to sign treaties, and direct control of the military.
- The new constitution and continuing Westernization result in a more concerted effort to define precisely the "national polity." This emerged as several principles—including the primacy of the emperor, his filial piety and loyalty to his people, and an unbroken history of the Japanese family from the mists of Shinto memory. Controversy regarding the *kokutai* was to erupt dramatically during the Taisho and Showa periods.
- In China the actions of the Western powers leads to the Boxer Rebellion in 1900. The foreign legations in Peking are threatened but saved by a multinational force. Russia uses this situation to advance her influence in Manchuria.
- Japan triumphs in the Sino-Japanese and Russo-Japanese wars, defeating the Russian fleet at Port Arthur and the Straits of Tsushima in 1905. The United States mediates the Treaty of Portsmouth granting Japan a dominant position in both Korea and Manchuria.
- In 1906 the imperial government appoints two smiths to the Imperial Arts and Crafts establishment in an attempt to preserve the rapidly disappearing art and technology of Japanese sword making.

Taisho Period (1914 – 1926)

- By the conclusion of World War I, rampant inflation causes the price of rice to grow out of proportion to wages, creating hardship in both urban and country families. The resulting riots of 1918 are savagely put down and tens of thousands of people are jailed by the government, whose cabinet falls shortly thereafter, despite having halved the price of rice.
- The kokutai becomes imbued with the concept of subservience of the individual to the good of the imperialist national extended family (as defined by the military).
- Production of traditional blades (gendaito) picks up again as the militarists gain increasing influence, representing an increase in interest in swords and sword

techniques by the general population. Among the facilitators of this resurgence of sword making is the ultra-nationalistic Black Dragon Society (Koku Ryu Kai), and its mover and shaker, Toyama Mitsuru.

- On September 1, 1923, the Kanto Plain is stuck by a massive earthquake killing 100,000, destroying over 550,000 buildings and leaving 2 million homeless (Hunter, 1984). Martial law is imposed, and conspiracy theories implicating socialists and Koreans result in hundreds being killed by mobs. The economic setback resonates for decades.
- In 1925, the last open-pit smelter where sword steel (*tamahagane*) starts its life is closed.

Showa Period (1926-1989)

- Ultranationalism prevails, the army ignores any attempt at civilian control, and Manchuria is invaded, essentially without government consent.
- In 1933, the Yasukuni shrine establishes an open-pit smelter at Shimane to produce steel for sword smiths producing swords at the shrine forges for the graduates of the military academy. It is closed in 1944.
- In February 1936, a group of young officers attempt a coup to recreate a government closer to the ancient model of an all-powerful emperor they think ideal. Several ministers are killed and the officers are executed.
- The army grows geometrically and serves as a vehicle of both technical training and nationalism for the general public. By the end of the Pacific War it will have 200 divisions and 5 1/2 million men.
- The Pacific War begins (1941), ushering in the mass production of machine-made swords tempered in oil (*gunto*). Many old blades are remounted in modern military *koshirae* and carried by the officer corps. While the term *showato* is commonly used in a derogatory sense to describe the utilitarian war-effort swords mass-produced during this period, it is clear that the production of traditionally made art blades was rebounding from near oblivion during this period (e.g. Yasukuni Shrine blades).
- The Pacific War ends with the atomic blast in 1945 and with the emperor's publicly renouncing any claim to kami nature.
- Occupying forces ban the production of swords and the practice of all martial arts as well as artistic representation of warfare or ancient traditions. They arbitrarily destroy many swords of artistic or historic merit along with huge masses of gunto. The ban is eased 5 years later in order to allow sword smiths to produce 60 traditional swords for the special dedication of the Ise Grand Shrine, an event that had occurred every 25 years for the previous 1,000 years.
- In 1953, a new law allows the resumption of traditional sword making. The Japanese Art Sword Preservation Society (NBTHK, Nihon Bijutsu Token Hozon Kyokai) is founded in 1960.
- In 1975, the NBTHK reopens the Shimane smelter to produce *tamahagane* for the growing number of *gendai* smiths.

Heisei Period (1989 – present)

- Crown Prince Akihito is raised to emperor upon the death of his father, Hirohito.
- Modern sword smiths close the quality gap between old and modern swords, and art swords demonstrate yet another life renewal.
- For the 50th anniversary of Japan's surrender in the Pacific War at Tokyo's Nippon Budokan, with Emperor Akihito in attendance, Prime Minister Tomiichi Murayama refers to Japan's mistaken national policy of colonial rule and aggression and then states, "In the hope that no such mistake be made in the future, I regard, in a spirit of humanity, these irrefutable facts of history, and express here once again my feelings of deep remorse and state my heartfelt apology."
- On April 13, 2001, the then recently elected, somewhat unconventional prime minister, Junichiro Koizumi visited the Yasukuni Shrine, dedicated to the military dead of Japan. Enshrined there among

others are convicted and executed class A World War II war criminals, including Hideki Tojo. This visit, two days before the surrender anniversary, results in waves of international protest, especially in Asia. His actions are also condemned by ex-Prime Minister Murayama.

—Oscar Ratti and Adele Westbrook,
Secrets of the Samurai

HISTORY OF IAIDO

Confronted by limitations of effectiveness, the martial arts of the West responded with a continuous crafting of superior equipment. Confronted with similar limitations, the Japanese warrior responded by fashioning a better self. The bushi turned not to technology in making his sword a better tool for fighting. Influenced by contemplative aspects of Taoism and Buddhism and by the self-discipline of Confucianism, he turned inwards. He fine-tuned his body and his mind in order to better manipulate his sword.

—*Dave Lowry,* Sword and Brush

The origin of iaijutsu is lost in the mist of medieval Japanese budo development. It cannot be separated from, and its development can only be understood in the context of, the politics and culture of a thousand years of Japanese history. Early references to drawing and cutting in one action include the *i-ai* technique of Tsukuhara Bokuden (c.1490 – 1570), who was born near the Kashima Grand Shrine and was trained in Shinto ryu swordsmanship. He undertook what was the first described musha shugyo whereby he traveled widely seeking challenge, experience, and enlightenment in the sword arts. He developed his own style, of which little is known today, and near his 40th year defeated a fierce *naginata*-welding opponent by a technique of drawing and cutting he called *hitotsu tachi* meaning in this case "one stroke." Other early iaijutsu references include techniques of the Tenshin Shoden Katori Shinto ryu, and later, those of both the Tatsumi ryu and Takenouchi ryu, all antedating the mid-15th century (Wagner and Draeger, 1991).

The above not withstanding, the founder of the art of drawing the sword is popularly considered Hayashizaki Jinsuke Shigenobu (1546 – 1621). It is possible that his battojutsu techniques were not so dissimilar to that of his contemporaries, but were differentiated from them by his emphasis on defense and spirituality. Jinsuke's descendents named his technique shin muso Hayashizaki ryu. Eleven subsequent direct-line masters are recorded although it is likely that this occurred in retrospect as the subsequent early headmasters were to some extent contemporaries and founders of other schools. The second for example, the founder of the Tamiya ryu, served as an instructor to the first three Tokugawa shoguns. The seventh and best known of his successors was Hasegawa Mondonosuke Eishin. Eishin is credited with modifying the original techniques to accommodate the newly popular, shorter katana and the new way of wearing it edge-up, thrust through the *obi* (sash). He also is believed to have added the seated techniques (*Suwari waza*) in Muso Hayashizaki ryu to the original okuden techniques of the school (Taylor and Ohmi, 1997). He was honored by Hideyoshi Toyotomi following a demonstration of his technique at Toyotomi's newly constructed capitol in Edo. Clearly, the practical application of iaijutsu techniques blossomed as large-scale pitched battles between armored troops gave way to small skirmishes among warriors wearing civilian clothing, as was occurring during Eishin's lifetime. Without the need of a kabuto-cleaving tachi, one-handed drawing cuts and vertical strikes to the head with a katana became the preferred battle technique. While some of the modern sword techniques have remnants left from the days of armor, the vast majority of modern iaido developed as a result of this shift in sword styles and techniques.

The ninth master of the muso Jinsuke Eishin ryu, Hayashi Rokudayu Morimasa (1661 – 1732), was a retainer to the lord of Tosa (Yamanouchi Toyomasa). He learned the art in the Edo area but brought it with him back to Tosa where it remained a "secret school." For the next eight headmasters the curriculum was only taught to samurai from Koichi, the capital of Tosa. Thus Tosa, a seaport and trading domain on the eastern island of Shokoku, was primed to play a pivotal role in the development of iaido in later times. Hayashi had trained with Omori Rokurozaemon, a student of Eishin who later moved to Edo, and he introduced the Shoden kata from Omori ryu iai to Eishin Jinsuke ryu, making these seated forms the initial kata taught to students.

Following the 11th headmaster, sometime after 1750, the Eishin Jinsuke style split into two separate parallel lineages. The first, *shimomura-ha*, was associated with the higher ranking samurai in Tosa who had been retainers of the Yamanouchi clan prior to its ascendancy in the Tokugawa shogunate. Tokugawa had rewarded the Yamanouchi clan with Tosa kuni for its support 175 years before at Sekigihara. The other line, *tanimura-ha*, was associated with the landed gentry (*goshi*) and lower ranking samurai who had originally been retainers to the Chosokabe, the original clan of Tosa who lost that domain by not supporting the victorious Tokugawa clan. This dichotomy is interesting simply from the point of iai development, but it was highlighted by the greater events that led up to the fall of the shogunate and the restoration of the Meiji Emperor to power in 1868.

The 17th headmaster of the *tanimura-ha*, Oe Masamichi (1853 – 1927), reorganized Tosa iai, combining once again techniques of both lineages, particularly the omori influence of the seated kata. He took the heretofore secret Tosa techniques on the road. He was the first to coin the name muso Jikiden Eishin ryu and renamed many of the omori and okuden kata. He is also reported to have developed a method of performing the chuden kata (Eishin ryu) one after another without rising from the floor (Taylor, 1993). He named this technique fast-draw (*haya nuki*) and in his method he apparently only used a single hand for each *kirioroshi*. Variations of this technique survive today in many dojo of both lineages.

This history ignores such important streams of iaijutsu as Shinkage, Itto, Tamiya, Hoki, and hundreds of others that existed at one time or another, as well as the other schools that remain viable to this day. The only excuse for this is that these schools have had no known direct influence on muso shinden ryu as we know it now. It is clear from the history above, however, that they all share common ancestors during the development and growth of swordsmanship within the Japanese archipelago.

HISTORY OF MUSO SHINDEN RYU

It is spiritless to think that you cannot attain to that which you have seen and heard the masters attain. The masters are men. You are also a man. If you think that you will be inferior in doing something, you will be on that road very soon. Master Ittei said, "Confucius was a sage because he had the will to become a scholar when he was fifteen years old. He was not a sage because he studied later on." This is the same as the Buddhist maxim, "First intention, then enlightenment."

—*Tsunetomo Yamamoto,* Hagakure: The Book of the Samurai

As mentioned above, muso shinden ryu began as Jinsuke's shin muso Hayashizaki ryu and was modified by successive headmasters, most notably Eishin, Hayashi, and Oe. The greatest subsequent influence on iai was made by Nakayama Hakudo (1869 – 1958), 16th headmaster of the shimomura-ha. His definitive contribution to the ryu followed Oe's tenure as headmaster and consisted of the creation of a "way" of muso shinden ryu—iaido.

Following the proscription of the wearing of swords following the Meiji Restoration, swordsmanship and sword making hit an all-time low. As the Meiji government consciously introduced the concept of the Japanese nation led by the emperor to the public, a compromise between old historical concepts and those of a modern industrial state was struck. During the beginning of the 20th century, success in war and the nationalist and ultra-nationalist sentiment of the time actively generated under the auspices of the Meiji constitution went hand in hand with a resurgent interest in iaijutsu by a large segment of the general population. During the formative years of the rebellion against the bakufu, many of Nakayama's mentors had been active in the loyalist movement, picking up steam both in Tosa and in Edo itself. He had trained in many schools of iaijutsu with close ties to Tosa including both *ha* of muso Jinsuke Eishin ryu. Budo dojo had been one of the common sites for the clandestine meetings of the shishi prior to 1868. As an inheritor of this tradition, Hakudo was in a unique position to interpret iai for the masses. Nakayama was held in such esteem by his contemporaries that he served as a sword tester of newly forged blades, often under the name Nakayama Hiromichi. A tracing of the tang of a Showa-era sword (*oshigata*) containing the details of a cutting test by Nakayama can be seen in a text by R. Fuller and R. Gregory (1993). Nakayama and his students, under the umbrella of the *Dai Nippon Butokukai*, codified the techniques of many of the schools known and practiced in the Taisho era (1912 – 1926) and created a nonprofessional representative set for use by the general population, primarily kendo players. He coined the name muso shinden ryu for these modified techniques and was instrumental in the transition from iaijutsu to iaido. Other styles of modern martial arts, notably aikido, adopted some sword techniques as part of their curriculum, primarily to practice defensive strategy against them.

Following World War II and after the prohibition of traditional martial arts by the U.S. occupation forces was relaxed, modern budo schools emerged. The ZNKR emerged as the leading supervising umbrella organization for the sword arts, although the ZNIR was (and is) also active. To provide real swordsmanship for *kendoka* versed only in *shinai* kendo, seven basic kata were created as representative of the major schools of iaido active at that time. Under the direction of Otani Kazuo, 11 experts in several ryu-ha met in 1967 and created these seven seitei, or basic kata. Among those represented was Kamimoto Eiichi, Hanshi ninth Dan in muso shinden ryu. Ten years later, three more kata were created, bringing the total seitei to 10. In 2000, a committee of the AUSKF announced the addition of two more kata, bringing the current total to 12. These are currently used in inter-ryu competition and promotion testing within the ZNKR and the AUSKF.

Currently, the two most popular schools of iaido both in Japan and the United States are muso Jikiden Eishin ryu and muso shinden ryu. The Jikiden school is still primarily centered in the south and west of the Japanese nation reflecting its ties with the old Tosa *ryogoku* (Taylor, 1993). The muso shinden school is more closely associated with the Tokyo area, representing Hakudo's eventual influence there. These ryu are very nearly the same school with only minor differences in the techniques of the kata, although the names for each may be quite different. Dojo of both schools with lineages that embraced the ZNKR heritage compete among themselves with only slight differences in the *noto*, and the way the *sageo* is tied.

Section Two
Preparation

In what ever art you pursue the Way, if you are single minded and determined to accomplish what you set out to do, you are no longer pursuing the Way. Someone with nothing on his mind is a man of the Way. If you have nothing in your mind, you can easily do whatever you do. A mirror, always clear, with no form or shape of its own, distinctly reflects whatever faces it. The mind of a man of the Way is like a mirror; because it has nothing and is clear, it is "mindless" and is lacking in nothing. That is the mind in a natural state. Someone who does everything with his mind in the natural state is called a master.

—Munenori Yagyu,
The Sword and the Mind

Since I no longer think
of reality
as reality,
what reason would I have
to think of dreams as dreams?
—Saigyo
(From the Country of Eight Islands)

It is necessary to use the preparatory time before your practice to make the transition from the concerns of your ordinary life to that of sole concentration on iaido. Changing clothes should facilitate changing minds. The warm-up should be done in such a way that your attitude toward iaido and your fellow students and sensei is one of respect and complete openness. Iaido is an act of discovery, and a receptive, uncluttered mind is essential. The business of iaido is serious, and your demeanor in the dojo should reflect that fact. On one level you are (ritualistically) killing someone—and the loss of life is a solemn occasion. Also, the very process of seeking wisdom among others engaged in the same pursuit demands respect. Finally, protecting the single-minded purpose of the dojo is one way of showing respect for your sensei and your art.

In most martial arts the student has a sparring partner with whom to interact. This is not practical in iaido for obvious reasons. The iaidoka must imagine his opponent. His level of success in mentally picturing an aggressor and reacting appropriately toward this mental image is in large part what constitutes advanced skill in iaido. Observation (*metsuke*), wariness or awareness (zanshin), proper distance (*maai*), focus (*kiai*), and timing (*hyoshi*) must all be integrated in a realistic whole. This is the hallmark of a master and is what elevates iaido beyond pure technique (jutsu).

Iaido is not and should not be flashy. At its best it is boring to the uninitiated because appreciation of its highest levels requires insight usually limited to bugeisha. It is deceptively simple because it is purged of all unnecessary motion of both sword and body. It may be described as an understated elegance of harmonious motion, breath, mind, body, and sword.

ETIQUETTE

The basic meaning of etiquette is to be quick at both the beginning and end and tranquil in the middle. Mitani Chizaemon heard this and said, "That's just like being a kaishaku."
—Tsunetomo Yamamoto, Hagakure: The Book of the Samurai

"Rushing into action, you fail.
Trying to grasp things, you lose them.
Therefore the master takes action by letting things take their course.
She remains as calm at the end as at the beginning."
—J. Kornfield, After the Ecstasy, the Laundry

Iaido literally begins and ends with etiquette, *reishiki*. While dojo may differ greatly in size and form from one school to another, a basic pattern persists. In the center of a designated wall is the *kamiza*, the spirit seat. This is also called the *shinza*. In the United States this is often a shelf above eye level (Figure 2).

Figure 2: *Kamiza* with shrine, incense burner, and photos of sensei.

Figures 3A and 3B: Entering the dojo with the *shimo no ashi* and immediately bowing to the kamiza.

In Japan it is more often an elaborate niche in the wall. It may include a formal Shinto shrine and other religious accoutrements such as an incense burner, sacred rope, and folded paper prayers. In others it may consist of a likeness of the founder of the art or of the school, a scroll of calligraphy appropriate to the art, a seasonal flower arrangement, or a national flag. Buddhist shrines are not generally appropriate to a dojo. To the left and right of the kamiza are the shimoza (lower seat) and kamiza (upper seat), respectively. The wall to the immediate left of the iaidoka facing the kamiza is designated as where the emperor would sit if were he in attendance and is given due respect. In the United States entering should be done with the left foot; this is the less aggressive action. More traditionally, it should be done with the foot farthest from the kamiza (*shimo no ashi*) (Figure 3A). Whether this is the left or right foot depends on where the entrance to the dojo is relative to the kamiza. When leaving the dojo, the foot closest to the kamiza goes first (*kami no ashi*). Immediately upon entering and just prior to leaving the dojo a standing bow is performed towards the kamiza (Figure 3B). Shinto ritual also dictates which foot turns around the other to turn the body, depending on the position of the iaidoka in the dojo relative to a line starting at the kamiza and dividing the dojo into mirror images. These rules are not often applied in the United States even during tournaments.

A training session or demonstration begins with a bow to the kamiza. The command for this bow is usually given by the senior student after directing everyone toward the proper direction. This is followed by a bow to the sensei and then a bow to the sword. These bows vary with the dojo and may be performed either standing or from the "correct sitting position" (seiza). At the end of a session the reverse order is followed. During the opening bow to the sensei it is customary to request him to honor you with his attention by saying *"onegai shimasu."* During the closing bow to the sensei the student says, "Thank you very much for what you have done" (*domo arigato gozaimashi ta*).

While in the dojo an individual is courteous to the other iaidoka by not disturbing their concentration with loud or unseemly physical or vocal activity. Mental energy should be focused on the art itself and inward, not outward. One should refrain from interfering in others' practice or from walking in front of observers. When this cannot be avoided, it should be done unobtrusively while holding the right hand horizontally between the two individuals and the head slightly bowed. Upon requesting help from a senior, one should stand to the side without physically intruding until the individual recognizes your presence. Then briefly request help with humility. When approached by a senior, an iaidoka should immediately perform a noto (if sword is drawn), face the senior, and bow.

Another aspect of etiquette which, unfortunately, must also be mentioned is that of personal hygiene. Practice clothing and your own body should be clean, free of body odor, and neat when in the dojo. This represents yet another courtesy to your dojo and your fellow iaidoka whose concentration may be distracted by a strong odor. Japanese are aggressive bathers, and some believe that gaijin smell badly to begin with. There is no sense reenforcing this image. Consider the common practice during the Warring States period of placing perfume inside the battle helmet so that if the warrior was decapitated, his head would not smell badly to the victor, or the lord to whom the head might be brought. That sort of puts in perspective the level of affront body odor represents to a samurai.

The organization of a dojo is as an extended family or clan structure. Control begins at the top and passes down vertically in a prescribed fashion through the assistant teachers, senior students, and junior students. Respect is offered to all, but submission to seniors is the rule. All dojo protocol follows this etiquette. If you are a new member of a dojo, you should be very concerned with the degree that individual expression is accepted by your sensei. Until that is very clear to you, assume that a strict hierarchy exists and that you are the least important member of it. If you have been in the dojo a while it might benefit you to consider the possibility that you may have become a little too informal. What is acceptable behavior toward your sensei (who in some sense should be a friend, parent, and confessor) in a social situation away from the dojo is probably entirely inappropriate in the dojo. If you are visiting a dojo, you are not even part of the social structure. You should present yourself in the most humble of manners. Consider that each dojo has its own protocol that may be very different from what you are used to. To exercise less than exemplary manners and humility in somebody else's dojo demeans you, him, and your sensei. Consider also that a visitor to a dojo may be tested, for example, by being left in seiza for an extended period. Be prepared and be flexible.

Etiquette also serves a very practical purpose. Picture a room full of gunfighters with loaded revolvers in their holsters. An individual in that room needing to handle his weapon must move carefully and signal—clearly and unambiguously—his non-aggressive intent. He can neither handle his weapon recklessly nor can he allow another individual to feel threatened or insulted. To do so will undoubtedly result in his being cut down in error or anger.

Finally, bushido, the code that we as bugeisha must adopt, demands honoring even an enemy samurai's social status and personal courage and dedication to his liege lord (daimyo). Even assassination, for example, in the culture of feudal Japan was accomplished within certain social limits and courtesies toward the victim. Certainly we owe the same courtesy to our fellow travelers in the martial arts odyssey.

CLOTHING

Life/Soul is like a clear mirror; the body is dust on it.
Beauty in us is not perceived, for we are under the dust.
—*Jalaludin Rumi* (The Way of the Sufi)

Though the eyes can only see ahead the spirit can be aware on all sides. This awareness is apparent to the audience, not just in the fact that the (Noh) actor avoids collisions, but in the actor's appearance when his back is turned. As the actor enters and exits, and performs various dance movements on the stage, his back is often turned to large numbers of the members of the audience. Yet when the actor projects strong Ki, his appearance from behind never looks small. This has far more to do with the actor's ability than with the size of the costume. Though the actor is facing away from the audience, there is something powerful and unapproachable about his appearance.
—*William Reed,* A Practical Guide for Westerners

The only essential clothing item needed to informally practice iaido outside the dojo is a wide, long (three turns around hips) belt or obi, often 4 x 144 inches. This keeps the saya in the correct position during the kata. It should be wrapped around the upper hips rather than the abdomen to leave the *hara* (center of balance) unrestricted. Unlike a judo or karatedo obi, it is always tied in back, which keeps the knot and loose ends out of the way of the hands. This is the way an obi is always tied in traditional Japanese dress. When a *hakama* (culotte-like skirt pants) is worn, the knot supports its ties and the flat plate or *koshiita* in the back. In a pinch, a judo obi can be used, but the tip of the saya will tend to fall toward the floor.

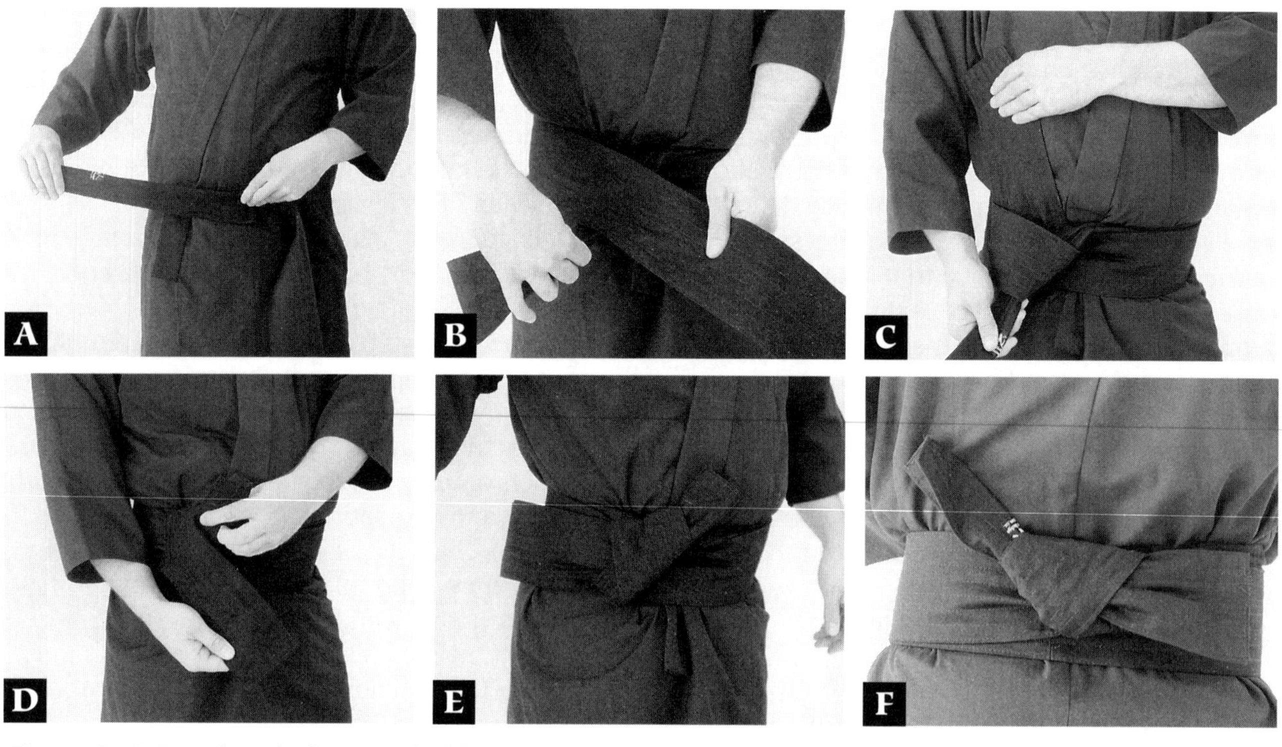

Figures 4A – F: Tying the iaido obi. One end is folded on itself for about 10 inches. The rest is wrapped clockwise three times around the hips. A square knot is used to fasten it, but the unequal width of the belt ends causes it to form the shape of a shell. The knot is then rotated to the back. Alternately, the ends can be tucked under the belt after the first half-hitch is tied, and then rotated to the back.

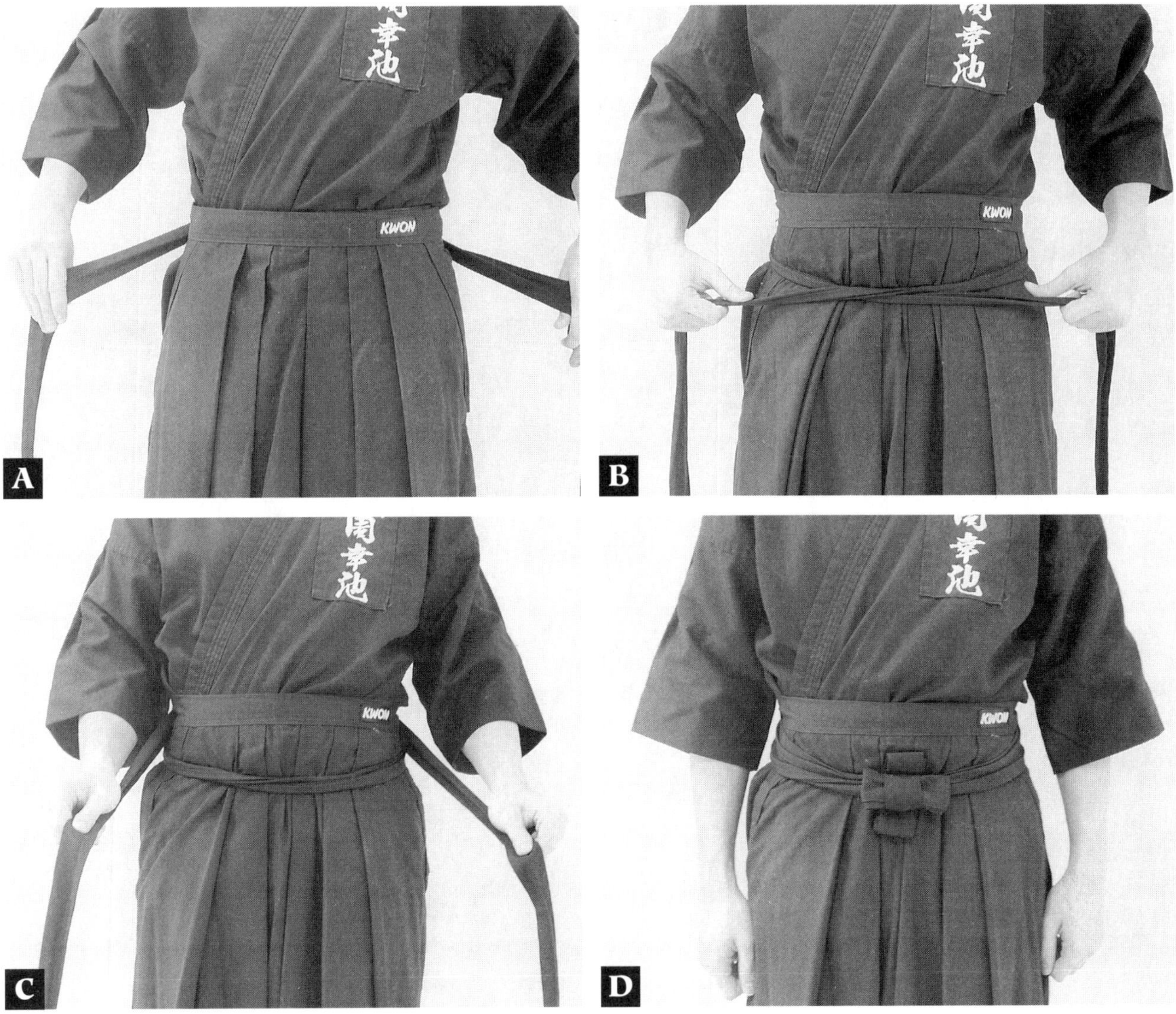

Figures 5A – D: One way of tying the hakama.
A: Front ties are crossed above the knot of the obi and brought to the front.
B: Front ties are twisted or tied in front 4 inches below the top and brought to the back and tied below the obi knot.
C: Back ties are passed under the front ties and are brought to the front where they are tied around the lower top ties.
D: One end of the back ties is rolled horizontally, and the other end wrapped around it in a vertical fashion, then passed behind the wrap to form a cross.

During practice in the dojo iaido is performed barefooted in a jacket-like short kimono, *uwagi*, and hakama (Figure 3A,B). When donning the hakama, it is traditional to step into them with the left foot first, then the right one. The uwagi in particular, combined with the obi suggests a combination characteristic of the work clothing of the lesser classes of the feudal Japanese. The hakama was more strictly a samurai or courtier item of clothing. Three-quarter sleeves are most practical for a practice outfit, although full-length sleeves may be worn. The hakama should nearly touch the floor and is worn over the tails of the jacket and over the obi. These should be all white, all black, all blue, or a white top with dark hakama. In some dojo, white is limited to the summer months and black to the winter. In others, white is limited to female iaidoka or kendoka. The belt should match the uwagi or hakama, its color having no rank significance.

Often a light cotton undergarment is worn

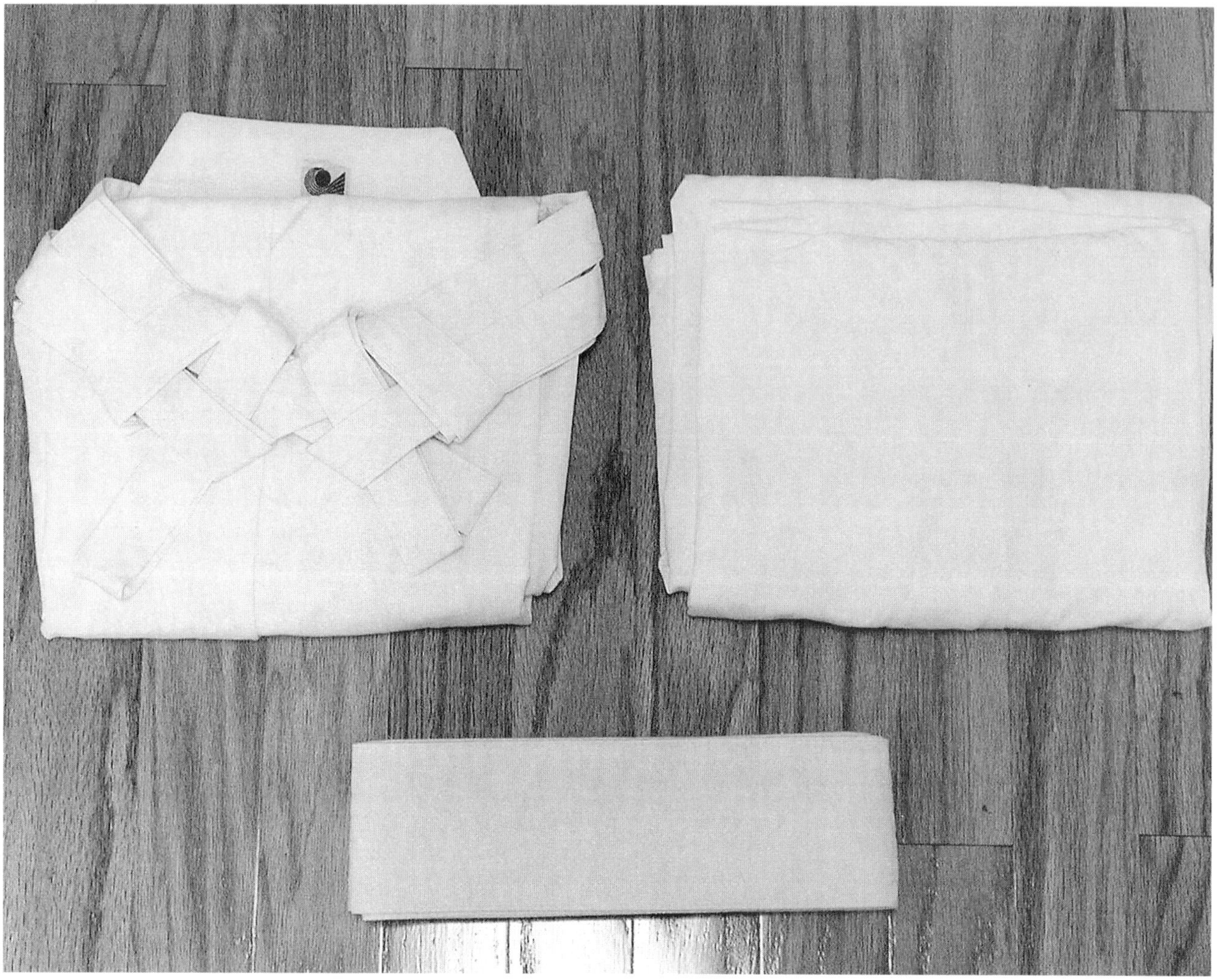

Figure 6: Iaido clothing (hakama, uwagi, and obi) properly folded for travel or storage.

beneath the uwagi. Traditionally this is white cotton. It is not proper to wear a Western crew neck T-shirt under the uwagi in many dojo or for any formal occasions. Light cotton is a practical material for the outer garment. Polyester or heavy duck are hot, although very durable. The formal iaido dress, which is really unnecessary in the United States, uses a silk jacket with full Chinese sleeves and family crests (*monsuke*). Gray or mustard-colored silk hakama are sometimes worn as part of the formal outfit by high-ranking iaidoka in Japan but should be avoided by U.S. students as they would appear rather presumptuous. The name of an American iaidoka in katakana script may be embroidered on the front left of the uwagi and on the right rear of the hakama, but no other patch, drawing, or lettering of any kind should be visible. Some Japanese will find the use of *kanji* characters for the name of a nonoriental budoka to be offensive.

Other useful items include a headband, if working out in the heat. White or black bicyclist or other exercise shorts may be worn under the hakama to fill out the gap left in the sides (flowered boxer shorts should not be visible). Although older sensei argue that if you control your balance properly they are unnecessary, kneepads are found to be very useful by most people. The kneepads are often forgotten when the rest of the costume is washed. They can become rather raunchy in a short period of time—you'd be amazed how much your knees sweat. Soaking them in

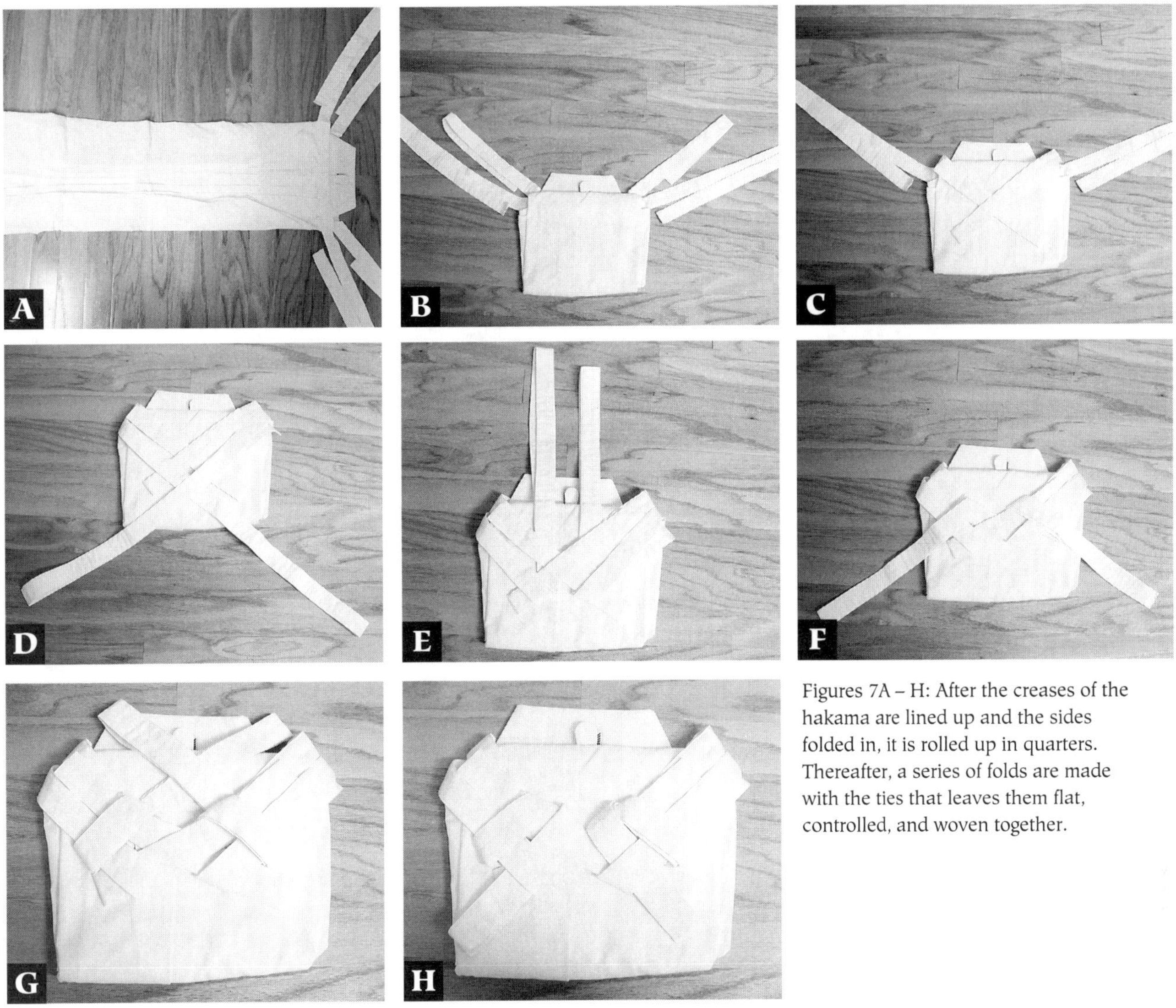

Figures 7A – H: After the creases of the hakama are lined up and the sides folded in, it is rolled up in quarters. Thereafter, a series of folds are made with the ties that leaves them flat, controlled, and woven together.

Woolite and cold water is a quick way of making them acceptable again. A bandana or kerchief may be carried inside the uwagi to wipe the blade or hands during practice (the space in front of your solar plexus, between the outer and inner wraps of the kimono is used like a pocket in traditional Japanese dress). Finally, don't forget to take off your wristwatch and all other jewelry (except a wedding band) during practice. Your goal is to lose your ego, not advertise it.

As might be expected, the care you take with the clothing you wear during practice, and especially at a tournament, is taken as a measure of your respect for the art. The hakama in particular has seven sharp creases that must be maintained. If you take your hakama to the dry cleaner, it might be wise to put tacking stitches in it to maintain the pleats in the proper arrangement until you are assured that the cleaner has some clue as to how it should look. If you plan to wash your hakama, make sure the koshiita is not made of cardboard, or it will dissolve in the wash, losing its shape forever. Parts of a gi may be patched, as long as it is done neatly and with an appropriate color cloth. Japanese dress, in general, is constructed in such a way that it can be easily folded and stored in a dresser drawer, rather than hung in a closet. So is it with the uwagi and hakama. Careful folding preserves the necessary creases and prevents wrinkling. Figures 6 through 8 demonstrate the proper way of folding both uwagi and hakama.

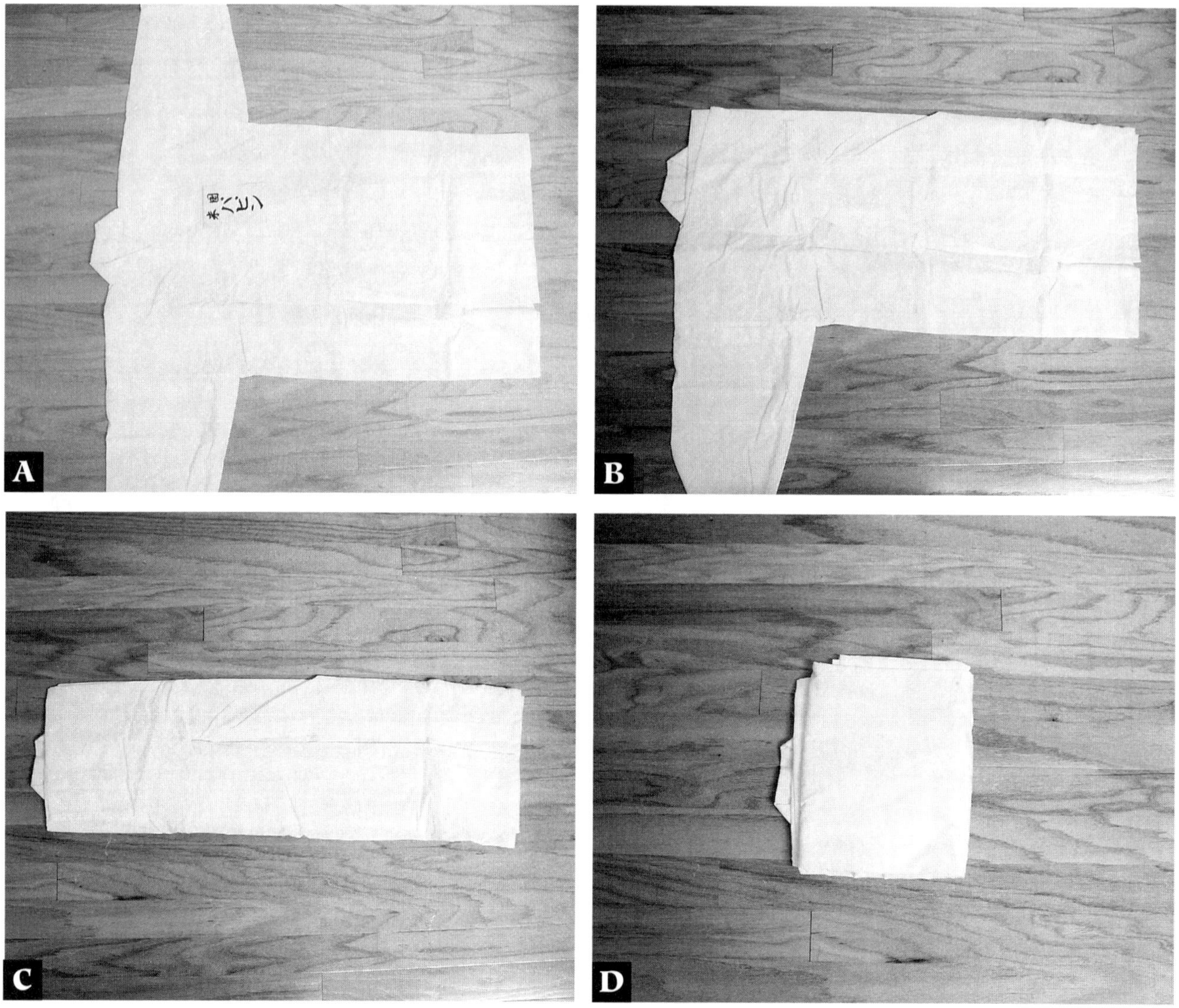

Figures 8A – D: To fold the uwagi the left sleeve and quarter of the trunk are folded across the midline and then the same thing is done with the right side. It is then rolled up into quarters.

RANK

Students here receive one belt and one belt only: the white belt. Those who put in the time, training, and effort will find their belt getting so soiled that eventually it turns black of its own accord. Only then will they have achieved black-belt status ... the true way of Zen Guitar asks black-belt players to redouble their training until their belt becomes so worn and frayed it begins to lose color and returns to white. Only through completion of that circle—white to black, black to white—can one know the depth of the Way.
—Phillip Toshio Sudo, Zen Guitar

The end of all our exploring
Will be to arrive where we started
And know the place for the first time.
—T. S. Eliot

For in much wisdom is much vexation, and he who increases knowledge increases sorrow.
—Ecclesiastes 1:18

The concept of rank as we understand it is a relatively recent development in Japanese martial arts. Jigoro Kano introduced the concept into his newly reorganized judo in the 1950s. It served the purpose of quantifying the growth of skill of his students of this classic jutsu reborn. He borrowed the idea of colored belts from the Koreans. This system was soon adopted by most Japanese budo ryu-ha. Prior to Kano Sensei, certificates by the master were issued to students of a budo upon the attainment of certain levels of expertise, usually three. These were called *menjo (*diploma) or *menkyo* (license). The final one qualified the recipient to open his own school. There are many stories about some of the unusual ways some sensei chose to express their concept of expertise in these documents, often expressing confusing Zen philosophy. For example, at least one student received a blank certificate, revealing a profound Taoist concept. One may wonder what practical value that document held?

In iaido, at present there is no absolute authority that supervises all promotions and therefore serves as a standard of rank. The AUSKF is the supervisory body setting standards in the United States for the majority of dojo. It closely follows the guidelines of the ZNKR, which is the largest oversight body in Japan. Both bodies make strong use of the seitei waza for all early ranks through second dan, *nidan*. After that, some *koryu waza* are introduced into the testing. Up to nidan, a candidate may be tested on an annual basis. After that, the number of years between testing is that of the previous rank. For example, a *sandan* (third dan) must wait 3 years to test for *yondan*. Promotions at the dan level must be tested by a minimum of five *godan* or above approved by the governing body. For the level of godan and above a nihonto (live blade), not an *iaito* (training sword), must be used by the candidate during the testing.

There are six kyu ranks (student ranks) from six to one, the highest perhaps corresponding to a high brown belt in judo or aikido. The dan ranks or instructor ranks go from one, the lowest, to eight, which is pretty much ceremonial. To put things in perspective, the first dan rank, shodan, is defined as a beginner with good basics. Attainment of black belt does, with no exaggeration, mean the beginning of the real journey. One is not considered ready to run a school until godan is achieved. In the final analysis, however, the master of the dojo is responsible for the rank of each student wherever or however the rank is earned and awarded.

The introduction of a rank structure into iaido is a mixed blessing. On the one hand it provides an outline for the student to measure his progress, so in the best of circumstances it provides positive feedback. It also may provide motivation. This is a Western tactic. On the other hand rank structure runs the risk of becoming the objective instead of the means. In Western culture, attaining "black belt" status has social ramifications probably not of significance to Kano Sensei who, of course, was dealing in an Eastern culture. It is very difficult for many Western students to feel comfortable in the traditionally vertically organized dojo social structure that comes naturally to the Japanese student. Throw in rank and competition often flares to the fore. The attainment of rank carries the seed of self-contentment, complacency, and vanity. The black belt who loses his "beginner's mind" because he thinks he has attained it all will never come close to his potential.

Ideally the student, either Eastern or Western, should practice iaido for its own sake. He or she may not be able to ignore rank, but it should be of minimal importance. The quality of the iaido should be the issue and what that means varies from one dojo or sensei to another. The Rev. Kensho Furuya speaks of an elderly student of his who practiced aikido solely for exercise following an illness. He quietly practiced with no thought or care of rank, apparently somewhat independently from others in the class. After some time a visiting sensei pointed out to the rest of the dojo the real level of this man's art (Furuya, 1996). The willingness to relate this story tells volumes of Furuya's attitude, which serves as a model for all of us. Morihei Ueshiba, founder of aikido, wore a white belt his entire career as a symbol that even he was a beginner. If you do iaido with humility you are in good company.

SWORD

Its cold blade, collecting on its surface the moment it is drawn the vapours of the atmosphere; its immaculate texture, flashing light of bluish hue; its matchless edge, upon which histories and possibilities hang; the curve of its back, uniting exquisite grace with up most strength; —all these thrill us with mixed feelings of power and beauty, of awe and terror.
—*Inazu Nitobe,* Bushida: The Warrior's Code

Watch the eyes of any child as a sword is drawn from its sheath. What you will see there expresses the power of the sword far more powerfully than any prose: the recognition of beauty, danger, and potential embodied in a gleaming, elementally cruel form.
—*John J. Donahue,* Complete Kendo

The Japanese sword (*to* or *ken*) had a special relationship to the samurai who carried it. Indeed the sword was considered the warrior's soul. It is a highly specialized yet deceptively simple tool designed to at once slice tissue and bone with as little physical effort as possible. As such it fits the Zen Buddhist's ideals of efficiency, simplicity, and single-mindedness, and so served as a model for the warrior himself.

The first swords found in archeological sites in Japan are of a mainland style: straight and double-edged (*chukuto*). The original "Japanese sword" (nihonto), the tachi, was developed later, during a period when samurai fought mounted on horseback and when the bow was the primary weapon. Transitional blades such as the famous "baby crow" were curved, but had an initial area back from the tip that was double edged. The tachi evolved into a long and deeply curved single-edged blade worn with the edge down, hanging from the samurai's obi. Its strong curve (*sori*) placed the cutting edge tangential to the target to be cut when swung from horseback. From the first modifications of the mainland sword by Amakuni, to the full development of the tachi, five distinct schools of sword making developed, named after their home domain. Called the *gokaden*, they consisted of Yamato, Yamashiro, Bizen, Sagami, and Mino. As the fighting styles changed and samurai fought more often on foot the tachi became shorter—a katana—and was worn edge upward thrust through the obi. This changed drawing the sword from an upward sweeping motion to a horizontal or downward maneuver. A shorter companion blade *(wakizashi)* was usually worn in a similar manner in front of the katana separated by the turns of the obi. This pair of swords (daisho) was the hallmark of the samurai until they were banned following the Meiji Restoration. On occasion a dagger (tanto) was substituted for the wakizashi.

Whatever its length, the Japanese sword was composed of a characteristic compound blade made of multiple welded layers of steel of varying hardness. The steel from which it was made was native iron sand, smeltered in an open pit and oxidized by the forging process. Each layer of the sword itself was made up of very thin welded layers of steel, much like Greek phyllo dough, created by folding the steel over and over during forging. Most often, a harder outer layer surrounded a soft core. After final forging, which created the curve, the blade was water-quenched with all but the cutting edge covered in clay. The overall effect was one of a layered (Damascus) blade with a hard cutting edge and softer steel "sandwiches" making up the bulk of the supporting blade. This unique structure ideally suited the twin needs of temper and brittleness for sharpness and softness, and shock absorbency for strength and to prevent shattering. Such a structure also reduced the amount of steel necessary, producing a blade light enough to be wielded quickly and accurately with one or two hands. This was the genius behind the fact that no other blade has ever surpassed the nihonto for cutting and flexibility. It also partially explains the deeply artistic nature of blade construction, and the individual characteristics of each blade including vitality, nobility, beauty, strength, and spirit. The specific techniques of producing such a blade were such a closely held secret that, for example, one assistant thought it a worthwhile trade to have a finger amputated as punishment for using it to determine the starting temperature of the quenching water prior to tempering.

Making the blade itself was (and is) a religious process practiced by the swordsmith often dressed as a Shinto priest and invoking the kami to help in the process. During its fabrication the blade is born of fire, water, earth, metal, and wood—the classic five elements of Taoist philosophy. In the process it acquires characteristics of the smith, the five elements including all they represent, and the gods and spirits of the forge, smith, and village. The blade then undergoes shaping and polishing by a polisher or *togarashi* and finally is invested in carefully crafted fittings, or koshirae, described below. An excellent description of the making and polishing of a nihonto and its koshirae has been presented by Leon Kapp, Hiroko Kapp, and Yoshindo Yoshihara (1987). During the history of warfare in Japan some swordsmiths were thought to produce "virtuous" blades, while others became infamous for producing "evil" blades. Perhaps the best example of the latter is that of Muramasa, whose blades were reputed to bedevil the Tokugawa clan during its rise to power at the end of the sengoku jidai.

Collectors classify Japanese swords by the era in which they were made, the province and the smith, as well as their size and shape. Many historic blades are characteristic enough that they can be identified even when they are unsigned or dated. Blades made through the sengoku jidai are called koto (old blades). Those from that point until 1781are called shinto (new blades). Those made during the last half of the Edo era are shinshinto (new new blades), and all those made after 1868 are considered modern blades (gendaito) or newly made blades (shinsakuto). This does not include blades made in way not conforming to the traditional materials or manufacturing methods. Thus a handmade blade of 1938, forged and water-tempered but made of Manchurian railroad tracks, would not be a gendaito, but a showato. Military blades of the Pacific War, many of which were machine made, are termed gunto (military blades). Neither of the later two examples can be registered in Japan.

PARTS OF A BLADE

...one of the most incredible aspects of the Japanese sword is that normally it has few if any straight lines or wholly plane surfaces. Not only are most swords composed of curved lines and curved planes, instead of uniform arcs of a circle, they have variously changing radii. These sections of parabolic lines and surfaces are so harmoniously combined that, no matter how one may examine them, at no point is there a break in the harmony of pattern or any harsh deviation. Amazingly, all this has been accomplished by simple handwork of hammer, scraper, and stone, guided by the eye and the instinct of the artist.

—Walter A. Compton

Figures 9 and 11 illustrate the common features of a katana blade. No attempt is made to describe the variations in shape of these features, different with each age, location, and swordsmith. Books that cover these details (Yumoto, 1958; Sato, 1983; Nagayama, 1997) are found in the Select Bibliography.

Mune—the back of the blade shown in Figures 9 and 10 (mu)
Monouchi—the first 10 inches or so of the blade used for slicing.
Ha—the sharp edge of the blade. Figures 9 and 10 (h)
Shinogi—the ridge on each side of the blade. Some blades, most often tanto (daggers) do not have such a ridge. Figure 9 (sg)
Nakago—the tang that is invested by the tsuka. Figure 10 (G).
Mei—the carved signature of the sword smith, which often includes his location. Figure 10 (Mon)
Shinogi-ji —the flat, usually parallel sides of the blade between the shinogi and the mune.
Munemachi—the notch on the mune side of the blade that the habaki butts up against. Figure 10 (E)
Hamon—the pattern of the junction between the brittle edge and the softer upper blade. Figure 9 (hn).
Hamachi—the notch on the ha side of the blade that the habaki butts up against. Figure 10 (F)
Hi, bo-hi—the groove(s) on the side of each blade to lighten it. Not all blades have hi.
Mekugi ana—the hole(s) in the nakago for the peg that locks on the tsuka. Figure 10 (H)
Kissaki—the tip of the blade. Figure 9 (ki)
Nakagojiri—the butt end of the nakago.
Yokote—the angle that delineates the kissaki between the planes of the kissaki and shinoji. Figure 9 (y)
Sori—the amount of curvature of the blade as measured by a line from Munemachi to kissaki
Kasane—the thickness of the blade

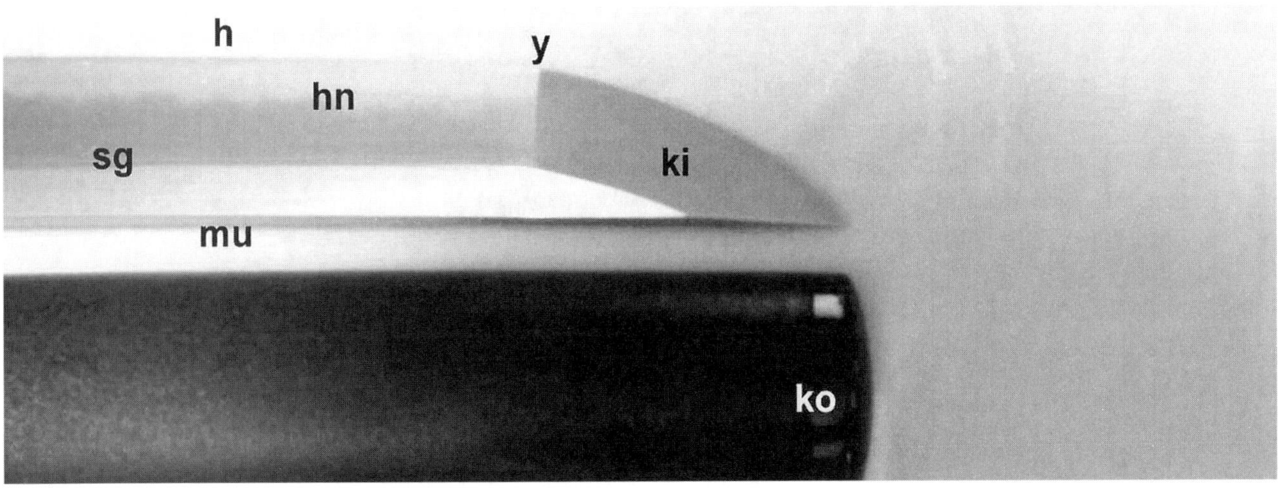

Figure 9: Parts of the tips of the sword blade and saya described in the text.

SWORD FURNITURE AND TSUKA

Furniture (koshirae) complement and enhance the natural beauty of the blade and express the personality of the swordsman as well as serving the fully functional purposes of protecting the blade and the hands of the swordsman. Figures 9 through 11 demonstrate a set of koshirae for a typical katana. (Military and tachi-style koshirae have other names.)

Tsuka—The handle or hilt of the sword. Figure 10 (Ts)
Tsuba—the handguard between the habaki and Tsuka. Figure 10 (B)
Kashira—the endcap or pommel of the tsuka. Figure 10 (P)
Habaki—the collar that butts against the tsuba and tsuka and wedges the blade tightly into the saya. Figure 10 (A)
Fuchi—the collar or cap at the tsuba end of the tsuka through which the nakaga passes. Figure 10 (J)
Seppa—the washers that keep the tsuba tight. Figure 10 (C).
Menuki—the talisman carvings or castings under the wrapping of the tsuka that provides grip. Figure 10 (M)
Mekugi—the peg that holds the tsuka to the nakago. Figure 10 (D)
Tsuka-ito—the cotton, silk, or leather ribbon woven around the samé of the tsuka. Figure 10 (K)
Samé—the ray skin leather that is wrapped around the wooden tsuka to strengthen it. Figure 10 (N)

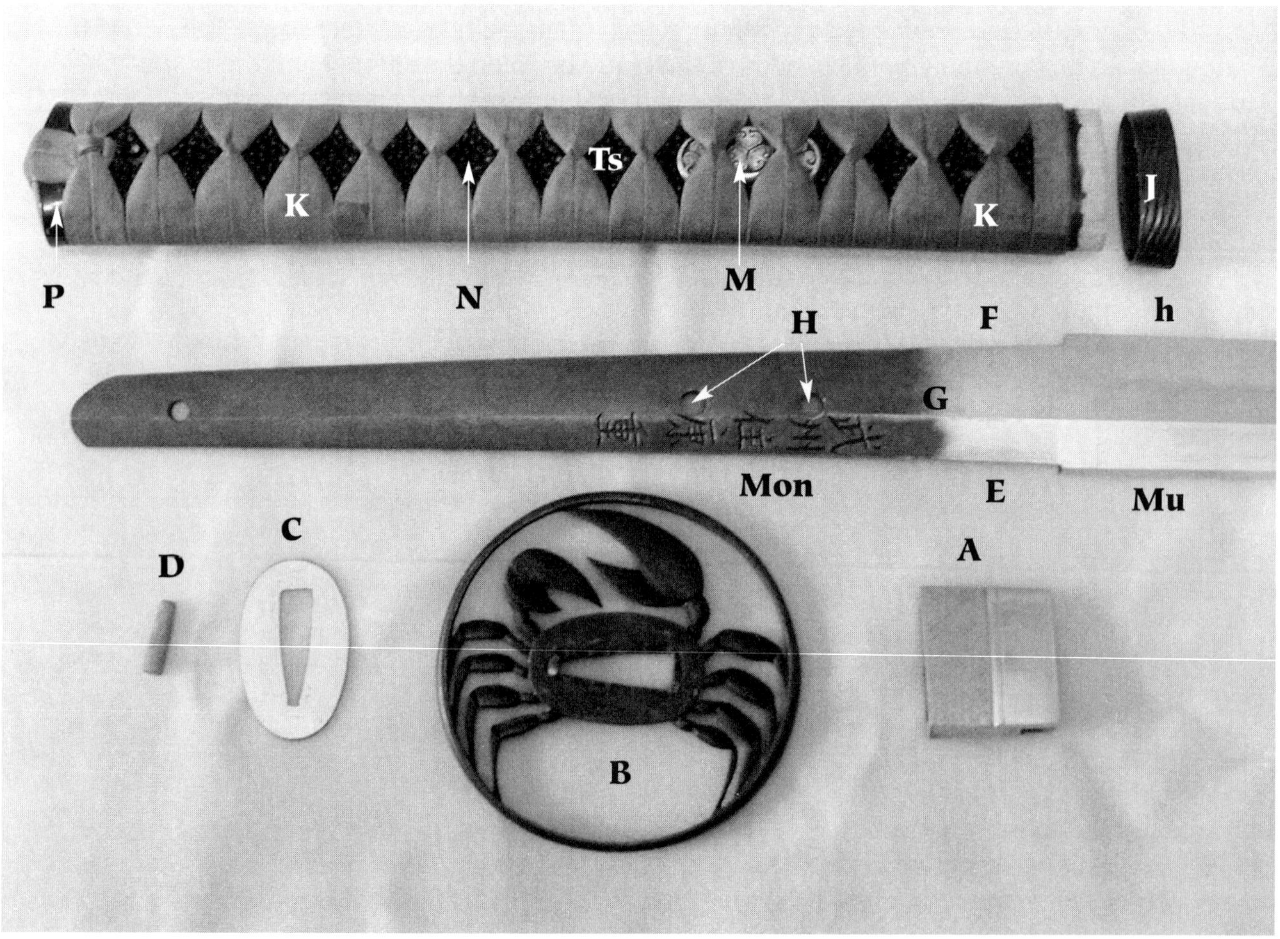

Figure 10: Koshirae (sword furniture) described in the text.

PARTS OF THE SAYA

A saya is constructed of two matched pieces of soft, nonresinous wood, usually Japanese magnolia, or *ho*. In this country poplar is a reasonable substitute. A groove for the blade is carved in each mirror-image face and the two then glued together. One piece is usually etched deeper than the other, thus putting the sharp edge of the blade or *ha*, off the seam. In a traditional saya, two- to three-day-old rice was mashed into a paste and used to join the two halves. This allowed the saya to be split open for occasional cleaning without damaging the wood. A receptacle was often carved into the inside of the saya past the tip of the blade (*kissaki*) to collect blood, oil, and dirt that might drip or fall from the blade.

The saya complements the blade and koshirae as well as protecting the blade. It is an essential and somewhat overlooked element in the practice of iaido. A poorly fitting saya will interfere with nukitsuke and noto as well as serving as a hazard to the general handling of the sword. A rattling of a blade inside a poorly fitted saya is extremely annoying, especially to judges. In some kata practiced by schools of kenjutsu, the saya is used to distract the enemy or to aid in blocking an attack. Even in some of the Muso Shinden ryu kata the saya is used to push the enemy into a position of disadvantage.

All saya were not used to wear the sword. *Shirasaya* (white saya) were unfinished saya with matching tsuka used to store the blade for long periods. Often a wooden blade was used to hold the working saya with koshirae together for display. Since the time that wearing swords was forbidden in the empire, most art blades came in shirasaya only. It is only recently that full koshirae have become fashionable again. It is not uncommon in martial arts supply catalogues to see shirasaya touted as ninja equipment; they were never used for anything but storage.

Figures 9 and 11 illustrate the parts of a working saya for a katana.

Koiguchi—the mouth of the saya. Figure 11A (g)
Kurigata—the fitting on the omote side that the sageo is attached to. Figure 11A (ku)
Shitodome—the metal fitting lining the hole in the kurigata through which the sageo passes. Figure 11A (sh)
Sageo—the woven cord used to tie the saya to the obi. Figures 11A and B (sgo) On the left, it is tied in a decorative slip knot for display. When worn, it is attached to the kurigata by a simple overhand slip knot with both ends of equal length and attached to the kurigata of the habaki by a single half-hitch, as illustrated on the right. (Figure 11B)
Kojiri—the tip of the saya. Figure 9 (ko) Sometimes it is covered by a fitting.

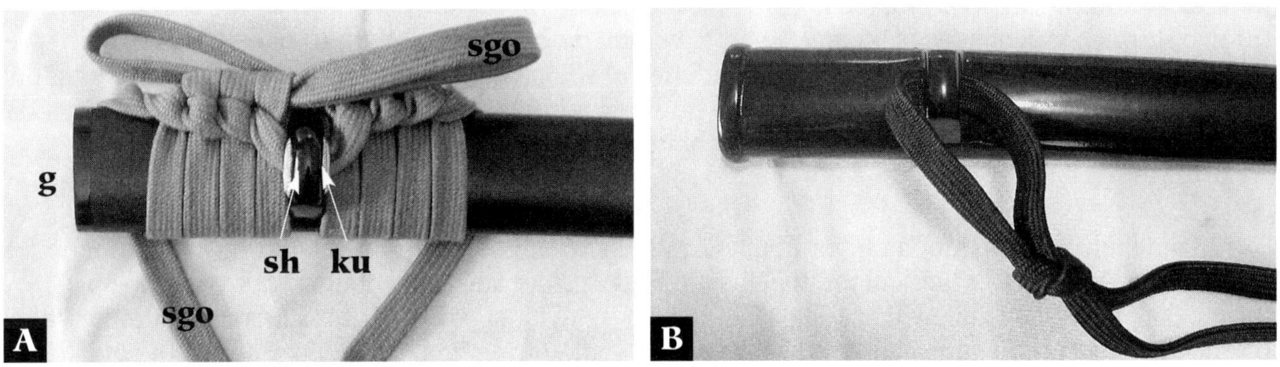

Figures 11A and B: Parts of the koiguchi end of the saya. On the left, the sageo is tied in a decorative knot for display. On the right it is tied in an overhand slip knot, ready to be worn for iaido. The saya on the right has an overhanging koiguchi cap that is stronger and preferred by some iaidoka.

CHOOSING YOUR SWORD

Security is mostly a superstition. It does not exist in nature, nor do the children of humans as a whole experience it. Avoiding danger is no safer in the long run than outright exposure. Life is either a daring adventure or nothing.
—Helen Keller

The present life is but the joy of self-deception.
—Qur'an 57:20

WHAT TO CONSIDER

Aside from the aesthetics of a sword, which after all will represent nothing less than your soul, the choice of a proper sword is related to the physical properties of both you and it. The sword's variables are safety, length, weight, balance, shape, fittings, and price. Your variables are height, strength, skill, and wealth.

Safety

Do not ever swing a sword not specifically manufactured for cutting or iaido practice. Never! Most Japanese military swords of World War II origin (gunto) are safe to practice with, but should first be inspected by a knowledgeable polisher for signs of weakness or damage and to guarantee that the blade is in fact what it is purported to be. The obvious dangers of using a sharpened sword should be kept in mind. Both the left hand and the saya take a real beating while the iaidoka is learning to respect a live blade, not to mention the potential danger to furniture, ceilings, and spectators. Most iaidoka who use a live blade started with, and stayed with, a training sword (iaito) for a long time. Training swords are for most if not all of us. They can be acquired from several well-known suppliers of iaido equipment. This has been greatly facilitated by the Internet.

A special warning must be emphasized about cheap "display swords" freely available from martial arts and novelty stores and from mail-order catalogues. Most "samurai" swords available in this manner are made for *display only*. Neither the metal nor the handle is adequate to take the severe stresses of being swung. Two particularly weak points are, first, near the junction of the blade and tang within the handle and second, near or through the retaining peg hole. Most of these "swords" have handles wrapped in embossed plastic ray skin (samé) along with tangs that do not extend through the entire handle. When the sword is held horizontally and wiggled side to side the end of the tang can be felt pushing against the plastic in the palm of the hand. This can result in the handle splintering, as well as a loose blade if it is swung. An unsharpened toy blade can still be thrown through a person, kissaki first. Even a well-made blade may break under some circumstances. The author has had the experience of seeing a senior student of his sensei break the blade of a quality and proven Japanese iaito by simply dropping it horizontally on a hardwood floor. Metal fatigue may have played a big part in that incident.

Length

This depends pretty much on your height and length of your arms. Feudal swords were made for people rarely over 5 feet tall and are too short for an average modern American. A good rule of thumb is to hold the tsuka with the right hand right up against the tsuba and then place the kissaki on the floor in front of your right foot with your hand alongside your leg (Figure 12). If the angle the blade makes is less than 15 degrees off vertical, it's too short. If the angle is 20 degrees or more, it is too long.

Figure 12: An easy way of determining if a sword fits you. The angle of the blade with the tip on the ground should be between 15 to 20 degrees.

Blades are usually measured in an old Japanese system of length similar to our English system, but a little "off" what we are used to.

A *shaku* is a little less than 1 foot.
(11.93 inches)
A *sun* is a little more than 1 inch.
(1.19 inches) 1/10 of a shaku
A *bu* is a little less than 1/8 inch.
(0.119 inches) 1/10 of a sun

The designated length of the blade disregards the tang. For example:

The blade the author (who is 5 feet 11 inches) uses is designated 2.6, which is 2 shaku 6 sun and is actually 31 inches long from kissaki to hamachi. The sword's overall length is 40 inches from kissaki to kashira, and 2 inches longer than that when in its saya.

The length of the tsuka is usually between 8 and 9 inches, although some iaidoka prefer the leverage and balance a longer handle offers. A rough rule of thumb is one-third the length of the blade.

Weight

The average iaito weighs between 800 and 1,000 grams, depending on the mass of the blade. Most beginners usually start with a fairly light blade, which allows them to gradually build up the necessary muscles, particularly of the right arm and wrist. A light blade is quick to start and stop; unfortunately, it is easier to bully and has less momentum to aid its power during a swing. A heavy blade is harder for a beginner to get going, but once moving is less likely to be disturbed in its path by mistakes. This is useful if the sword is launched in the proper direction and plane in the first place. "Sword-Spirit-One" means we try to learn not to fight our sword, but blend with it. One way to change the weight of a sword is to change the tsuba, but be warned—that changes the balance as well.

Shape

The shape of the blade is always a gradual curve, but during different periods of history, the curve varied in degree and pattern. Most, if not all, iaito blades have the point of greatest curve off a horizontal line at the midpoint between kissaki and hamachi. This may shift in either direction on antique live blades. A greater curve allows easier cutting by bringing the blade tangential to the target. In iaito it is more a matter of aesthetics than anything else.

Most iaito have grooves down both sides of the blade. On a tempered blade, these are to lighten it. On an iaito they not only lighten it but also allow it to "swish" when swung properly. The swish is a useful tool to help you on the way, but be warned: "swishing" can become addictive! Most swords made for cutting (*batto-do, tamishigiri*) do not have grooves (*bo-hi*) because they are narrow and light enough to start with. The grooves also weaken the blade, making it more susceptible to bending or breaking. These grooveless blades cut just fine with the application of proper technique.

Balance

The balance point of a sword is usually 7 or 8 inches in front of the tsuba. This is a personal choice, but extremes should be avoided. There is a tendency to chop with a tip-heavy sword. A light-tipped sword can be whipped around more easily but will tend to lack authority. Many iaito, expensive or not, have never had anyone really try to balance them, and the koshirae are often a matter of chance or cost, not balance. An easy but limited way to change the balance of a sword is to use a lighter or heavier tsuba.

Fittings

Iaido is a traditional art, and the sword should express the style of feudal Japan and be restrained in both color and decoration. Since the sword is such a personal thing, it is very appropriate for it to express the tastes of the iaidoka so long as those tastes are consistent with tradition. It is enlightening to learn the significance of the many decorative motifs used on swords, and if you have an opportunity to choose them for your own sword, so much the better. For example, a common theme, *botan-shishi*, peony-lion, illustrates the contrasting traits of strength and delicate beauty inherent in an ideal warrior. Many purveyors of iaito offer a limited choice of koshirae with some blades. Alternative fushi-kashira, menuki, and tsuba, either of modern manufacture or even authentic antiques, are available on the market as replacements. One thing to keep in mind when choosing a tsuba is the texture of the omote surface. The upper left quadrant is the surface the base of your thumb will be in intimate contact with while during kata. The tsuba shown on the left in Figure 13A is likely to be kinder to your skin than the one in 13B. A variety of fittings can be seen on the swords illustrated in Figure 15A through D.

The tsuka deserves a special note since it also is not entirely an aesthetic consideration. Handles are traditionally wrapped first in ray skin, which provides grip and strengthens the wood underneath. This was all some original swords had. Most often the samé was overwrapped by a ribbon of some kind,

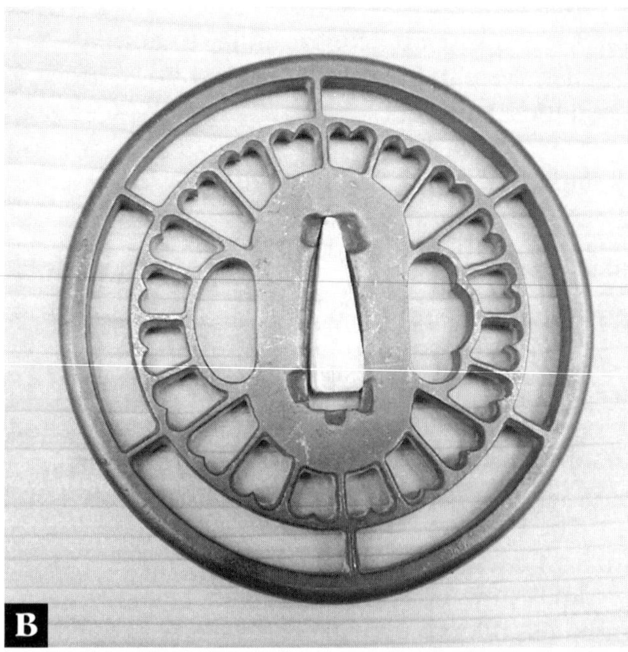

Figures 13A and B: The tsuba on the right is much more likely to abrade the base of your thumb than the one on the left.

tsuka-ito, to hold it in place and to add further strength and improve the grip. Some inexpensive iaito have synthetic (plastic) samé. This may look fine but its strength is marginal and it does not absorb perspiration. With lengthy practice it may be very difficult to keep it from slipping from your grip and should be avoided. Most often the overwrap is cotton. This absorbs moisture well without getting slippery but wears out fairly quickly and stains or discolors easily especially if it is not black. Having a tsuka rewrapped properly can cost as much as the blade of an iaito. Leather and silk are the other two options. Leather on modern swords is usually treated so that it does not absorb moisture; because it can't be pulled tightly it is glued in place. It looks beautiful but it can become rather slippery and wears out relatively quickly, particularly when gripped too tightly (as all beginners do). Silk is ideal, but expensive and depending on the style of weave, may tend to snag up loops which can get pretty ugly quickly on less expensive wraps. While most if not all modern shinken and iaido are wrapped in the fashion shown in Figure 10, a variety of wrapping patterns were used in the past.

Price

What you need is a safe sword of the proper length and weight for your size. If finances dictate skimping, do it first with fittings and style, never with safety. The sword should appeal to your sense of aesthetics but keep in mind that it is humility that permeates all Zen Buddhist-inspired arts. A plain sword of quality says much about your spirit, taste, and priorities.

Because of the fluctuations of the value of the yen to the dollar, any discussion of prices can only be approximate. A smaller, serviceable iaito can be purchased for about $250. A heavier, fancier iaito will average around $500 but can cost as much as $2,000. A reasonably preserved and physically sound machine-made gunto of World War II vintage can cost $500 and up. Non-Japanese (usually Chinese) forged and tempered blades suitable for cutting and iaido are becoming widely available and can be found for $800 on up, but the quality varies greatly. Be advised that the hamon on such blades may be created with acid etching, rather than the inherent qualities of the steel. That does not affect safety, but scratching or polishing will remove the "hamon." Also, acid treatment makes the blade more likely to rust if

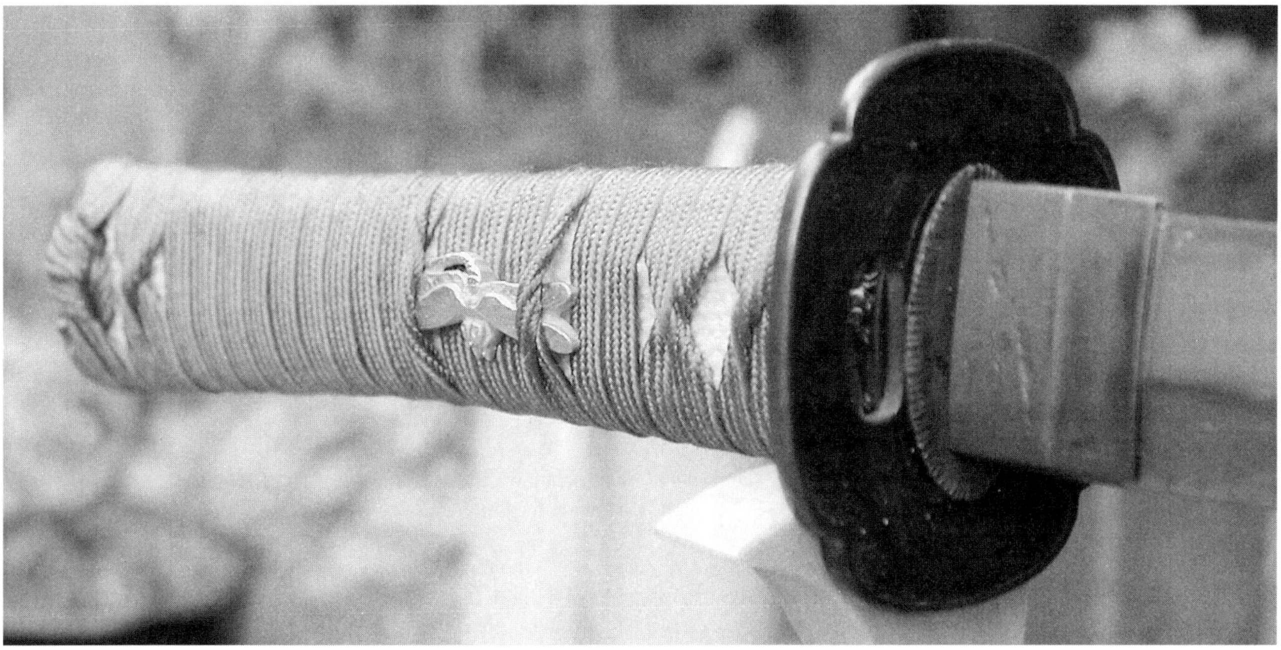

Figure 14: A presentation-style tsuka-ito wrap on a Koto wakizashi.

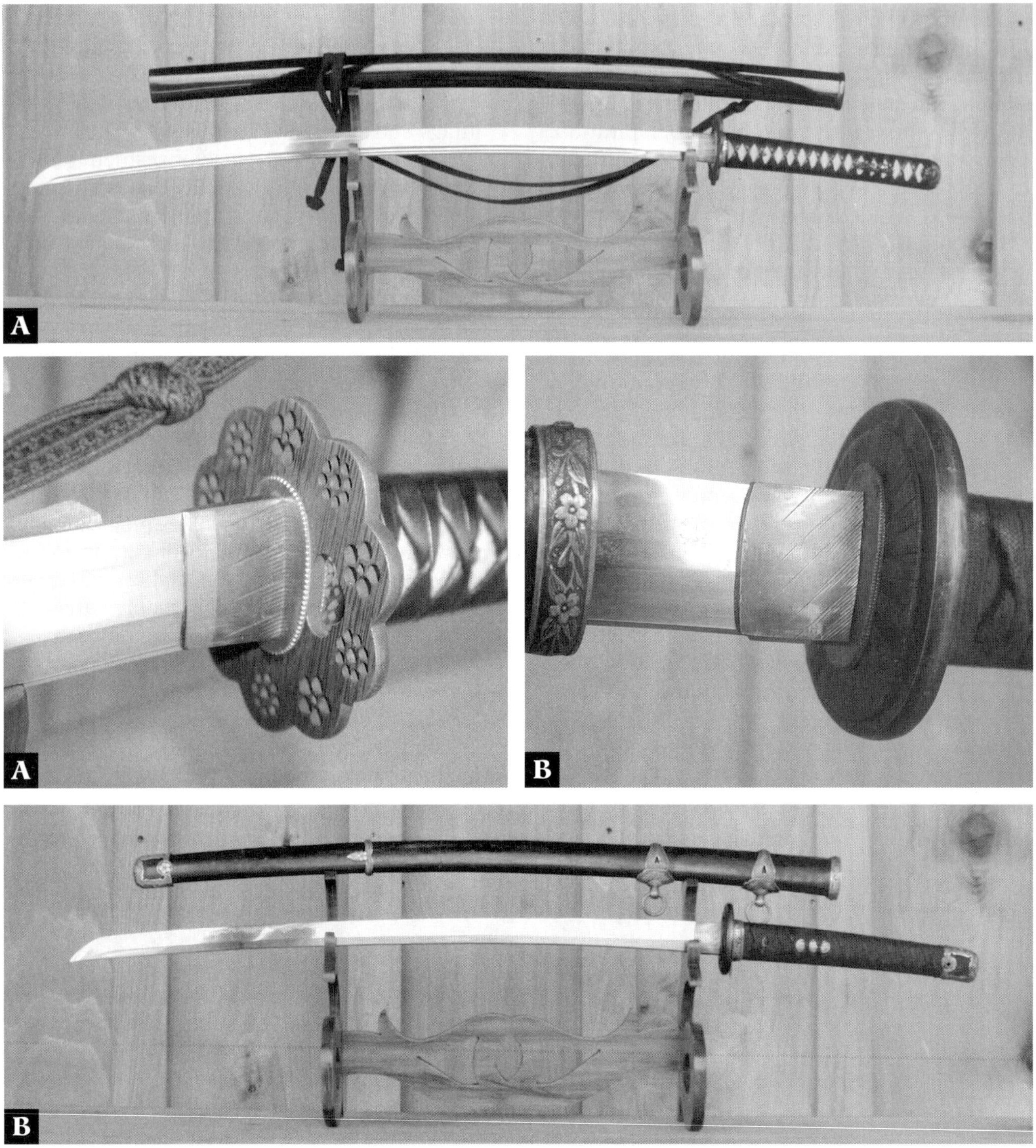

Figures 15A and B: A variety of swords can be used for iaido.

Figure 15A shows a modern Japanese lightweight (800gm) iaito with leather tsuka-ito (28-inch blade). The blade is nonferrous and has a bo-hi. The "hamon" was made by grinding. It cost $400 shipped from Japan.

Figure 15B shows a prePacific War kai gunto (naval sword) in military koshirae (26-inch blade). The blade is hand-forged and signed but only semisharp and has no bo-hi. It could be used for iaido with a different saya, but more properly it should have all its koshirae replaced for that purpose. It cost $1,200 from an American dealer.

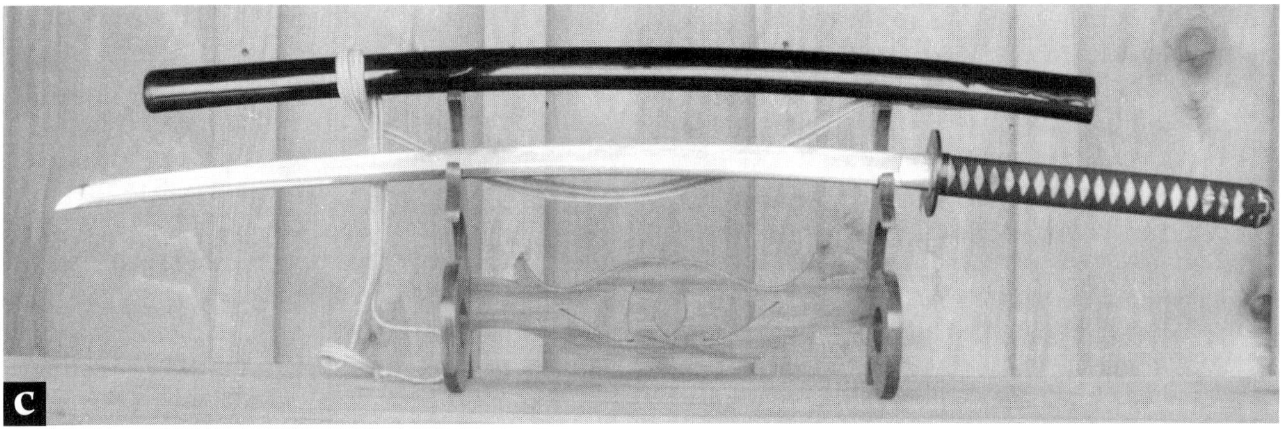

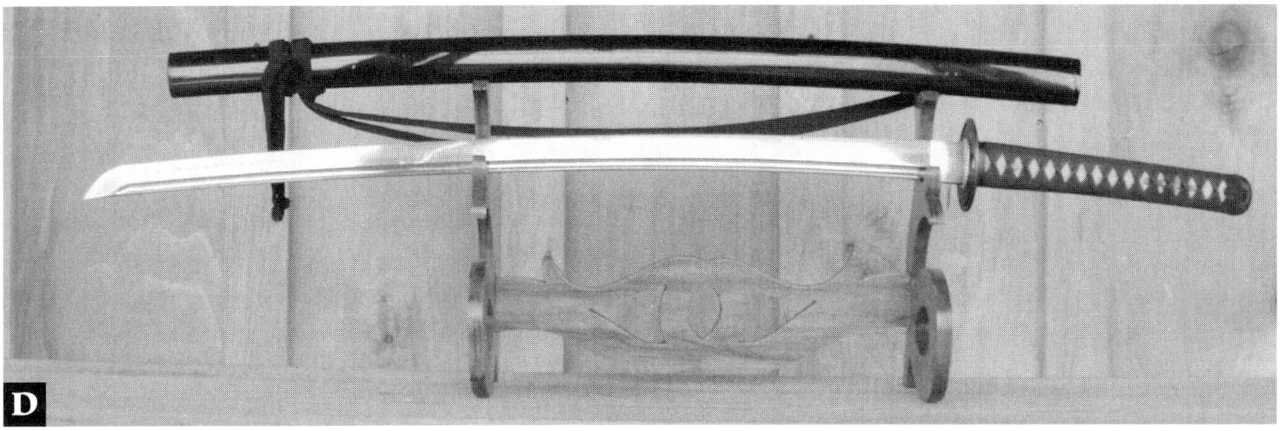

Figure 15C shows a forged-iron sword made in China (30-inch blade). It is sharp enough to cut with. The "hamon" has been created by acid etching and the blade has no bo-hi. It cost $800 from its first owner and was offered on the Internet. The author has subsequently shortened the tsuka.

Figure 15D shows a modern forged and signed shinsakuto made for tamishigiri (28-inch blade). It is sharp, slightly tip-weighted, has an active hamon, and has a bo-hi. It cost $3,200 from the same dealer as the sword in Figure 15B.

not cared for properly. Modern Japanese forged-iron blades designed for iaido or batto-jutsu (shinken or shinsakuto) will cost from $2,000 to $3,000 or more. They should not be compared with art swords at all but considered a special-purpose tool with which to practice iaido or cutting. Those designed especially for cutting usually have heavier, tip-balanced blades while those designed for iaido are usually lighter and more centrally balanced. Those with a bo-hi will come at a higher price.

Art swords of current production (gendaito) cost $4,000 and up (mostly up!). A good argument can be made for not using an art sword for iaido because of the exposure of the blade to almost constant handling. Ancient nihonto can range from worthless and/or unsafe (full of forging defects, stress fractures, poorly cared for, overpolished, or otherwise misused by amateurs) to priceless treasures. Old is not necessarily valuable. Any sword other than an iaito should be purchased from a dealer with a good reputation who offers a refund period, and a knowledgeable polisher should appraise the sword beforehand. The Internet has greatly increased the availability of all swords to the non-aficionado, since most of us can't afford to travel to sword shows with any regularity to buy equipment. The corresponding danger is that there is no way to really know what you are getting other than by trusting the reputation of the dealer on whom you are completely dependent. The experience of others in your dojo, especially your sensei, with different dealers should be an invaluable first step to finding your blade.

One final point is worth making. You do not perform iaido with a blade alone; the saya is an integral and somewhat neglected necessity. If the saya is not made properly it may disfigure a nihonto or iaito and at the worst, bind the blade and prevent a smooth nukitsuke. More common is rattling, caused by the saya's either having been made improperly, or just being worn out. Nukitsuke and noto should be silent, and saya noises are very distracting both to the iaidoka and to observers, especially judges. A common problem with a saya is the loosening of its grip on the habaki over time. This is not really a failing of the saya, just a bothersome side effect of aging. To some extent, the grip of the saya on the habaki will vary with ambient temperature and humidity. The necessary habit of keeping the thumb on the tsuba at all times is testimony to how ubiquitous this problem is now and was in the past. The life of a saya can be prolonged by carefully painting the inside of the koiguchi with one or more layers of clear nail polish (lacquer). If done in an irregular manner this may lead to a few more scratches on your habaki, but that is a small price to pay for preventing your sword from hitting the deck unexpectedly or worse, severely cutting your palm.

HANDLING YOUR SWORD

In my strategy, the training for killing enemies is by way of many contests, fighting for survival, discovering the meaning of life and death, learning the Way of the sword, judging the strength of attacks and understanding the Way of the "edge and ridge" of the sword.
—*Musashi Miyamoto,* Book of Five Rings

What then is the "combat mind-set"? It is that state of mind which insures victory in a gunfight. It is composed of awareness, anticipation, concentration and coolness. Above all, its essence is self-control.
—*Jeff Cooper,* To Ride, Shoot Straight, and Speak the Truth

A sword should be carried in the left hand, the arm straight down with the tsuka forward and the ha upward. This position is called *sageto* (Figures 16A and B). The kurigata should be in your left palm, and your thumb should be extended with its tip holding the top of the tsuba. The tsuka is brought slightly in front of you so that the entire sword and saya are at about a 35-degree angle off straight ahead. The sageo should be neatly coiled and either held with the index finger or looped around the thumb. Care should be taken not to let the loose ends of the sageo dangle below its loops. When entering the dojo, moving around the dojo, or moving to or from a *shinza* or *embu* the left arm should be flexed to the sword is held at the level of the obi. This position is called *teito* (Figures 16C and D). The sword is also lifted into teito in preparation for a bow or to place the sword in your obi.

A drawn sword is to a samurai what a loaded and cocked gun is to a modern warrior. It should not be drawn except for a specific purpose, which is usually to cut someone. If it is drawn for any other legitimate purpose, such cleaning it or examining it, especially around other persons, it must be handled in a formal ritualistic fashion. This both shows the bystanders you know how to handle a sword safely and that you are honoring them by putting yourself in harm's way so that you do not place them in danger. It also demonstrates respect for the sword itself. This is the same as opening the breech of a firearm in front of the person to receive it so that all can see it is empty, or by being cautious never to point the muzzle of a firearm toward anyone, loaded or not.

When transferring a sword to another, the sharp part of the blade (ha) is always turned toward the bearer, never at others. After all, you are not going to pass your sword to someone you do not trust. When transferring a sword, sheathed or unsheathed, the tsuka is handled with one hand,

Figures 16A through D: Front and side views showing the difference between sageto (upper two photos) and teito (lower two photos). Notice in both positions that the loose ends of the sageo are not dangling.

Figure 17: The proper way to pass a sword to another. The sword is going left to right. The ha is pointed toward the swordsman offering the blade, and he is holding it at the end of the tsuka. He controls the sageo with the other hand. The receiving swordsman grasps the tsuka near the tsuba and nods his assumption of control.

usually the weakest, so that it is easier for the receiver to strike the bearer with the blade than vice versa. This is usually accomplished as shown in Figure 17. The sheathed sword can also be offered horizontally using both hands, ha toward the bearer, tsuba held in place with the thumb. In either case, if the saya has a sageo, it is held in the nonessential hand and handed to the recipient after he has received and stabilized the sword. Always check the mekugi to make sure it is well seated before passing a sword to anyone. When giving and receiving a sword, a short bow, or at least a nod tells the other person involved that you or he then has control and the sword will not be dropped. Also, make sure the transfer occurs in a large enough area that it is unlikely to be interrupted by other people or furniture.

WEARING YOUR SWORD

As a string of the kithera vibrates purely, emitting only that note of the musical scale which is its alone, so must the individual warrior shed all which is superfluous in his spirit, until he himself vibrates at that sole pitch which his individual daimon dictates. The achievement of this ideal, in Lakedaemon, carries beyond courage on the battlefield; it is considered the supreme embodiment of virtue, andreia, of a citizen and a man.

—*Steven Pressfield,* Gates of Fire

The sword is worn on your left side, ha upward, thrust through the obi with the kurigata an inch or two above and in front of the obi. Under most circumstances, you should keep the tsuba at your midline. This places the tsuka in an optimal position to be reached with the right hand for a draw. It also causes the kojiri end of the saya to flare out slightly from your hips. When walking about while wearing a sword, you must allow for a little extra clearance room on your left side. To accidentally strike another's saya with yours (*saya ate*) is a real faux pas.

Before placing the sword in your obi it is proper to bow to it by holding it horizontally aloft in front of you with both hands, the tsuka to your right and the sageo coiled in your right fingers (Figure 18). Make sure the free ends of the sageo do not extend below the level of the coils. Then bend your head and waist slightly without moving the position of your hands or the sword.

To place the sword in the obi, continue to support it and the sageo with your right hand keeping it as horizontal as possible. At the same time bring your left hand with the kojiri to the obi at your

Figure 18: Bowing to the sword (torei) before wearing or after removing your sword.

Figures 19A through F: Sequence of placing the sword in your obi.

midline. Separate the second and third layers of your obi with your right thumb and thrust the kojiri between them. As the kojiri comes out beneath the obi at your left side, slip one of the ties of your hakama under it. This will help support the saya when it is empty, preventing it from slipping vertically when the weight of the sword has been removed. Unobtrusively bring the sageo to your right side and make the ends of it fast to one of your hakama ties on this side. Then pull on the middle part of the sageo to make sure it is secure before bringing your right hand to your side. Finally, grasp the koiguchi of the saya with your left hand and place your thumb, extended, on the top of the tsuba (Figures 19A through F). To remove the sword informally, such as when standing at the end of practice, stabilize the sword with your left hand, with your thumb on the tsuba, and pull the end of the sageo loose with your right hand. Bring the sageo to your left hand and slip it under one of your left fingers. Then withdraw the sword and saya about 6 inches at a 45-degree angle toward your right. Grasp the koiguchi and sageo with the right hand and place your left palm flat on the obi over the saya. Extract the sword and saya from your obi with your right hand, grasp the kojiri with your

Figure 20: Placing the sword along a wall temporarily to perform some task better done without wearing it. Never leave a sword where it can be stepped on.

left hand as it comes out from beneath the obi, and hold it up above you for a bow as described above.

If you are removing the sword during practice to adjust your clothing, to exercise, or to switch to a bokken, but will be putting it back on later, remove it as described above and then step to the nearest wall keeping it on your left side and parallel to the sword. Slide your left leg backward and kneel on your left knee. Place the sword against the wall with the ha facing it and the sageo along the saya, bent over itself so that it does not extend past the kojiri. Then stand and go about your business. To recover the sword from the floor, kneel on your left knee with the sword to your left and the tsuka forward of you. Pick it up by grasping the sageo first and then the koiguchi end of the saya with your left hand. Stabilize the tsuba with your thumb and bring the sword to your left side in the carry position. Then stand, dragging the rearward foot forward as you do (Figure 20).

Handling the sword in this fashion not only shows respect for your sword and the dojo, but also allows you to maintain zanshin. It keeps you and your sword in an optimal position for a quick draw if attacked during the maneuver. A final note is in order as far as safety goes. The need for keeping your thumb on the tsuba has been discussed earlier. Unfortunately, most of us are less than diligent at times and the possibility exists that the sword may slide tsuka first out of the saya toward the floor. Let it go! The habits you develop will last whether you carry a live blade or not, so always act as if you are. Trying to stop a sword from hitting the ground by reflexively gasping the blade has cut many kendoka. You can stop a blade from coming out of the saya by pushing on the side of the blade with your finger, but it is smart just to let it hit the floor and stop moving before you try to pick it up. An embarrassing clatter is a lot better than a trip to the emergency room for sutures.

EXAMINING AND CLEANING YOUR SWORD

Uchidachi teaches shidachi by sacrificing himself, training as if he were going to be killed at any moment; this self-sacrifice embodies the spirit of teachers and parents. Kata training is of no use without understanding this. It is this spirit that allows shidachi to grow and polish his or her own spirit. Kata bujutsu teaches neither victory nor defeat, but rather how to nurture others and pull them to a higher level. That is budo.
—*Nishioka Tsuneo,* Sword and Spirit

As with all other sword activities there is a proper way to examine a sword. Since this is the first step to cleaning one, the two are treated together. You examine a sword sitting in seiza, with any implements needed close at hand. The *ura* side is toward you, convex edge up (as worn), the tsuka in your right hand. Bow to the sword by holding it slightly above your forehead and then flexing your waist without moving your arms. Look at the entire outside (omote, uma) first. Unsheath the sword when it is safe and after obtaining any necessary permission. It is impolite to examine a sword half sheathed. Remove the saya by pushing it off along the mune using your left hand and set it alongside your left thigh. You may then examine the habaki and the adjacent blade. You may also look along the side or edge of the entire blade as long as it does not bobble around in the process.

Figures 21A through E: Sequence of examining a blade. Note that no pieces of furniture or people are nearby.

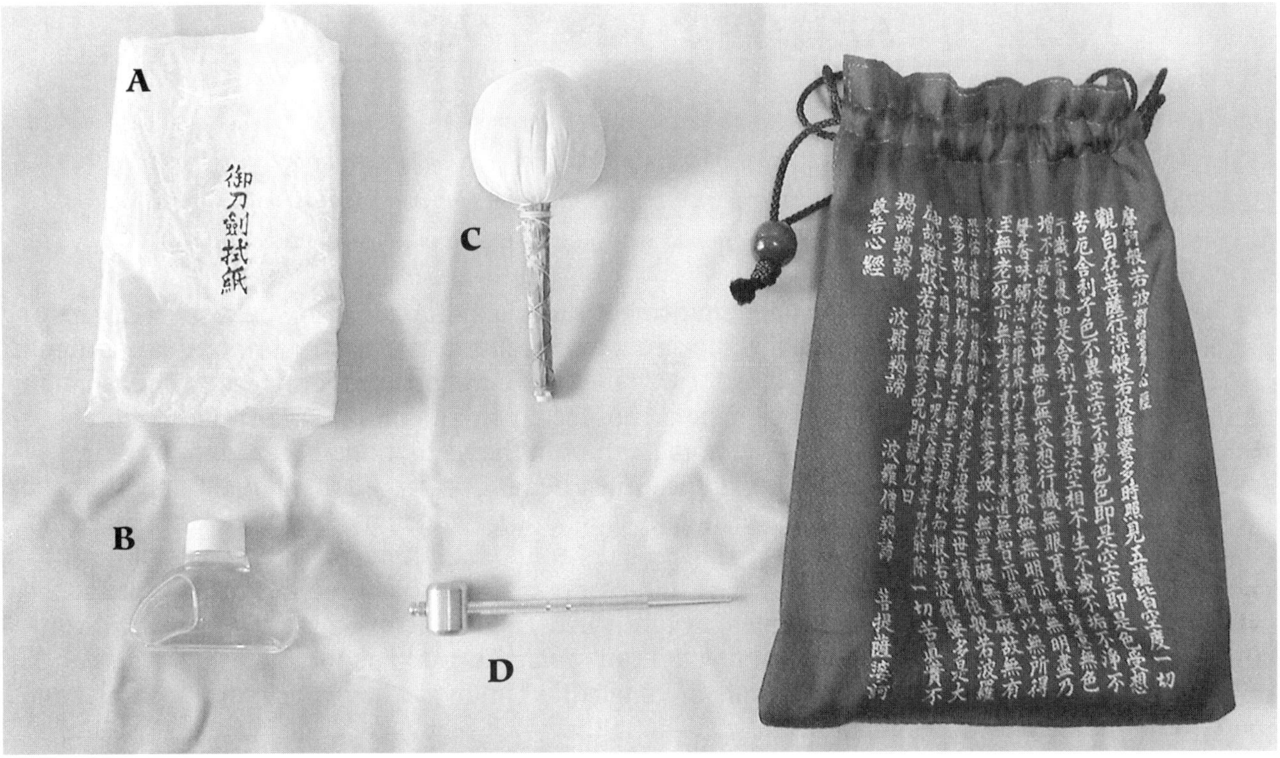

Figure 22: Contents of an average sword care kit including paper (a), choji oil (b), uchiko powder in a silk application ball (c), and a tool for removing mekugi (d).

To closely examine the monouchi and kissaki it is necessary for you to support the blade. Do this with your left hand using a clean, lint-free cloth or paper between your fingers and the steel. Fingerprints can etch a blade in one hour. Do not sneeze, blow, cough, or sweat on the blade, either. The blade is cleaned with the cloth or paper if necessary and then sheathed in the reverse order.

Any cleaning and/or oiling are done after the blade has been examined as described above. The following applies to the care of a live blade. Abrasive powder should not be used on an alloy blade and light mineral oil is adequate for lubrication. The shinken blade is first wiped with paper bent around the mune from habaki to kissaki, ha upward, to remove old oil and any grit. If more cleaning is necessary, *uchiko* powder is sprinkled on to the blade with an applicator ball and wiped off as above using multiple strokes to affect a mild polish. Craig states the proper number is 40 to 45 (Craig, 1981). New oil is applied to the paper first, then the blade with the same near-to-far motion, not back and forth. Any high-grade oil can be used, such as that for sewing machines, but the best is made in Japan and scented with clove (*choji*). If wiping a particularly auspicious blade, you should soften the paper first by crushing it in your fingers before applying the oil.

If the nakago is to be examined, the mekugi is driven out of its hole with a punch designed for that purpose. The tsuka is grasped firmly in the right hand, blade vertical, kissaki up, and the right wrist struck with the left fist. If this does not loosen the tsuka, it may have to be beaten off with a brass, wooden, or plastic hammer. When loosened, the blade is replaced in the saya before lifting off the tsuka. Then the nakago may be thoroughly examined, moving it around with the saya. After the examination the tsuka is replaced, the saya removed, and the kashira struck on the left palm to seat it. Be very careful to reseat the mekugi firmly, because the sword is very dangerous should it fall out. Figure 22 shows the contents of an average sword care kit including oil, paper, uchiko powder, and a punch.

CARE OF YOUR SWORD

Now, with an arsenal of small stones of ever-increasing fineness, he is able to make visible and attractive all the details of the smith's metalwork. It is the polisher who defines the lines of the blade, enlivens the hamon, brings out the grain of the steel (jihada), exposes its color and texture (jitetsu), and burnishes the top and back to a mirror finish.

Leon Kapp, Hiroko Kapp, and Yoshindo Yoshihara, The Craft of the Japanese Sword

A typical iaito requires very little maintenance but lots of care. Aside from the respect always due it by the iaidoka for what it represents, its structure requires avoiding any unnecessary trauma. Japan has strict export laws for swords and regards them as a national art form. For this reason iaito blades are usually made from nonferrous metals, most often an aluminum-zinc or boron alloy, which is then plated with chrome. This exempts them from the regulations because they are not "swords." Swords must meet several criteria: they must be ferrous, forged, tempered, more than 8 inches in length, and have a hole in the nakago *(mekugi ana)*. Plated iaito get scratched and chip easily, and the plating can peel off. All these blemishes are difficult to repair and just as difficult to camouflage. Polymers can fill in defects but result in permanent discoloration. Any attempt at polishing out scratches is bound to create a bigger defect. Thus any unnecessary contact or flexing can result in damage that is far easier to prevent than repair. The iaito should be wiped with light mineral oil before and after use. Fingerprints are unsightly but do not have the same connotation they would if they were found on a live blade. Oiling the blade regularly lubricates the saya over time, facilitating a smoother, quieter draw. It also cleans the blade periodically, keeping it from filling the saya up with debris, which can eventually split the saya or scratch the blade. As reported earlier, original saya were glued together with a rice paste, which allowed splitting them open without damaging the wood so that they could be cleaned from time to time and then stuck back together. That can't be done with most modern saya.

Nihonto or real or "live" blades, are composed of welded layers of variably soft and hard steel that discolors and oxidizes easily. This happens very quickly if in contact with the oils and salts present in the perspiration on human skin. Since the beauty and value of a well-made blade depends upon the condition of its steel, maintaining a proper polish and preventing rusting or staining is a time-consuming but extremely important process. There is a great deal to be lost by improper handling or care of a live blade. Though details are outside the scope of this book the basics can be reviewed. After use a live blade is lightly dusted with a very fine abrasive and absorbent powder (uchiko), wiped clean with rice paper and then lightly coated with the finest of oils scented with clove. It is never touched by bare skin unless in battle or practice. If it must be handled, special paper (nugui) or cloth patches are used. Obviously, during use in battle this could not be done, but there is a grace period of about an hour or more when a cleaning delay will result in no damage.

A live blade should be carefully stored away from corrosives, moisture, or abrasives and regularly inspected to catch any unsuspected deterioration early. If not to be used for a long period of time, it is usually removed from its fittings (koshirae) and placed in an unadorned unfinished wooden storage saya (shirasaya) with a matching tsuka over the tang. Japanese magnolia was used for this not only because it was easily to work and didn't split but also because it did not contain any corrosive oils of its own, as do pine or cedar. A wooden model blade is used to keep the fittings together for display. Even with the best of care a fine blade probably needs to be repolished by an expert every couple of hundred years.

MINOR REPAIRS

When a warrior fights not for himself, but for his brothers, when his most passionately sought goal is neither glory nor his own life's preservation, but to spend this substance for them, his comrades, not to abandon them, not to prove unworthy of them, then his heart truly has achieved contempt for death, and with that he transcends himself and his actions touch the sublime.

—Steven Pressfield, Gates of Fire

There are relatively few injuries you can try to repair on an iaito and none you should consider touching on a nihonto because an iaito is a nonferrous blade coated with chrome. Eventually, the chrome is likely to flake off. Excessive flexion will speed up the process. This construction makes it very difficult to repair chips or nicks in the blade. These defects are usually just cosmetic issues, although a nick in the ha near the kissaki may interfere with a smooth noto. Forget otherwise common ways to repair nicks in metal like soldering. The heat will do terrible things to the plating. The other problem is that the chrome layer is very thin, so any attempt to polish or file irregularities out of the blade it will go right through the chrome and you will find you have a very funny colored spot on your blade. The best method I have found is to use some of the epoxy putty available in hardware stores or plumbing or automotive supply stores. The one I have used is EP-400 Epoxy Putty made by Rectorseal. You have to mix the two separate parts to get it to cure. This stuff WILL NOT look like the rest of the blade (it is dull black) but it will fill the nick and is very hard when dry. After curing it can be filed down to match the edge, which then can be lightly buffed with 600-grit emery cloth. This epoxy can also be used to fill gaps between the tsuba and the nakago if the tsuba is loosened. Do not put the sword together until the epoxy has dried, or you will never be able to take down your sword again.

Another common problem that can be repaired easily is the eventual wear you get between the habaki and the koiguchi; a new saya is usually a little tight, and the habaki may not go in all the way. With use, the koiguchi will wear looser, eventually allowing the blade to fall out of the saya when upended. Painting the inside of the saya with clear lacquer, either with a brush or spray, can reverse this. Be sure to mask off the rest of the saya before using a spray. If you overdo it, you can always remove a little lacquer with a file or sandpaper. Another approach to the loosening of the habaki in the saya is the use of a thin wooden shim glued into the koiguchi. This works particularly well for large mismatches. Refinishing an entire saya is another thing altogether. Most saya are lacquered and can be sanded down so that the nicks and scratches are sanded off, or if deeper, filled with epoxy and then repainted. Don't expect, however, to get the smooth lacquer surface back without a LOT of resanding and respraying. Remember that a new coat will always soften the previously dry lacquer, so it's risky to paint over with a different color.

If a saya splits but there is no lost wood, you can wedge the split apart, work carpenter's glue into the crack and then wrap the area tightly with a shoestring or other soft cord. Keep in mind that some refinishing is probably going to be necessary because of the bead of glue and scratches that remain. Tightly wrapping with cord will also crush the soft wood of the saya. If wood is lost, another method of repair is to fill it with epoxy. With a saw, first take the cap off the koiguchi and then run a cut along the top of the saya through the crack, removing it completely. Grease the blade and habaki and place a piece of paper about 1/2 inch wide and slightly longer that the cut on the edge of the blade and habaki adjacent to the crack and place them all into the saya. Make sure the paper completely blocks the inside of the saya from the crack. Then pour quick-setting epoxy into the crack, partially filling it but not allowing it to escape over or around the top of the koiguchi. When the epoxy is starting to set, remove the blade and habaki. The paper will stay. Do this immediately if at any time the epoxy appears to get past the paper into the saya proper. After setting is complete glue the cap back onto the koiguchi with more epoxy and fill the saw cut completely this time. When set, the epoxy can be shaped with a file, sanded and painted. The result will be the same size and stronger than the saya was originally. The manufacture of a new saya is also not out of the question. It may actually prove easier to make a new saya than get a good repair on an old one (Babin, 2000).

Rewrapping a tsuka or even making a new tsuka for an iaito is difficult, but not insurmountable but is beyond the scope of this handbook. Several methods of wrapping can be found by searching the Internet. Repairing loose tsuka-ito can be relatively simple, however. The main problem with inexpensive or homemade wraps is that they are usually too loose. With use, the crossover points drift and the wrap can become distorted, which can actually impair your grip. The best solution is a professional wrap, but if that is impossible, you might consider coating the tsuka-ito with water-soluble transparent cloth glue, which is available at fabric or hobby stores. Leather wrapping cannot be pulled very tight without tearing it so it is often lacquered after wrapping. You can do that to your cotton wrap too, if it gets loose. Try to keep the lacquer off the samé. A similar method can be used to fix an end knot that keeps coming undone. The author has used superglue for this with great success and it is cosmetically quite acceptable. Such a process would be totally unacceptable on a nihonto with koshirae of any intrinsic value.

Sometimes, with long use, a tsuka becomes loosened, which causes the tsuba to make an unacceptable rattling sound. One solution is to add another seppa, but the space may not be wide enough for that. If so, make one or more cardboard seppa out of a 3 x 5 filing card, of about 2-3mm smaller diameter that the metal seppa and place it (them) between the seppa and tsuka. This will cushion each and stop the noise. Another approach is to fill the extra space in the tsuba's nakago ana with the epoxy paste used for filling nicks in the blade. Molten lead can also be used as long as the tsuba and its decorations can tolerate the heat (around 400 degrees Fahrenheit). Fill the nakago ana with lead well away from the blade and let it cool, then drill and file it out for the nakago just enough so that you have a tight fit. A temporary solution to this problem, for example at a tournament, is to wrap dental floss tightly into the seam between the tsuba and a seppa.

The mekugi may loosen up and even fall out, which is extremely dangerous if not caught before the sword is swung. If a mekugi does not fit well, or is lost, it is very easy to whittle a new one from a bamboo chopstick (*hashi*). If an iaito has a plastic mekugi, it should be replaced immediately with one of bamboo and be examined to make sure there are no other safety factors, such as a short tang.

The tsuba, fuchi, and kashira of an iaito are often made of a base metal and then electroplated with copper or silver. The plating then may be antiqued with chemicals or lacquer. With continuing abrasion from the iaidoka's fingers, the antiquing and even plating will wear off these metal pieces leaving the underlying metal exposed. It is probably best to accept this as testimony to your experience. Buffing the metal parts will most likely become a disaster. If you absolutely must have them restored, take them to a reputable plating company, or learn how to electroplate (copper is easy and safe, silver uses cyanide salts and is pretty dangerous). Dented or twisted fittings can be hammered out with a wooden or plastic mallet if they are iron, copper, or brass, but not if they are pot metal. You can determine if they are iron with a magnet. There are two products available at gun stores made by Beachwood Casey: Plum Brown for use on iron, and a product containing selenium dioxide for use on copper, bronze, and brass parts. The latter will also darken sterling silver. Depending on the base metal of your fittings, these products can be used to recreate their oxidized color.

If a blade rattles in the saya, the saya doesn't fit properly. One method of stopping this is to put a small strand of cotton on the tip of the sword and push it into the end of the saya. You can continue to do this until the rattling stops, but remember that if you overdo it, you'll have to take the saya apart to remove the excess cotton. If the nakago moves within the tsuka, thin shims of wood or cardboard may be strategically placed and taped to it to fill up the extra space. Make sure, however, that the loosening is not due to a broken nakago or a split in the tsuka.

Section Three
Bringing Life to Your Sword

GRASPING YOUR SWORD

When you take up a sword, you must feel intent on cutting the enemy. As you cut an enemy you must not change your grip, and your hands must not "cower." When you dash the enemy's sword aside, or ward it off, or force it down, you must slightly change the feeling in your thumb and forefinger. Above all, you must be intent on cutting the enemy in the way you grip the sword.

—*Musashi Miyamoto,* Book of Five Rings

The way in which you grasp your sword greatly influences its subsequent path and force. It is impossible to practice even mediocre iaido with an improper grip.

Your left hand should be closest to your hara with your little finger near but not off the end of the tsuka (kashira). The back knuckle of your left index finger should be almost on top of the sword, so your wrist needs be cocked to a considerable extent. This places the fleshy part of the base of your left thumb on top of the tsuka. This is essential in controlling and especially stopping the sword.

Your right hand grasps the tsuka with your index finger near, but not pushed up against, the tsuba. The web between your right index finger and thumb is back from the tsuba about 1 inch and is centered on the middle of the top of the tsuka. Thus the fingers of the right hand are not parallel to the tsuba but tilted back some as if pointing with the sword, and your right hand is not as rotated over the tsuka as your left hand.

The grasp is tightest with the fourth and fifth finger of each hand. Your index and middle fingers should be loose. This allows some rotation within the hand, causing a brisk tip motion as well as preventing a chopping action with the sword. It also softens the shock to the arms when your blade contacts the enemy or his blade.

Keeping the proper degree of finger tension and relaxation is an acquired skill. Keeping your fingers too tight, especially your index finger, results in an awkward, jerky motion and bouncing at the end of the cut. Trying too hard to relax them may result in a fluttering of the fingers during the cut and the danger of throwing the sword. Safely experiment with both extremes until a comfortable compromise is adopted.

Beginners usually grip the tsuka too tightly. Among other things, this tends to wear out the tsuka-ito too quickly. That is a good argument for beginners not getting expensive tsuka for their first sword. They may also choke up on the tsuka and cause the second knuckle of their right thumb to be abraded by the tsuba. Most iaidoka have a callus at this location. With practice, this becomes less of a problem, but a beginner may need to put a little moleskin on his right thumb or on the back left face of the tsuba at first.

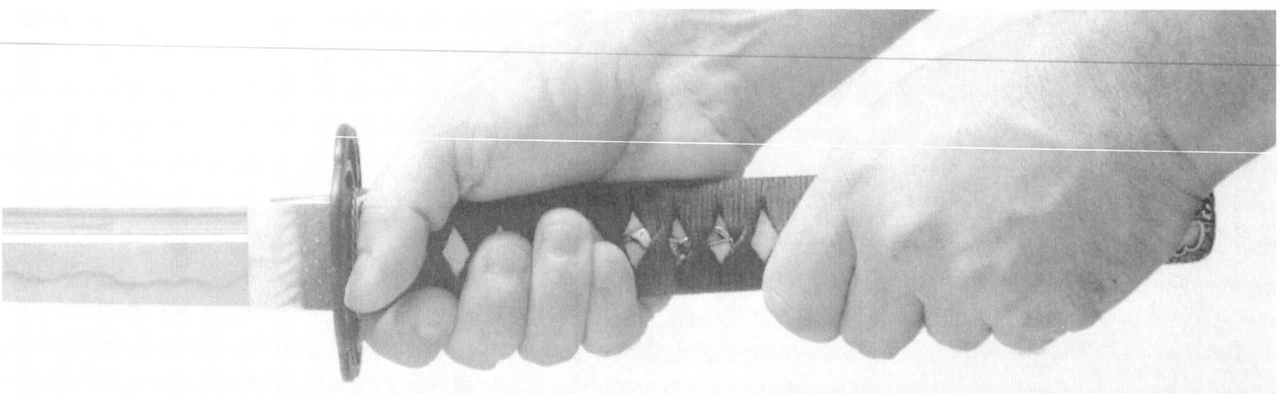

Figure 23: The correct grip for cutting, called te no uchi. The fourth and fifth fingers of each hand are the tightest. Note that the first knuckle of the left index finger is on top of the tsuka in order to support it.

CUTTING–KIRI

"Swing with the inner body." He helped me make an arc with my arms to hit an imaginary golf ball. "Swing from the part that's full o' new life, the part of ye nearest the light of yer soul. That's the part smarter than this flesh. Has more power, rhythm, music. ... It'll serve ye longer than these arms," he whispered. "It's played this game a long, long time. It was there before ye were born."

—Michael Murphy, The Kingdom of Shivas Irons

If you try to wield the long sword quickly you will mistake the Way. To wield the long sword well you must wield it calmly.

—Musashi Miyamoto, The Book of Five Rings

A blade cuts by being dragged tangentially over the recipient tissue (Figures 24A and B). This is accomplished either by pushing it, as in kendo, or drawing in toward you, as in iaido. Simply chopping with the blade will not only result in a poor cut but also may break or trap the blade. Cuts should originate from the contraction of your abdominal muscles rotating your pelvis under your body. This is followed immediately by the action of your left wrist flicking the tip out prior to movement of your arms. During overhead cuts, the kissaki shoots past the top of the target and then is dragged back across it by the action of lowering the arms in an arc that moves the hands (and tsuka) closer to the body (Figures 42A through F). Power in the cut comes from the hips and the shoulders, not the arms. Horizontal cuts slice in a similar fashion by comparable arm and wrist actions and are driven by hip rotation (Figures 39A through H).

All downward vertical cuts whether straight, as with a *sho-men* cut, or diagonal as in *yoko-men* begin with the sword held directly above the head. The hands set the path at the onset of the swing. This prevents both too early a commitment to the cut and telegraphing it in advance to your opponent. The initial power in a vertical cut should come from the left hand and arm; the right hand simply guides the path of the blade. Beginners often try to get power into their cuts by tensing up and using muscle power rather than body power. This usually results in a jerky motion, as well as cutting too close to the body and bending the waist when stopping the blade. As they become aware of that error, beginners then try all kinds of maneuvers to force relaxation. Often these take the form

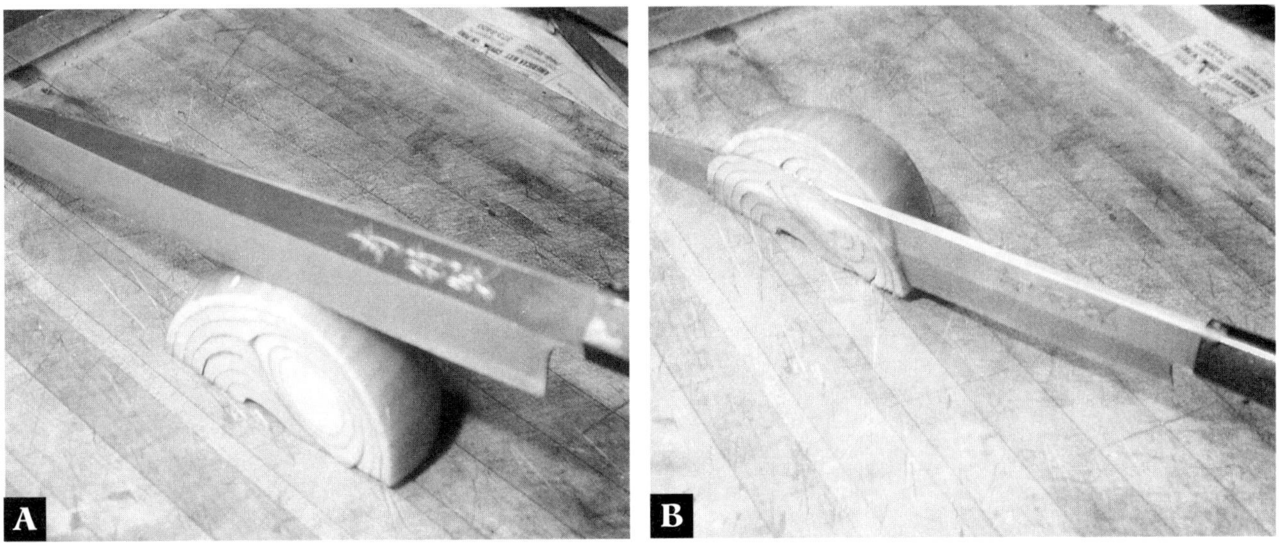

Figures 24A and B: Cutting with a sword should be a slice, not a chop.
A katana cuts in exactly the same way this sushi knife does, not as if it were a cleaver.

of extraneous body movement, usually of the fingers. Beware of loosening your grip too much or wiggling your fingers just prior to kirioroshi. Likewise, it is common to see the left fingers wiggle during *chiburi* or noto. When a master performs a cut no conscious thought or effort guides or drives the blade (mushin or *muto*).

An initial cut (*nukitsuke*) or a block begins when the kissaki clears the saya. The timing of that event is controlled in large part by the action of the left hand sweeping the koiguchi backward and behind the back of the obi as the blade goes forward. This saya motion is called *sayabiki*. It balances the action of the blade and adds power to the cut or block. Lateral or diagonal cuts begin after the left hand has rotated the saya into the proper angle to allow the draw in the correct direction without twisting the right wrist to get it there. At the completion of the cut the kissaki must not be allowed to extend past a line extending straight out forward from the shoulder. This guards against a countercut toward the center by keeping pressure, or *seme*, on the opponent. It also favors a secondary attack if the first is unsatisfactory.

Most students of iaido have never had the opportunity to engage in practice cutting, *tamishigiri*. Most iaidoka who have done tamishigiri using mats or bamboo have never cut flesh. When surgeons teach students to cut and suture lacerations, they often use fresh pigskin because it is the closest to human skin in texture, thickness, and tenacity. Pig's feet are cheap (or free) and readily available from a butcher or slaughterhouse. If you really want to know what makes your sword work, pick up some pig's feet and slash them with a straight razor or equally sharp knife. See what it takes to cleanly cut skin, fat, muscle, and tendons and see what happens when your blade encounters bone. You will acquire an entirely new respect for both the nihonto and for the *kaishaku*. After working with the pig's feet, imagine feeling the same sensation as you swing your iaito to cut your imaginary opponent. You'll never "chop" with your blade again. "If your want to know bamboo, study bamboo."

STARTING POSITIONS–KAMAE

Indeed, we are a collection of cells that behaves like a "thundering buffalo herd." Because "our chief exemplar is always the person we were just a moment before," most of us cannot slow down sufficiently to hit a golf shot or caress a lover properly.
—*Michael Murphy,* The Kindgom of Shivas Irons

Seiza is the formal "proper" way to sit. For Westerners it's really more like kneeling. The lower legs are flat on the ground from knee to instep. The body is upright, sitting on the ankles lightly just above the feet that are big toe to big toe but not crossed. The knees are one fist-width apart. The hands lie flat, palms down on the thigh halfway between the knee and the hip with the fingers together and pointing toward the opposite knee. The back is straight, the head held as if suspended from the ceiling, the chin tucked in slightly. The shoulders are relaxed. The center of gravity is pictured mentally as being low in the hara, and a "root" can be imagined actually extending your body below the surface of the floor. All the body's weight is not draped over the ankles but held above in anticipation: a sheet of paper should be imagined lying between the gluteus muscles and the heels. This is a hard position for beginners to maintain. When informally observing floor action in the dojo it is usually permissible to sit off-center on the floor to the side of the feet. This should not be done in highly formal events or when you are honoring a guest. When a kata begins from seiza, the first action of the legs is almost always to rise into a kneeling position with the buttocks off the feet and the feet up on the toes (*kiza)*. It is very important not to let the knees drift too far apart before starting a kata from seiza. Keeping the knees close together prevents the left foot from getting too far to the right of the left knee when rising up to cut.

The process of sitting is accomplished by bending both knees and gently sweeping first the left and then right hakama leg outward from behind your knees with a quiet twist of your right hand. The knees then continue to bend without moving your feet. First your left and then your right knee touches the ground without a "clunk." As your body sits on your legs your feet are flattened so that the insteps are flat on the floor. The sword, which has been held horizontal during the process with your thumb on the tsuba, is then brought in toward the obi with the tsuba at the level of your navel in the midline. During this entire procedure, your back should be as straight as possible and your shoulders relaxed. To stand, lift your buttocks off your feet (kneeling) and bring your toes up on the floor. Shift your weight to your left knee and step your right foot no farther forward than the left knee. Stand straight up without bending forward and bring your feet together. When doing this you

Figures 25A – C: Three views of the formal sitting position, seiza, while wearing a sword. Notice the fingers are mid-thigh and pointed toward the opposite knee. The buttocks should not rest on the heels, but be held just above them. The tsuka should be in the center of the abdomen.

Figures 26A – J: Basic sequence of dropping straight into seiza from the standing position. Notice that pushing the hakama is gentle, the back is kept as straight as possible and the left knee drops down first, then the right. A slightly different sequence is used when performing koryu waza.

Figure 27: Swordsman in kiza beginning to draw.
He can cut or block in any direction from this position.

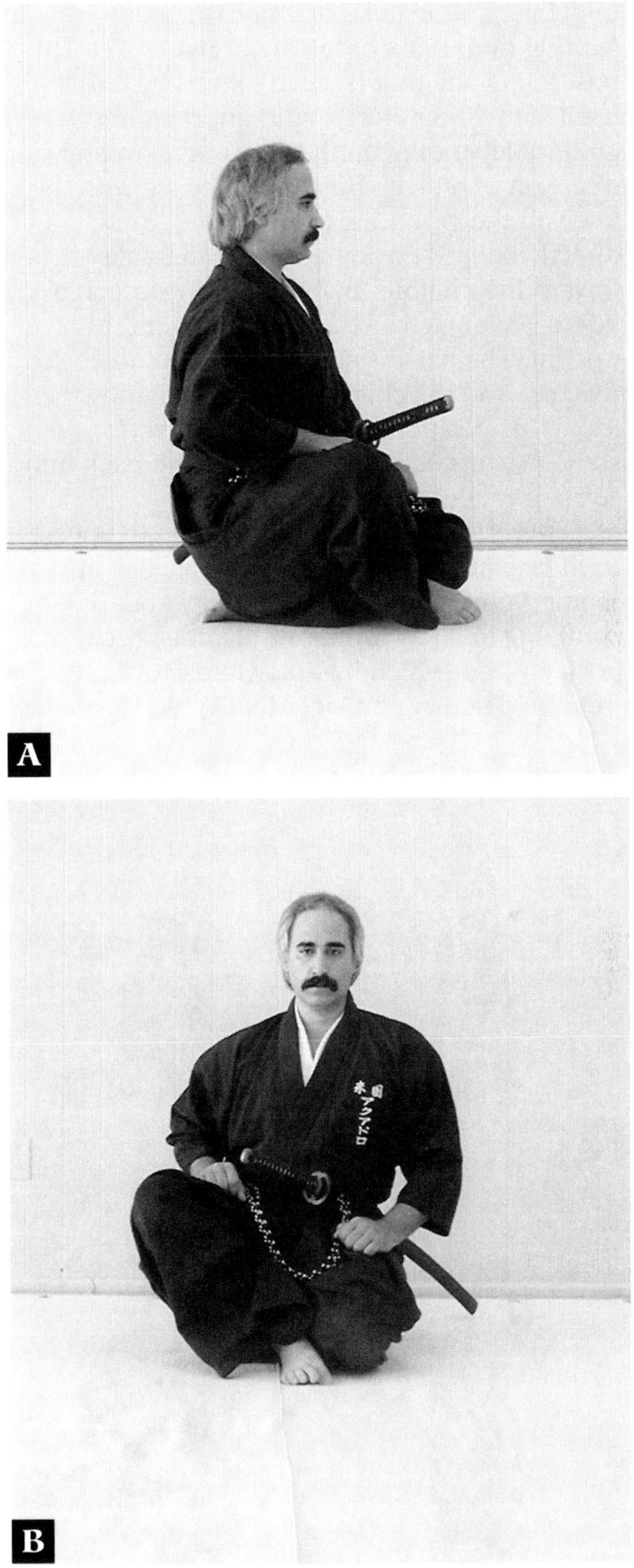

Figures 28A and B: Tatehiza. Note that the left foot is flat on the floor and the swordsman is sitting on it. The right foot is against and not forward of the left knee. The hands are close to the center to facilitate a quick draw.

can stabilize your upper body with your right hand on your right thigh if absolutely necessary and only if it is done unobtrusively.

For informal sitting, most dojo allow sitting with each foot under the opposite knee (cross-legged) with hands in the lap. This is like the "lotus" meditation posture except that both the feet are below, not above, the knees. It must be remembered that in the Orient, showing someone the bottom of your feet is impolite. In all instances, after attaining the sitting position the sword is brought to the right side with both hands and then laid on the floor, not the hakama, with the curve toward the leg and the tsuba even with the knees. The sageo is kept close to the saya and not allowed to extend past the end of it. The sword is brought back to the left side with both hands before arising. The right foot is brought forward to, but not past, the left knee, and the body moves straight upward without bending.

Kiza is an intermediate posture that is used

to deliver a nukitsuke or kirioroshi when starting from seiza or tatehiza (Figure 27). This position is one that is clearly kneeling and is used with either one or both knees on the ground depending on the flow of the kata or direction of attack. The foot of the leg with the knee on the ground is up on its toes and directly behind the knee, not at an angle toward the midline. Both knee joints are at a 90-degree angle whether on the ground or upright. The back is straight; the shoulders are relaxed, and the chin is tucked in slightly. From this position, you can easily rise to standing, turn to either side, or settle back into seiza or tatehiza.

Tatehiza is a semi-sitting position that was used by samurai when dressed in medieval armor (yoroi), which was too bulky and confining to allow formal sitting. It is also a position from which it is easy to rise or move from for defensive action. Most Western budoka find this very uncomfortable at first. There is no solution for this except to practice it frequently for increasingly longer periods to allow both muscles and ligaments to stretch.

You start into tatehiza as with seiza, by bending your knees and sweeping the hakama from behind them with your right hand thrust between your knees. You then sit on the medial side of your left foot and ankle with your left buttock without moving your right foot. Then bring your right foot up against the inner surface of your left knee with your great toe slightly forward of it. Your hands are placed on each mid-thigh, with your fingers loosely closed, palms down. In some other ryu for their koryu the hands are placed with their backs down on the thighs, fingers curled. Tatehiza usually takes some practice to get limber enough to perform it fluidly.

To stand from tatehiza pull your right knee vertical while tightening your buttocks and

Figure 29A – H: An alternative way of assuming seiza or tatehiza used when doing koryu. Notice that instead of dropping straight down on the left knee, the motion is initiated by moving the left foot back. This prevents the inadvertent forward motion that occurs with the basic technique.

lifting your body. Put your weight on your left knee and rotate your left foot from under you to behind your left knee and your toes, left toes upright on the ground. Then step out with your right foot so that your right knee is at 90 degrees. Finally, pull yourself up with your right leg sliding your left leg forward to meet it. In Muso Shinden ryu, both seiza and tatehiza are assumed in a manner different when performing its koryu. To use this technique slide your left foot behind some 10 to 12 inches, sweep the hakama leg laterally as above, and drop to your left knee. Then bring your right knee or foot, depending on the end position desired, even with the left knee and allow your body to settle back on one or both feet.

Tachi, or standing, is a relaxed position, not military-like as in the West (Figures 29A and E). The knees are slightly bent, the feet flat on the floor parallel to one another and slightly apart. The hips are rotated in, with the lower back straight. The shoulders are relaxed and slightly forward, not back pushing out the chest. The head is straight, chin pulled slightly in. The eyes are defocused, taking in the periphery for motion. The right hand is down along the leg, the left around the koiguchi with the thumb straight on the top of the tsuba.

There are numerous positions used for defense and offense during sword fighting. While iai does not start from any of them, an iaidoka use them during the performance of kata.

Chudan no kamae (Figures 30A and B) is a midlevel position, right foot forward, left back with the heel off the ground and with equal weight on each foot, both of which are forward and parallel. The tsuka is held at the midline about obi level and the kissaki is elevated, pointed directly toward the opponent's eyes. This is not only intimidating (seme), but keeps your enemy from accurately judging the length of your sword. Most ryu-ha consider this the basic sword position with the greatest number of options, offensive and defensive, and it is used extensively in kendo.

Jodan no kamae (Figures 31A and B) is the high position, left foot forward, right foot back and close enough that the body is a little

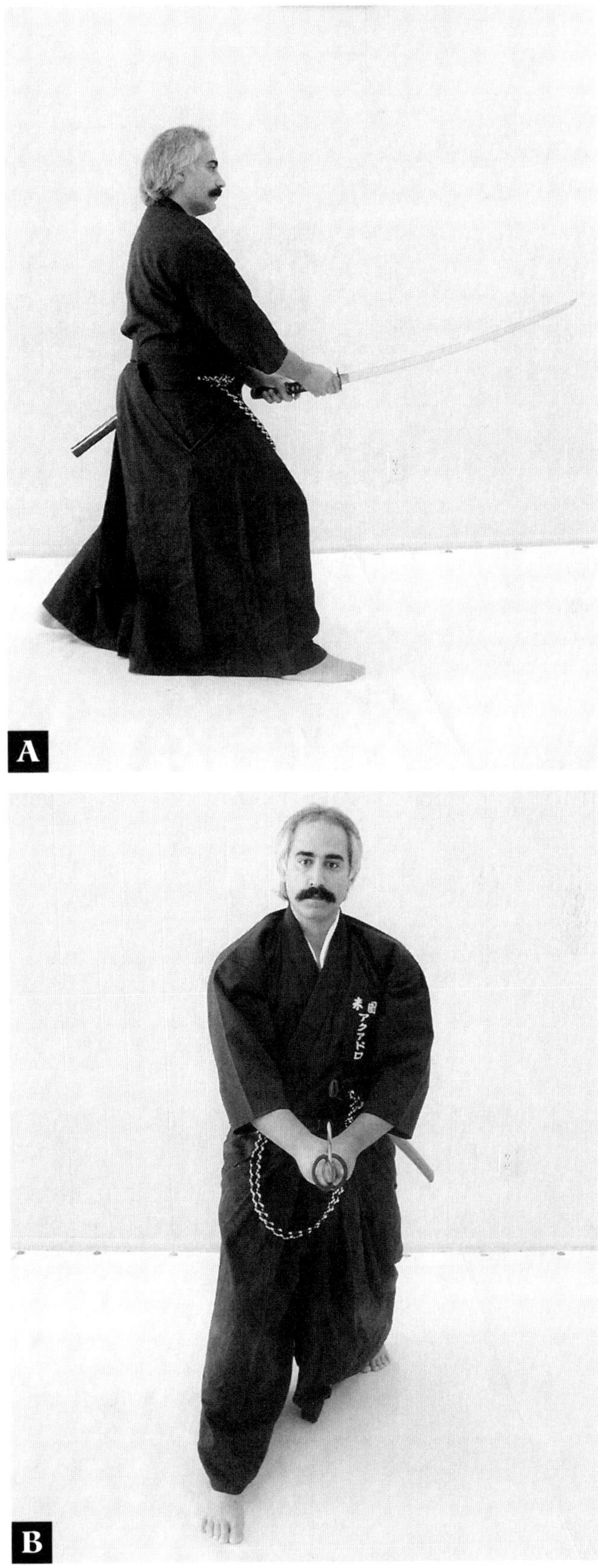

Figures 30A and B: Chudan no kamae.

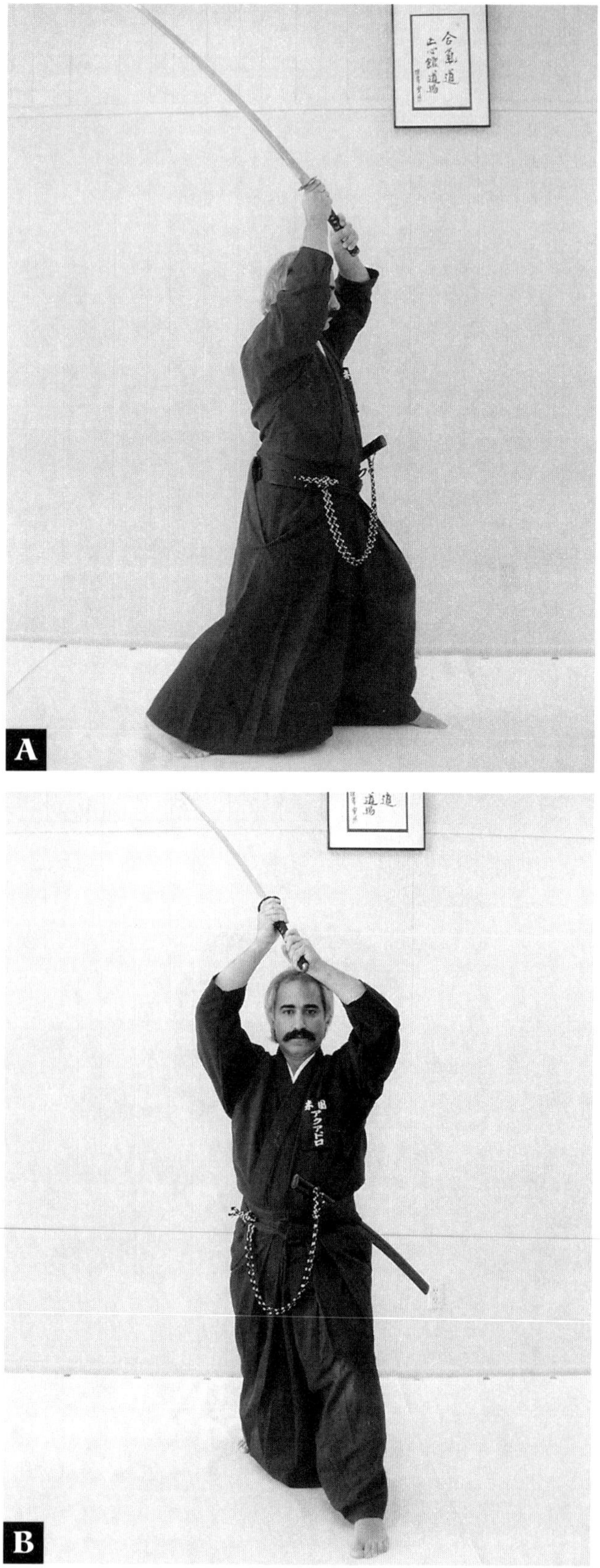

Figures 31A and B: Jodan no kamae.

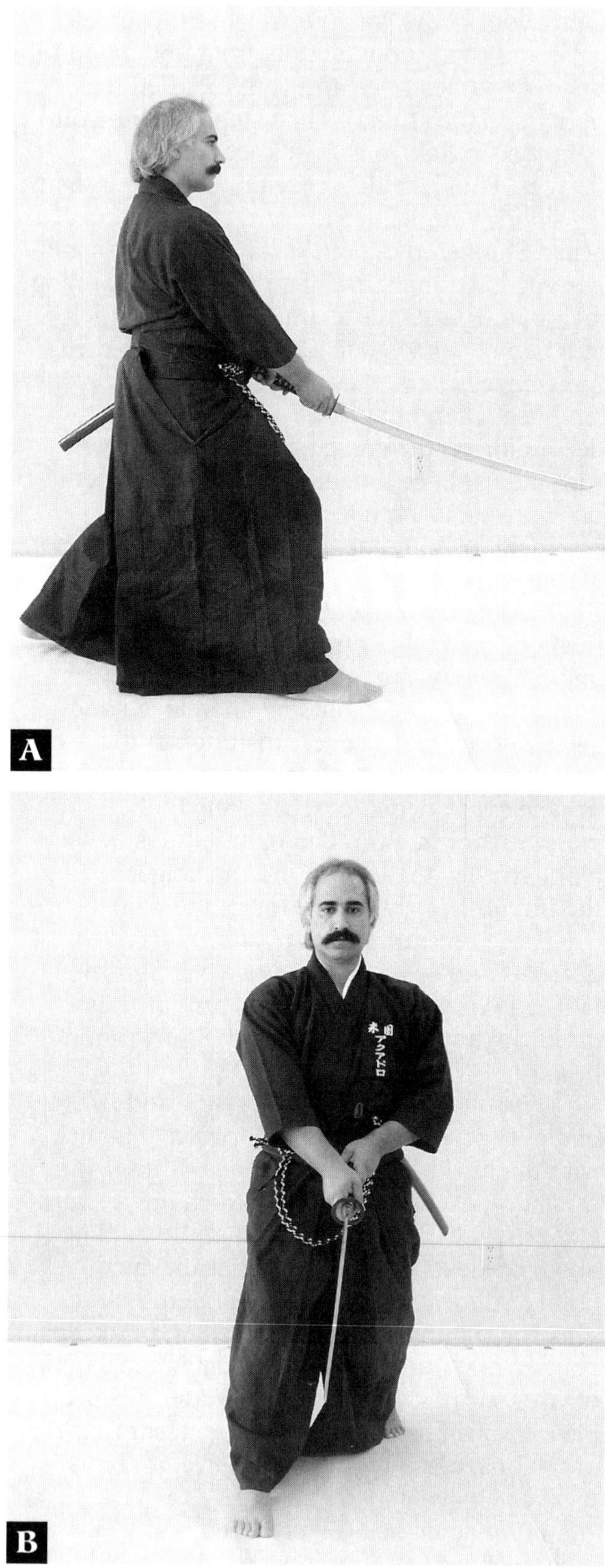

Figures 32A and B: Gedan no kamae.

higher than in chuden. The sword is held over the head, leaning slightly to the right and back about 45 degrees, the ha pointing straight ahead. The upper body is rotated slightly to the right but the head looks straight ahead, daring the opponent to try something. This is a strong position from which to launch a sho-men or yoko-men strike, but leaves the lower body exposed. In iaido it is often used as a transition position allowing the iaidoka to exhibit zanshin until all danger has passed and the chiburi leads to sheathing the blade.

Gedan no kamae (Figures 32A and B) is a low position, right foot forward, tsuka and hands at midline, and kissaki pointed about a meter in front of you. It appears to be weak defensively, leaving the upper body unprotected. It facilitates quickly rising strikes, however, which can be devastating.

Hasso no kamae (Figures 33A and B) is another midlevel position with the left foot forward, the right one back, and a slight body twist to the right. The sword is held with the kashira and left hand at the midline, and the right hand is against the tsuba at the level of the corner of the mouth. The blade is tipped slightly to the right and back slightly off true vertical and, like jodan, the ha is pointing straight at the opponent. Like jodan, hasso is used as a defensive position exhibiting zanshin from which either to launch an attack, or retire from the conflict.

All of the above kamae use the traditional grip that has been described earlier. This is impossible with *waki no kamae* (Figures 34A and B). In this position the sword is pointed to the rear and held behind the right leg. The front of the tsuka is held by the right hand with its back against the iliac crest with the palm upward. The ha points away from the leg. It grasps only with its fingertips underneath and thumb tip on top of the tsuka. The left hand loosely holds the kashira end of the tsuka palm down and keeps the blade directly behind the body, down at about a 45-degree angle. This position hides the blade from the opponent's vision. Not only can't he tell its length, but also he can't tell what kind of strike you plan to launch. It could also be used to disguise a

Figures 32A and B: Hasso no kamae.

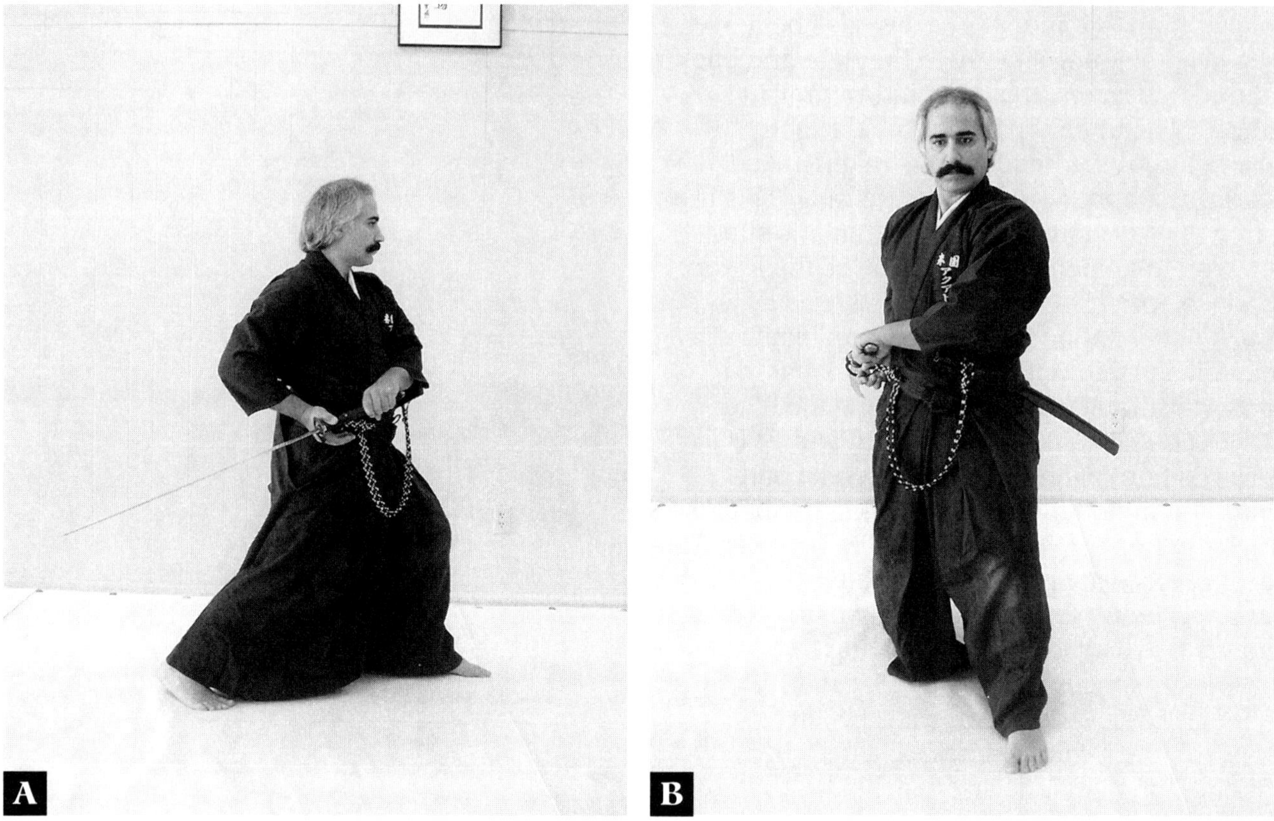

Figures 34A and B: Waki no kamae.

damaged blade. From it, either a vertical or horizontal cut is easily initiated.

There are many other kamae used by other ryu-ha, and the number of sword positions that might be used during a real conflict is endless. For example, the blade is sometimes rested on an elbow, the mune of the blade lying across the chest, body half turned with the kissaki pointed toward the opponent's eyes. This, like waki no kamae, keeps the enemy from measuring the blade's length or condition. The same strategy is used in other ryu-ha by resting the mune on an open palm, with the blade's tip pointed at the enemy's face. Jodan, hasso, and waki can all be done from the other side of the body, just as an overhead strike can come with the right leg back, not forward. Muso Shinden ryu uses none of these, but that does not proscribe their potential use in prolonged combat, which is the realm of kenjutsu, not iaido.

BALANCE, POSTURE, AND MOVEMENT

The truest center o' gravity is not the center of the Earth. It's at the center o' the soul. And because it's everywhere, Michael, it gives us our deepest stability.
—*Michael Murphy,* The Kindom of Shivas Irons

If you stop thinking of some place to put it, you mind is bound to extend and spread all over and fill your whole body. Without putting your mind in any place, you must let it serve wherever it is needed at each moment, depending on your opponent's move.
—*Muninori Yagyu,* The Sword and the Mind

The term "balance" is ubiquitous in martial arts literature and yet it is applied to so many different concepts that it may lose its usefulness in the dojo. In the *physical* art of iaido, balance refers to the maintenance of stability in the environment in which the conflict occurs. This allows quick and powerful actions of the body and sword in response to the actions of an opponent. Balance provides the base from which power can be projected through the sword. Pure physics dictates that a wide base and low center of gravity increase stability and, therefore, balance. Thus an upright posture and a low, wide stance are the tools used by the iaidoka to maintain balance. Balance, however, is not solely a static phenomenon, but must be maintained during a variety of movements, both defensive and offensive. In the human, bent limbs, relaxed muscles, cautious stepping, abdominal breathing and a flexible mind-set also play a big role in allowing a warrior to maintain control while moving thorough the unpredictable events of a conflict.

In the *mental* art of iaido, balance involves an appropriate compromise between strength and softness, action and inaction, advance and retreat, and commitment and anticipation. In other words, balance is the Taoist state of health or well-being. A mind focused on a single goal, such as a sho-men strike, is inflexible and will doggedly pursue that attack instead of responding

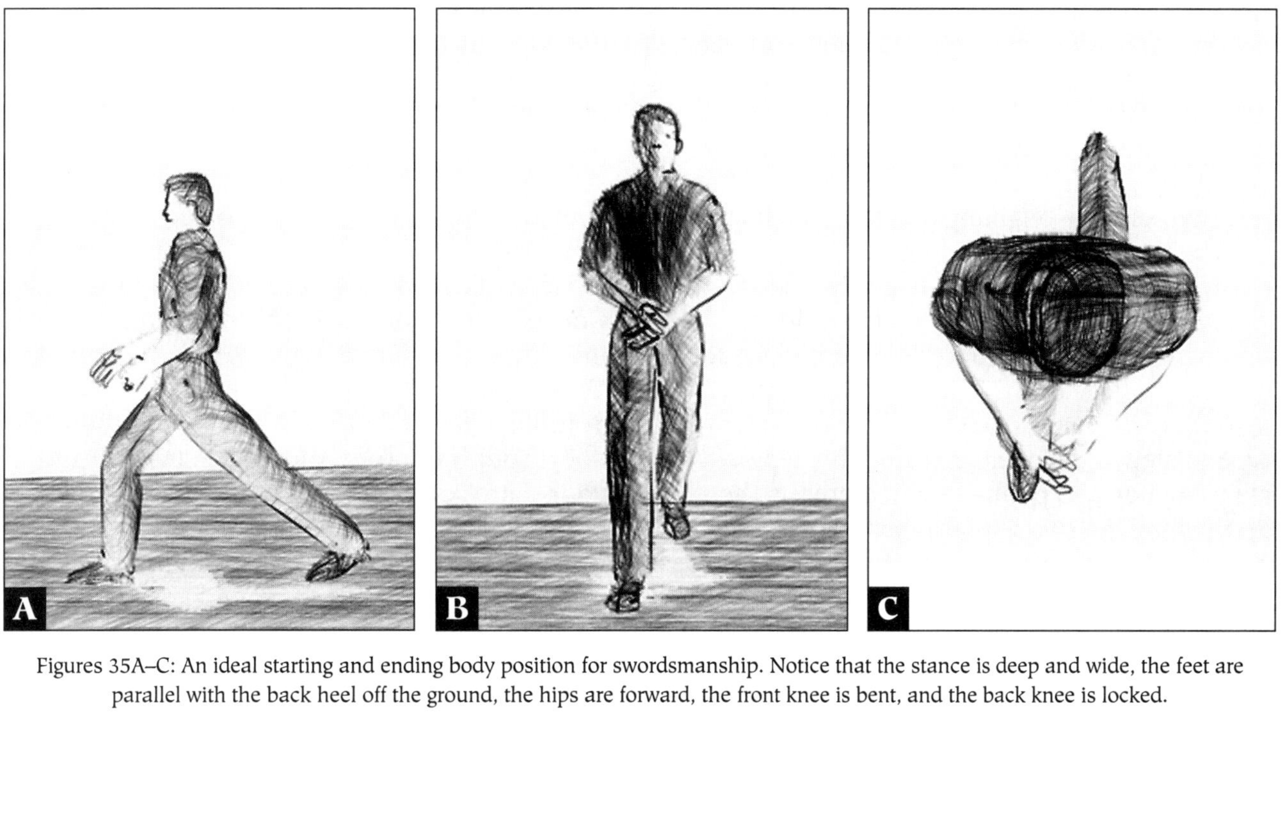

Figures 35A–C: An ideal starting and ending body position for swordsmanship. Notice that the stance is deep and wide, the feet are parallel with the back heel off the ground, the hips are forward, the front knee is bent, and the back knee is locked.

appropriately to the constant change inherent in any conflict situation. Concentrating on the present instead of the future frees the mind to instantly take advantage of a lapse in the opponent's attention. It is assumed that as a samurai, you have already decided that the fight you are going to engage in is important enough to spend your life on, otherwise you should be elsewhere. Therefore you are not fighting for survival but for your will to prevail. This also frees your mind to deal with the here and now rather than the future and to stay in harmony (balance) with the moral and ethical dictates of your society and the universe.

We can learn a lot about body position during iaido from watching kendo, for if the fight is prolonged past the first cut, iaido becomes kendo. Both feet are kept parallel toward the opponent and on a broad base. The back heel is raised off the floor about an inch to facilitate the quickest response, offensive or defensive, without the need for adjustment. Movement is begun with the forwardmost foot sliding and the action, usually a strike, made as the trailing foot comes back into position. This type of step, in which the feet do not change their relative position to one another, is termed *okuriashi*. It is almost always used when making a sword movement and allows for very quick changes in direction and protects a neutral balance at all times. It allows strong actions without overcommitment or other errors such as crossed legs, an awkward body position, or overweighting one foot. Such steps may be performed in a long forward or rearward series, somewhat like skipping.

When covering ground to close with an opponent or when simply going from place to place a traditional stride is used where by the lead foot alternates one side to the other. This type of step is called *ayumiashi*. This type of stepping has two points of vulnerability: the first, where the two legs are next to one another, the other when the forward foot is starting to accept the weight of the body. Whichever type of step you are using, keep your toes and the balls of your feet on the floor when stepping—in other words, slide rather

Figure 36: Stepping heel-to-toe during iaido is not only wrong, but opens you up to ridicule. Feet should slide along the floor with the toes remaining in contact with it.

than picking up your feet. This is most often forgotten with movement of the trailing foot. The worst thing you can do is let your heel hit first and then slap your toes down like a duck or Bozo the Clown. This is considered very "American" (in the worse possible context) by Japanese. *Gaijin ashi* literally means "foreign feet" and ridicules this practice.

You must think and act as if your center of gravity is just below your belly button (hara, *dan tien, tanden,* one point): your back and neck should be straight. Think of your head as suspended by a string from the ceiling with your spine and hips dangling from it. Your stance should be stable and rooted, with your center of gravity in the middle or very slightly forward of the middle of your foot stance. Consciousness of this is called "centering" in the Chinese arts and "the one point" in aikido. Your forward leg should be bent at the knee. Your back heel should always be slightly off the floor. Your back knee should be straight, and your buttocks should be rotated under your body. You can best maintain the proper back foot position by consciously pushing with the straight leg into the floor behind you. There are a variety of mental exercises used in martial schools to help maintain a stable stance. One that is applicable to iaido is to think of your

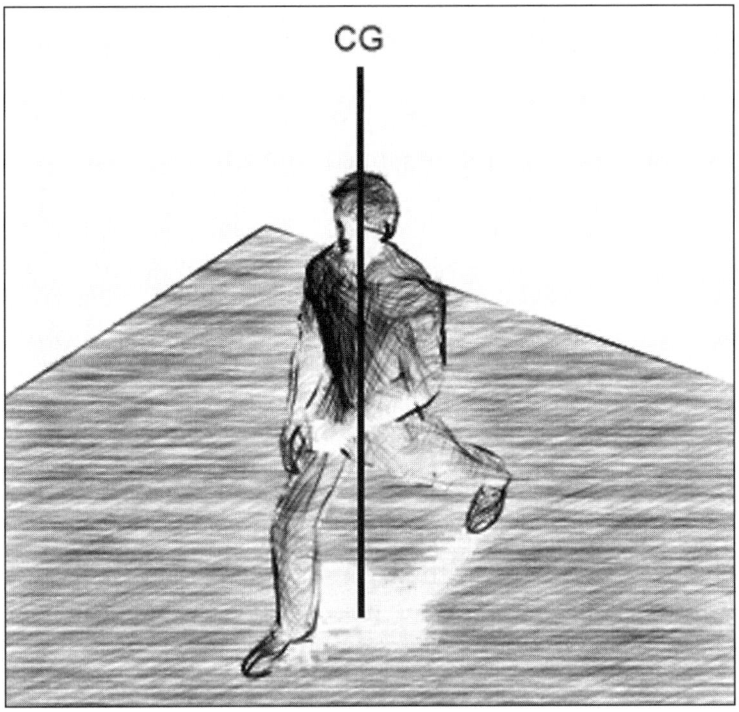

Figure 37: Placement of the vertical axis (CG) of the center of gravity slightly closer to the front foot than midline, and as low as possible. Notice the line runs through the head, neck, torso, and hara.

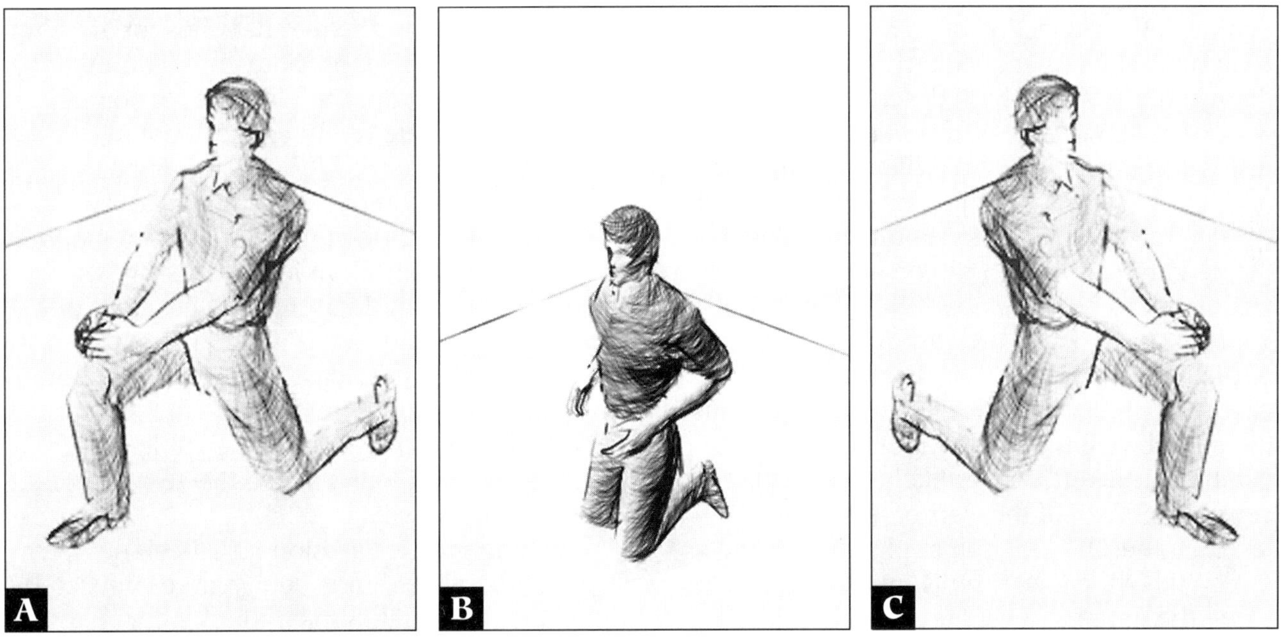

Figures 38A – C: From a transitional kneeling position (B), a stable forward position can easily be assumed (A). Alternatively, the body can be pivoted around one knee for a kneeling response to one side or the other (C) or even a reversal.

feet having roots that spread out under the surface of the floor and then use the image to support your body. A comparable kneeling position is illustrated in Figure 38A.

It is difficult for Western iaidoka to keep their feet parallel while moving them. Particularly when stepping to the rear, there is a tendency for beginners to angle the feet laterally rather than keep them straight. It is much easier to think about keeping your pelvis pointed forward, which will unconsciously point your feet properly. Another trick in learning to position your feet during a backward step is to lead with your heel. When you step back, also step outward to broaden your stance. With hips straight and heel leading, your feet will automatically slide along the ground trailing your heel at the proper angle.

Stepping forward is accomplished by symmetric hip rotation and upward tilting of your pelvis anteriorly by contraction of your stomach (rectus) muscles, thereby tucking your buttocks under your hara and dragging the following foot forward. Do not push off with your back foot; that will make your head bounce and your trunk tilt. When you tuck your buttocks under your body, your shoulders are naturally forced to relax and drop. Your back must be kept straight no matter what your arms are doing. It may help to think that you are leaning back a little during forward sword motion.

Weapon techniques, including iaido, must deal with the projection of energy through the weapon to the target opponent. Starting with the use of the stable base described above, a warrior must wield his weapon in such a fashion that balance is maintained in the face of a strike that transfers the maximum possible power. Bare-handed arts demonstrate that a fist, te-katana, or grasp can be applied with the greatest power and flexibility when they are kept within a narrow area around and in front of the hara (centered). This is even more the case when holding a sword or polearm because the added weight of the weapon makes extending the limbs more likely to upset the center of gravity of the warrior. Also, the leverage that the hips can apply through the arms in moving a weapon is much greater when the hands are held in close. In iaido, keeping the tsuka close to the center is not limited to facilitating a quick draw with a sheathed blade. Many of the basic stances and sword movements described later in this book start and end with one or both hands and the tsuka at the swordsman's center. Some examples include the middle-level ready position (chudan no kamae), horizontal cuts in both directions (*yokogumo*) and the finish-position of numerous vertical cuts (kirioroshi).

Another feature of movement in iaido, especially in the muso shinden ryu is the coordination of the movement of different parts of the body. This is closely related to the timing issues discussed in the next chapter. Whenever two events are taking place, for example a draw and a step, both begin, progress, and end at the same time and rate. This is one of the reasons it is difficult to describe the individual actions of the kata in words. Another example is the simultaneous movement of the left and right hands during the beginning of the noto. The sword is brought to the midline by the right hand just as the left hand brings the koiguchi of the saya to the midline to receive it. This is an important aspect of the style of muso shinden ryu, but more importantly, it is part of the overall tactics. Simultaneous motions are more difficult than sequential ones for an opponent to fully appreciate and counter.

In feudal Japan, the pleasure section of each city was referred to as the "floating world." This is a good term to remember because all your motions during iaido kata should look as though you are floating around, not stepping around. In iaido, walking is always relaxed and natural, not hesitant, or a jerky, exaggerated "ninja walk." Like the floating world of the past, your motions should have a "not quite there" quality that appears effortless, mysterious, and irresistible. Taken to extremes, if you look like a ghost to a samurai, you might just win.

A long practice session for a beginner may result in a blister on his left great toe caused by pushing off with it. Some moleskin taped to a base of celoidin (liquid bandages) should be considered as a preventive. Likewise, knees can get blistered under pads if it is hot and the legs sweat excessively. This is another place that could use moleskin or at least some talcum powder if a long session is contemplated, such as during a teaching seminar.

TIMING, RHYTHM, AND VISION

Though he knew almost nothing of kendo, Honda grasped that there was something like a coiled spring within this young boy that gave off a dark blue glow. The vigor of his spirit manifested itself without a trace of disorder, and, whatever the resistance, created a vacuum within his opponent's resolve, if but for an instant. And the usual result was that, just as air is drawn into a vacuum, so this weak spot of this opponent drew Iinuma's shinai.

—*Yuko Mishima,* Runaway Horses

In strategy it is important to see distant things as if they were close and to take a distanced view of close things. It is important in strategy to know the enemy's sword and not to be distracted by insignificant movements of his sword. ... It is necessary in strategy to be able to look to both sides without moving the eyeballs

—*Musashi Miyamoto,* Book of Five Rings

Because iaido is practiced against an imaginary opponent it would appear that the iaidoka has the luxury of setting his own speed, timing, and rhythm. While this is true in a superficial sense, the natural mechanics of the human body and the physical properties of the sword dictate certain limits. Add in the necessity of being true to the iaidoka's own inner primal beat and harmonizing with the cycles of the universe while ignoring trivial influences, and it becomes obvious that the iaidoka must be both spontaneous and in harmony with his environment.

Timing is one of the ways that the iaidoka can manifest his spirit and is closely related to mental preparation. Many of the kata can be artificially separated into steps, each of which has its own rhythm. The initial draw (nukitsuke), for example, starts very slowly and methodically, gradually quickening but preserving the option of replacing the sword, until it reaches a point of no return when "the missile is launched." Then action stops for an instant. The raising of the sword and downward cut that follow, taken as a unit, also start slowly and crescendo into a rapid movement, which stops suddenly. Replacing the sword in the saya (noto), on the other hand, starts slow and gets slower and the iaidoka allows the "battle mode" to be put away with the sword and to recover his peaceful demeanor. The speed with which the timing changes, the length of the intervals between moves, and the overall pace of the kata all speak to the mental state or spirit of the iaidoka. The phrase *jo ha kyu* refers to the variation of pace within a single kata.

When you first learn to put the various parts of a kata together into a single form, your task is to integrate them into a single smooth, continuous flow. You should avoid jerky, isolated actions. This facilitates a relaxed body, which is also an important characteristic to develop. Usually, as the movements smooth out the timing emerges as a slow, continuous, predictable pace. This is desirable at first. As your performance of the kata matures, however, the emotions appropriate to the actions needs to overlay them. An important aspect of this is the timing of the final cut (kirioroshi). In order to work in the real world, the cut must strike the enemy seemingly from nowhere. If your movements are choreographed to a single rhythm your opponent will know when you are about to strike. If your sword goes into an overhead position too quickly and hesitates there, your opponent knows you're not going to slash his belly. As you gain confidence in the natural flow of your movements you should attempt to delay the final cut a fraction of a second longer than a strict, steady rhythm would dictate. This adds more energy and emotion to your actions.

One trick to accomplish the above is to consider the vertical cut actually starting in the opposite direction from a sword position halfway between chudan and jodan. For a walking kirioroshi you step with your right foot and start to bring the sword up with your arms, threatening your opponent with the forward motion of the kissaki for as long as possible. Do not bring the sword over your head yet. At the very last moment, just as you start to move the back foot up, whip the sword, first up over your head and then forward and up, into the cut. This is exactly the timing you would exercise if you suddenly took advantage of a momentary loss of concentration or other opening in your enemy's defense. When you first do this successfully, you will be amazed at the increase in strength this gives your cuts. Even the sound of the swish will be different. Be warned, however, that when you first start to do this you may start to bend forward with the cut because of too much right-handed power and/or you may tend to dip the blade too far behind your head. Practicing with a mirror will help prevent this. One of the ways this concept has been described in the ZNKF literature when the direction of attack is changing is by using the term *ukenagashi* (receive and return) meaning there should be a smooth transition from a block to a cut (see appendix A). Ukenagashi is the name used for several kata at different levels in both muso shinden and Eishin Jikiden ryu.

Other factors also influence the timing. The iaidoka must look for an unexpected response to his actions. He must not commit himself through an action and lose defensive options until he is relatively sure it is safe to do so. Delays of this sort demonstrate zanshin, or "continuing mind." A good example of this is a hesitancy to raise the kissaki from the enemy's face when moving into jodan no kamae from the end of a kirioroshi even after starting the appropriate foot motion for the next step.

Another related factor is metsuke, or the attention of the vision. The opponent is imaginary, but does not appear so while watching a skilled iaidoka. He is there and the swordsman watches him, following his body or sword with his eyes as he demonstrates zanshin. Of course this should not be exaggerated. Different kenjutsu ryu recommend keeping your eyes on different parts of the body such as the eyes, hands, or hips. Other schools of swordsmanship, and indeed Musashi himself, recommend not following any one object with the eyes, but trying to keep everything within the peripheral vision, which is most motion sensitive, also known as "distant mountain sight," *enzan no metsuke* (Shimakabura and Pellman, 1995). The authors also describe five levels of "sight," depending on the degree of understanding that sight involves. One way of summing up the way the body should move toward a target is that the head moves first, then the shoulders, hips, and the feet, in that order, and only then the blade.

A final factor that influences timing is the breathing cycle. The theory of this is discussed in the next section. Suffice it to say the iaidoka has some limitations to control over the length of the parts of the respiratory cycle. Control of respiration and its integration into movement is a major part of the mastery of most Asian martial arts.

BREATHING – KOKYU

If the breath is dispersed, then it is not stored and is easy to scatter. Let the breath penetrate the spine and the inhalation and exhalation be smooth and unimpeded throughout the entire body. The inhalation closes and gathers, the exhalation opens and discharges. Because the inhalation can naturally raise and also uproot the opponent, the exhalation can naturally sink down and also discharge him. This is by means of the mind, not the strength, mobilizing the breath.

—Li I-Yu

Iaido, as other oriental martial arts, is strongly influenced by Taoism. In Taoist physiology, one characteristic of life itself is the spontaneous circulation of a life energy (ki) from the dan tien (hara), where it is produced from water and heat and travels throughout the body via the acupuncture meridians and vessels and out to the limbs. Other sources of available but limited ki include what an individual inherits from his parents, what he receives from ingesting and processing food and water, that which is absorbed from the environment, and local ki produced by muscular activity. In Traditional Chinese Medicine, the smooth unimpeded flow of ki throughout the body is the definition of health and balance. This circulation can be consciously augmented by the action of the mind of a martial artist. The power can even be transferred from the bugeisha's body to another person whom it acts upon for either healing or injury. One of the most powerful ways to maximize the movement of ki is through proper breathing.

Taoist theory states that during inspiration, the body absorbs the ki of heaven, earth, and other individuals or objects into the body with a defensive, nurturing, and yin effort. On the other hand, during exhalation the body projects its ki into heaven, earth, and its environment, as well as any object of interest. This is an offensive, taxing, and yang part of the cycle. The *kiai*, or shout, at the time of a strike in many martial arts is an expression of this theory and aids the proponent in projecting his ki and focusing his attack. Note that "nonbreathing" is not part of the normal cycle. At least in most Chinese martial arts the breath is never held. To do so is believed to remain in a condition in which the body is weak and vulnerable. Some modern iaidoka attempt to hold their breath during most if not all of each kata; this does not seem consistent with good Taoist concepts.

Taoist breathing is one variety of abdominal breathing that is also called reverse abdominal breathing. It is very yang and rapidly strengthens the practitioner. On inhalation the abdomen contracts as the back and limbs straighten. During exhalation, the abdomen expands and tightens, the hips rotate under the spine, the back curves forward, the knees bend, and the shoulders curve gently inward. One common example of reverse abdominal breathing in Western culture is that breathing pattern often used when straining, such as pushing a heavy object such as an automobile. This kind of breathing is believed by traditional Chinese medicine to circulate ki up the spine (governing vessel) and down the front of the body (conception vessel) as well as out to the limbs and deep into the bone marrow. It is also believed to specifically strengthen the girding vessel, a horizontal pathway around the hips that is essential for the maintenance of strong balance. During the opposite of reverse breathing, or Buddhist breathing, the abdomen expands with inhalation and collapses with exhalation. It is a breathing pattern that lends itself to relaxation, not strength, and may be used during *zazen* to balance yin and yang.

For iaido to follow Taoist principles, inhalation should be made during the preparation for nukitsuke, kirioroshi, or chiburi. The actual cuts should occur during exhalation. In this regard, the hoki ryu-ha of iaido actually uses kiai during cuts. The ZNKR kendo kata also use vocalizations during offensive actions in a similar fashion. These should be integrated into a reverse abdominal breathing pattern.

The Chinese practice of *chi kung* consists of a series of repetitive limb and body movements coordinated with the breathing cycle during either reverse or standard (Buddhist) abdominal respiration, depending on the desired effect. It not only represents an excellent warmup exercise for any martial art, including iaido, but it leads to the gradual recognition of the subtle, and sometimes not so subtle body sensations related to the flow and control of ki. Once you have achieved this body awareness, merging breath and intent will become second nature to you and your sword will serve as an extension of your body and your mind.

Regulation of breathing during iaido is a pretty advanced concept that is probably unnecessary for even intermediate students. However, beginners should implement the concept of using the breath to help relaxation, such as the relaxing breaths before starting a kata. Likewise, exhaling softly during the noto, where aggression as well as the sword is being put aside, should be incorporated early in training to set the proper spirit. Zazen, or seated meditation with abdominal breathing, either Taoist or Buddhist, is an excellent way of preparing to practice iaido. Be sure to breathe from your hara, relax your entire body, clear your mind, and keep the tip of your tongue on your palate.

ZEN AND THE ART OF IAI

Yesterday is dead and gone
And tomorrow's out of sight,
It's so sad to be alone,
Help me make it through the night.
—*Kris Kristofferson,* "Help Me Make It through the Night"

Because it (the sword) is a weapon, it confronts us with the terror of mortality and considerations of moral action, often making the linkage between the two painfully real and present.
—*John J. Donahue,* Complete Kendo

If you decide to study shakuhachi seriously, you will find that as your practice deepens there may be moments of liberation. Don't attach yourself to such fleeting trivialities. Liberation is not the goal. Liberation is the practice in this moment; it's in everything we do.
—*Ray Brooks,* Blowing Zen

The previous sections discuss the techniques of moving the sword in concert with the various parts of the body. They also consider the timing and feeling of those movements relative to the imagined opponent. Further, they outline the relationship between the physical and conceptual sword and the iaidoka wielding it. Up to now all of this has skirted the direct issue of the relationship of Zen Buddhism to iaido.

Zen, from the point of view of most Americans or Western Europeans, is a philosophy derived from Buddhism that has as its goal the release of all the false concepts and perceptions of reality that an individual has inherited and/or learned from his culture. This release, whether a slow, deliberate process or a sudden insight (*satori*) is believed by Buddhists to lead to the state of nirvana, a state of true understanding of how we relate to the universe often referred to as "enlightenment." It can be characterized as the act of throwing off all that is superfluous in our lives and thoughts. This leads to coming to grips with observed reality during every individual moment we are living it.

The means of striving for this goal through Zen varies to some extent depending on the sect an individual might follow but, however it is approached, it is an irrational process. In some sects riddles (*koan*) are used to jar the student into different thought processes. In other sects the process is one of concentrating on the mundane acts of living. Common to most is the act of sitting meditation (zazen). The goal of zazen is to learn to put aside the constant stream of superfluous mental conversation we all have with ourselves long enough to really experience the here and now. Usually, we are so involved with either reliving and reinventing memories or projecting fantasies into the future that we do not pay attention to what we are experiencing in the present. Ritualized motion can also be used alone or in conjunction with zazen to focus the mind on the present (e.g., chi kung, tai chi, yoga, the spinning dance of a Sufi dervish).

The practice of iaido is one type of ritual motion used by the Japanese to approach an appreciation for the here and now by using the imagery of individual battle. Since virtually any activity can be used to this purpose, iaido is far from unique. However, it now serves the purpose particularly well for modern individuals of most nations because it has become an impractical activity, that is, one that is no longer really useful for other purposes in their cultures, including self-defense. Because of this it is easier for us to adopt it as a means of mentally focusing on the present than, say, washing the dishes. And yet, if you read Zen literature, washing the dishes is a frequently mentioned activity in which to seek reality. The process of insightfully practicing iaido, or thoughtfully washing dishes for that matter, can be greatly enhanced by preceding it by five minutes of zazen. How "good" the meditation might be is not critical for the purposes of most iaidoka. It will still make a difference and besides, it will improve with practice.

The zanshin, metsuke, maai, and hyoshi described in previous sections can now be seen in the context of Zen to be the outward expression of an aware mind completely in tune with its current surroundings and activities. The state that exists when our outer aspect (omote, or body) exactly represents our inner aspect (ura, or mind) is termed *majime* and is the goal of the iaidoka. Such a state allows an instant response to changes of reality (for example, a sudden attack). This state is not simply good acting, at least in the Western sense. In Japanese No theater the actor changes his ura to match the outer manifestations of the part he is playing, thereby projecting the energy of the character. Perhaps the Western equivalent is "method" acting. The No actor produces a stage presence of great strength (ki). The same characteristics will exist in a master of iaido, *chado, shodo,* or aikido, or in masters of *bonsai, shakuhachi, go,* or *ikebana* for that matter. These expressions of inner awareness of the moment, to the extent that they shine through the technique or product, are what Iaido and Zen are about. In the best of circumstances this is what is judged during *shinsa* of any of the "ways." The attainment of rank, a student's position in the hierarchy of his dojo, any awards he may have won, or the classy monsuki or nihonto he may have acquired, have nothing to do with the purpose or practice of iaido, which is an individual iaidoka's journey toward himself.

Section Four
Basic Movements

The only aid the individual can bring to the budo he follows (to preserve it) is to set aside his personal predilections and desires, and attempt to pursue it with a pure heart, staying as closely as possible to the course set by those who've gone before him. Through study, through interaction with his seniors, teachers and masters, and of course, through incessant and selfless training, he must make the effort to comprehend the true meaning of the budo, and to follow it unswervingly.

—Dave Lowry,

Bokken: Art of the Japanese Sword

SAFETY

No set of rules will compensate for a lack of common sense or carelessness. Both the sword and the iaidoka should be kept in good repair and technique should constantly be improved and interiorized. The following precautions are a starting point for a personal checklist for safe practice.

- Use a proper blade, not a cheap imitation or a damaged shinken.
- Keep your thumb on the tsuba whenever you are carrying or wearing a sword.
- If the blade falls out of its saya, don't try to catch it; let it fall.
- Always exercise zanshin and metsuke. Know where all the people in the dojo are, what they are doing, and where your and their blades are at all times.
- Do not draw your blade around anyone but budoka.
- Never use your blade for anything but practice.
- Check the mekugi before practice or passing the sword to another.
- If your tsuka or tsuba sudden becomes loose or noisy, stop practice until the cause is discovered.
- When you get tired enough that your technique deteriorates, quit and rest for a while.
- Always place your sword flat on the floor against a wall, not propped up against a wall or furniture. Never step over another's sword on the ground.

WARM-UP

Iaido is a noncontact, low-impact activity. It can be done by individuals of any age or of either sex, and even by people with some degree of disability. On the other hand it is exercise. Iaidoka work their entire body, but the legs, knees, and ankles take the brunt of the exercise because of all the dropping to the floor and rising that they do. Furthermore, most Westerners are not used to the degree of pelvic rotation necessary to perform these motions properly and have relatively weak lower backs. Such movements are done in precise postures without the ability to augment either specific muscles or balance by varying the motions. Muscles and tendons must be limber enough to assume the kneeling and sitting positions and remain in them for a while before rising, and strong enough to rise with precision and control keeping a straight back all the while.

Parts of the upper body are also put under stress. The right arm in particular is worked hard by iaido, mostly during one-handed cuts and especially the Omori chiburi. One structure taking a lot of strain during cutting is the tendon of the long head of the biceps muscle that can be found in a bony grove in the humerus just at the edge of the deltoid muscle on the front of the upper arm below the shoulder. The right elbow also takes considerable pressure. As the chiburi gets stronger, it is the forearm muscles, attached to the elbow that have to work harder and harder to stop the sword at the end of the cut.

Other structures that may take a beating are the big toes. Most seiza and tatehiza kata include a kneeling position in which the big toe is bent backward against the floor. During a cut, this toe pushes the body forward. Most beginners need some conditioning to be able to bend the toes to this degree and often use it too much in the act of stepping forward. The big toe of the rear foot is often rubbed raw by prolonged practice of okuriashi stepping, as is common in kendo. For a long practice session, for example a seminar, it is wise to tape the sole of these toes to prevent blisters.

Preparing for iaido should consist of basic flexibility and range-of-motion exercises for all joints, including the spine. In particular, the hips, knees, and hamstrings should be progressively stretched. The author uses elements of Chinese chi kung and a few hatha yoga techniques for loosening all the joints and improving breathing during practice. This also helps to relax and mentally prepare for training. What is important is not how you loosen up, but that you do it, in order to prevent injury and keep your movements fluid. It is also recommended that the aspiring iaidoka regularly perform exercises that strengthen the low back and abdominal muscles. These are often called "Williams Exercises" by physicians and instructions can be obtained from your doctor, a physical therapist, or a chiropractor.

NUKITSUKE

Drawing Cut

Nukitsuke is the initial cut made as part of withdrawing the sword from the saya.

A forward motion of the right leg always accompanies a forward nukitsuke. If the initial starting position is standing, you step forward with your right leg and cut as the back leg moves up. If starting in seiza, you come up into kiza during the draw and slide your right foot forward, cutting on the motion of pulling your left knee forward to maintain the 90-degree angle of left and right knees. In AUSKF seitei waza the nukitsuke is done when the right foot hits the floor with no "pull-up."

- Bring the fingertips of your right hand to the top of the tsuka, keeping them straight and parallel. This motion should be kept close to your body, protecting your wrist with the tsuka.
- At the same time, grasp the saya between the koiguchi and kurigata with your left hand and break the habaki loose by pushing the tsuba forward with your left thumb.
- Push the sword away from you with your fingertips; do not pull it out of the saya. As the sword

is withdrawn, the tsuka should be gradually pushed to the left of your center and rotated into the horizontal plane. This leftward drift is pronounced when doing koryu, and minimized in seitei waza.

- When the kissaki approaches the koiguchi pull the saya backward with your left hand. This begins the nukitsuke. Support the kissaki with your left index finger onto which it should drop. You then continue the nukitsuke by sequentially contracting the fingers of your right hand and angling your right wrist. This sends the kissaki out first, propelled by your wrist and hand, not by arm motion.
- The initial starting point of this cut is just to your left of the enemy when doing koryu, and straight at him when performing seitei.
- Once the kissaki is all the way forward, it and the monouchi part of the blade are dragged across the opponent's body by motion of the locked right arm toward your right.
- As the cut is made your left hand continues to pull the saya against the obi and the koiguchi is dragged around it, pointing the koiguchi toward your left and forcing the tip of saya to the right behind your back. This motion (sayabiki) should result in the saya and sword winding up at right angles to each other at the completion of the movement. It adds balance and strength to the strike.
- Reach out with your right arm as far forward as possible during the cut without leaning your trunk forward or twisting your hips. This combined with the sayabiki gets maximum power and distance out of the horizontal cut without compromising readiness for further action.
- Do not lean forward.
- At the end point of nukitsuke your right arm

Figures 39A – H: Left to right, the sequence of events occurring during the drawing cut (nukitsuke). Notice that the tsuka is pushed out of the saya and that it drifts to the left as the draw continues to allow room or the cutting action to follow. Also notice the accompanying sayabiki.

is extended at the height of your shoulder at about 45 degrees to your right of forward with your elbow locked. Your wrist is straight, not cocked up or bent backward. The kissaki is slightly lower than your shoulder pointed at a spot about 10 feet in front of your midline. This keeps it within the confines of lines projected forward from your shoulders, protecting your center.

- All sword cuts must stop crisply, without bobbing. This is facilitated by relaxing the driving arm and shoulders (and the rest of the body) before the cut is completed. In nukitsuke this is just as the kissaki is passing the opponent's midline.
- With beginners there is a tendency to drop their center by bending their knees when performing a standing nukitsuke. This should be avoided; the energy goes forward, not downward.

For beginners, the nukitsuke is an opportunity to split their saya. This is especially true on draws like that used in the kata *kasagiri*. The kissaki must come out of the saya completely before the right hand begins the cut or the mechanical leverage of the entire blade will cause its first 3 or 4 inches to split the saya down its upper seam. The best way to avoid this is to make sure the koiguchi is pulled off the kissaki with the left hand as a sayabiki is begun. Some better (i.e., more expensive) iaito come with a saya reinforced with bone or a hardwood at the koiguchi. It may be cheaper in the long run for a beginner to find someone who can make an inexpensive "disposable" saya out of poplar or other soft wood, and save his original saya until he has learned how to prevent this injury. Iaidoka of all levels can be misled by events into this error—usually by haste.

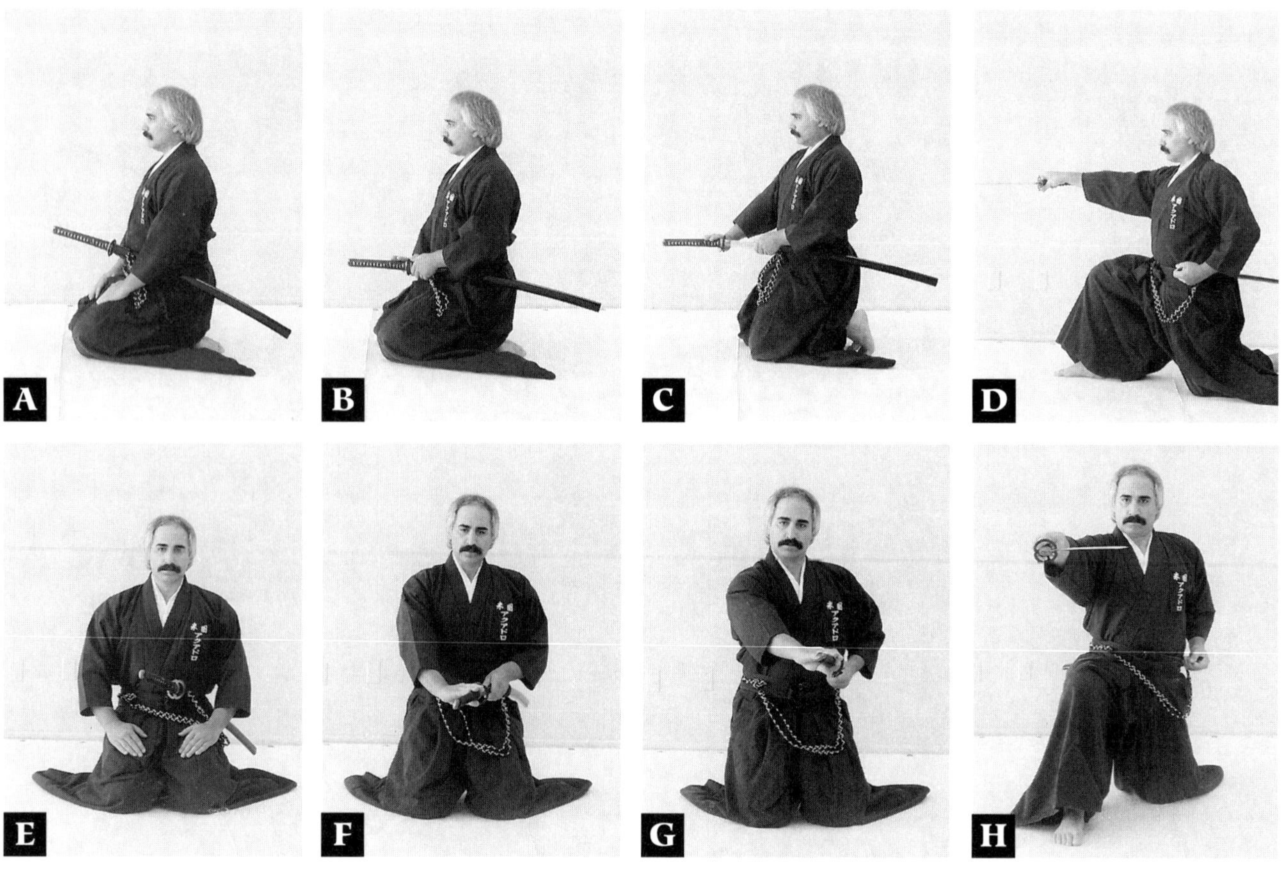

Figures 40A – H: Sequence of performing Nukitsuke from seiza. Notice that as the tsuka is pushed from the saya by the right fingers it drifts to the left as well and forward, the swordsman moves into a kneeling position up on his toes, and as the cut occurs, he steps out with his right foot.

FURIKABURI

Raising the Sword

Furikaburi means bringing the sword overhead for a vertical cut. This is almost always done in conjunction with either a slide forward or a rotation to redirect the following cut.

- The basic starting position for this movement is the end of a nukitsuke.
- You first move the kissaki as if you were trying to strike your left ear with its mune. You do this with motion of your right wrist prior to any motion of your arm. As the blade moves toward you, rotate the sharp edge upward (90 degrees).
- As the tip glides diagonally by your left ear your right hand with the tsuka is lifted opposite the middle of your forehead and then smoothly raised over and behind your head. Your right hand should not move farther to the left than the midline during the entire sequence. The sword should ideally be held at an angle of about 45 degrees and directly before and behind your head. The kissaki must not be allowed to drop below the tsuka at any time during the movement and is ideally always higher.
- Your left hand leaves the koiguchi of the saya and grasps the tsuka just as it reaches

Figures 41A – F: Furikaburi is the act of raising the sword over your head in order to make a vertical cut. Notice that the left hand does not reach the tsuka until the blade is in position to begin a downward cut.

its apex over your head. This timing means your left hand must start to move before the sword gets over your head.

- You are often moving forward during this maneuver and your body should slide under the tsuka as it is elevated instead of moving the tsuka over and behind your head. The cut is initiated immediately as the tsuka is gripped by the left hand.
- Do not relax your grasp with the fourth and fifth fingers of your left hand prior to the cut. Doing so would cause the tip to drop below horizontal just before the forward action. Such "cocking" of the cut is improper.
- Be careful not to wiggle your fingers in an attempt to relax your hands prior to the cut.

KIRIOROSHI

Definitive or Finishing Cut (Literally, Storm Cut)

Kirioroshi is almost always done while moving forward on the back foot (koryu). Whether you are standing or kneeling, your right foot slides out forward first and the cut is made while the back foot or knee slides up. During seitei waza the cut may be made with a foot movement that does not actually move the body forward.

Figures 42A – F: Kirioroshi—the basic midline vertical cut. Note how high the tip of the sword goes initially, and then how t he hands move toward the body as the arms drop, causing a slicing action essential to the efficacy of the cut. The force in the cut comes from the shoulders and the hips, not the arms.

- A vertical cut, be it sho-men or yoko-men, begins from the midline vertical, behind and above your forehead, not in front of it. The furikaburi should have just gotten it there immediately before you begin the strike.
- The cut starts with your wrist and ends with your arm motion. There should be no initial downward or backward motion of the sword prior to the cut. It should come out of nowhere. Your arms must be relaxed and your grip correct to do this.
- The kissaki should go up as it goes out, the apex of its arc occurring above the strike point. Think about throwing tip of sword at the ceiling above and beyond your target. (Other ryu-ha may insist on a more horizontal cut.)
- During a vertical cut your hands are twisted toward each other around the tsuka as if wringing out a wet towel (*shibori*). This brings your elbows, which were far enough apart at the beginning to contain your head and kabuto, closer together. This action results in the blade being drawn back across the target, aiding cutting by slicing and eliminating chopping. It also adds strength and stability to the last part of the cut by putting force on the top of the tsuka, and keeps it more accurate.
- By the time the cut is completed your right arm and both shoulders should be relaxed. This is what stops the sword cleanly without bobbing.
- Most vertical cuts should end with your hands midline at your hara and the kissaki slightly higher that the tsuka in a "water holding" position (*suihei*).
- Emphasize the slicing aspect of this cut. From the point that the kissaki reaches its position over the target, farthest from you, your arms and hands should move toward your hara as well as down. This is what drives the cut, preventing a chop. Your shoulders should also drop naturally during this action, but you should not drop your hips by bending in iaido, such as might be used during cutting practice (tamishigiri).

KAESHI

Reversing Attack

It is frequently necessary for you to cut in one direction and then immediately turn and cut someone behind you. This occurs in kata at all skill levels.

- Following a kirioroshi done with the right foot forward, first turn your head to the left and immediately thereafter step your left foot 180 degrees around behind you, keeping your knees bent. You don't just step but slide your left foot out, moving with the step toward your new target. As you do this, do not move the tip of your sword (it is stuck in a body!) or bend your upper body in the process.
- It is useful to consciously keep your left arm straight across your chest as you turn so that you don't inadvertently lift the sword over your head too soon. This also helps prevent twisting the blade side to side.
- Your right foot then steps out past your left and at the same time that you raise both your arms to move the blade over your head. Be sure to lift the left arm close to your body, keeping the kissaki pointed toward your last opponent. It is useful when starting to learn this reversal to picture your feet on either side of a line on the floor. After the turn around, your feet are still straddling the same line, but they are on the opposite sides.
- Furikaburi ends when the right foot is planted on the ground, and that is also when your left hand first begins the next kirioroshi. The tempo of the furikaburi should be slow enough that the cut is not begun until the right foot is forward and the left is ready to slide forward with the cut. If it is too fast, the sword will have to hang over the head for a time while the lower body catches up. This signals your

intentions to your enemy. It should, in fact, appear to your target as if your blade came out of nowhere.

- It is not easy to develop a technique that prevents your head from bouncing up and down while doing these movements. One trick is to practice in front of a mirror and watch the top of your head. The "cure" for bouncing is in keeping the knees bent like shock absorbers—especially the lead knee. Think in terms of sliding forward as if on roller skates, or floating.

Changing Directions While on the Floor

Several of the kata require striking one or more enemy not immediately in front of you while remaining on the floor in a kneeling position. The common thread is first to immediately rise into kiza as you start to draw the blade and look toward your first target (Figure 38). You then pivot around the knee farthest from the target and step out with the near foot to assume the kneeling striking position. The body, feet, and sword should all stop at the same time. Use the momentum of the back leg and foot swinging behind you for power during the cut. Depending on the direction in which you are turning, the rotation of your trunk will either aid your cut or detract from it. In the latter case, it is especially important to use the energy of the back leg in conjunction with a crisp sayabiki for both balance and power.

UKENAGASHI

Blocking and Striking (Receive and Return)

One common defense you can employ against an overhead sword attack is to first draw and block the blade with the side of your blade, effectively redirecting it away from you. Then you can use the energy of the striking blade to flip your blade up into a quick, returning offensive strike.

This may be done as you rise from the floor, or as you step backward away from a frontal or side attack. It is a component of kata at all levels of the muso shinden ryu and is always a one-handed technique in this school. Basically, you draw your blade horizontally between you and your attacker and then push it above and in front of your head and left shoulder. The distance from either is best judged by picturing a hard strike coming down on the blade and adjusting the position so that a collapse of the block will cause your blade to hit your shoulder. This will prevent the attacking blade from

Figures 43A – D: Reversing the direction of attack following a sho-men kirioroshi and setting up for a second one.

Figures 44A – D: Ukenegashi. The block may begin from a sitting or kneeling position and is immediately converted into a kirioroshi by swinging the blade over the head and grasping the tsuka with the left hand. Notice that the head is tilted toward the right for further protection against the strike.

hitting your head and causing it to slide down the tilted blocking blade.

It is appropriate, and part of the kata, to tip your head away from the blade to make room for its eventual collapse. The AUSKF kendo kata and other schools of iaido have in their repertory two-handed and/or back-handed blocks that are not strictly ukenagashi but work in a similar fashion.

Choking Up on the Blade

One of the skills you must acquire as a swordsman is to always maintain a distance from your opponent optimum to bring your sword into play (maai). A sword is a middle-distance weapon, most effective when the combatants are about 4 feet apart. Knowing this, an opponent is likely to try to get inside this practical distance to neutralize your sword technique.

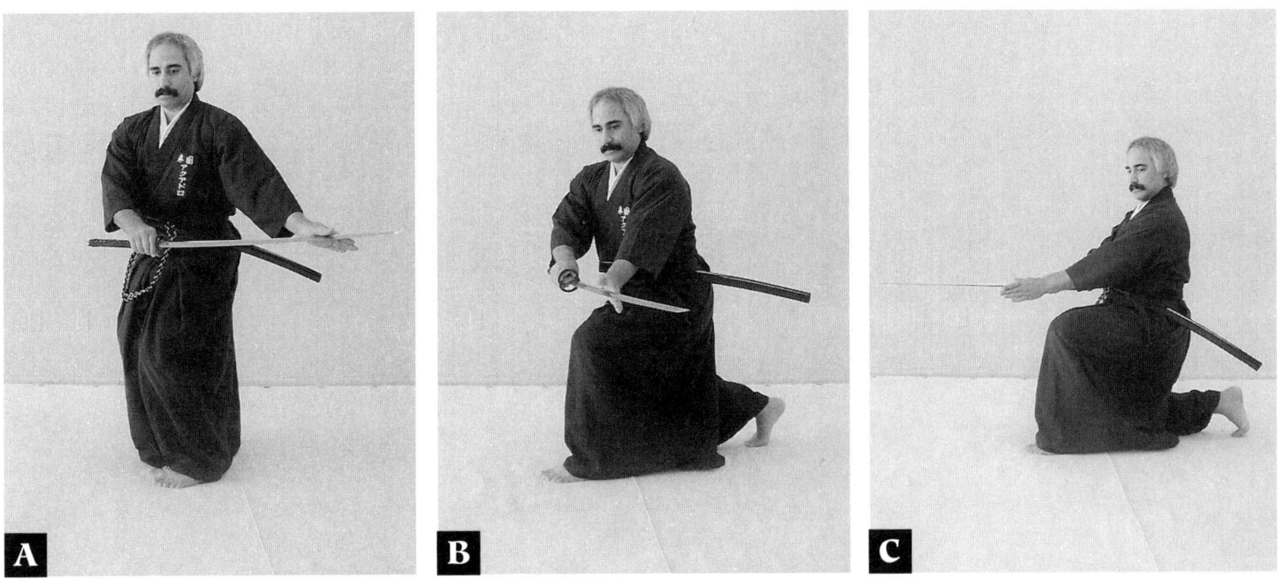

Figures 45A – C: Left-to-right slash done by choking up on the blade in order to work within the usual striking distance of a katana. In this instance, the swordsman follows the opponent to the floor. Power comes from the hips.

One way of dealing with this is to choke up on the blade, which has the effect of turning a katana into a wakizashi-length weapon. This technique is usually begun after the blade has already been drawn. In one variation, you make a horizontal cut by pulling the tsuka close to your right hip and stabilizing the mune of your blade with your left palm. You then twist your hips, cutting horizontally from left to right. As this is done, your left hand slides down the mune toward the tsuba. A similar maneuver is performed as part of several of the Eishin ryu waza. You can adjust the direction of cut to cover several different conditions, including diagonal and vertical cuts, and you can remain standing or follow an opponent to the floor as the cut proceeds. Figures 45A through C depict such a cut from Eishin – Yonhon Me. This technique has the further use of adding power to an otherwise spent one-handed cut when it has failed to adequately penetrate the enemy's tissue.

YOKOGUMOGIRI

Horizontal Cut (Cloud-Cover Cut)

Traditional sword-cut targets are those areas of the body over which Japanese armor was weakest. Thus the neck, armpit, and wrist are point hits in a kendo match as well as prime targets in medieval battle. That is a legacy of the *sengoku jidai* that survives in modern iaido. Much later, kendo and iaido added the most important, or difficult, strike depending on the presence of a helmet (kabuto): the head.

The helmet was a barrier that 15 centuries of swordsmiths designed blades to overcome. Another relatively armor-deficient area was just below the breastplate (*do*). A horizontal cut below the do would be expected to enter the lower abdomen wall, spilling the bowel and entering the urinary bladder, generally a slowly fatal wound unless deep enough to sever the aorta. Depending on circumstances the cut may be made left to right or right to

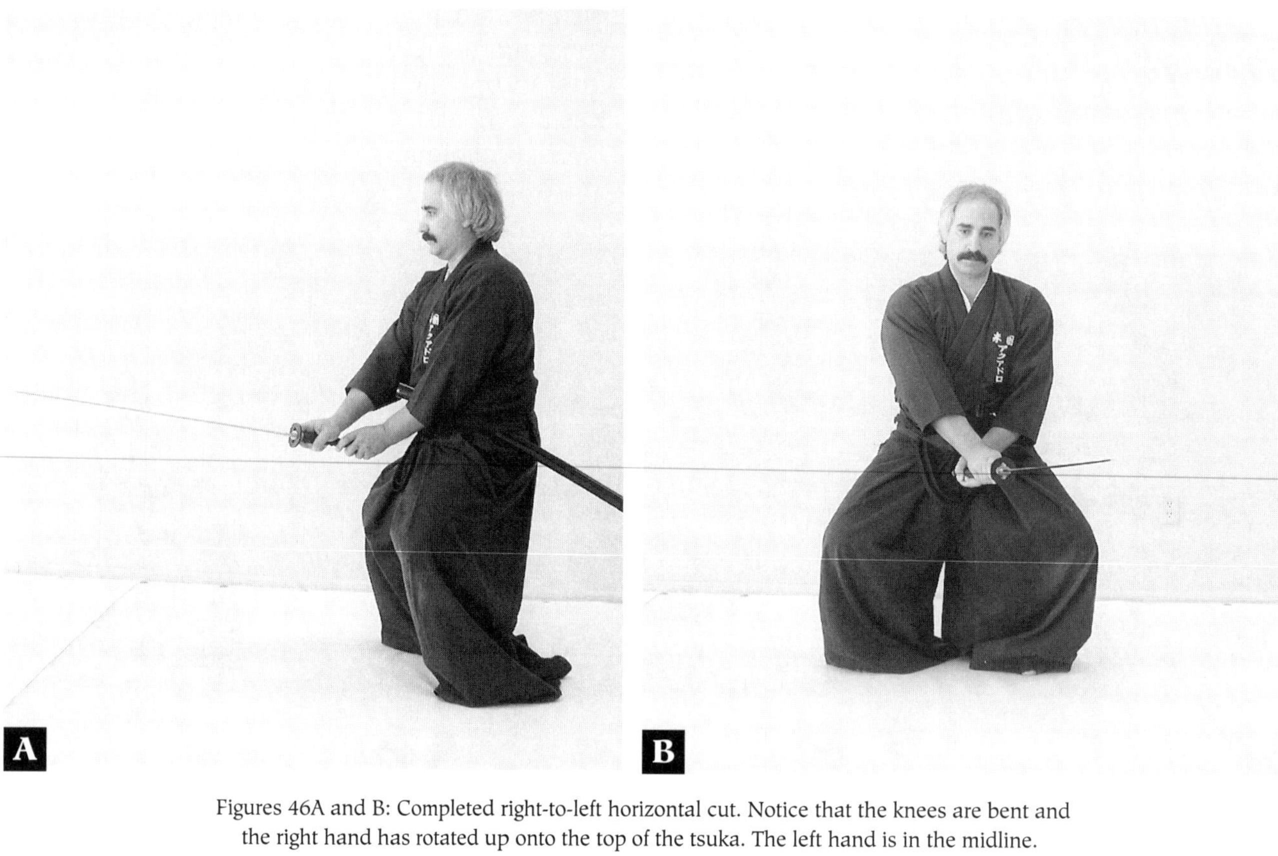

Figures 46A and B: Completed right-to-left horizontal cut. Notice that the knees are bent and the right hand has rotated up onto the top of the tsuka. The left hand is in the midline.

Figure 47A and B: The starting position for a left-to-right horizontal cut. This may be done in conjunction with a step with either foot. Notice that the left hand and tsuka is in, and stays in, the midline.

left, with either foot forward. Often a right-to-left cut starts with a one-handed swing with the right hand during which the left hand grasps the tsuka to provide additional power (ryuto). The last half of this swing is somewhat like swinging a baseball bat, with power coming from the hips and shoulders. During the cut, the right hand migrates to the top of the tsuka and both hands end up remaining in front of the hara, with the cut ending at its exit from the abdomen. To strike the target directly it is often necessary to bend the knees to a considerable extent, keeping the weight equally between the feet.

The sword is usually transferred from the right to the left side over the head when a left-to-right cut is needed. As shown above, the power for the cut comes from hip rotation and the hands remain in the mid-line. Cutting in this direction, the kissaki may be allowed to move way to the right in anticipation of bringing the sword overhead for a following sho-men cut.

TSUKI

Thrusting the Blade

A tsuki is a horizontal thrust of the blade point-first into an opponent. It can be done to the front, but is often used to dispatch someone closing behind or to the left of you, in which case an overhead strike is awkward. It is a one-handed technique even though the opposite hand may add support to the blade. Because a simple thrust makes a small hole that may miss vital organs it is usually combined with a downward vector that enlarges the cut or a twist, doing considerably more damage.

Thrusting to Your Left

- Put your feet together with your left thumb on the tsuba.
- Bring your right fingers up to the tsuka as you break the habaki with your thumb and look to the left.
- Draw the blade horizontally as far to your

Figures 48A and B: Thrusting to the left. Notice how both hands move to the midline and the left upper arm stabilizes the mune of the blade. The weight is equally distributed and the back remains straight.

right as you can, keeping it against your front. Near the end of the draw, clear the kissaki with a sayabiki. Immediately raise the mune up to you nipple line.

- Step sideways to your left with your left foot, keeping your head level and your knees bent. As you narrow your stance with your right foot, thrust the blade horizontally across your chest to your left as you simultaneously bring the koiguchi to your hara. This saya action not only adds power to the tsuki but your left biceps guides the mune in the proper direction. This action also causes the kojiri to push your target into the path of the kissaki. (Be sure to start the thrust before moving the biceps too far forward—many iaidoka have a hole in the left sleeve of at least one of their gi tops.)
- At the completion of the thrust, the kissaki should not be behind you but to your left, and the tsuka should be locked into your chest by the undersurface of your forearm. Weight should be equally distributed, knees bent and shoulders relaxed.

Thrusting Forward

This is done with either the left or the right hand providing the power and with or without support from the other hand. The basic concepts include keeping your hips and shoulders perpendicular to the target for stability, using a shift of weight from back to front and hip action for power, adding a vector down to increase the damage and locking the elbow of the thrusting arm. In Kamimoto-Ha, one-handed thrusts are made from the midline of the body with the thumb on the side of the blade, pushing against the tsuba. Virtually all the thrusts used in muso shinden ryu kata are aimed at the solar plexus (and heart).

ATE

Striking with the Kashira

From either a standing or a sitting position, the right fingers are placed on the top of the tsuka parallel to one another and at 45 degrees to the tsuka and direction of attack (which increases the distance of the strike).

Forward motion of the body is initiated,

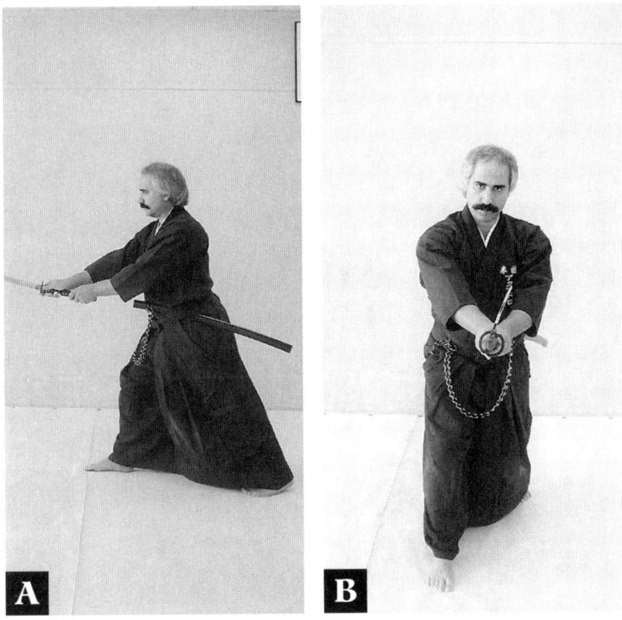

Figures 49A and B: Two-handed forward tsuki. Notice that the upper body is slightly forward, supported by the back leg, and that the sword is rotated slightly counterclockwise. In AUSKF Seitei waza neither the twist nor the leaning are acceptable.

Figures 51A and B: Supported, short forward tsuki. Notice that the blade is parallel to the ground both before and after the thrust but that the kissaki has been lowered slightly, increasing damage.

Figure 50: Forward tsuki from a kneeling position might be used when the swordsman is under a porch or in a cave with limited height. Power still comes from the left leg.

Figures 52A and B: Two variations of ate. On the left, a standing ate to the face, on the right a kneeling ate to the solar plexus. Notice that the right fingers are flat on the top of the tsuka and angled forward.

either as a step or rising from sitting. The back foot's movement and strong hip action are used to drive the tsuka and saya, as a unit, into the face or solar plexus of your enemy.

The trajectory of this thrust must be straight from the obi to the target. Raising the tsuka too high at first will allow the opponent to simply block it with his hand.

Since this action is almost always followed by a definitive strike, the target is held at bay with the kashira while the saya is slipped backward off of the blade.

YOKO CHIBURI

Throwing Blood off Blade by a Lateral Flick

- The classic starting position for this is from the end of a kirioroshi with your right foot forward, a position which is essentially *chudan no kamae*.
- Turn the blade counterclockwise with your right hand so that the ha points out and down toward the right (loosen the grip with your left hand and rotate the tsuka with your right hand). In the process, push your right hand up against the tsuba. This will help you keep your right hand in the proper finish position.
- Snap the entire blade firmly but smoothly out to the right and down without flicking the tip by itself.
- Simultaneously move your left hand horizontally to the koiguchi, touching it with left thumb and then sliding your thumb and palm back about 1 inch. Keep your fingers together and pointed slightly out from parallel to your leg in order to keep your fingers from getting tangled up in your hakama.
- Push the saya down with your left thumb until it is horizontal (parallel to the ground).
- Keep your body perfectly upright with your hips rotated forward and your shoulders relaxed, down, and back. Your weight should be equally distributed with your back heel off the ground slightly. When

Figures 53A – F: Yoko chiburi. Notice that the blade is rotated counterclockwise inside the left hand before it is pushed sideways at the level of the obi. (The open left hand in the upper middle photo is exaggerated.)

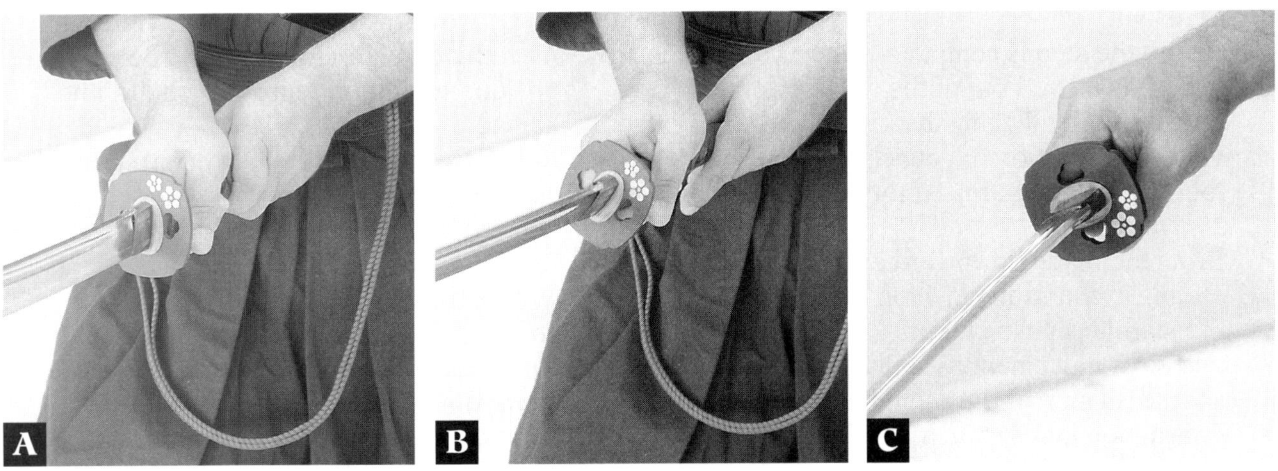

Figures 54A – C: Details of the hand and tsuka positions during yoko chiburi. Notice in the final frame that the back of the hand is flat with the wrist, not cocked up, which is a common error.

starting it may be helpful to actually picture yourself leaning back a little with your shoulders during the maneuver.

- The final sword position should be with the blade tilted clockwise at 45 degrees with its tip down, pointing at a spot on the floor about 10 feet and slightly to the right of just in front of you. The kissaki should be within the line of projection of your right shoulder.
- Both hands should be at the same (obi) level and the top of your right hand should not project above the plane of your right arm. In other words, it is incorrect to have your wrist cocked back at the end of this movement. This will be aided by the proper adjustment at the beginning of the movement. Your right arm should be 30 degrees forward of your shoulder line.

Yoko Chiburi from Hasso No Kamae

- Grasp the koiguchi with your left hand, covering and concealing the inside of the saya. At the same time, square up your shoulders parallel to your enemy and rotate the blade so that the ha is about 30 degrees to your left.
- Start to slide your left foot back, leading with your heel and keeping your toes pointed forward. As your body and head move backward, leave your right hand where it is; you will gradually step away from it moving your head behind the plane of its cut.
- Before the step is completed when your head has moved out of the way, perform the chiburi by flicking the kissaki out to your left by action of your right wrist followed by your arm. At the same time do a sayabiki.
- Bring the blade downward and to the right, ending in the same position described for the standard yoko chiburi. Both the sword and saya movement as well as your feet should all stop at the same time.
- This action is very much like Omori chiburi, which is described in greater detail below.
- This action can only succeed if the blade is in the correct position before starting it forward and the head is out of the way. Once the plane of the cut is established, it cannot be changed without extraneous movement of body and sword.

Yoko Chiburi from Jodan No Kamae

- This is just as described above for hasso no kamae with three exceptions. First, the timing of the left step and chiburi is a little different because the blade has a greater distance to travel. Second, you do not grasp the koiguchi first, but initiate the chiburi with both hands on the tsuka by twisting the upper body parallel to your enemy and rotating the blade 30 degrees counterclockwise. Last, you augment the wrist flick by pushing on the kashira end of the tsuka with your left fingers just before sliding them down to the top of the saya.
- To emphasize setting up the plane of the cut one more time, the initial movement is just like that of a yoko chiburi from hasso no kamae. As the left foot starts sliding backward, the shoulders and upper body rotate toward your left until your shoulders are parallel and the blade is rotated with the ha toward the left about 30 degrees.

OMORI CHIBURI

Flicking Blood off the Blade by Throwing the Blade over Your Right Shoulder and Then Making a Diagonal Cut across Your Body

- As with yoko chiburi, the basic beginning position for Omori chiburi is chudan no kamae.
- Rotate the blade with your right hand in a clockwise direction this time, loosening your grip with your left hand.
- Immediately after, hold the tsuka firmly with your left hand and jam the fingers of your right fist firmly against the tsuba. In Omori kata you should allow a slight forward movement of the kissaki that initiates the movement of the sword over your right shoulder.
- For seitei waza, the kissaki does not move forward and your left hand slides at obi

level onto the saya pushing it horizontal before the blade moves. In Omori ryu the left hand and the sword move at the same time just like as with a yoko chiburi.

- Move the kissaki first with your right wrist, then using your arm to briskly flip the entire blade, tip first, over your right shoulder keeping your right arm forward of your shoulder line. This should be done with the energy of any other sword thrust.
- When this is completed your arm should be fully extended and locked, and the sword should be pointing at a 135-degree angle relative to straight ahead and with the kissaki slightly higher than your right hand.
- Without any pause, immediately flex your right elbow without allowing it to drop down (keep your upper arm at shoulder level as if saluting) and bring the tsuka to the level of your eye about a fist's width away from your face. You can check this during practice with your right index finger without letting go of the sword. At this point the blade should be tilting slightly back and toward your right, the ha slightly toward your left somewhat similar to a one-handed hasso no kamae.
- Cut forward to the left across your face. The tip should move first and is then followed by the arm whose elbow should lock out straight before the blade is dropped at all. Beginners usually lift the elbow in an attempt to gain mechanical advantage, which is wrong.
- You then continue the cut with your left arm fully extended, bringing the sword to the same final position as in yoko chiburi.
- The net effect of this movement is a diagonal cut across a potential opponent standing in front of you from his right shoulder to left hip.
- Once the sword is put into motion the plane of the cut should not change, so the blade position during the hasso-like part of the stance must be near perfect.
- Do not elevate your right elbow as the sword moves. This will invariably result in a cut that is too horizontal and too close to your head and body.
- At the end of the cut the right arm should be relaxed so that the blade does not bobble. Your right wrist should be straight, not cocked back.
- Your head should be straight, your eyes at a point on the floor 10 feet ahead of you. Your back should be straight, your buttocks pulled under your hips, and your stance deep and solid.
- Timing is critical in this motion. Once the sword starts its rotation the tempo should continue to increase in speed, but smoothly and without any starting and stopping or jerkiness (crescendo).
- In seitei waza, the chiburi does not cross your midline. In koryu waza, the chiburi goes farther to your left and is more of a cut across your body on its way to its final position.

The Omori chiburi is a rather involved way of accomplishing the goal of throwing off the blood on the blade, and one might suppose that it would tie up the swordsman during its execution. At any stage of the process, however, it may be converted to a response to an attack from most any direction. Using the above illustrations, you can picture rotating the body on its vertical axis and turning the final thrust into a cut. Also, if an attack comes earlier in the sequence, the position of the blade over the shoulder can easily be converted into a sho-men or yoko-men strike either to the left or the right.

NOTO

Returning the Sword to the Saya

A basic precept of doing whichever noto is appropriate is that no one is to be able to see into the inside of your saya. What is within your koiguchi is considered a secret to be hidden from view with the fingers of your left hand.

- Starting at the end of whichever chiburi was performed, you move the kissaki toward your left hand beginning with right wrist action alone. Then move the sword to your left with your right hand and arm. At

A

B

C

D

E

F

G

H

I

Figures 55A – L: Omori chiburi. Notice how the sword is first thrust firmly backward, then forward, as high as is done during a sho-men cut and then down to the same position as a yoko chiburi. Also note how the left thumb holds the saya into a horizontal position.

the same time rotate and twist the saya forward around your waist until the koiguchi is horizontal and at your midline. As the blade slides back to your left, the mune is placed on the web between your thumb and first finger of your left hand right at the midline of your body.

- The above is accomplished in all but the reverse chiburi by simultaneously dropping the tsuka into the fingertips of your right hand (forming a horseshoe shape with your fingers and thumb) while beginning the left hand movement of the saya.
- The part of the mune first touching the left hand varies with the set being performed. In seitei waza it is right at the tsuba. In Omori it is about one third out toward the kissaki; in Eishin about one half to two thirds; and in Okudan the kissaki goes directly into the saya (Figures 59A through D).
- As soon as the mune touches your left hand you extend the tsuka at arm's length 45 degrees to your right, drawing the blade across your left hand. You cannot do this if your fingertips do not loosely hold the tsuka. You rotate the koiguchi posteriorly around your left hip at the same time. Eventually the kissaki will drop onto your left index finger, and then into the koiguchi.
- When the tip drops into koiguchi you reverse the direction of both the sword and saya. You first rotate the saya back onto the kissaki and then start to slide the sword back into the saya with your right hand.
- Do not change the angle of the sword from the body as you do these maneuvers.
- The rate of return also varies with the set being performed. For seitei the rate is slow all the way, but as the sets get more advanced more of the blade is replaced rapidly before slowing at the end.
- As the sword approaches being two-thirds sheathed, the saya is rotated with the left hand in a clockwise direction, timed so that the saya comes vertical as the blade is completely sheathed. Do not try to rotate the sword directly with your right hand.
- The left thumb does not move until the tsuba is within a centimeter of it, then it simply elevates to accept the tsuba sliding underneath it, facilitated by a slight cocking of the wrist.
- All four fingers of the right hand are on the top of the tsuka as it is slid in toward the saya. They are all together and straight, pointing at a 45-degree angle to the tsuka until all movement of the blade stops.

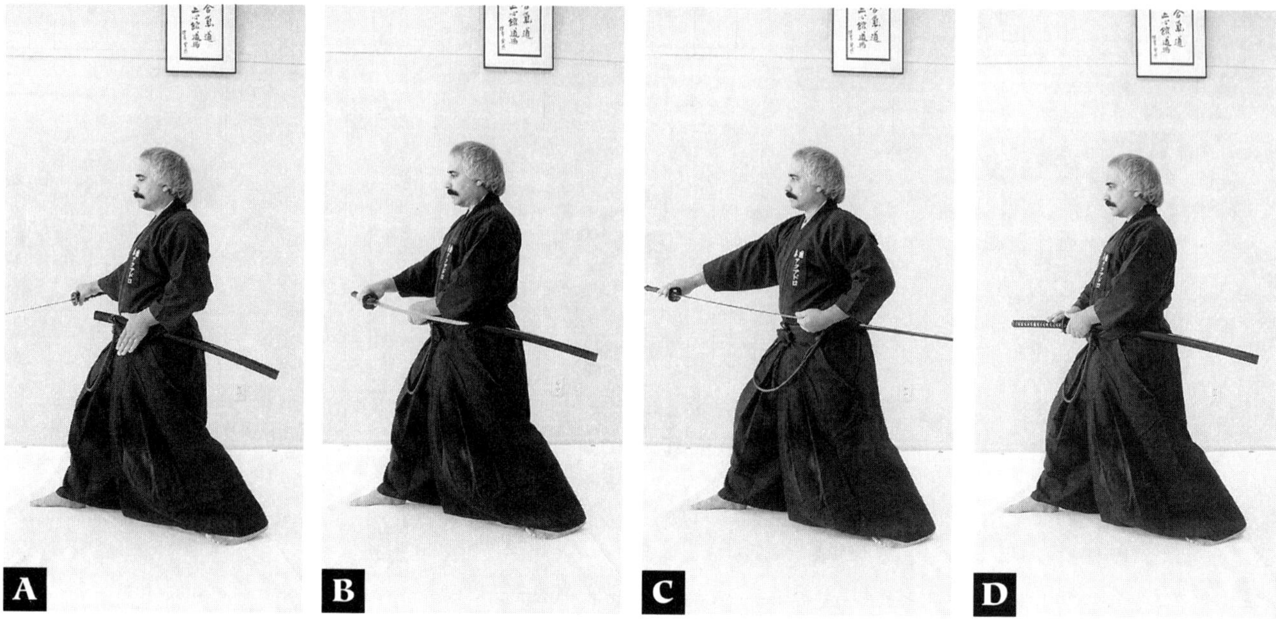

Figures 56A – D: Noto from the side. Notice that the body turns very little and the saya motion is critical for success.

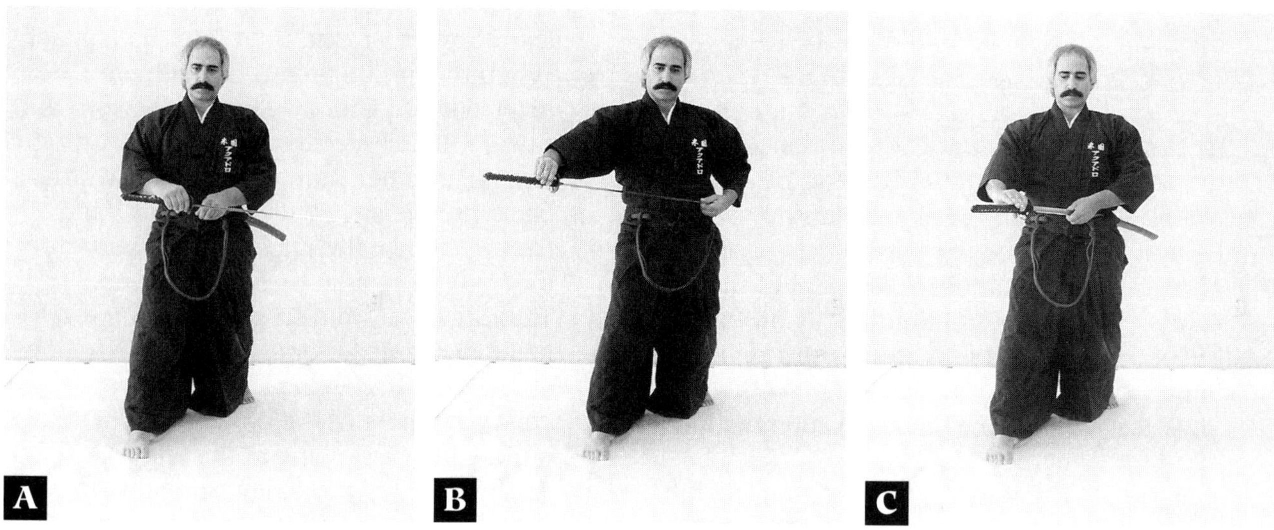

Figures 57A – C: Noto from the front. Notice that the hands come to the center at the same time and the sword first goes out, then in at the same angle to the body. The saya is rotated to the vertical by the left hand as the noto is completed.

- Your rear foot is then pulled forward to your front foot by action of your hips. Your right hand is still on the tsuka.
- The right hand is then unobtrusively dropped along your thigh until it is vertical along your upper leg, fingers together. If the tsuba is in the midline where it belongs, then the tsuka protects your right hand from being struck.
- Noto not only sheaths your sword but it sheaths your aggression. It should always be done thoughtfully and slowly while you gradually relax your entire body as it progresses toward completion. You should never be rush or trivialize the action. It should actually get slower as is proceeds toward completion. At the same time, you should behave as if you may still be

Figure 58: The hand position at the completion of a noto. As the habaki is pushed into the saya by the right fingers the left thumb unobtrusively captures the top of the tsuba.

attacked at any time from any direction thereby maintaining strong zanshin.

- In many kata, the noto is accomplished while assuming a kneeling position.

Noto is the other opportunity, along with nukitsuke, for the beginner to damage his saya, this time not by splitting it but by stabbing the top of the koiguchi with the kissaki. This does not affect the function of the saya as a split does but it does detract from its aesthetics. Some saya come with a cap of copper to prevent cutting the koiguchi. This is a nice touch for a beginner's saya, but it is hardly essential to the art. The problem goes away as the beginning iaidoka learns some accuracy (as do the little cuts on the web and index finger of the left hand).

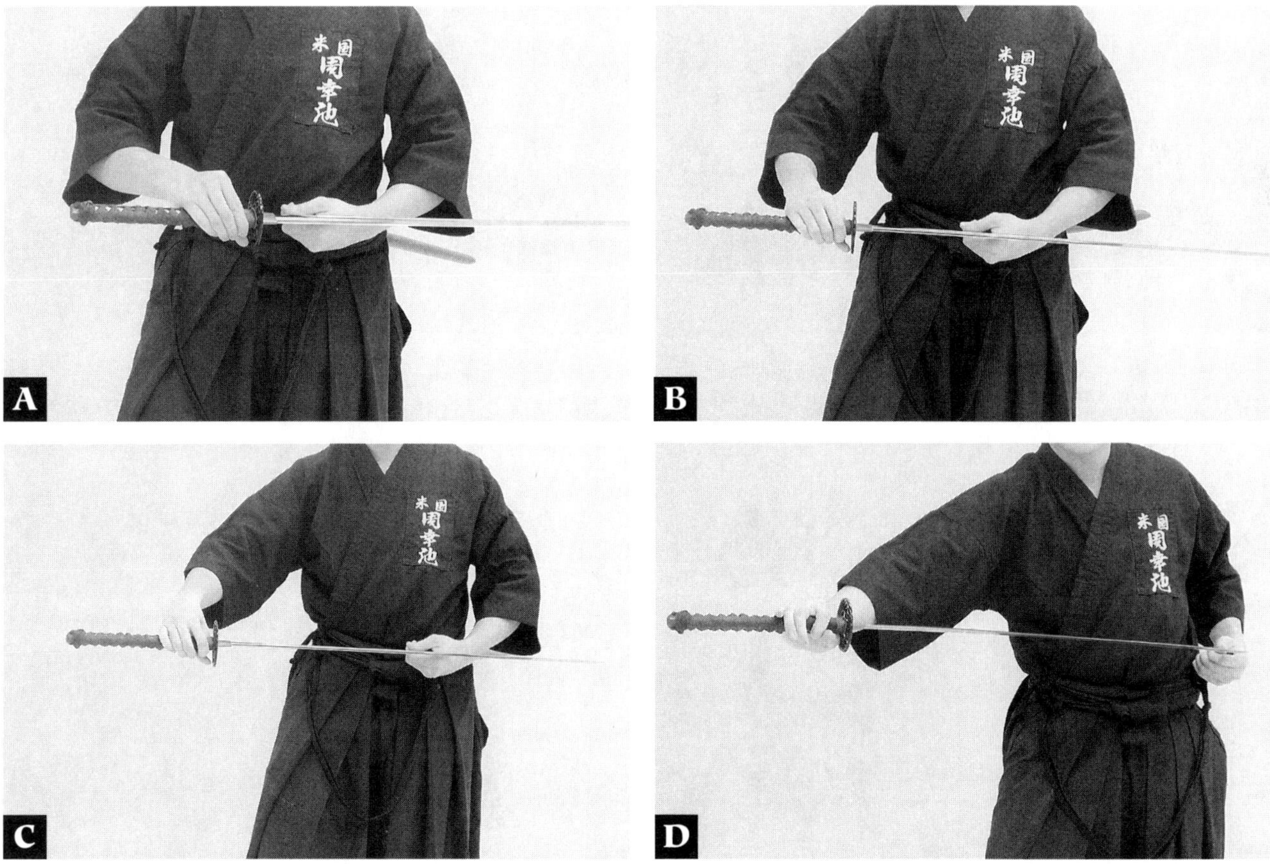

Figures 59A – D: Progressively speedy noto by adjusting the part of the mune first touching the koiguchi: Seitei (A), Shodan (B), Chudan (C), Okudan (D). Notice how in all cases the mune is supported by the left index finger.

Figures 60A – L: Reverse chiburi. Note how the blade is returned to the saya back-handed.

REVERSE CHIBURI AND NOTO

Getting Blood off the Blade by Holding It Tip Down in front of Your Right Leg and Then Wiping It on Your Hakama before Replacing It in the Saya Back-Handed

- Following kirioroshi take the tsuka to your left side, keeping it and your left hand at shoulder height, your left arm locked at a 45-degree angle to your left. In order to accomplish this, your right hand must be turned palm up, holding the tsuka with your right and thumb fingertips only. The kissaki goes to a position against the middle of the right thigh, ha downward. This should be done in a manner that keeps the ha of the blade pointed toward your grounded enemy.
- You may to some extent actually wipe the blade against your thigh with an upward motion while positioning it, stopping when the left arm is horizontal.
- At any time during the process described above, the tip of the sword can be swept to your right to block a strike coming from the floor.
- Next you reverse your right hand on the tsuka, putting it palm down draped over the tsuba holding the tsuka with thumb and fingertips.
- Without moving the sword or your right hand, grasp the koiguchi with your left hand.
- Flip the sword over by rotating your right wrist clockwise, palm up, and swing the kissaki toward your left until the sword is horizontal, mune toward you.
- Simultaneously, rotate the saya counterclockwise putting it in the horizontal plain and bring the koiguchi and the mune of the blade together in front of your hara.
- Hold the tsuka loosely with the fingers of your right hand and pull it out, away from your right side at a 45-degree angle, allowing the mune to slide over your left hand.
- As the right arm approaches its extremity, perform a sayabiki, allowing the kissaki to enter the koiguchi.
- Slowly and thoughtfully return the blade to its sheath rotating it vertical as it goes in by rotating the saya, not the sword, with your left hand.
- As the noto continues, drop to your left knee. It should hit the floor as your tsuba hits the saya.
- As the sword goes in, the fingers of your

Figure 61: Hand position during reverse noto. Note the right index finger is parallel to the tsuka.

Figures 62A – L: Vertical chiburi and noto. Notice how the sword must be brought to the left over the saya.

right hand should be oriented with the index finger along the ura side and parallel to the tsuka, the other fingers curled loosely below it. The thumb should rest loosely upon the top of the tsuka.

- During the entire chiburi and noto, your eyes remain on the body of your enemy on the floor 5 feet in front of you (metsuke). Following standing after the noto, disengage and lift your eyes to a level direction.

VERTICAL CHIBURI AND NOTO

Throwing the Blood off Your Blade and Sheathing It in a Tight Space

This chiburi and noto is used when there is an obstruction on your right side preventing a standard chiburi, or when the sword must be kept close and controlled because of darkness. Its formal use is limited to Okudan kata but it is a useful tool in a crowded dojo. It is usually employed following a vertical kirioroshi.

- Your left hand slides to the koiguchi as your right hand firmly grasps the tsuka and carries it to your right side keeping the blade horizontal, the ha downward. You firmly elevate and lower the kissaki by right wrist action in a vertical direction, without changing the position of your hand relative either to the tsuka or your body.
- The noto starts by pulling the saya forward about a foot out of your obi with your left hand as you elevate the koiguchi.
- Simultaneously elevate the kissaki a second time with your right wrist and arm and flip the kissaki mune first over your left shoulder, bringing the mune of the blade at the habaki to the web of your left hand. You then lift the tsuka up vertically toward your left, keeping the mune in the web of your hand. Be sure you bring the tsuka far enough to your left to allow the blade to go into the saya.
- Pull the koiguchi back down toward your obi (this is really started while the sword is still going upward). When the kissaki drops into the koiguchi, allow the sword to drop vertically into the saya, keeping it to your left side. As the sword is sheathed you rotate the sword and saya to the horizontal, stopping as the tsuba hits the saya.

Section Five
Muso Shinden Iaido Kata

INTRODUCTION TO KATA FORMS

One such point is eliminating excess sword and body motions. Iaido is an art form and is designed to affect the character of the individual practicing it. Eliminating impurities in the form ties directly into the process of refining the character, so it is of utmost importance that the student concentrates on this aspect of training.

—Nicklaus Suino, The Art of Japanese Swordsmanship

"When a man is a beggar, he thinks that small change is a fortune. It is not. In order to rise above beggar-hood, he must rise above small change, even though he uses it as a means. Used as an end, it will become an end."

—Ibn Ikbal

Kata, or form training, is a teaching aid used by all Japanese and probably all Oriental educational systems. For example, copying famous calligraphy or watercolors is used in Japanese art schools to a much greater extent than in the West. The concept of copying art in the East is considered far more of an art in itself than it is in Western culture. In a physical art, such as the martial or the theater, the idea is to allow the body to develop "muscle memory" of each action long before any attempt toward creativity is considered. In the martial arts it can be argued that since modern proponents do not risk their lives to argue the value or effectiveness of a technique, we do not have the right to change the techniques of those that have. Having said that, it probably is impossible for a martial art to be passed down generation after generation without substantial unintended changes being introduced by each subsequent headmaster and indeed by every practitioner.

The description of the kata in this section is an attempt to put into words what probably only exposure to a good teacher over a long period can really express. The process of description artificially breaks the action into a "by-the-numbers" experience, a method best shed as quickly as possible. On the other hand, when we first learn kata that is how all of us first think of them. Steps help to tweak the memory of the beginner and to a lesser extent the intermediate student. The eventual loss of the step-wise thought process and the development of the ability to just let the action happen automatically is called mastery.

Some of the kata, for example, Seitei-Ippon Mai, are prototypes for many of the others. These kata are described below in much greater detail than the others, even at the risk of a certain redundancy. It should be remembered that the great detail in these descriptions is an expression of what is considered important to one American dojo (Memphis) that sprang from one Japanese dojo (Nagagaki Sensei) that embraced one interpretation (Kamimoto Sensei) of one arm (Shimomura-ha) of one traditional ryu (Jinsuke Eishin) at a single point in Japanese history (Taisho era). As the descriptions that follow progress to the more senior forms, a certain familiarity with basic movements is assumed.

Dojo of the same original stream (e.g., muso shinden) may or may not embrace the seitei kata. Those whose forbears followed the leadership of the ZNKR generally do. Those whose traditions follow the ZNIR generally do not. Ryu of both muso shinden and Jikiden Eishin traditions compete regularly at AUSKF tournaments using seitei techniques despite minor differences in handling noto, rei, and sageo. Other dojo of both ryu-ha do not accept the concept of seitei. This artificial distinction, however, is not intended by the author to suggest that the koryu of one group is in any way more or less "genuine" or "pure" than that of any another. Likewise, accepting seitei kata is mostly a historical accident rather than the conscious choice of most current sensei. One teaches what one was taught.

There is a characteristic of kata forms in general that is very confusing until you understand what the form is trying to prepare you for. Each kata has a practical situation (*bunkai*). However, each of the steps of the kata, as the situation develops, has a variable outcome. For example, if your nukitsuke were always successful, you would never need to do a finishing cut. If your finishing cut always worked, you would not have to do a chiburi in a way that still protected you. This is explained in some instances as the possibility of another swordsman showing up, which it certainly could represent. Remember though, that the kata is trying to always prepare you for the next possible necessary technique. For example, in Seitei-Juippon Me, do you really need to cut this guy five times? The kata is an exercise that is actually preparing you to recover and restrike following a variety of misses, not necessarily a series of them. In my descriptions of the kata I sometimes refer to an imaginary or potential opponent. This is only to say that you might find yourself in a situation at that point in the action where there is some threat there, not necessarily the same person you just cut.

BOWING IN AND OUT

I do not love my Empire's foes,
Nor call 'em angels; still,
What is the sense of 'ating those
'oom you are paid to kill?
So, barrin' all that foreign lot
Which only joined for spite,
Myself, I'd just as soon as not
respect the man I fight.
—Rudyard Kipling

Formal Standing Bow (Hairei)

Stand with your feet together, body upright, and shoulders and chest relaxed. Your sword is held in your left hand down at arm's length with the convex edge upward and the tsuka toward the front (teito). The sageo is looped under your left thumb, which is on the top of the tsuba, or beneath your left index finger. It is important that the full loops of the sageo are longer that the hanging, unlooped ends.

Before exercising the standing bow you must transfer the sword to your right side. Take your left hand with the sword held as above and bring it in front of your midline with the sword vertical and the convex side toward your hara. Reach over your left hand with your right hand and grasp the saya and sageo from the concave surface side. Let go with your left hand and return it to your left side as your right hand brings the sword to your right. This transfer should occur exactly in the midline. The tsuka is now to the rear, the convex edge is down and the kojiri is down and pointing forward. In this position it is very difficult to draw the sword quickly. Crushing its loops against the saya with the right hand should control the sageo.

Now bow forward from the waist. When you do so the sword must not move. It does not bow with you. If bowing to the kamiza, bow deeply (about 30 degrees). If bowing to a person, bow less deeply and keep your eyes on the person. It is generally best to bow slightly longer than your sensei or senior student.

After straightening up, reverse the process of moving the sword. Bring the sword in front of your hara and as you do, twist your right wrist 180 degrees counterclockwise. Grasp the saya with your left hand on the concave surface, capturing the sageo in the process and putting your thumb on the top of the tsuka. Then return the sword to the beginning position on your left side.

Seated Bow before Wearing the Sword (Torei)

Assume seiza holding the saya and sageo as described above. Grab the saya at the kurigata with your right hand, fingers below, keeping the sword still and drag the sageo down and past the saya to your rear completely straightening it out with your left hand. Support the saya and sageo at their distal end by encircling them with the fingers of your left hand. At the same time place your right thumb on the top of the tsuba and lift the entire saya and sageo, moving it directly in front of you. As the sword moves to the right rotate your left hand so that its fingers are on top of the saya and the thumb below, with the sageo draped over it. You then place the sword on the floor in front of you, offering it with the right palm upward and the left palm down. Place the tsuba in front of your right knee and out farther that the other end of the saya with the convex side away from you. Do not place it an uncomfortable distance from you. You only need about a foot of space to bow into. Let go of the sword with both hands at the same time, being careful not to let it rock back and forth

Figures 63A – G: Formal standing bow (heirei) to Shinza. Note that the sword is kept unobtrusively close to the body during transfer from side to side. The sword remains motionless during the bow.

Figures 64A – O: The sequence of bowing to the sword (torei) and then placing it in your belt. This sequence follows the bow to the kamiza (heirei), and begins any practice, demonstration or tournament.

in the process. Keep the sageo on your thumb and subtly bend it double so that it does not extend past the kojiri. All of this should be done while keeping your eyes forward, not on the sword.

You bring your hands back to the middle portion of your thighs, each pointing to the opposite knee. Place your left fingertips on the floor immediately in front of you, then the right ones to form a triangle with your index fingers and thumbs. This should not be an equilateral triangle; the side made with your thumbs should be shorter than those formed by your fingers. Arch your back, bend at the waist, and place your head immediately above your index fingers. It is not necessary to touch the ground and you must avoid sticking your rear end up in the air. Keep yours eyes as forward as possible without extending your neck (zanshin). Rise, bringing your hands back in the reverse order as before, right first, left next. The idea is to keep the right hand away from a (imaginary) companion sword (wakizashi) in your obi for as short a time as possible.

Replace your hands on the sword exactly as you put them there in the first place, right hand palm up with thumb on top of tsuba and the left hand palm down with fingers above the saya and the thumb under supporting the sageo. Lift the sword, hold the right hand still in extension of the tsuka and bring the opposite end of the saya (kojiri) with the sageo to your hara, immediately above your obi in the midline. Place the kojiri under the top of the obi with your left thumb and slide the saya to your left under the obi and over the lower tie of your hakama until the koiguchi is in the midline and the kurigata touches the obi. You may guide the kojiri with your left hand, which is still holding the sageo. Transfer the sageo to your right hand by passing it under the sword and tie it to one of the hakama ties near your right hip. Some judges emphasize tugging lightly on the sageo with your right hand after it is tied to guarantee its security. You are now ready to begin a seiza kata, or stand up.

The reason for not placing the sword down perpendicularly to you is based on the dojo standard that states that the imperial family, if present, would be seated watching you from your left side when you are facing the kamiza. If you place your sword at right angles, the kissaki is pointed at the emperor, which is an act of treason.

Seated Bow Following Removing the Sword (Torei)

Assume seiza while wearing the sword and place your hands on your thighs. Reach to the knot of the sageo on the right side with your right hand and pull the knot loose. Transfer the sageo to your left hand by using your right hand to drape the sageo over your left thumb. Place your right hand on your obi above the right hip and pull the saya out of the obi about 8 inches with your left hand. Take your right hand off the obi and slide its thumb under the sageo, taking it off the left thumb and grasping the ura side of the saya with the right index finger on top of the tsuba, pointing toward the kashira. Your left hand then goes, fingers open and together, to the left side of the obi above your hip. Draw the sword and saya the rest of the way out of your obi and place the kojiri on the floor just to the right of your right knee, sword vertical and sageo dangling from your thumb. Keep your left hand motionless on your obi. Lift the saya slightly and turn the sword horizontal while laying it on the floor, tsuka to the left and convex side toward you. When loops of the sageo first touch the floor, push the tsuka slightly away from you, angling the sword. This technique places the sageo behind the saya. After the saya is stable on the floor you then straighten and bend the sageo over, using the fingers of your right hand to prevent its extension beyond the kojiri. You bow in exactly the same fashion as when putting the sword on.

Following the bow, you grasp the saya between the kurigata and koiguchi with your right hand, palm down and with the index finger on the top of the tsuba. Lift the sword and saya to the vertical position and place it on the floor in the midline, allowing the sageo to hang straight down the omote side of the saya. Take your left hand and stroke the omote side of the saya, straightening the sageo and eventually

A
B
C
D
E
F
G
H
I
J
K
L

Figures 65A – R: Sequence of removing the sword from the obi, bowing to it (torei) and preparing to stand in preparation for a bow to the Kamiza. Notice that the sword lies on the ground with both the edge and the tip in the opposite direction from the beginning bow.

capturing it between the left fingers and thumb. Raise the sword with your right hand, stabilizing it with your left hand on the end of the saya, and then drag the kojiri to and past your left side, putting it in the usual carry position. Grasp the sageo 6 inches from its end with your left hand and drag it up to the koiguchi, which you then grasp, returning your right hand to your thigh. You are then ready to stand.

Seated Bow to Instructor or Fellow Student (Shirei)

At times you may bow to the sensei while seated. Likewise, when you start a tournament, your bow to your partner before assuming your place on the floor. To do this, you assume seiza while holding the sword at your left side in the carry position and controlling the sageo with your left thumb. You then put your right hand on your right thigh. Next, raise your left hand and tsuka above and in front of your hara allowing the sword to become vertical with the kojiri just above the floor with the convex side pointed toward you. Grasp the saya and sageo with your right hand between the koiguchi and kurigata and then sweep the kojiri past you to the right. As you do this, control the sageo with your left hand. Place the sword on your right with the convex side toward you and the tsuba just to the right of your right knee. Place both hands on your thighs.

You then bow just as in the previously described seated bow, left hand first and then right. Be sure to keep your eyes on the person you are bowing to. You then reverse the entire process, bringing the sword to your left side in the carry position before you stand up.

Figures 66A – C: Shirei between two iaidoka, for example, before a tournament. The sword is shifted to the floor on the right, keeping it off the hakama. Then the two swordsmen bow to each other without taking their eyes off each other.

Less Formal Standing Bow (Tachirei)

Stand as described above with the sword and sageo in the teito position. Bow from the waist about 15 degrees without moving the sword. If bowing to a picture keep your eyes lowered; if bowing to a person, keep your eyes on him. Then straighten up without disturbing the sword position.

Figure 67: Group of iaidoka exercising tachirei at the end of practice.

Bokken Etiquette

As a general rule, if you are carrying and using a bokken in the dojo you treat it as if it were a sword. There are, however, some traditional differences. The bokken is routinely carried on the right side, ha upward with the tsuka forward and your right arm extended along your right thigh. It remains in this position when you perform hairei rather than reversing its direction as you do with a sword. When bowing to your sensei or another student, you raise the bokken vertically in front of you with your right hand and grasp it with your left hand below your right, which then returns to your right side. You bring the bokken to the left carry position at your left side at obi level and bow. If you are not going to use the bokken immediately, you return it to your right side before moving. When seated in seiza or more informally, the bokken is kept on your right side, ha toward you, tsuka level with your knee. You do not move it to your left side before rising, but keep it on your right side until you are ready perform a kata, or place the bokken on a rack.

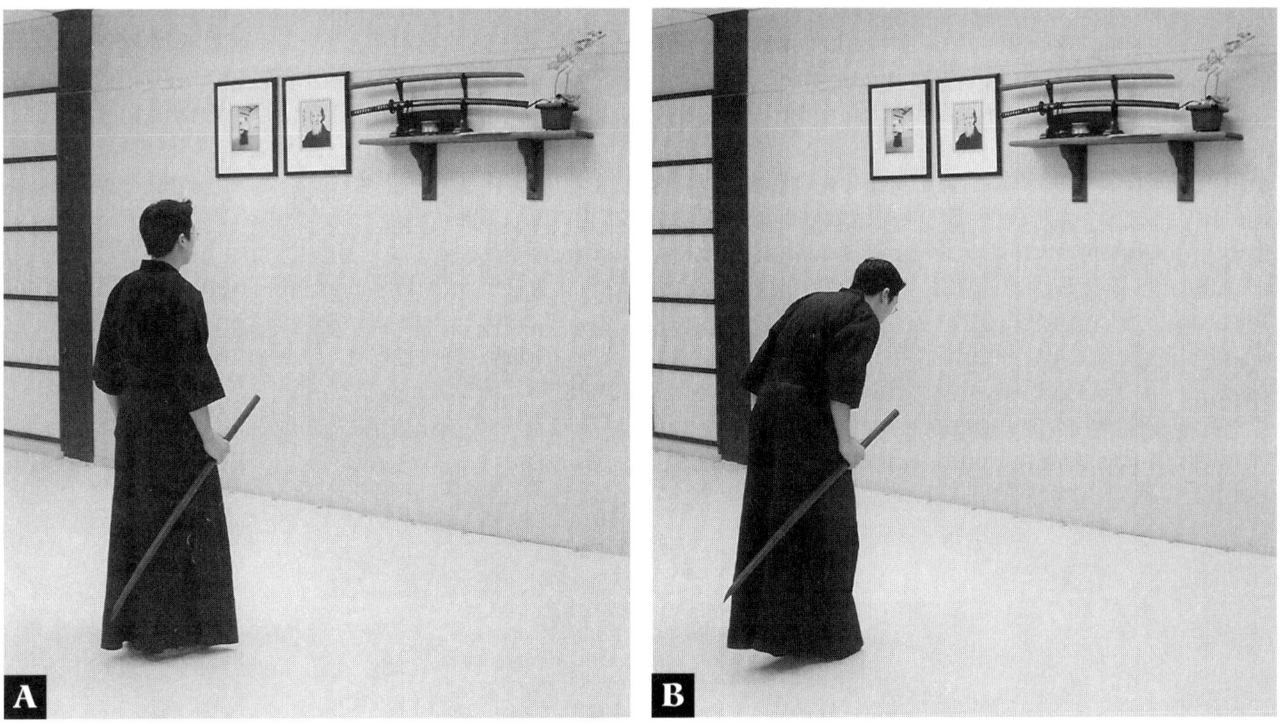

Figure 68A and B: Heirei using bokken etiquette.

SEITEI

制定

His power came from a unified body, all parts working in harmony, relaxed, totally relaxed until the moment of focus, when the edge of the blade would have struck the target had there been a real one. At that instant, Sato-san turned his body to stone and then just quickly relaxed it again as he slid forward in a shuffle to complete the action of the kata with another stroke, this time vertical, of his weapon. This was a demonstration at high level of settsuku, or "body connection," one of the mysterious qualities of the Japanese martial disciplines that make them so compelling and dynamic.

—*Dave Lowry,* Persimmon Wind

When you have exhausted all the various forms and piled up accomplishments through training and practice, movements come to exist in your arms, legs, and body, not in your mind; and whatever you do you do freely, in disregard of the forms, but not violating them. When you reach that point, you do not know where your mind is—even the Demon of Heaven or a heretic won't be able to pinpoint its whereabouts. The forms exist for reaching that state. When you have acquired them, they cease to exist.

—*Munenori Yagyu,* The Sword and the Mind

As mentioned above, seitei waza or "basic techniques" are not old at all, but were created in 1968 by a committee of members of the ZNKR (All-Japan Kendo Federation) representing several different ryu. These kata were created out of pieces of techniques typical of these several schools to serve as a standard for all schools. They were never intended to replace the traditional kata (koryu) of any school. Their purpose was to provide a set of kata representative of the art in general with which members of all schools could compete among themselves on equal footing. They were also conceived to provide a basic understanding of iaido for kenshi who were not formally studying iaido. Originally seven in number, after 10 years they were increased to 10 and, recently, to 12.

Generally, all seitei kata should be performed in a "big" manner using large arcs for cuts. Wide arm movements should be used, even for those that are secondary, such as placing the left hand on the saya during chiburi. Steps should be long, especially when leading to a kirioroshi, or reversing the direction of attack. Stances for chiburi and noto should be deep. Vision should be all-encompassing. Other specific characteristics of the seitei waza that differentiate them from koryu including kneeling directly down to the floor, a nukitsuke that stays more in the centerline, not advancing the knees during kirioroshi, placing the left hand on the saya before starting an Omori chiburi, and a noto in which the habaki is brought to the koiguchi.

The following, by Kazuo Oya, director of the ZNKR, is taken from the preface of an English version of the original committee report that was presented at the Second World Kendo Tournament held in Los Angeles in 1971.

Iai-do and Kendo are inseparable. The sword-drawing techniques of Iai, and the spirit within the attack and defense postures, are fully applicable to the practice of Kendo.

In Japan Kendo trainees are often asked, "Do you practice Iai?" If the answer is no, the inquirer will look puzzled, while the person who was asked may feel embarrassed. For people in general conceive of Kendo and Iai as the same art. It follows then, that Kendo students should know and practice Iai.

Yet within the scope of Iai practice there are many different ryu-ha, or schools. A lifetime of study would not permit the mastery of all these styles. Consequently, it may be beneficial to students of the sword arts to learn the essentials of each school in synthesized form, and thus to understand the basic techniques, especially the art of drawing the sword.

The plan for this text was completed in May 1968. Eleven Masters associated with the All-Japan Kendo Association united the basic techniques of the various ryu-ha into seven forms. Suitable for beginning students, these forms contain ninety percent of the fundamentals of Iai. By this synthesis we trust that those who love the sword arts may learn the first principles of the art.

Iai is not confined to these forms alone, however. We would encourage all students to pursue a deeper sturdy of Iai. The inmost meaning becomes clear only through intensive training within the old ryu-ha, where the true spirit of the art is full manifested.

—Kazuo Oya, Director
All- Japan Kendo Federation

IPPON ME – MAE (FRONT)

前

Bunkai

You are sitting in seiza when you perceive a threat from an opponent seated in seiza facing you. You draw slowly, making your intentions known but giving the opponent an opportunity to withdraw; he does not. Your nukitsuke cuts toward his eyes, driving him back and you slide forward and, taking advantage of his loss of concentration, finish him with a sho-men strike. You then toss the blood from your blade as you stand, nudge him with your toe for any response, and replace your blade.

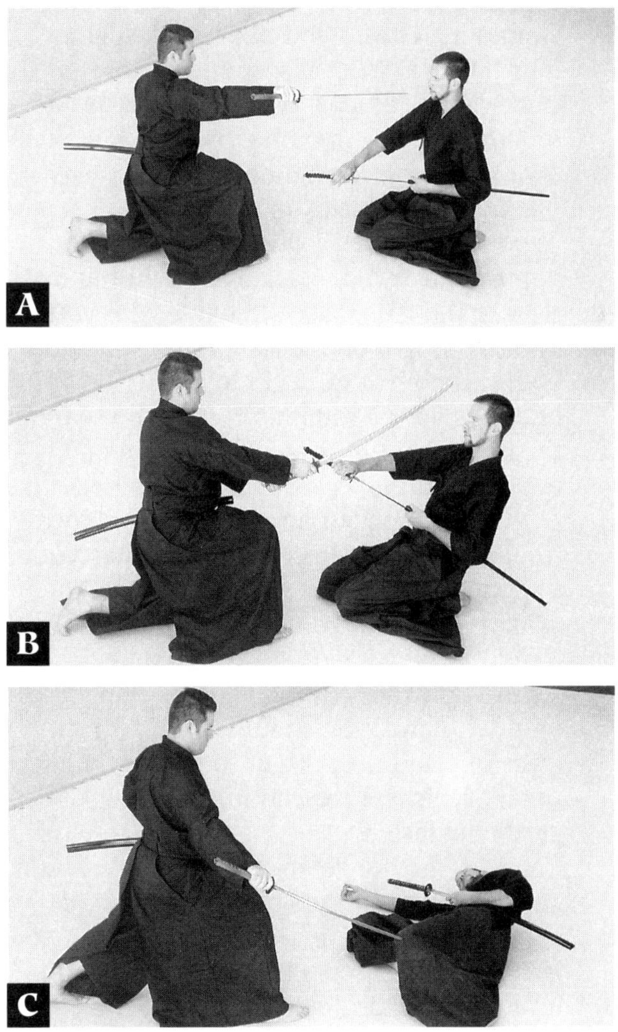

Figures 69A – C: Some steps in the sequence of mae.

Technique

- Assume seiza from the standing position by bending both your knees and keeping your back as vertical as possible. Your left hand should hold the saya with your thumb on the tsuba. Place your right hand between your knees and subtly flick your wrist left, then right, quietly pushing your hakama out from within your knee joints. Kneel without making a thumping noise with your left, then right side while keeping up on your toes. Then sit back, flattening your feet with your insteps on the floor, toes touching but not crossing, knees about one fist's width apart. The sword is placed with the tsuba midline and your hands are placed on the middle portion of your thighs with your fingers pointing toward the opposite knee. Your back is straight, shoulders relaxed and back, chin slightly in, neck straight as if suspended from ceiling. Take at least one good relaxing breath with your mouth closed and relax all over while still remaining alert.
- The action begins by imagining your opponent's aggression and making appropriate eye contact. Your right hand rises to the tsuka close to tsuba with your fingers straight on the top of the tsuka and your thumb below. Begin to rise up on your knees as your left thumb breaks the seal of the habaki to the saya. The tsuka remains in your midline as the sword is pushed out of the saya by your fingertips straight away from your body. This action pressures your opponent. Simultaneously, you rotate the saya into the horizontal using your left hand, keeping it close to your obi.
- By the time the sword tip is at the fingers of your left hand, you should be upright, kneeling, and up on your toes. The timing of all of this is a crescendo, getting gradually faster.
- You start the horizontal cut (nukitsuke) by contracting the fingers of your right hand sequentially starting with the fifth one immediately after pulling the saya back into a sayabiki, ending at 90 degrees to the sword. At the same time the right foot slides out from the body so that the knee stays at 90 degrees and the left leg and foot move to the left directly behind your right knee. Ideally, there is a slight forward motion to your entire body imparted by your left foot. Your back is kept straight with your chin in. There is no bending forward. The action is as if all the elements of your body are moving around the axis of your left knee and thigh.
- The cut shoots out, tip first to the center of your target and then is smoothly brought across the opponent's eyes with the sword very slightly inclined tip down. It stops crisply with the tip inside the line made by projecting your shoulder forward. This is done while a reciprocal motion of the left arm sweeps the saya backward twisting your shoulders slightly and extending the sword a little farther forward. Pause.
- Your next motion, furikaburi, is threefold: you move the kissaki first with your right wrist, keeping your arm extended at first as if going to strike your left ear with the side of the blade. You then move the blade and right hand backward, blade to your left side. When your right hand gets opposite the midline of your forehead, raise it over your head with the tsuka above and behind, not in front of, your forehead. Then twist the saya back to the carry position and bring the koiguchi forward with your left hand. Your left knee is dragged forward by the action of your right leg flexing at the knee until it overlaps the right heel. At the last minute your left hand is brought up to the tsuka just as the sword reaches its highest point.
- Your right foot slides forward so that your knee is at a 90-degree angle.
- You pull your body forward with your hips as the second cut, kirioroshi, is made vertically without dipping the blade, but flicking it out above and past your target. Then bring your arms, fully extended, down in front of your body causing the sword to slice the target. The sword stops with the kissaki slightly lower than your hands, about 6 inches off the floor. Your hands should be below your right knee. Pause.

- Blood is thrown off the blade (chiburi) by rotating the blade toward your left side with your right hand while keeping the left loose. Your left hand then clamps down on the tsuka, your right hand is pushed up against the tsuba, and then as an extension of that same motion, the wrist is extended throwing the kissaki forward slightly and then over the right shoulder so that it winds up 135 degrees from forward and the tip 30 degrees higher than horizontal. During this motion, your left hand moves to the saya with your thumb on top of the saya and the fingers together, straight and slightly away from the vertical. From this position, the right arm is flexed bringing the hand within a finger's length of the right side of the head, keeping the wrist stiff and the sword tilted back and to the right of upright. The tip is then thrown forward, first by wrist action alone and then by the following of the wrist by the arm, which remains horizontal until locked in full extension. Stand up without moving the feet. The arm is then brought down, keeping the cut in the same diagonal plane and moving the entire blade as a unit across your front by the arm as it assumes a position to the left and in front of the body with the top of the wrist flat, at the same level as the obi. The tip is pointing at a spot on the floor about 10 feet directly in front of you. Pause.
- You then change step by sliding your right foot even with the left keeping your head at the same level by bending your knees. Keep your back straight with your hips tucked under your waist. This should result in a slight movement of the kissaki forward, which exhibits both semé and zanshin. Then slide your left foot back and to the right assuming a deep, wide stance with the left heel slightly off the floor and the center of balance low. Your shoulders should be loose and your back straight. Your left hand is still on the saya.
- Replace the blade in the saya (noto) by flexing your right wrist to move the kissaki back and to the left of your left hand and then simultaneously bring the koiguchi and habaki together in the midline with the mune of the blade resting on the web between your left thumb and forefinger. Your right hand then forms a "horseshoe" with the fingertips and thumb of the right hand holding the tsuka that is then thrust out away from the body at the level of the obi at arm's length, forming a 45-degree angle. The koiguchi is forced back and close to the obi by a full sayabiki that allows the kissaki to fall into it. The saya is then swept back onto the blade, and the blade is slowing placed within the saya as it is gradually rotated from horizontal to vertical.
- During the last move of the noto, you slowly kneel so that your right knee hits the ground just as the sword is fully ensheathed. Your thumb slides onto the tsuba and you stand, dragging your back foot forward to meet the front one.
- Your eye position is shifted upward, your right hand is unobtrusively brought to your side and your left foot steps backward to prepare for the next kata.

Technical Notes

- The first thing to move are your eyes, the second is your right hand moving unobtrusively up to the tsuka.
- You should simultaneously break the habiki loose and start up into a kneeling with your feet up on your toes (kiza).
- The sword is pushed out by the fingers of your right hand, not pulled.
- Be sure to rotate the saya horizontally while drawing the blade, keeping the hips straight but twisting the shoulders slightly.
- Don't begin the nukitsuke until the kissaki clears the koiguchi. That is accomplished by pulling the saya back with the left hand.
- Pivot your body around your left knee and make any body corrections around this point while making the horizontal cut. Both the left and right foot should be kept straight in front or behind your body, or moved to this position during the cut. If not, when you stand during the chiburi you will be unsteady because of too narrow a base. Keeping the knees no farther apart

than one fist's width before nukitsuke is one way to prevent this.

- Power comes from your wrist first, then your upper body during the sayabiki. Don't forget the sayabiki.
- During your draw don't lean forward; if anything, lean back, keeping your chin tucked in slightly.
- End the nukitsuke relaxed. This will stop your blade without wavering or bobbling.
- To start the second cut move the kissaki first with your wrist, then bend your right arm.
- The monouchi of the blade should approach your left ear and when your right hand is in front of your nose; lift the sword with your right hand as a unit above and slightly behind your forehead. As your left knee is sliding forward at the same time, the net result is that your head slides under the raised hands, which essentially stay in the same space.
- Just before your two hands come together on the tsuka, slide your right foot out so that the knee is at a right angle. You may stamp this foot for emphasis.
- Get the blade well over your head before meeting it with your left hand. When your left hand touches the tsuka begin a kirioroshi immediately.
- Don't dip the tip before starting kirioroshi. This can be avoided by keeping the last two fingers of each hand gripped tightly on the tsuka throughout the movements leading up to the cut.
- The power of kirioroshi comes from the hips, transmitted via the left arm. The right hand and arm only guide the direction of the cut. Putting too much power into the cut with the arms will cause you to bend at the waist like a puppet soldier. Putting too much power into the right hand during the cut will cause the upper body to rotate toward the left with the right shoulder dipping.
- During kirioroshi the kissaki first goes out horizontally, driven at first by the left wrist. It then goes down from left arm action. During the lowering of the blade, the arms are kept extended at the elbows and the wrists "wring" the tsuka like a wet rag by rotating the thumbs toward each other. This puts the hands on top of the tsuka at the end of the cut, adding to the power. Because of this motion the elbows come slightly toward each other as the sword descends from its highest point. The hands (and tsuka) are brought toward the waist at the end of the cut, emphasizing the slicing action of the monouchi. At the end of the cut make sure your left wrist is low enough that it forms a right angle with the tsuka. There is a strong tendency for beginners to keep it high to keep from hitting the floor. Being relaxed at the end of the cut best prevents this.
- At the end of the cut, the hands should be at the level of your obi and the kissaki should be slightly lower than that.
- Begin chiburi by rotating the blade clockwise and then pushing the right hand up the tsuka against the tsuba. The kissaki goes out toward the opponent before going to the back. Once started, chiburi is a continuous motion, but different parts go at different speeds. The left hand's position, fingers together and out a little from vertical, is designed to keep your fingers from getting tangled in the two sageo of the pair of swords (daisho).
- During chiburi there is a tendency for the beginner to push the sword too far behind him. At the completion of the first movement of chiburi, your right hand and tsuka should be within your peripheral vision.
- When the right hand is brought toward the head before the diagonal cut that ends Omori chiburi, the position of the blade fixes the plane in which the blade will travel from that point on. If this is not correct, the only way to get the blade in the proper end position is by twisting the arm, wrist, or sword, or all of them, which looks terrible.
- In seitei chiburi (as opposed to Omori ryu), the sword does not cross the midline, but takes a much more vertical course than that used in koryu waza.
- Beginners often raise their right elbow at the start of this cut, probably in the mistaken belief that it will add power to the

cut. This interferes with the path of the sword, causing it to drop quickly rather than extending outward first.

- In the process of changing feet, adjust the bend in your knees so that your head stays at the same level during the entire maneuver instead of bobbing up and down. Your feet should slide, not step, with your toes staying down on the floor. When the final foot position is assumed, your feet should be widely and deeply placed with the weight evenly divided and your back leaning slightly back if not perfectly straight. The back heel is slightly off the floor and the back knee is locked to enhance stability.
- If you have a tendency to lean forward after the change of feet the problem is with your hips. Your buttocks are not under your waist enough. This can be corrected by making sure that the back leg is locked in position and the front one is sufficiently bent. This will force you to rotate your hips, opening up your lower back and pulling your shoulders back.
- Begin the noto by moving both hands toward each other at the same time. The left thumb slides along the top of the saya with the fingers horizontal to the omote face of the saya until the koiguchi can be grasped by the index finger and thumb. The right hand starts the movement toward the left by flexing the wrist and causing the kissaki to move first, and then moving the right hand and habiki toward the left, at the same horizontal level (the obi).
- Care must be taken to push the koiguchi down with your left hand. This keeps the saya horizontal during the noto—a characteristic of muso shinden ryu.
- The mune of the blade adjacent to the habaki is supported in front of the koiguchi by the left index finger.
- Following the noto, your back foot is brought up level with the other foot while your right hand is still on the tsuka. When your foot motion stops, your hand is brought down to your right side by keeping it close to your thigh. Doing it this way keeps the tsuka in a position to protect your hand from a sudden cutting attack.
- Your left hand should completely cover the koiguchi during noto so that the inside cannot be seen. Any attempt to use the fingers of your left hand to help positioning the sword can be suppressed by concentrating on keeping the index finger tip and thumb together in a solid ring.
- At every point in the above description where it says "pause," you should read that as "pause and relax everything but your attention." Go right down your anatomy relaxing neck, shoulders, abdomen, lower back, and knees.

NIHON ME – USHIRO (REAR)

後

Bunkai

You have just turned and assumed seiza when you perceive a threat from an opponent sitting in seiza to your rear. You slowly rise to your knees and then turn around, making your nukitsuke to his eyes just as you face your opponent. You then slide forward and finish your opponent with a sho-men strike, stand, and throw off the blood from your blade, nudge the opponent with your foot, and replace your sword.

Figure 70: Halfway through the turn at the beginning of ushiro. Notice that the right knee has been placed in front of the left knee so that no lateral shift occurs during the turn.

Technique

This kata is very much like mae except that it starts with a counterclockwise rotation and thereafter is a mirror image of the first kata.

- From the standing position, with your left thumb on the tsuba, turn clockwise starting with the right foot. Keep zanshin to the front until your right foot starts to turn around.
- Assume seiza exactly as in ippon me.
- Your right hand moves toward the tsuka and your eyes move toward the left.
- You begin to rise up on your knees and then the toes.
- The habaki is cracked with your left thumb at the first movement of the body by pushing the sword out of the saya with the fingers of your right hand on top of the tsuka.
- As soon as you are on your toes, your right knee is moved in front of your left one, swinging your right lower leg into about a 30-degree angle with the other and keeping your weight on your left knee. At this point your blade should be less than one-third drawn and horizontal. Your fingers are not yet grasping the tsuka but rest on top of it.
- Weight is then transferred to your right knee; your left knee is raised off the ground and rotated toward the left with your left toe remaining on the floor but your heel reversing directions. Your body spins around your right knee, while your fingers finish the draw with the kashira pointed toward your opponent, with the tsuka horizontal.
- As your right leg swings behind your hips to a position parallel to the forward line, nukitsuke is performed by the action of sequentially flexing your right fingers around the tsuka and pulling the saya off the kissaki with a sayabiki.
- Make the cut at eye level with the kissaki slightly down. Remember, you are higher that the opponent so "eye level" is not your eye level. End it inside the anterior projection of your right shoulder. Pause.
- Begin furikaburi by moving the kissaki, initially with only your right wrist, toward your left ear. Then bring your right hand and arm first toward the left, and then back over the midline of your forehead, extending the kissaki rearward. Do not allow your right hand to go farther left than your midline. As this occurs, the koiguchi is brought forward by your left hand and your right knee is dragged forward by your left leg to reach near your left foot.
- Your right hand raises the tsuka, keeping the kissaki even higher, as your head slides under the tsuka by the action described above.
- You then slide your left foot forward to a position that leaves your right knee at a right angle. This is completed as the left hand reaches the tsuka.
- As soon as your left hand grasps the tsuka you begin kirioroshi by rotating your hips forward so that the angle of the left knee remains exactly 90 degrees. Cutting thus, the movement of your hips puts the weight of your body behind the cut and leaves you more latitude for subsequent reaction to circumstances. Pause.
- At the end of the cut the sword should be in exactly the same position as in ippon me with the hands at the obi and the kissaki slightly lower. The only difference is that your left knee, not your right, is forward.
- Chiburi is done exactly as in ippon me. Because the left knee is forward, however, it is more likely that your left fingers will be in the wrong position after they are brought to the left side, lateral to the omote side of the saya. They should be together and as straight as your left thigh allows them to be.
- The change of step is exactly like, but the mirror image of, that in ippon me.
- Likewise, noto is performed as in ippon me. Because of the change of step the left thigh does not interfere with the movements of your hand, sword, or saya. You kneel in conjunction with the sheathing of the blade, your right leg forward, and your left knee meets the floor as the tsuba hits the saya. Pause.
- You stand and then your right foot is

brought up even with your left one, your eye contact is broken and raised, and your right hand slides down to your side. Pause.
- You then step backward using your left foot first to reposition yourself for the next action.

Technical Notes

- When turning around before assuming seiza, zanshin is demonstrated with the eyes and head by keeping attention directed toward the original forward direction until the body is nearly turned around and then bringing both to bear on the new forward direction.
- As with ippon me, the eyes (not the head) move first, the right hand second. The head moves to the left with the rest of the body. When you are halfway around, you pick up your opponent with your peripheral vision.
- The position of your right knee and leg prior to spinning around is going to determine the final direction of the body, so early attention to exactly where to place them is essential to learning this kata. Without putting the right knee in front of your left, when you spin around you will be off the line by half a body width, and will miss your opponent with the nukitsuke.
- The draw occurs slowly as your body rises and turns. At the point your shoulders are at right angles to the new forward position the kissaki should be out less than a third. As your right leg swings around your right knee, the cut is launched to take advantage of this torque to strengthen it. This extra power is very important to this kata.
- If the draw proceeds too rapidly in the turning process the tsuka will collide with the warrior sitting next to you.
- The mechanisms of foot and knee movements are different from ippon me but attention should be directed toward getting your feet in sufficiently broad a base that, when you stand during the chiburi, you are stable.
- In sliding the left hand back with the thumb over the saya during chiburi, the fingers may bump into your left thigh. This is not an issue in ippon me. Keep your fingers as straight and perpendicular to the floor as possible.

SANBON ME – UKENAGASHI (FLOWING BLOCK)

受流

Bunkai

You are sitting in seiza when you become aware of a standing opponent in jodan no kamae attacking you from your left side. You block his cut with the side of your blade as you stand up. As his blade slides off yours to your left and his body bends forward, you bring your sword vertical and without hesitation cut downward into his neck. You wipe blood off your blade with your hakama and sheathe your blade using a backhanded technique.

Technique

- While standing, turn 90 degrees by moving the left foot first and continuing to maintain zanshin to the original direction until your body is nearly completely turned to the right. Then move your head and eyes to the new forward position.
- Assume seiza just as in the preceding kata.
- Bring your right hand up to the tsuka and incline your head to the left and up to watch the opponent's sword. Release the habaki with your left thumb.
- Get up on your knees and toes and start to push the blade out with your right fingertips, with the tsuka somewhat elevated from the horizontal. Keep the kojiri from hitting the floor.
- Bring your left foot to but not past your right knee with the foot at 90 degrees to the attacker and parallel to your right leg.
- As you start to rise, finish the draw and place the sword in a blocking position perpendicular to your opponent, blade at a 45-degree angle, kissaki out in front and above your left shoulder with the blade horizontal, mune forward.
- As you continue to rise, pushing the block above you, step with your right foot to a point just in front and perpendicular to

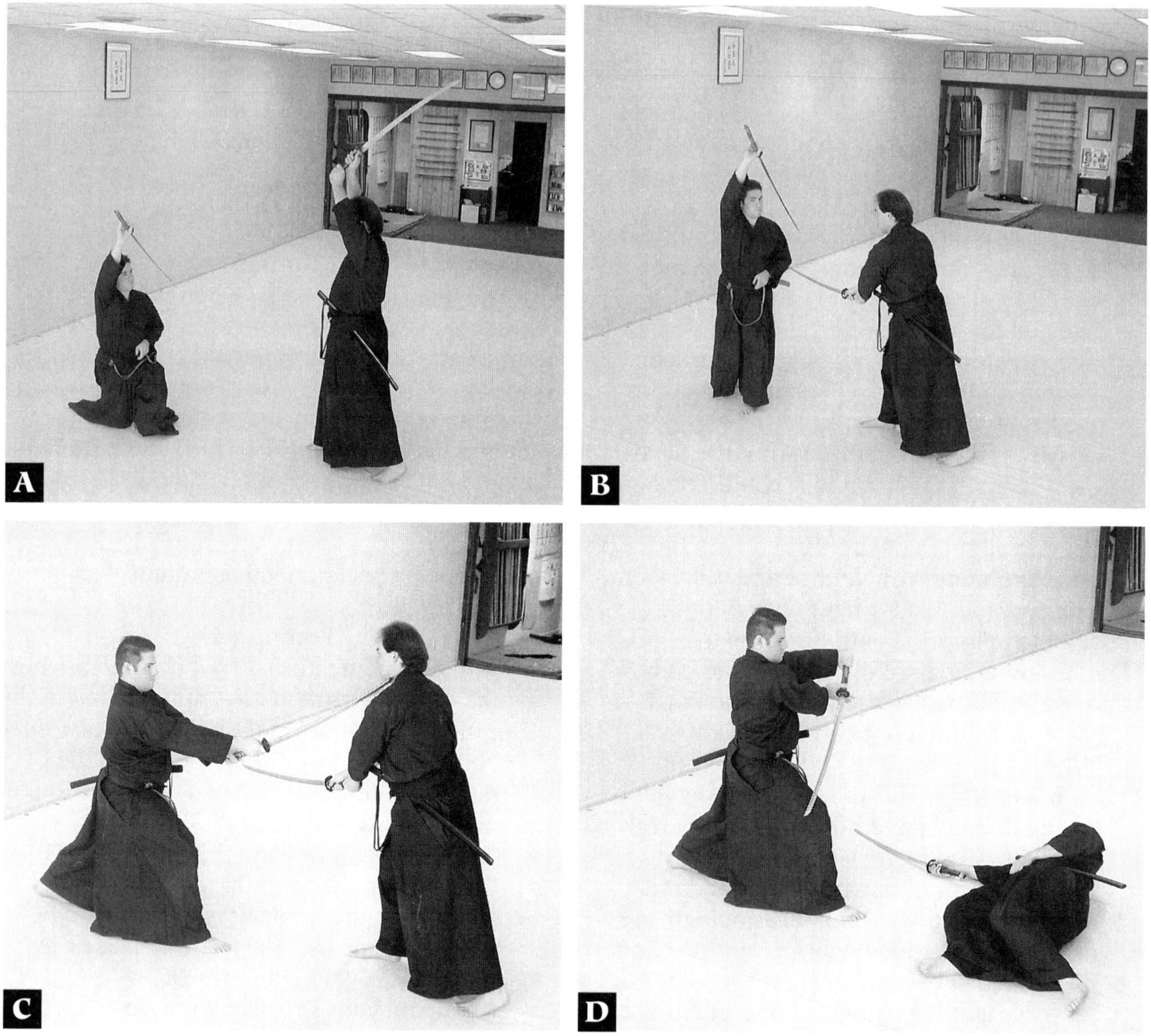

Figures 71A – E: Some of the steps in the kata ukenagashi.

your left foot. This step should be completed as the block reaches its highest point. Your right arm should not be completely extended, but at a slight angle. Immediately flip the tip of the sword upward with wrist action without otherwise moving your right hand.

- As soon as the sword is vertical, step to the rear by sliding your left foot back parallel to your right, keeping the toes of both feet on the floor and your left leg parallel to your right foot. At the same time as your left hand grips the tsuka begin your cut, moving the tip first with power from your left wrist without dipping the kissaki backward. The step and the cut end at the same time. The cut follows a diagonal from your right to left at about 15 degrees from vertical. The end position of the sword is off of straight ahead to the left by 10 degrees. Your hands should end up at mid-abdomen with the kissaki slightly lower. Pause.
- The grip of both hands is loosened and the kissaki is brought to the right of your right leg with the blade resting flat against your middle thigh. Your left hand, holding the tsuka is extended so that it is on a straight line with your shoulders to the left. This will draw the blade across the hakama, wiping it, and will bring your right arm across your chest. If you were to continue to hold the tsuka in the same right grip, your right wrist would be twisted in sharp extension. Therefore the wrist is kept straight and the tsuka held between the thumb and base of index finger with the right palm upward.
- You release your right hand, turning it over, and regrip the tsuka with your fingertips, palm down, index finger toward the kashira.
- Your right wrist is then extended and twisted clockwise, throwing the blade to the left of the body as your left hand releases the tsuka, grasps the koiguchi, and rotates it into horizontal.
- The koiguchi and mune just below the habaki are brought together in the midline with the mune on the web between your left thumb and index finger, supported by that finger extending past the koiguchi.
- Your hold the tsuka loosely in the fingers of the right hand and shoot it out to the front right at an angle of 45 degrees, keeping the blade horizontal. Simultaneously, your left hand rotates the koiguchi into sayabiki allowing the kissaki to fall into it. The saya then slides back onto the blade and you complete the noto by bringing your right hand in toward the saya, keeping the sword and saya horizontal.
- You slowly assume a kneeling position with your right knee forward and at 90 degrees, rotating the blade to vertical with the saya under the control of your left hand. Your blade hits home as your left knee hits the ground. Pause.
- Your right hand should hold the tsuka with the index finger parallel to it along its ura. Your thumb sits loosely over the top with the remaining fingers curled under it. Your wrist will be extended perhaps an inch from the tsuba.
- You stand, left thumb on the tsuba, and bring your left foot even with your right one. Drop your right hand to your side and step back with your left foot, preparing for the next activity.

Technical Notes

- Proper metsuke demands that you keep your eyes on the opponent's sword, not his body, as you block. So look up as you begin the block, and, as you stand, adjust your eyes for your increasing height.
- The draw is started, and your left foot simultaneously begins to move up to meet your right knee.
- When your left foot meets your right knee you start to stand, then you finish your draw and set the block as you are rising.
- The proper position for the blade during the block is with the right hand above your head, a little to the right and in front of it. Your right arm remains slightly bent with the wrist cocked to the left. The blade is at a 45-degree angle to the floor, kissaki above and forward of your left shoulder. The blade must be held sufficiently in front of you as well as above, so that the force of the

opponent's blade will not move it behind you, which would result in your being cut.

- Avoid pushing the blade up too high during the block and extending your arm. This gives an exaggerated appearance to the motion and delays the downward cut.
- You block with the side of the blade upright to receive the attacking blade on the shinoji. This minimizes damage to your blade and maximizes the chances of the opponent damaging his.
- Weight is shifted to your left foot and you finish standing, pushing up the block as you do so.
- The opponent's blade hits and slips off your block as you reach your full height. It will impart a "bounce" to your blade. You use this energy captured from your opponent to immediately flip your blade to the vertical and step around with your right foot. Keep your knees bent while you do this so that your head stays at the same level from the swords' contact to the end of the kirioroshi.
- After the block your metsuke should shift to the body of your opponent.
- There should be no delay between assuming the vertical sword position and the kirioroshi. It is this timing that befuddles your opponent, allowing you to prevail.
- The kirioroshi is to the left of your midline because that is where your opponent's body was pitched when he slipped off your block. So be sure the blade is pointed that way.
- In an attempt to rush the vertical cut several mistakes can be made. There may be a pause while you regain your strength, or worse, while you dip your blade backward in a misguided attempt at power. You have lost your advantage. The other common error is to start the cut with power from the right arm. This will be weak. Finally, it is very easy to misgrasp the tsuka with the left hand, not getting the thumb and index finger completely around it. This will cause your blade to travel at a different angle than the cut, making it ineffective.
- Use you body weight that is shifted downward by the rearward step to add strength to your kirioroshi.
- Be sure to draw the tsuka in toward your body at the end of your kirioroshi for a slicing action.
- When moving from the kirioroshi to the chiburi, keep the kissaki between you and your enemy. Exercise lots of zanshin. You are using this particular chiburi because it offers good defense from an enemy close to you on the ground. Any flamboyant movement going into the chiburi opens you up to potential attack.
- The noto of this kata will tell you a lot about the size of your sword. If you cannot put the kissaki on your mid-thigh and keep your left arm horizontal, your sword is too short for you.
- As you finish your noto you must turn your sword to the vertical using your left hand via the saya. If you try to do it directly with your right hand, your final right hand position will be way off.
- At the end of the noto, your right index finger should be parallel to and against the tsuka and the other fingers coiled loosely underneath it.

YONHON ME – TSUKA ATE (HILT STRIKE)

柄当

Bunkai

You are sitting in tatehiza when you are threatened by two opponents, one sitting facing you in front and one behind you. You kneel and strike the one in front with the kashira, draw the saya off the blade and thrust into the one behind you. You then turn and finish the one in front with a sho-men strike, throw off the blood, and sheathe the blade using Eishin ryu-like techniques for the chiburi and noto.

Technique

- From a standing position you do *hakamabiki* while dropping to your left knee. While moving to sit on the inner

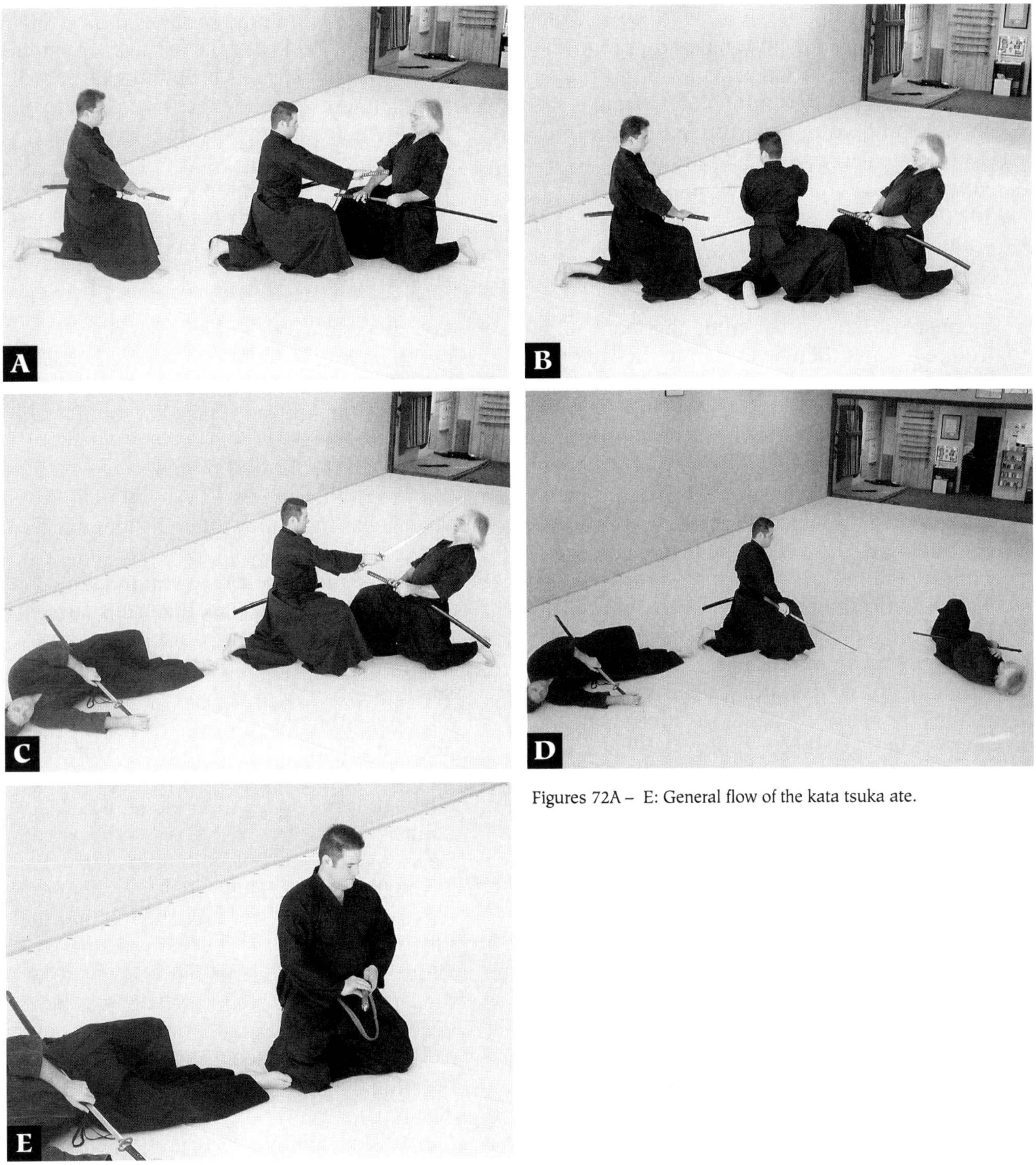

Figures 72A – E: General flow of the kata tsuka ate.

side of your left foot, bring your right foot straight to the right side of your left knee. Your right knee is up with your lower leg at a 45-degree angle from the floor. Your hands are closed into loose fists, palms down on the top of each thigh drawn loosely to your abdomen.

- Move your eyes to the front opponent; raise your right hand to the tsuka and your left to the koiguchi while squeezing your knees toward each other, which facilitates raising your body upward. You strike the opponent's solar plexus with your kashira at locked arm's length by moving both sword and saya through your obi. At the same time your right foot slides straight forward and you pivot your left leg around your left knee, bringing it parallel with your right leg. All movements stop with the strike.

- Immediately start drawing the saya down off the blade toward the obi while holding the sword motionless as if pushing it against your just-struck front opponent. Your eyes and then head turn to the left as the saya begins to move to the rear.
- When the kissaki comes free of the koiguchi, elevate the sword to a horizontal position with the mune on your chest. Simultaneously pivot your left foot 90 degrees behind you while rotating your hips and saya toward the left, thereby clearing a path for the kissaki.
- The thrust is made along the line of the chest, and, as the right hand goes backward with the tsuka, the left hand holding the koiguchi comes forward under it. This rotates the distal tip of the saya into the opponent just stabbed. It also stabilizes the thrust blade, keeping its path directly toward your left instead of curving too far behind you. Pause.
- Your head, shoulders, and waist rotate to the front, and the left foot and lower leg rotate around the left knee to bring the entire body into a forward alignment. This rotation is used to pull the blade out of the opponent behind and get it over the head.
- The front opponent is finished with a sho-men kirioroshi that ends up below the right knee with the kissaki only 6 inches from the floor. Pause.
- A yoko chiburi is performed low, again with the sword ending up well below the right knee and the left hand on the saya with fingers together and the thumb at right angles to them along the top of the saya. Pause.
- Noto is performed just as in the first two kata, but while you are kneeling. As the blade is slowly thrust into the saya, your right knee is extended outward as you sit on your left heel with the left foot up on its toes. Your right foot is brought adjacent to your left foot as you sit backward, and your body remains facing forward. The right hand remains on the tsuka.
- Following the noto slide your right foot forward so that your right leg forms a 90-degree angle at the knee and your left foot, still up on its toes, is rotated directly backward.
- You then stand, weight on your right foot, and pull your left foot up even with it. Then raise your gaze, drop your right hand subtly to your side, and step back left foot first.

Technical Notes

- Start to rise for the first strike by pulling your knees together, which lifts your body out of tatehiza.
- The strike must not cause you to lean forward. Keep your back and arms straight.
- As your saya slides off your blade, your head turns to the left and then back at the same rate.
- Do not let the blade move away from your chest at any time before the backward thrust. The thrust should extend past your elbow, but not so far that you lean or lose control.
- Be sure you keep your shoulders relaxed during the thrust. This keeps your center of gravity low and better prepares you for the following action.
- When the kissaki clears the koiguchi and the left leg swings back at 90 degrees before the thrust, a conscious effort must be made to keep the right knee forward rather than flopping over to the left. This is not just aesthetics, because if you lean your knee to the left, the enemy on the ground can push it over causing you to lose your rooting. This can't happen if the knee is upright.
- Be sure that the sword starts forward before the left biceps muscle moves forward. Many iaidoka have gotten at least one hole in their left sleeve by mistiming this step.
- At the completion of the thrust, the tsuka should be tightly tucked against and

beneath your right forearm and against your chest.

- There is a tendency to cut over the shoulder rather than over the head during this kirioroshi. Do not do this.
- If you don't relax while making this kirioroshi, the sword will hit the floor for sure.
- The chiburi is not horizontal, but more horizontal than most chiburi in these kata. After the kirioroshi there is a short period of zanshin, during which you elevate your blade preparing it for the chiburi.
- At the completion of the chiburi the kissaki is below the knees, with the tip below the obi and within the shoulder line, pointing at the forward enemy.
- The act of sliding your right foot and knee backward during noto accomplishes two things: it moves you back from the enemy to your front and, by rotating the saya, keeps the two enemies from grabbing either your kojiri or kashira.

GOHON ME – KASAGIRI (DIAGONAL CUT)

袈裟切

Bunkai

As you are walking forward you are threatened by a standing opponent drawing for a head-cut as he approaches you. You flip your saya upside down and draw vertically from below, striking upward while walking in order to either cut his hands or force him backward. You immediately reverse the direction of the blade and cut back down again before he has a

Figures 73A – D: Kasagiri. The up and down vertical cuts should be parallel, and there should be no pause between them. The hasso no kamae is an expression of zanshin.

chance to recover (*kirigaeshi*). You step backward with your right foot and assume hasso no kamae to exercise zanshin and evaluate the slain enemy. You then throw the blood off your blade and sheathe it. This kata is named for the kesa, or robe, worn over the left shoulder of certain monks.

Technique

- From the standing position step out with your right foot.
- Step again with your left foot as you grasp your saya with your left hand and touch the tsuka with your right hand and start to push out the blade. Get it about halfway out without bending your body forward.
- Take your third step with your right foot, flip the saya over with your left hand, and draw and cut outward (very important) and then upward, putting a little hip rotation to the right during the upward sweep.
- As the sword goes up, your left hand rotates the saya back to the starting position. Do this before the sword has reached its apogee. Start your left hand up after the tsuka.
- As the blade attains a vertical position, immediately grasp the tsuka with your left hand and cut down in kirioroshi without "cocking" the blade first. Rotate your hips back to the left during the cut. The end position of the blade is with the tip slightly below that of your hands. Pause.
- Step backward by sliding your right foot to the rear keeping your toes on the ground. Do not move the sword until you are ready to shift half your weight to the back foot.
- At this point bring your sword back to hasso no kamae while demonstrating zanshin. Pause.
- Chiburi from hasso no kamae is done with your right hand only. Start to step backward with your left foot while maintaining zanshin. Don't move your right hand (with the sword) but allow your head and body to be drawn away from it. First rotate your hand in front of you slightly by squaring up your shoulders and hips. This will rotate the ha from straight at your enemy, to slightly to your left of him. Then perform a yoko chiburi by cutting out to your left with your right wrist first followed by the arm, which brings the blade to the usual chiburi position. Do not raise your right elbow. Perform sayabiki simultaneously with your left hand. Pause.
- Perform a level, thoughtful noto, keeping your metsuke on your enemy until completed.
- Then look level, drop your right hand, and step backward with your left foot to prepare for the next activity.

Technical Notes

- Be sure to walk in a level, relaxed fashion.
- Don't bend over during the draw; draw outward first, then upward.
- As the blade goes up, the left hand turns the saya to the usual position.
- There should be no gap between the up and down cuts. This will occur if too much time is taken reversing the saya, or if that action is started late.
- Don't "cock" the blade prior to the down cut.
- While cutting down, don't twist the hips so much that it lifts your left heel further off the floor.
- The angles of the up and down stroke are the same.
- While moving into hasso no kamae, remember that you are wearing a kabuto, a large helmet with flaring neck and shoulder guards like wings. You will have to move the sword in above these wings and then lower it into hasso. This action should not be exaggerated.
- In hasso no kamae the left hand is in the midline and the right hand is a fist's width away from the right cheek. The edge of the blade is pointed directly at your enemy.
- Yoko chiburi from hasso no kamae is performed much like that from jodan no kamae. First, the ha of the blade must be rotated toward your left to put it into the plane of the chiburi. Then, as the head and body move backward, the kissaki moves out to the left first by wrist movement, and then is followed by extension of the arm in the same direction. At the point that the

Figure 74: The length and direction of the up and down parallel cuts used in the kata Kasagiri.

arm is fully extended, it is lowered into the right-side sword position with a slight slicing motion.

ROPPON ME – MOROTEZUKI (TWO-HANDED THRUST)

諸手突

Bunkai

While you are walking forward you are threatened not only by an opponent directly in front of you, but also by someone to your rear. You draw, forcing the enemy in front backward, and thrust toward him, pushing him back farther. You turn and cut the enemy behind, and then turn and cut the one in front. You shake the blood off your blade and sheathe it.

Technique

- Begin walking forward with your right foot, keeping your toes on the ground.
- During the second (left-foot) step, grasp the tsuka with your right hand and draw the blade high and to your left so that you can see your opponent between the blade and your right arm. The sword should be positioned so that the cutting edge is rotated toward your left about 30 degrees from vertical.
- After your right foot has made the third step, cut up and out at a 30-degree angle as your back (left) foot comes forward. The cut goes from the opponent's right forehead to left axilla. Perform a sayabiki with the cut. Pause.
- As your left foot comes up even with your right foot, your left hand brings the saya forward, and then continues on to grasp the tsuka, which has been brought to the midline by the right hand. At this point the kissaki should be pointed at the enemy's chest.
- Step out with your right foot and on the back (left) foot's motion forward thrust the tip of the blade into the opponent's solar plexus. It should be driven by the hips and a slight downward action of the tip.
- Without moving the sword at first, step with the left foot around and out in back of you

Figures 75A – E: Representative steps in the kata morotezuki.

180 degrees. As you turn your body use the rotation to withdraw the sword straight out of the first enemy.

- Step through with your right foot and cut on the left foot motion to a high sho-men position.
- Step around as before and cut on the back foot to the front in a low sho-men position. Pause.
- Perform yoko chiburi. Pause
- Do a nice, thoughtful noto, keeping metsuke on the enemy on the ground.
- Bring your left foot up to right and raise your eyes to the forward position. Drop your right hand to your side.
- Step back with your left foot for your next motion.

Technical Notes

- Slide your feet forward—no duck feet.
- Make your first cut high and up, then down. It should fit between lines forward from each shoulder. The body should be turned slightly to the left, right shoulder downward.
- Releasing the sayabiki and grasping the tsuka with the left hand should all be one smooth, continuous motion.
- If you bend at the waist slightly during the thrust, as originally done in our ryu-ha, do not lift up your left heel.
- When you step to the rear each time you should slide your foot out as far as you can while maintaining stability to get as much motion away toward the rearward opponent as possible.
- You should be careful not to bounce your head and/or body as you make these movements. Use your bent knees, particularly the lead knee, to keep your head and shoulders on a flat plane.
- When turning and moving to the rear do not allow the sword to be pulled off midline. The blade is supposedly stuck in your enemy, so the kissaki cannot drift sideways by the rotation. It is extracted straight from the body by your forward motion only as you start your furikaburi.
- Both kirioroshi are complete, stopping at the belt level.
- You must remember to step out far enough with your right foot so that when you stop and make your second kirioroshi on the back (left) foot motion, you are still in a deep stance.
- The original way of doing the thrust in our ryu-ha consisted of rotating the sword 30 degrees counterclockwise and bending slightly. This served the dual purpose of allowing the sword to snake over any attempted block, and to break the vacuum holding the blade in the enemy.

NANAHON ME – SANPOGIRI (THREE-WAY CUT)

三方切

Bunkai

You are walking forward and three enemies close in on you from the front and both sides. You start to draw toward the one in front while continuing to walk, keeping him occupied with your slow draw. You are monitoring the other two with your peripheral vision. At the last minute, without warning you step out to your right cutting that opponent with a left yoko-men cut. You then immediately spin around and cut the opponent to your left without stepping. You then step and cut to your right 90 degrees, finishing the enemy originally to the front. You step back with your sword in jodan no kamae, assessing the situation, and finally toss off the blood on your blade and sheathe it.

Technique

- Take four steps forward starting with your right foot. By the fourth step (left) you should be aware of the enemy on your right but still be applying semé to the one in front. Begin to draw your sword as you step with your right foot angled toward the right and a little in front of your left one. At this point you turn your body to the right and draw.
- The draw is made high enough to see the enemy under it, and proceeds at an angle about 15 degrees off vertical, left to right, and stops at the shoulder level, continuing to cover your front.

Figures 76A – E: Diagram of the steps and cuts of sanpogiri.

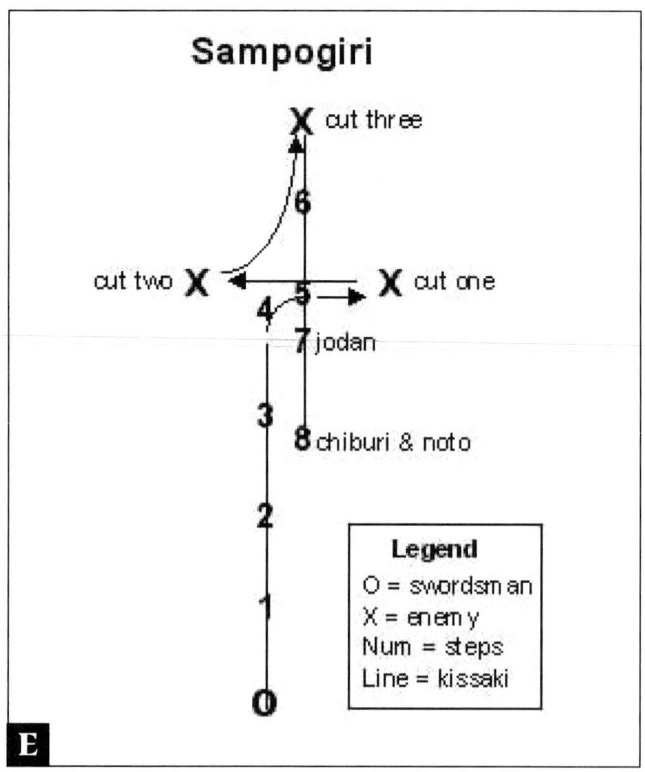

- Do a sayabiki during the cut. Pause.
- Look forward to your left.
- Immediately turn your body 180 degrees to the left by rotating your right foot around on its heel while returning the saya to the front.
- Following the turn do a full sho-men cut (without stepping). Pause.
- Turn 90 degrees to your right (original front) while positioning the sword over your head. Step out with your right foot and perform a low sho-men cut on the back foot motion. Pause.
- Maintain zanshin. Step back into jodan no kamae deeply with your right foot. Do not raise the sword into position until you are nearly reweighted in order to guard against unforeseen action by the opponent. Pause.
- Perform chiburi from jodan no kamae. Move the kissaki first in a plane off to your left, follow it with your arm, and then sweep the arm down to complete the chiburi while settling into a deep, long stable stance. Pause.
- Do a standard noto.
- Bring your left foot up to right, drop your right hand to your side and look forward.
- Step backward starting with your left foot to position yourself for the next move.

Technical Notes

- Forward steps should be natural and relaxed, keeping the ball and toes of your feet on the ground.
- Keep from bobbing your head by moving with your knees bent and your pelvis tucked under your body.
- Begin nukitsuke as if you are going to cut the enemy in front with a horizontal move, but position your feet to make the sudden direction change toward the right.
- Be sure to tilt the saya during the draw to put it into the plane of the cut that is about 15 degrees off of vertical.
- Perform sayabiki during the right-handed cut.
- Set up your second cut by pivoting your body 180 degrees. The first move is to look to the front with your head and eyes without moving anything else.
- The pivoting occurs by rotating the right foot along with saya and then the rest of the body. The feet do not step, just pivot.
- The timing is such that the left and right cuts are made explosively with little time between them. The third cut is set up a little more formally.
- You should assume jodan no kamae near the end of the step rearward to exhibit zanshin. Keep the kissaki at neck level until the last minute.
- Because chiburi from jodan no kamae is started with both hands, you can use your left hand to augment the kissaki movement by pushing on the tsuka during the start of its rotation before lowering that hand to the saya.
- You must delay the start of the chiburi until the left-foot step rearward is nearly completed, allowing the body and the sword to stop at the same time.
- Moving your left foot outward as well as rearward will help you keep your balance and keep your feet parallel as well.
- The original way of doing the first two cuts in our ryu-ha consisted of more of a follow-through of the first cut, and a partial shuffle-step with the left foot prior to the second cut.

HACHIHON ME – GANMEN ATE (FACIAL STRIKE)

顔面当

Bunkai

While you are walking forward enemies from both front and back threaten you. You strike the face of the opponent in front with the kashira by sliding the saya forward through your obi. You then spin around 180 degrees while unsheathing the blade and step out and thrust into the rearward enemy's solar plexus. You turn around again and finish the first enemy with a sho-men cut, shake the blood off the blade, and sheathe it.

Technique

- Begin to walk forward starting with your

Figures 77A – E: Steps in the kata ganmen ate.

right foot. On the beginning of the third step place your right fingers on top of the tsuka at 45 degrees to the forward direction.

- As the rear (left) foot moves forward at the end of the third step, the saya and sword are pulled part out of the obi briskly at an angle to strike your forward enemy's eyes.
- Hold the sword immobile and sweep the saya off the blade with your left hand. As the saya moves rearward, so do your eyes and head.
- As the kissaki comes out of the koiguchi, your left foot steps around and out at 180 degrees from forward.
- The blade is twisted 90 degrees counterclockwise during the above movement to place it horizontal. The

kissaki stays right in front of the koiguchi during the first part of the rearward step.

- Tuck the tsuka firmly against your obi with the mune toward you and place your thumb on top of the habaki with its tip against the tsuba.
- As soon as your body and the blade are squared up in the new direction, without pause step out with your right foot.
- On rear-foot action, with your body neither twisted nor bent, the kissaki is held directly in front of your body and thrust (tilted slightly upward) into the solar plexus of the enemy. Sayabiki is performed at the same time. Pause.
- Turn 180 degrees by first rotating your right foot around on its heel with your body and head following and bringing the saya back to the forward position.
- Step out with your left foot, pulling the sword out of the rearward enemy and over your head without waving the blade side to side.
- On the rear-foot movement perform a sho-men kirioroshi. Pause.
- Perform a yoko chiburi. Pause.
- Bring the left foot forward, raise your eyes, and drop your right hand to the side of your right thigh.

Technical Notes

- Each step may be made a little more quickly leading up to the strike (crescendo).
- Hand position on the strike is very important. The fingers are on the top of the tsuka, straight with your fingers at 45 degrees to the tsuka, not grasping. This increases the forward distance the sword can go, faking out your opponent who thinks he is not in your personal space. This drives him backward.
- Your head and saya should move fluidly together to the rear, with no movement of the blade until it is completely unsheathed. The tsuka keeps pressure against the first enemy's face during the first part of the turn around while the saya is being withdrawn.
- As your body turns around following the step with your left foot to the rear, the blade must be kept right alongside your body. Pinching the kissaki between your left thumb and index finger while still holding the koiguchi facilitates this.
- At the end of the rotation the tsuka is pulled right against your obi with the blade horizontal and mune toward you. Do not pause.
- The thrust is accomplished with your body untwisted and square to the rear. The kissaki is moved to directly in front of your midline as you thrust. There is no twisting of the blade. Originally in our ryu-ha, the tsuka was moved to the midline, allowing the entire body to power the thrust.
- Rotating the body, pulling the saya forward out of sayabiki, and pulling the blade straight out of the body all occur together.
- The rear step should accomplish some forward movement, during which the sword blade must not waver but go straight over the head. Do not make a distinct pull on the blade as if to disengage it from the enemy.
- Make all the body motions with the knees slightly bent to keep the head on an even plane during the kata.

KYUHON ME – SOETEZUKI (REINFORCED THRUST)

添手突

Bunkai

You are walking forward when an opponent threatens you to your left. You turn, draw, and strike diagonally, forcing the enemy backward. You then pull both your right foot and sword backward drawing your enemy toward you. You suddenly and strongly thrust your blade into his abdomen while supporting the mune with your left thumb. You tilt and withdraw the blade, enlarging the wound and allowing the body to slide off the end, toss blood off the blade, and sheathe it.

Technique

- Start walking with your right foot first.
- Your right hand comes up to the tsuka as your left foot makes the second step.

Figures 78A – E: Soetezuki. Notice how the first cut pushes the enemy back, then the sword moving to the rear sucks him into range for the supported thrust.

- As you twist your body to the left and bring your right foot up to your left one, pointing just off to your left of the enemy the sword is drawn from the saya high enough for you to be able to see the enemy under it and your arm. At the same time twist the saya so that it is angled to allow a high diagonal cut (yoko-men).
- Simultaneously step back away from the enemy with your left foot and strike the enemy with the diagonal cut to the right side of his head, ending with the blade nearly horizontal. Pause.
- Pull your right foot back not quite to your left and twist your toes so that they point to your right at about 30 degrees. At the same

time put the tsuka back against your right side past your obi. As you do this, place your left hand on top of the mune halfway between the kissaki and the tsuba, keeping the sword parallel to the floor.

- Step out with your left foot parallel to the right foot, pointed off to the right of the enemy. On a back-foot forward motion thrust the sword into the enemy, keeping the sword parallel to the ground and the tsuka stabilized with your right forearm and bolstered by your left hand. There should be a small downward vector to this tsuki to do greater damage. Pause.
- Without moving your left hand, lift and extend your right hand so that the blade slides under your left thumb until your right hand is at shoulder level and at a 45-degree angle to your forward plane. Pause.
- Holding the sword motionless, slide your left hand softly to the koiguchi, remain in zanshin for a moment, and then step your left foot back into a deep stance and perform a yoko chiburi.
- Perform a noto while still watching your enemy. When completed, bring the left foot up level to the right one.
- Immediately step back and twist the left foot toward the original forward direction while dropping your right hand to your thigh. Follow it with the right foot so that you are standing with feet together pointed in the original direction and ready to step off to the next movement.

Technical Notes

- The head and eyes should engage the enemy just before making the second (left) step.
- Bringing the right foot up and drawing the sword should occur smoothly together. The kashira can be thought of as striking the enemy's face during the turning draw.
- Step into a deep stable stance with the left foot and make the cut with a lot of wrist action down through the opposite side of the opponent's body to hip level.
- At this point, both feet should be parallel, pointed toward the enemy on your left.

Figure 79: The angle and length of the nukitsuke used in seitei kata six, seven, and nine.

- Pulling back your sword and right foot together is a feint to draw the enemy into attacking you.
- The sword should be held parallel to the floor with the tsuka extended behind the back just prior to the thrust.
- When you step forward with your left foot and thrust, both feet have shifted and now are parallel and pointing toward the enemy on your right.
- The thrust is primarily forward with a good advance of your feet, but there is also a downward component, not of the tip alone, but of the entire blade, which is kept parallel to the ground during this entire maneuver.

- The supporting left hand is kept flat on top of the mune, but in a real strike the body sliding up the blade would bend the fingers down. The back of the hand and knuckles would then be used to push the body off the end of the downward sloping blade.
- As the right hand and arm are elevated toward the right the left hand does not move. The rightward motion not only changes the angle of the blade, but slides it over your left thumb. This motion cuts the initial stab wound into an elongated "J" shape. The left hand is in such a position that the enemy lying on the ground cannot see into the koiguchi.
- When stepping back to chiburi, be very careful to slide the feet, keeping the knees bent and the back straight and not allowing the head to bob.
- The first movement of chiburi is to cover the koiguchi with your left hand. Thus it is still protected visually. Then demonstrate zanshin by pausing to look at your opponent's body without moving the sword. Then do your chiburi, zanshin again, and the noto.

JIPPON ME – SHIHOGIRI (FOUR-WAY CUT)

四方切

Bunkai

You are walking forward and notice the threats from four enemies converging on you, each from a different direction. You strike the hand of the one diagonally to your right as he starts to draw, then turn and thrust into the one behind you. You turn back to finish the original opponent with a sho-men strike, turn 90 degrees to the right, and hit the head of a third opponent. You then turn 180 degrees, hiding your blade in waki no kamae, step forward and finish the last enemy with a sudden sho-men strike. You raise your sword into jodan no kamae, appraising the situation, and then throw the blood off your blade and sheathe it.

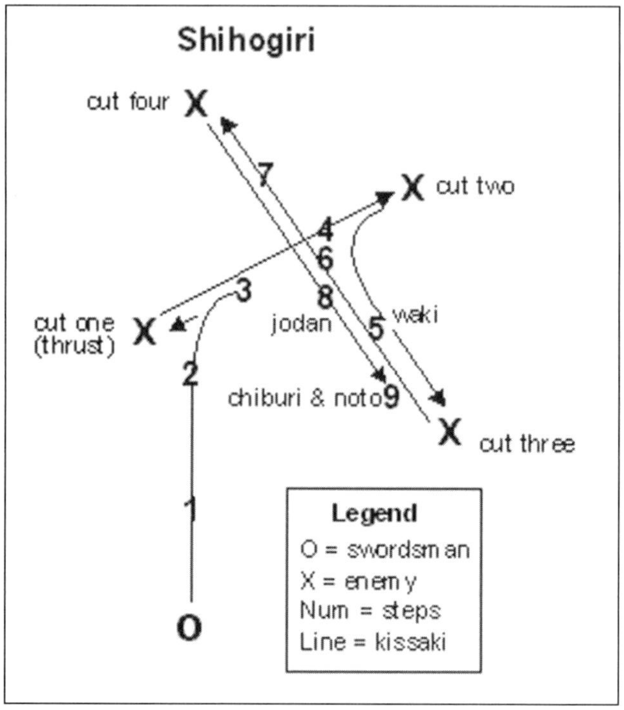

Figure 80: Diagram of steps and cuts of shihogiri.

Technique

- You step out with your right foot, left thumb on the tsuba, take a second step with your left foot and turn your eyes, head, and then body toward the enemy at 45 degrees to your right.
- You stamp down with your right foot toward this enemy and at the same time turn your tsuba counterclockwise 90 degrees and slam it down on his wrist, thus blocking his attempt to draw.
- Begin to draw the blade out by pushing the struck enemy away with the kashira. At the same time, pull the saya back off the blade, keeping the latter in close to your body. Turn both feet 90 degrees to your left, right heel slightly off the floor with weight equally distributed on both feet.
- Bring the mune of the blade up to your chest so that it is horizontal to the ground.
- Step sideways with your left foot and thrust the blade along your chest into the second enemy as the right foot slides to the left to "catch up."
- As you thrust with your right hand, you

Figures 81A – C: Some steps in the sequence of shihogiri.

bring the koiguchi forward to your hara, rotating your left shoulder and biceps in toward your chest. The thrust stops after the tsuba passes your left biceps.

- Turn both your feet back 90 degrees to your right and step through with your left foot. On the motion of your back-foot cut down the original enemy with a sho-men cut.
- Turn 90 degrees to your right and step out with your right foot. On the back foot motion, cut down the third enemy with a sho-men strike. Pause.
- Rotate your body as you step out behind with your left foot 180 degrees to your last cut. As your hips come around, your right hand comes to your waist palm up, the back of the hand against your hip, fingers loose and holding the sword with fingertips in waki no kamae.
- Step through with your right foot, keeping the sword straight behind you, and on the back-foot motion quickly bring the sword over your head and cut the last enemy with a sho-men cut. Pause.
- Step back with your right foot and bring the sword to jodan no kamae. Pause.
- Step back with your left foot into a wide deep stance, with your back straight and eyes toward the last enemy. Then perform yoko chiburi. Pause.
- Do thoughtful noto, bring up your left foot and drop your hand to your side.

Technical Notes

- When exercising the first strike, the opponent's hand is hit with the side of the tsuka. Your right fingers should be straight, together, and at 45 degrees on top of the tsuka for maximum distance. The force is directed forward and down the foot stamp timed to add to the force. It ends with the sword close to horizontal.
- As you turn your body to your rear, you push the first opponent away with the kashira as part of your draw.
- You control the sword by keeping it in close to the body. You then raise the mune to the nipple line, keeping it horizontal as you do a sayabiki and thrust out your chest a little.
- Originally, our dojo stopped the thrust when the tsuba struck the left biceps muscle. More recently we have been extending the thrust farther out. When doing this technique it is very important to tuck the tsuka tightly into the right wrist and forearm for stability.
- In turning around, you start with your right foot flat and your left heel up off the

ground. You turn on the balls of both feet and end with the left foot flat and the right heel off the ground. Your feet should be parallel both before and after stepping for the thrust.

- When you step to thrust your feet move sideways. Do not lean your body into the thrust. Keep your feet planted in what is called a horse stance (*ma bu*) in the Chinese arts.
- The kashira of the tsuka is kept tucked into your right wrist as you make the thrust. This also stabilizes the blade, maintaining the proper direction and preventing wobbling.
- Moving both arms together when doing the thrust and sayabiki serves these purposes: the blade is stabilized by the left upper arm keeping it from curving behind you, the joint actions mutually balance the body (reducing overthrust), and the sayabiki pushes the enemy into the path of the thrust.
- As in all direction changes, the head precedes the hips, shoulders, and sword in the next three direction changes and cuts.
- Following the cut to the third opponent the sword is held in waki no kamae. In this position the enemy cannot see it, therefore he cannot tell if you intend to strike vertically or horizontally, or even how long your sword is. This is why you wait to the last minute to strike him from this position.
- Be sure to get the sword over your head before you cut.
- When going into jodan, keep the kissaki in your opponent's face for as long as possible to discourage him from moving in (semé).
- Jodan no kamae is a guarded position poised to either cut or quit depending on what you see. Maintain strong zanshin.
- When performing the chiburi from jodan no kamae, your left hand should push against the tsuka toward your right forearm, thus increasing the snap to the initial movement of the blade forward and to your left. It then should slide along your chest to the top of the saya, not hop to it. Upon reaching the saya it should push the koiguchi down, thus keeping the saya parallel to the ground.

JUIPPON ME – SOUGIRI (ENTIRE CUT)

総切

Bunkai

You are walking forward and you are threatened by an opponent at your immediate front. You draw with an overhead block, allowing his cut to pass in front of you, and immediately convert your block to a right yoko-men strike. You strike again, progressively lower, left and right, make a sweeping cut across his hara, and finish him with a sho-men strike. You toss the blood off your blade and replace it in the saya. An alternative interpretation considers multiple attackers.

Technique

- Step off with your right foot, both your hands at your sides.
- As you make the second step (left foot) bring your left hand to the mouth of the saya and your right to the tsuka, placing your fingers on top, not around it.
- As you step again with your right foot, push the tsuka forward, unsheathing the blade.
- Raise the sword into a block as in ukenagashi and, at the same time, bring your right foot back almost but not quite even with your left.
- The minute your left hand reaches the tsuka, step forward again with your right foot and cut while on your back foot to the left side of the opponent's head, stopping at the level of the jaw.
- Raise the blade over your head and shuffle again with your right foot and cut while on your back foot to the opponent's right shoulder, stopping at the solar plexus (suigetsu).
- Raise the blade yet again as you step again with your right foot and cut while on the back foot to the opponent's left trunk, stopping with the sword horizontal at his hara.
- Withdraw the sword over your head and step out again with your right foot as you

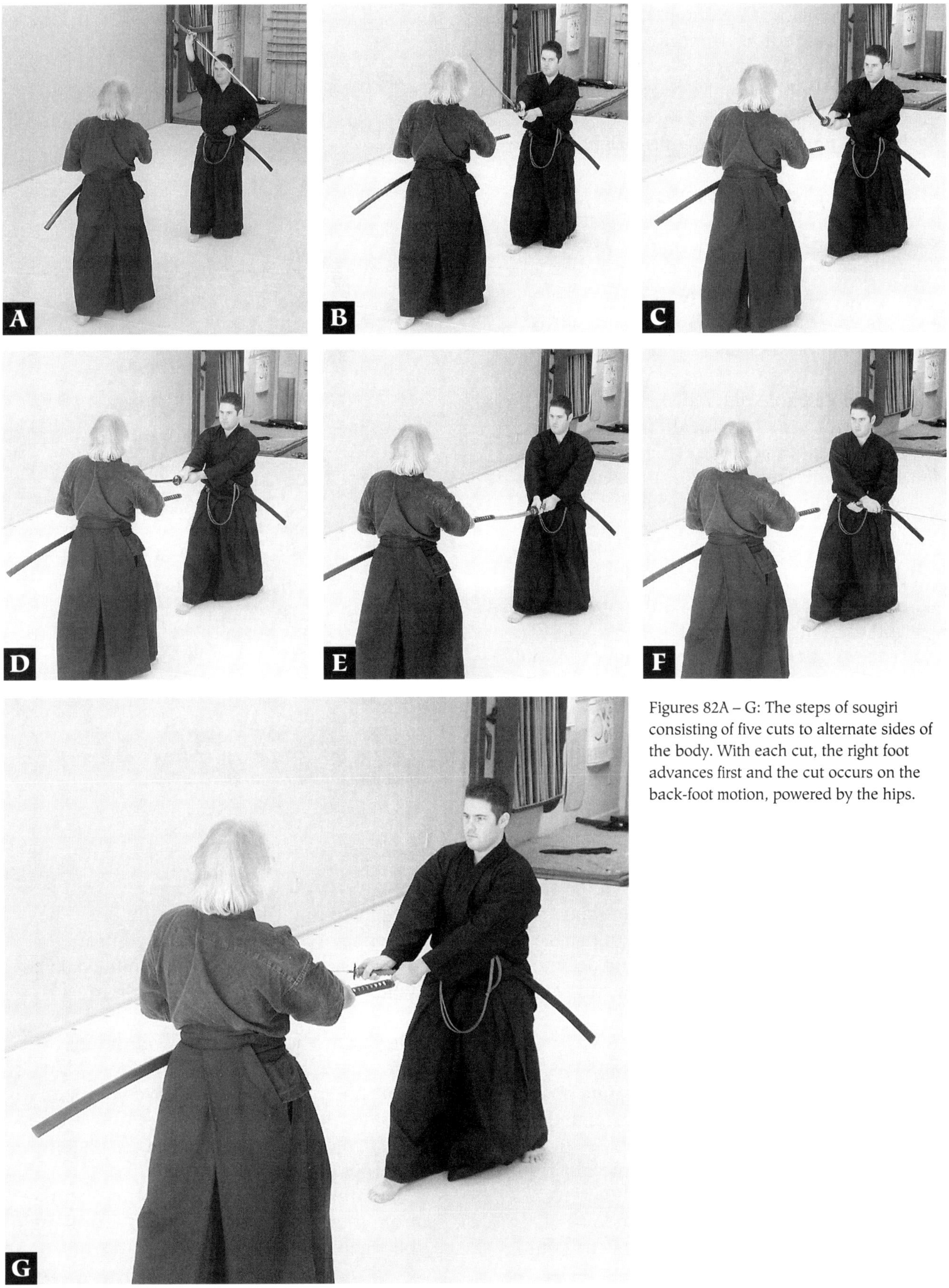

Figures 82A – G: The steps of sougiri consisting of five cuts to alternate sides of the body. With each cut, the right foot advances first and the cut occurs on the back-foot motion, powered by the hips.

bring the sword down to just above your left hip and cut horizontally across the opponent's abdomen.

- Without stopping, raise the sword over your head and finish the enemy with a sho-men kirioroshi as you make a final right-footed step.
- Perform yoko chiburi and noto as usual.
- Bring your left foot up to your right, drop your right hand to your side and step back.

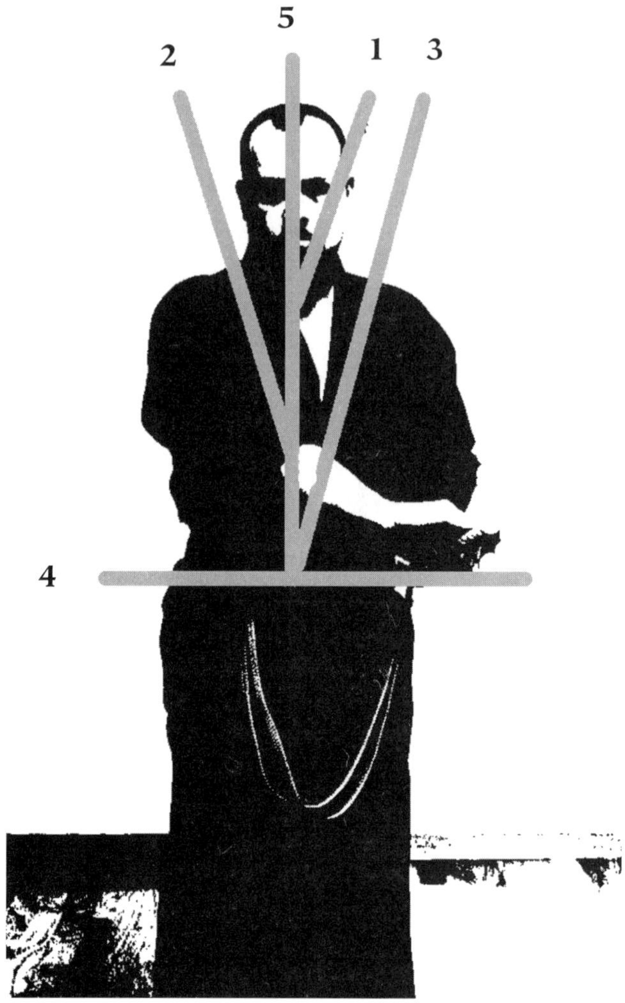

Figure 83: The sequence, angle, and length of the cuts used in sougiri.

Technical Notes

- This kata is familiar to students of muso shinden ryu iaido as a modification of the okuden kata sanbon me—somakiri. The most noticeable difference is that the horizontal step is made on yet another right footstep, not a left one. This makes it a series of five right steps of the *okuri ashi* type. The chiburi and noto are of the seitei variety.
- As the block is begun as part of the draw, the right foot steps back briefly to allow the opponent's blade to pass in front of you and then moves forward again as you strike. The trunk and hip movement should be like a wave, moving back, then forward in a smooth continuous flow without interruption.
- The tsuka should not be drawn to the right but should remain in front of your face. It should be raised up, not forward, because the opponent is very close to you.
- Each of the vertical strikes is at a separate angle, but each should start from the same overhead position. Failing to do this telegraphs your intent before your strike.
- Each strike must end cleanly and accurately. There is a very slight stop at the end of each cut except the horizontal sweep.
- Lifting the blade between strikes (furikaburi) is along the same plane as the previous cut, and back to the same position as mentioned above. It is the assumption of the kata that at least the first three cuts are slashing and do not imbed in the opponent's body.
- It is very important that the blade be rotated into the proper plane as each cut is begun so that the cut is a valid one. The essence of this kata is blade control.
- There is a slightly more pronounced stop when the sword is at the left hip to emphasize that position.
- During the horizontal cut your hands should not be excessively off the midline of your body, which would leave you open to counterattack.
- The level of the horizontal cut is just above the hips.
- The final cut must be a smooth transition from the horizontal cut without any stop in between.

JUNIHON ME – NUKIUCHI (DRAW AND CUT)

抜打

Bunkai

You are forced to rapidly cut an opponent immediately to your front. You draw into a block while stepping back slightly, immediately convert it into a sho-men strike, perform chiburi, and finish with a noto.

Technique

- From a standing position, with no stepping, bring both hands to your sword in the usual manner.
- Step back with your left foot and perform a vertical draw pretty much in the center of your body.
- Perform furikaburi as you step your right foot not quite even with your left.
- Step back out with your right foot as you reach for the sword with your left hand and immediately cut sho-men.
- Perform yoko chiburi as you step your right leg behind your left one.
- Perform a noto as usual.
- Step up with your right foot so that it is even with your left.
- Take one step forward, right then left.
- Drop your right hand.

Technical Notes

- This will be recognized as a standing version of the final kata of Omori, Eishin, and Okuden waza, all of which are performed from the seiza position.
- On the draw, the tsuka moves up near the midline. There is not much of a block; the main defensive move is the step backward.
- The right-foot and body motion is back and forth during the draw and cut, like wave motion.
- The right foot goes back into a deep stance during the chiburi and then comes forward again after the noto.
- The kata is completed by taking a right-left step to the starting position.

A

B

Figures 84A and B: Beginning and end of the nukiuchi kata of the seitei group.

OMORI RYU—SHODAN WAZA

大森流一初伝

The overall process (of teaching Budo) can be likened to teaching a child to ride a bicycle: The child does not innately know how to balance, pedal and steer, nor will he be likely to discover how on his own. At the same time, no one can fully explain any of these skills either; one can only demonstrate them and help the child practice them until he figures out for himself which muscles are doing what at which times to make the actions possible.

—*Karl Friday,* Legacies of the Sword

Many mistakes arise from self-consciousness—from too much focus on what the body is actually doing. When pitching a baseball, throwing a football, or shooting a basketball, problems always arise when the athlete tries to aim the ball. So it is with playing guitar. When the mind becomes preoccupied with what the hands are doing, it shuts out the music inside.

—*Phillip Toshio Sudo,* Zen Guitar

Omori ryu kata are the shoden, or beginning kata, of the muso shinden koryu. They almost all begin from seiza. As a group they differ from seitei in several important ways. Seiza is accomplished by sweeping the left foot backward and kneeling on it before carrying the hakama to the side with the right hand and dropping down into seiza by kneeling on the right. Another difference is in the timing of the chiburi. There is no delay while the left hand grasps the koiguchi; both hands move together, the sword twisting and raising as the left hand slides onto the top of the saya. An Omori chiburi does not stop at the midline, as is done in the seitei waza, but goes way to the left, cutting a potential opponent from right shoulder to left hip before stopping in the exact position as a yoko chiburi would There are more subtle differences. The cuts are fuller that those of seitei waza and somewhat more aggressive, and the noto is done quicker, moving the saya back slightly earlier in the sequence. The overall timing of Omori kata is quicker and more aggressive than that of seitei.

In most ryu-ha of muso shinden iai, the right hand is characteristically drawn toward the kashira at the end of the kata before returning to the side of the body. This is another representation of zanshin and can be performed before, during, or after standing at the completion of a sitting or kneeling kata. While not a characteristic of Kamimoto-ha, it is an important feature with which the student should be familiar. It is usually omitted during junto (nanahon me) because the swordsman is not facing an enemy.

Omori Rokurozaemon Masamitsu was a student of Eishin, as well as Ogasawara ryu etiquette (reishiki) and Shinkage ryu (Ratti and Westbrook, 1973). He created a set of 11 iai techniques originating from the sitting (seiza) probably derived from both Shinkage and Eishin ryu and modified by the Ogasawara ryu etiquette. The bunkai of these kata generally involve actions inside the court or some other assembly hall. These techniques appear to have been incorporated into the Eishin ryu prior to its' splitting into the two streams of Tanimura-ha and Shimomura-ha and they are found in both muso shinden and Jikiden Eishin ryu. This was most likely accomplished via the cross-pollination with the Tosa schools that had had a close relationship with Omori (Wagner and Draeger, 1997). Oe Masamichi, 17th grandmaster is credited with giving these waza new names, which are use by Jikiden Eishin ryu (Shimakabura and Pellman, 1995). The muso shinden ryu retains the original, earlier nomenclature, presumably that of Omori himself.

Figure 85: The characteristic movement of the right hand out to the kashira at the end of an Omori kata representing zanshin that is used by many streams of muso shinden ryu iaido.

IPPON ME – SHOHATO (BEGINNING SWORD)

初発刀

Bunkai

You are in seiza and threatened from the front. You rise, cut across your opponent's neck and slide forward once to push him backward. Then slide up again and finish him with an overhead strike. You then throw off the blood from your sword while standing up, kick your enemy's body for response, and sheathe your blade, kneeling as you do.

Technique

This is the Omori equivalent of the first seitei kata (or vice versa). In Eishin ryu it is called mae, but it is different from mae in that your nukitsuke starts farther to your left and is thus longer, you slide forward during kirioroshi,

Figure 86: Shohato. Note at this point it looks like seitei–ippon me, however the body movement is more aggressive and there is more forward movement during the cuts in this kata.

the timing of the chiburi is somewhat more continuous, and the noto is quicker.

- You drop into seiza by kicking your left foot out behind you as you perform hakamabiki with your right hand and then kneeling on your left knee.
- You grasp the hem of your hakama with your right fingers and put it gently to the right as you bring in your right knee even with your left and a fist's width from it. Settle back on to your heels and place your hands on your thighs, halfway between your knees and hips, pointing at the opposite knee.
- Take a calming breath or two and engage the enemy in front of you with your eyes. Move your right fingers to the tsuka and as they touch it, break the habaki free from the koiguchi with your left thumb.
- Begin pushing the tsuka out of the saya with your right fingers as you begin to rise up on your knees. Allow the tsuka to drift to your left as you do so.
- By the time your blade is nearly out of the saya you should be up on your toes with your body straight. The saya and blade should be horizontal. The tsuka should be about on a vertical line through your left shoulder, but lower.
- Slide your right foot out past the point where the knee is at a right angle.
- Begin nukitsuke by pulling the koiguchi off the kissaki with your left hand.
- Pull your left knee up with your right leg as the cut develops to a position where both your knees are bent at 90 degrees.
- Sequentially flex the fingers of your right hand, driving the kissaki out to your left of the enemy and then crisply bring it across his neck with your right arm locked. Don't bend forward.
- Perform sayabiki synchronously with the cut.
- As you cut, extend your right arm out as far as you can without actually twisting at the waist or bending forward.
- Stop the nukitsuke cleanly with the tip slightly lower than the tsuka and inside the forward projection of your shoulder. Pause.
- Without moving your right arm or the sword, slide your right foot farther out in front of you. Pull your body forward with your right leg pushing the kissaki toward your enemy's face.
- Simultaneously bring the koiguchi out of sayabiki toward your hara, pull your left knee forward with your right leg to within 6 inches of your right foot, and finally move the kissaki first, then the blade, toward your left ear with your right wrist to begin furikaburi.
- As your right hand comes in front of your face, lift the sword up above your head as your body moves under it. At the same time the blade moves from your left to your midline above your head.
- Slide your right foot out again past the right angle.
- Perform a big kirioroshi while pulling the left knee up with the right and tucking your hips in under you until your right knee is at a right angle.
- Stop the cut with the tip 6 inches from the floor and your hands directly in front of you at obi height. Pause.
- Perform an Omori chiburi by rotating the ha toward your left through a loosely held left hand.
- Grasp the tsuka with the left hand and push the right hand up against the tsuba. Continue this motion by letting go with the left hand that then slides to the top of the saya, pushing it to the horizontal.
- You push the kissaki a little forward by this action, and then your wrist pulls the tip briskly back over your right shoulder, the arm following. The end position is with the right arm locked and straight out laterally from the right shoulder. The blade forms an angle of 135 degrees from forward, the kissaki pointing up at 45 degrees from the horizontal.
- Unlike the seitei Omori chiburi, the left hand does not precede the right, but both movements are made simultaneously.
- Without a pause your right elbow is flexed as in a salute, bringing your right knuckles and tsuka even with your right temple, a

finger's length to the right. The blade is not quite vertical, leaning both to your right and behind you, the ha rotated slightly toward your left.

- Flick your wrist out to your left, propelling the kissaki first, then followed by your arm and the rest of the blade. The blade will cut across your midline toward your left.
- After your arm is fully extended, bring it down so that the blade ends up where it would be in a yoko chiburi. This results in the blade's making a continuous cut across the chest of a potential opponent. Pause.
- Change step as in seitei kata.
- Perform a noto. In the Omori ryu, the koiguchi and habaki do not meet in front of the hara, but about a quarter to a third of the blade is left between where the mune touches the koiguchi and the tsuba, just before the sayabiki and extension of the sword arm occurs.
- After allowing a sufficient time to demonstrate zanshin, you drop into a kneeling position. Your right knee should touch the floor just as the tsuba hits the koiguchi.
- Stand as in seitei.

Technical Notes

- The movements into seiza are delicate and dignified. The hakamabiki should be subtle. Try to keep your body straight up and down while performing it.
- You should not make a big step backward with your left foot going into seiza; just 6 to 8 inches are enough to get you down onto your knees.
- It is desirable if a little fold of the hakama is left standing when released from the right hand.
- The nukitsuke is not performed straight ahead like a threat as in seitei, but as a legitimate cut by causing the tsuka to drift to the left, so that at the moment of sayabiki, when the blade is released, it can cut widely across the enemy.
- Delaying the furikaburi slightly while beginning to slide forward allows the kissaki to apply semé to the opponent by threatening his face.
- The forward slide and hip movement allow much more energy to be transferred to the cut.
- The noto of this group is a little quicker than the last because there is less blade movement. This follows a trend that becomes obvious as the more advanced kata are studied.
- If the right hand is to be brought to the kashira at the completion of the kata, it may be done before, during, or after standing following the noto. It should be done in a slow, contemplative fashion.

NIHON ME – SATO (LEFT SWORD)

左刀

Bunkai

You are seated in seiza when you perceive a threat from an opponent seated to your left. You rise to your knees, spin around 90 degrees to your left, and cut him at neck level with nukitsuke. You then slide forward and finish him with a sho-men strike. You then toss off the blood from your blade and sheathe it.

Technique

This kata is most like seitei's ushiro, except that you only turn 90 degrees to your left instead of 180. (In Eishin ryu it is called migi.)

- From a standing position toward the front you turn 90 degrees to your right by stepping with your left foot.
- You keep your eyes forward until you are turned in order to demonstrate zanshin, and then turn your head and eyes to your new forward direction.
- Assume seiza as in shohato.
- Take several relaxing breaths.
- Bring your right hand to the top of the tsuka, fingers together and straight. As soon as your fingers touch the tsuka, turn your head slightly to the left and pick up your opponent in your peripheral vision.
- Release the habaki with your left thumb

Figure 87: Halfway through the turn in the kata sato. This is just like shohato except that the swordsman (on the left in this picture) starts with his left side toward his enemy.

and push the tsuka out of the saya toward your left as you rise up on your toes.

- Then spin your body around, pivoting on your right knee and stepping out with your left foot.
- Begin your nukitsuke by pulling the saya backward off the kissaki and swing your right foot until it is exactly behind your right knee. Use this motion to add energy to your cut, which is launched to your left and then sliced across the enemy.
- Stop without bouncing with the kissaki slightly lower than your right hand, pointed toward a spot on the floor about 20 feet in front of you (in other words, down and forward). Pause.
- From this point on, you do exactly what you did in shohato, except that the forward foot is reversed (i.e., cut and chiburi with the left foot forward—noto with the right).

Technical Notes

- The first motion, as always, is moving your right hand to the tsuka, the second, moving your head.
- By the time your body has turned around your kissaki should be at the koiguchi. Do not start the cut itself until your body position is perfectly lined up on the enemy. Then begin it by pulling the saya off with the left hand.
- On kata like this one where the left leg is forward, right below the koiguchi, it interferes to some extent with keeping the left fingers perpendicular to the floor during chiburi. Do your best but keep them straight and together even if angled forward somewhat.
- Remember that the Omori chiburi starts with both hands at once with no pauses and that the noto does not put habaki and koiguchi together but separates them by one-third sword's length.

SANBON ME – UTO (RIGHT SWORD)

右刀

Bunkai

You are seated in seiza when you are threatened from a seated opponent to your right. You rise to your knees, turn and cut him across the neck, slide forward, and finish him with a sho-men kirioroshi. You toss the blood off your blade, nudge the body with your toe, and sheathe your sword.

Technique

This is the opposite of nihon me. (In Eishin ryu it is called hidari.)

- Turn to the left using your left foot first, and drop into seiza using Omori technique.
- Take several relaxing breaths.
- Bring your right hand up to the top of the tsuka keeping your fingers straight and together.
- Look to your right as you continue to push the blade out with your right hand as you rise up onto your knees (kiza).
- Pivot around ON your left knee and step out with the right leg. Use this rotation to put power into your nukitsuke. Pause.
- Perform furikaburi and kirioroshi, chiburi, and noto as in ippon me.

Technical Notes

- The key issue in this kata is the timing of the start of nukitsuke and the spinning of the body. In nihon me, the nukitsuke is started after the body comes to a halt because it reverses the direction. In this kata the body motion is incorporated into the draw and makes it much stronger.

YONHON ME – ATARITO (STRIKING SWORD)

当刀

Bunkai

You are seated in seiza when you perceive a threat from your rear. You rise up, spin around and force your opponent back with your nukitsuke. You then slide forward and finish him with kirioroshi, toss the blood off your sword, and sheathe it after kicking the body for response.

Figure 88: Halfway through the turn of uto. This also is just like shohato except that the swordsman (this time on the right) starts with his right side toward the opponent.

Technique

This is almost exactly like seitei – nihon me with these exceptions: you assume seiza in the Omori manner, you do the continuous Omori chiburi, and you use Omori timing. (In Eishin ryu it is called ushiro.)

GOHON ME – INYOSHINTAI (YIN YANG ADVANCE RETREAT)

陰陽進退

Bunkai

You are sitting in seiza when you are attacked from the front. You kneel and do a nukitsuke that misses. You then stand and take a step forward striking your enemy with a sho-men cut that does not kill him. He drops to the floor in front of you, and you drop down into a kneeling position, perform yoko chiburi, and begin a noto. At this point, your enemy starts to move. You slide your left foot back to gain distance and deliver a low horizontal cut from left to right, slide forward, and finish the enemy off with a kirioroshi. You then perform an Omori chiburi and noto.

Technique

This kata provides some guidance in what to do if your first (and second) cut doesn't connect or finish your opponent. You don't hesitate, but continue forward immediately into another strike. (In Eishin ryu, inyoshintai is called yaegaki.)

- Assume seiza in the Omori fashion.
- As you recognize the threat from the front raise your right fingers to the top of the tsuka.
- Break the hold of the habaki with your left thumb and start to rise up onto your knees, pushing the tsuka out and to your left with your right fingers as you rise.
- The sword should be nearly out of the saya as you attain kiza.
- Begin nukitsuke by pulling the koiguchi off the kissaki and sequentially contracting the fingers of your right hand around the tsuka, from little finger to index finger.
- Slide your right foot out in front of you as your wrist flicks the kissaki to your left of the enemy, and then use your arm to draw it across his face. At the same time pull the koiguchi back along the top of your obi with your right hand into sayabiki, rotating it horizontally with your left wrist.
- At the conclusion of this action, the saya should be at right angles to your forward axis and horizontal. The sword should be slightly down at the tip from exactly horizontal, your right arm horizontal and about 45 degrees off the forward axis. The kissaki should be within the line projected forward from your right shoulder. Pause. Up to this point the action has been exactly as in Omori – ippon me.
- Begin furikaburi as you stand up. Continue it as you step forward with your left foot.
- You perform a high sho-men kirioroshi as your back (right) foot moves up. There should be a little overreach, with the body leaning forward from the waist.
- Drop to your right knee, straightening your waist as you do so. The sword stays in chuden until just before your right knee hits the ground. Perform a yoko chiburi with sayabiki so that your body, saya, and sword all stop at the same time. Pause.
- Begin an Omori chiburi by rotating the koiguchi forward around your obi and bringing the mune of the blade, about 1 foot from the habaki, to the web between your left thumb and index finger.
- Push the tsuka away from you at 45 degrees to your right off the forward axis allowing the mune to slide over your thumb.
- As your right arm reaches full extension the kissaki should drop into the koiguchi, aided by some sayabiki from the left hand.
- Begin to sheathe the blade and at the same time rise up and put your weight on your right foot.
- Slide your left foot backward in time with the blade.
- When about one-third of the blade is sheathed, redraw the blade and make a horizontal cut at about the level of your

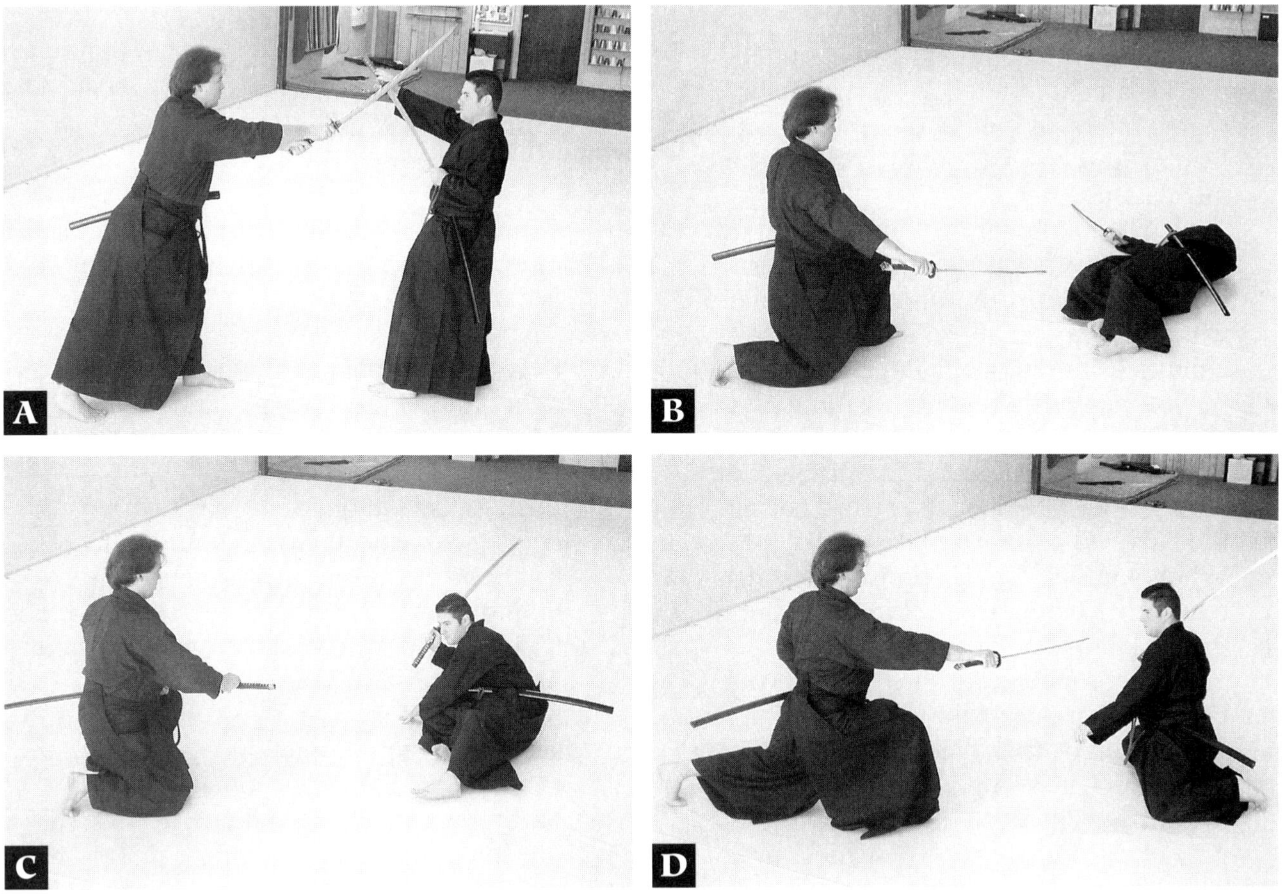

Figure 89A – E: Inyoshintai. After a missed nukitsuke, the swordsman pursues the enemy, striking him down, but he comes off the floor attacking and must be dispatched with a second kirioroshi.

knees as your left leg slides rearward and you keep your left knee off the ground.

- Drop your left knee to the ground.
- Perform furikaburi as you bring the saya forward with the left hand and draw your body forward with your left leg.
- As the sword reaches its upward limit bring your left hand up to meet it.
- Slide your right foot forward past 90 degrees of knee flexion.
- Begin a sho-men kirioroshi as you slide your body forward, again on your left knee. Pause.
- Perform Omori chiburi, change steps, and do an Omori noto as you drop to your left knee.
- Stop your sword and body at the same time. Pause. Stand and bring your left foot up to your right one.
- Drop your right hand to your side.

Technical Notes

- Nukitsuke is exactly as ippon me.
- The kirioroshi that follows is unusual in that you stretch your body forward, actually leaning at the waist. Cut on the back-foot movement.
- As you drop to your right knee, your body straightens out, with you tucking your buttocks under your waist. The sword drops with you, staying horizontal until the yoko chiburi is started. Don't forget the sayabiki.
- As you begin the first noto, you must first rock back on your right foot, bringing your right heel off the ground, and then slide your left foot back as the sword goes in the saya.
- When your left foot is opposite your right, redraw the blade. Don't start the cut until the kissaki is free of the saya.
- You must concentrate hard to keep your body upright during the low horizontal cut. There is an overwhelming urge to bend over, which is wrong. This low cut is to stop the enemy who is on the ground from the previous kirioroshi but is reaching toward your knees with his blade.
- You must keep your knee off the ground during the cut. When you finally put it down don't let it thump.
- You then finish as if it was the end of Omori – ippon me.

ROPPON ME – RYUTO (FLOWING SWORD)

流刀

Bunkai

You are in seiza when an enemy rushing toward you from your left with his sword overhead attacks you. You block a downward cut to your head and then avoid it by stepping backward. You then open your opponent's belly with a right-to-left horizontal cut. You follow his body down with your kissaki, wipe the blood off your blade on the right leg of your hakama, and sheathe your sword backhanded.

Technique

This is a more complicated version of the seitei waza ukenagashi with a more involved block and counterstrike. (In Eishin ryu, it is known as ukenagashi)

- Turn your body to the right as you did in nihon me and assume seiza in the Omori fashion.
- Take a couple of relaxing breaths.
- Become aware of the attack; bring your right hand, fingers straight and together, to the top of the tsuka as you look at the enemy's sword.
- Push the sword out of the saya with your right fingers and step with your left foot in front and to the left of your right knee.
- Stamp your left foot as you push your blade up into a blocking position just as in seitei - ukenagashi.
- Step to your right with your right foot and keep both feet parallel and facing forward. Lean your body away from your left putting your weight on the right foot. At the same time bring the mune just past the habaki to your right deltoid muscle, holding the sword parallel to the ground with your right hand only. Your left hand remains on the saya.
- Rotate your left foot to your left and make a kind of roundhouse step to your left with your right foot as you begin a right-to-left horizontal cut with your right hand.
- As the body and blade come around to your left, grasp the tsuka with your left hand.
- Keep your knees bent and your feet pointed away from each other at 45 degrees and at about a step apart. As the cut moves across the enemy's abdomen, rotate your right hand up to the top of the tsuka that should be at your hara with your hands.
- At the end of this cut you should be facing the enemy, knees bent, feet pointing off center by 45 degrees and about a foot apart. The tsuka should be in the midline with the kissaki just to your left of your enemy. Pause.
- Rotate your feet forward as you rotate your

Figures 90A – C: Ryuto. In this version, the swordsman blocks, leans backward to avoid a downward cut, and then finishes with a right-to-left horizontal cut before a reverse chiburi/noto.

hands around the tsuka into a conventional grasp, keeping the kissaki pointed at your downed enemy.

- Slide your left foot back as you drop the kissaki over the enemy's head, keeping your back straight. Sword and foot stop together. Pause.
- From this point on you end as in ukenagashi, except that the reversed noto is a little different than that in seitei. The habaki and koiguchi do not meet in the midline in Omori ryu, but the hands slightly cross right over left in order to begin the noto.

Technical Notes

- There is a progression of stamping the foot in this kata: one-two-three, left foot forward, right foot back, right foot around to left.
- The left foot comes out a little farther forward of the right knee than in ukenagashi.
- When you step out sideways with the right foot, you immediately move all your weight to it and your body over it and keep the left foot unmoved but unweighted. This allows you to sidestep the vertical cut coming down on you.
- The timing of the third step coordinated with the hands in the horizontal cut takes a lot of work to develop.
- Do not allow the hands and tsuka to go to the left of midline.
- Rotate the tsuka with the right hand as you keep your left hand loose in order to reestablish the traditional grip on the tsuka. Also rotate the right foot on the heel as you make the hand movements.
- When you follow the head down with the kissaki as you step back with the left foot, do not bend your upper body forward.
- To set up for the noto, the blade is swung from the position on your thigh toward your left, in front of your left hand, while keeping the ha pointed toward your enemy. As this is done your right hand crosses over your left, which has brought the koiguchi slightly to the right of midline. The end of all of this

is that the mune near the habaki winds up lying on the web between the left index finger and thumb right above the koiguchi. The sword is stretched out along your left forearm nearly parallel to the saya.

- During the noto, the sword is returned to the vertical position by rotating the saya with the left hand. The right hand is supporting but not clenching the tsuka. As the tsuka rotates through the right hand the index finger stretches out parallel to it, with the other fingers loosely curled under the tsuka and thumb to the right of the top of the tsuka.
- As you do your noto, you drop to your left knee, sword and knee stopping at the same time. Continue to keep your eyes on your enemy. Then drag your back foot forward with your right leg. As your feet come together, your eyes lift and your right hand drops to your side.
- This type of large, horizontal cut is sometimes referred to as yokogumo (cloud cover), which is also the name of a chudan kata (which does not contain that type of cut!).

Note: In many (or maybe most) ryu-ha, the swordsman steps farther forward with his left foot for the block, does not lean backward, and makes the definitive cut a diagonal one, to an opponent to the left of his midline using both hands from the start.

NANAHON ME – JUNTO (ORDERLY SWORD)

順刀

Bunkai

You are serving as a kaishaku, a second in ritual suicide. It is your job to strike off the head of the person performing *seppuku* after he has thrust the short sword into his hara and cut up into his liver. He is not an enemy, but family or friend, and he has picked you personally to perform this last service for him, as distasteful as it may be to you. Both your reputation and the reputation of his family and clan are at stake in your performance. All your motions are dictated by the timing of the actions of the individual performing seppuku. You sit quietly as he composes his poem, then you draw and hide the sword, stand, and ritually wash your face with your hand as he grasps his short sword. You step forward raising your sword unobtrusively as he prepares to perform hara-kiri. After he has cut himself substantially you cut through his neck or his neck and head with a two-handed kirioroshi. (In some ryu this is a one-handed cut). You initially leave enough anterior skin to keep the head from rolling away, which would be an insult to the family. You follow the body down with the kissaki and perform a reverse chiburi and backhanded noto in a slow, respectful fashion.

Out of respect for its solemnity and for those samurai who have participated in it for centuries, it is the custom of our dojo never to practice this kata when we have visitors and never to perform it for display (*embed*). In choosing to describe it in detail the author profoundly wishes that this respect will be followed by those students who use this handbook. In Eishin ryu, this is known as kaishaku.

Technique

- Every action in this kata is performed slowly and with dignity, not with zanshin.
- Drop into seiza in the standard Omori fashion.
- As you start to draw your sword pivot your body to the right around your left knee, keeping the sword horizontal to the ground along your left leg during its drawing.
- As you stand upright following the draw, rotate your entire body to the left (forward) while keeping the sword horizontal in front of you.
- As you draw your right foot toward your left, ritually wash your face clockwise with the tsuka, and end with your feet together and the sword held vertically with your right hand, tsuka alongside your head. (Your left hand should be at your side.)
- When the time comes, simultaneously step

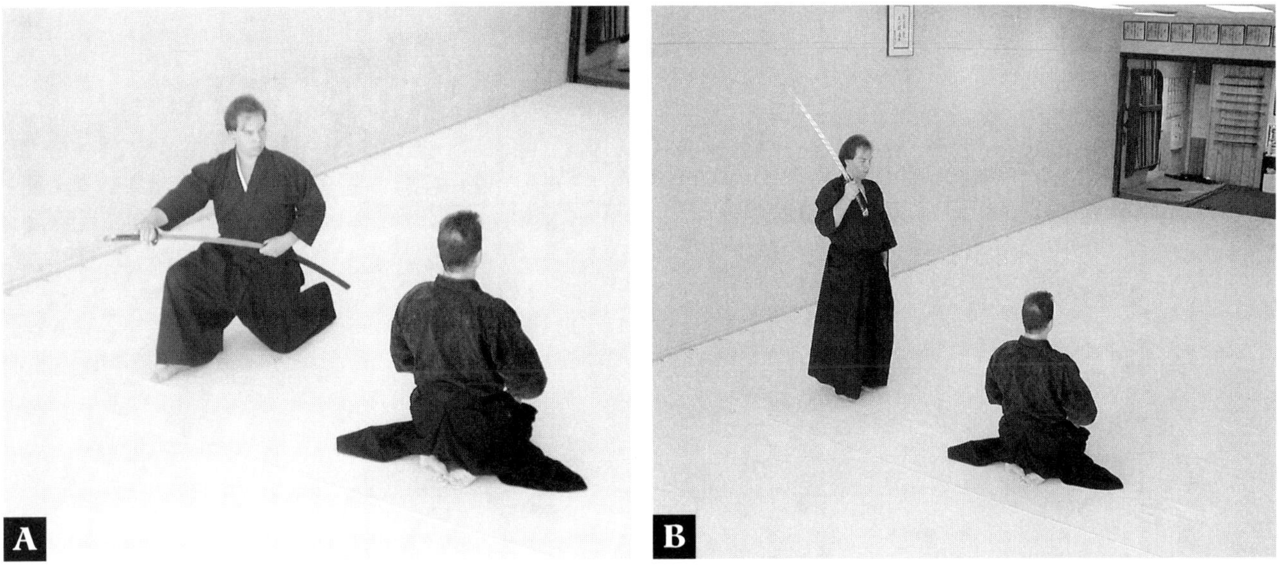

Figures 91A and B: Getting into position as kaishaku in the kata junto.

out with your right foot and raise the sword over your head, holding the sword with both hands.

- Perform a kirioroshi, cutting nearly, but not completely through the anterior neck skin.
- Then rock back with your hips as you cut the last connection between head and neck.
- Follow the body down with the kissaki of the sword.
- Do a reverse chiburi and noto, then stand.

Technical Notes

- It takes some time to determine where to position yourself so that you wind up in the right place after drawing and standing. Only practice can give you this skill.
- The "face washing" done in this kata may be unique to Kamimoto-ha.
- The angle of the kirioroshi varies with the rank of the person performing seppuku. If the person is of high rank, it is done vertically, if of lower rank, it is done at a progressively lower angle.
- There is obviously a very subtle difference between solemnity and zanshin and the iaidoka must make the adjustment in his attitude for the difference to become apparent during the kata.

HACHIHON ME – GYAKUTO (REVERSE SWORD)

逆刀

Bunkai

You are sitting in seiza when an opponent moving toward you with his sword raised attacks you. You move backward as you stand and block his first cut, and then chase him, cutting him with a sho-men cut after the second step. You pause and go into jodan no kamae to further watch him. Finally, you drop to your right knee and stamp on his hand as he reaches for your knee. Reversing your right hand on the tsuka, you spin your body to the right and stab him in the head while supporting the blade with your left hand, palm upward. You then wipe the blood off your sword on your left thigh as you do a modified reverse noto, sitting back away from the body as you do it.

Technique

- Drop into seiza using the Omori method.
- You perceive a threat from a standing enemy. You bring your right foot up slightly forward of your left knee. At the same time

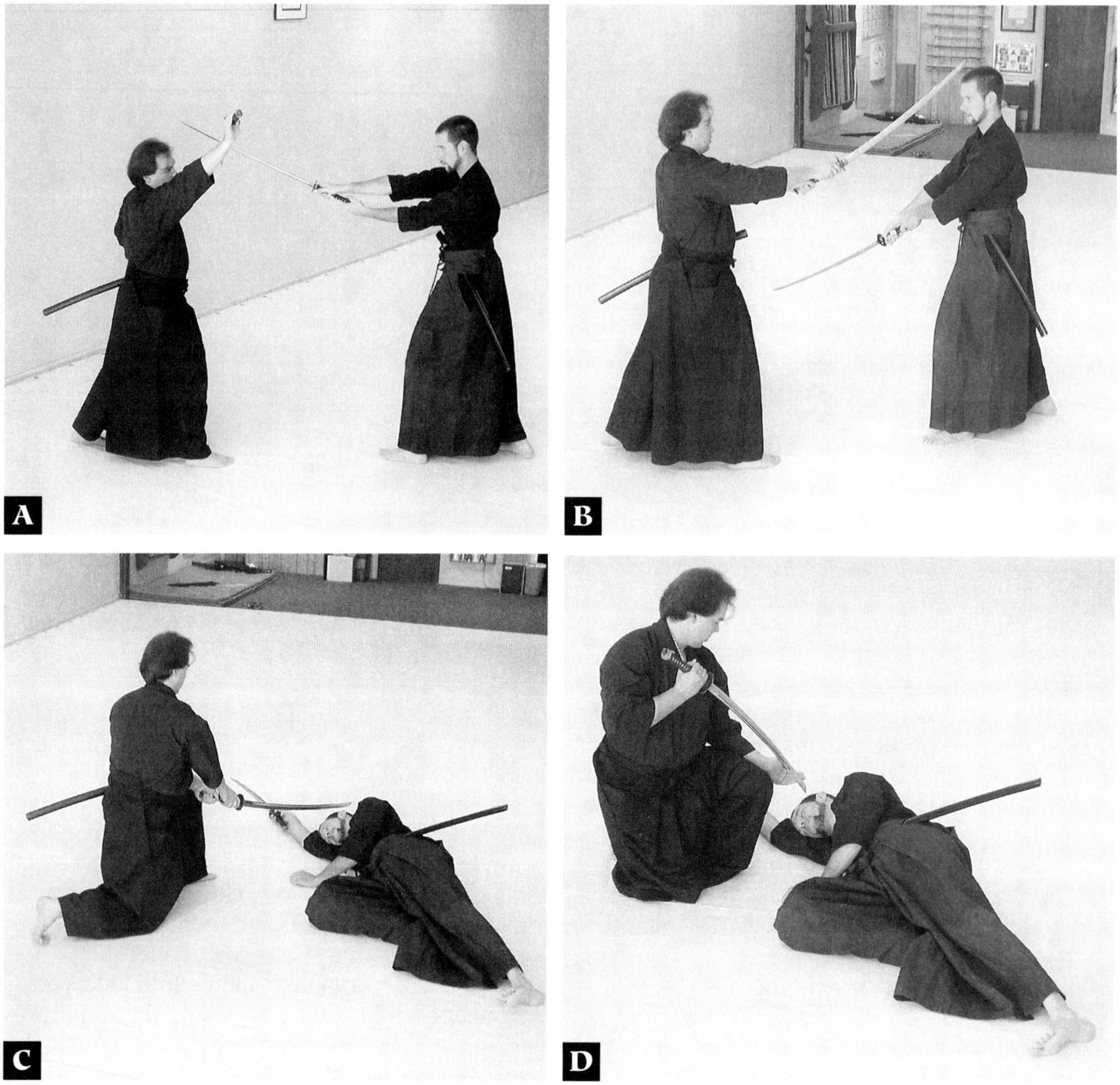

Figures 92A – E: Many of the steps of the kata gyakuto. After the opponent is felled, the kissaki is used to stab the head. In another version, it is used to sever the carotid artery in the neck.

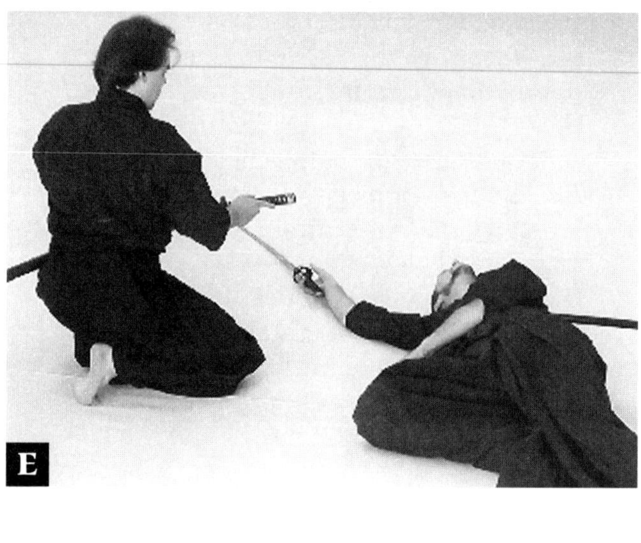

you bring your right fingers up to the tsuka keeping them together and straight.

- In pushing the tsuka out of the saya with your fingers, you point the tsuka down toward the ground barely avoiding touching the kashira to the ground.
- Then raise the tsuka above the level of the saya and push it up into a block as you stand, stepping back with your left foot.
- Then step out with your right foot performing a high sho-men kirioroshi, driving your enemy back.
- Follow the opponent, keeping the kissaki in chudan no kamae during your first step with your left foot. You step through with the right foot and raise your sword over your head in furikaburi and again cut with a full sho-men cut on the back-foot motion of the second step. Pause.
- Leave your sword unmoved and step with your left foot, bringing it up to your right.
- Step back with your right foot, bringing your sword up to jodan no kamae. Pause and exhibit zanshin.
- Drop the kissaki to level the sword and then drop down into a kneeling position on your right knee as you stop the kissaki over the opponent's head.
- Stamp your left foot and then reverse your right hand on the tsuka.
- Turn the sword 180 degrees, mune down, by rotating your right hand and wrist. Place your left hand under the mune in front of your left knee, aiming the kissaki at the enemy's head.
- Pull the sword back with your right hand and then forward into the head briskly and forcefully.
- Bring the sword back a second time and as it moves, rotate it to a horizontal position keeping the ha away from you and dragging the kissaki over to the koiguchi with your left hand.
- Move your right leg back behind your right knee as you perform a sayabiki with your left hand and engage the kissaki in the fingers covering the koiguchi.
- Sheathe the sword as you twist your body toward your left with your knee sticking up at 45 degrees and leaning back away from the body, sitting on the right foot, and exhibit zanshin.
- Move your left knee to the front and straighten your right leg, then stand, pulling your back foot up to your left one.

Technical Notes

- The motion upon arising and cutting the first time should be a smooth back and forth motion of the body like the surf coming in and then going out again.
- After the first cut is made, the next two steps should be fairly rapid as you are chasing your opponent.
- The second cut is made at the last minute; do not move forward with the sword over your head.
- Exhibit a lot of zanshin.
- When you drop to your knee out of jodan no kamae keep your back straight.
- After stamping on the enemy's hand, rotate your hips so that the right leg is at a right angle to your left leg as you slide it under you.
- Lift the sword up slowly and stab quickly and with intent. Be careful not to hit the floor.
- Withdraw the sword slowly and then take control of the kissaki with your left hand, dragging it over the saya as you straighten out the right leg by rotating it around its knee.
- Try to continue that rotation into the movement of the left knee to the left as the noto continues.
- Some ryu-ha do not make a distinct stab, but instead simulate cutting the opponent's carotid artery in the neck before doing the reverse noto.

KYUHON ME - SEITYUTO (ENERGY CENTER SWORD)

勢中刀

Bunkai

You are walking forward when you are threatened from the front. You perform nukitsuke and follow up with kirioroshi while continuing to walk forward uninterrupted. You stop briefly to toss off the blood and then sheathe your sword. You then continue on your way.

Technique

This is like doing seitei – ippon me in an upright position. It is called tsukikage in Eishin ryu.

- From a standing position begin walking with your left foot. At the same time reach up with your right fingers to the tsuka and release the habaki with your left thumb.
- Perform nukitsuke as you step forward with your right foot.
- With your next step (left foot) perform furikaburi and on the next step (right foot) perform kirioroshi on the back foot. Pause.
- Perform Omori chiburi, change foot and do an Omori noto.

Technical Notes

- Begin with your left foot for timing. A short step gives you enough time to break the habaki and perform nukitsuke while stepping forward with the right foot. If this maneuver were being done for real, you would already be walking and would begin to reach for your sword when putting your left foot out.
- The tempo of this kata should be a steady progression of movements coordinated with the steps. The sword motion fits the timing of the stepping, not vice versa.
- Be sure to keep your back straight as you cut. You must keep your arms and wrists soft for this to flow properly.
- Keep your knees bent to prevent your head from bobbing.
- The second step of the "step change" is not as deep as it would be if you were planning to drop to one knee during the noto.

Figure 93: The nukitsuke of kata seityuto, which is a standing equivalent of shohato.

JIPPON ME – KORANTO (TIGER DISTURBANCE SWORD)

虎乱刀

Bunkai

You are sitting in seiza when a standing enemy threatens you on your right side and is holding a raised sword. You spin to the right, staying close to the ground, and make an arched nukitsuke cutting your opponent's wrists. You then stand, bring your feet together, and finish him with kirioroshi during a short step forward. You throw blood off your blade and sheathe it.

Technique

- Turn your body toward your left, using your left foot first, and assume seiza using Omori technique.
- Become aware of the enemy on your right and reach for your tsuka, keeping your fingers straight and together. Turn your head to watch the opponent and begin to draw your blade.
- Rise up on both knees (kiza), rotate on your left knee, and step out with your right foot to put you in the familiar 90-degree kneeling position. At this point the kissaki should be at the koiguchi, held steady by the index finger and thumb of your left hand.
- Make the cut as you stand up off your left knee without moving your feet.
- Stand up and bring your left foot up to the right.
- Slide your right foot out and perform kirioroshi on the back foot. Pause.
- Change step, perform Omori chiburi, and noto.

Figure 94: The definitive cut in the kata koranto. Notice that the back knee is off the floor.

Technical Notes

- The rotation to the right is necessarily fragmented in its description but in its exercise it is a continuous motion. The body and leg and foot motions up to the point of the cut are exactly as done during Omori – sanbon me.
- Coordinating the draw with the body movement in this kata is a major undertaking accomplished only with lots of practice.
- The cut has been described as following the rising and setting of the sun. It is high and 45 degrees forward, but the kissaki is kept within tight lateral limits. Its path is an arc that comes up to the first wrist and down through the second. This is done as the enemy's blade is just beginning to come down toward your head. Because he is committed to his cut, when you cut his wrists he continues to move toward you.
- Do not cut wide or you will be open to the enemy's continued forward motion.
- Your enemy is quite close to you so that you cannot step out wide to cut him. Therefore, your kirioroshi is done following a short step forward.

JUIPPON ME – INYOSHINTAI KAEWAZA (YIN YANG ADVANCE RETREAT/ CLAM TECHNIQUE)

陰陽進退—替業

Bunkai

You are sitting in seiza when a seated enemy threatens you from the front. You force him back with nukitsuke but do not cut him. You stand and lean forward striking him with kirioroshi. You then drop to your knees and perform yoko chiburi. As you start to do a noto your enemy, who is lying in front of you, tries to cut you from your right side. You throw a

Figure 95: In the kaewaza form of inyoshintai, a block to a cut to the right ankle is substituted for the horizontal cut in the former kata. Notice how the tip blocks near the habaki of the threatening blade gaining the most mechanical advantage.

strong block with the side of your sword aimed at the enemy's hand, or at least the back of his blade, drop to your knees and slide forward finishing him with kirioroshi. You then toss the blood off your blade and sheathe it.

Technique

This kata is exactly like Omori – gohon me described earlier except for the substitution of the block for the low cut. Therefore only this aspect will be described here. (In Eishin ryu, this is known as gohon me.)

- At the point where you begin to perform your first noto kneeling on your right knee, left leg forward, your enemy starts to strike toward your right ankle from the floor.
- You put your weight on your right knee and begin to slide your left foot back as you take your blade out of the saya and lay it along your left side while pulling the koiguchi in front of your hara with the left hand.
- As your left foot slides all the way to the rear without touching your left knee to the ground, throw a block out in front of your right foot with the side of your blade powered by both the foot motion and a strong sayabiki.
- Drop your left knee to the floor and slide forward, performing furikaburi. Step out with the right foot and finish your enemy with kirioroshi.
- Complete the action as in gohon me.

Technical Notes

- This is a powerful block delivered with the flat of the blade close to the enemy's tsuba, which gives you a mechanical advantage through leverage. Its power comes from three sources: you "cock" the block by bringing your sword way to the left before firing it, you combine it with a brisk sayabiki, and your body is braced by the slide of your left foot to the rear.
- Your grip on the tsuka for the block begins by grasping the tsuka right up against the tsuba with the right hand at right angles to the blade. This is in contrast to the usual way of placing the fingers on top of the tsuka. You brace your grip by placing your thumb against the ura side of the blade just in front of the habaki.
- It takes particular effort to keep your back and upper body straight while doing the block. Do not bend over.
- The kissaki should be as far out in front of your right foot as it will go without stretching and about 10cm (4 inches) off the ground.
- In other ryu-ha, the block comes straight from the saya, not from a position along the saya, and at its end the blade is pulled backward along the right side.

JUNIHON ME – NUKIUCHI (DRAW AND CUT)

抜打

Bunkai

You are in seiza preparing to bow to an enemy your liege lord has commanded you to kill. You grasp your sword, lift it into a block during furikaburi and bring it down into a shomen kirioroshi. You toss the blood off your blade with a yoko chiburi and sheathe it.

Technique

This is one of the few purely offensive kata. Whether invoking the "I'm just following my lord's orders" defense is justification for you or not is a personal decision. In terms of bushido, that is reason enough, and absolves the samurai from the blame of taking a life.

- Assume seiza in the Omori style.
- Bring your right fingers to the top of the tsuka as you release the koiguchi with your left thumb and rotate the tsuka in front of you.
- Push the sword out of the saya while you assume kiza in a more or less horizontal and low position, left to right.
- Raise the sword as a block and then swing it over your head in the manner of ukenagashi.
- Cut straight down, remaining on your toes but widening the distance between your

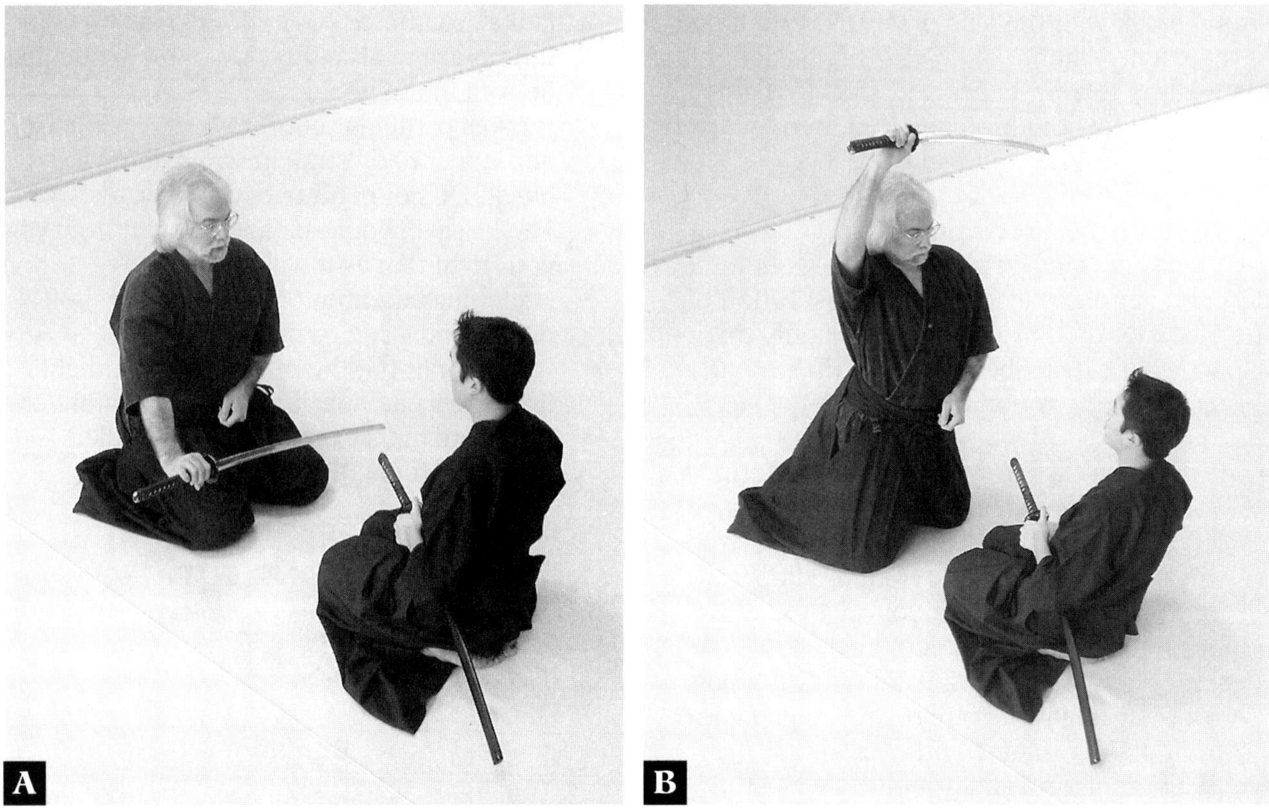

Figures 96A and B: In the Omori version of nukiuchi, the sword is drawn low in defense against a grab and then raised into a block that is converted into a sho-men finishing cut.

knees dramatically in the process, adding power to the cut. Pause.

- Perform a low yoko chiburi just over the top of your right knee with the kissaki ending up 10cm from the floor. Pause.
- Perform a noto. During the first quarter, you bring your left knee in toward the center, during the second quarter you bring your right knee in, during the third quarter you drop back on your feet from off their toes and finish by sitting back onto your feet as the noto ends.
- Place your hands on your thighs again, assuming formal seiza.

Technical Notes

- Be sure to keep your back straight during the entire process.
- Your arms and shoulders will have to be relaxed by the end or this low kirioroshi will hit the floor for sure.
- The method of using body weight to power this cut has changed. Originally the method was to rock back onto the feet during the block and fall back onto the knees with the downward motion. This resulted in numerous knee injuries over the long run, so the ZNKR adopted the present method.

Author's Note: The nukiuchi kata of each level is different, but there seems to be little uniformity in these differences among ryu-ha. One variation of this particular kata is that the enemy opposite you is reaching for the tsuka of your sword. As his hand approaches, you unsheathe your blade and slice his wrist. You then raise the blade into the block and immediately make a sho-men cut. In the chudan variety of nukiuchi, the blade is drawn more vertically in a central position and the block is less well developed. In the okudan variety (*itomagoi*), the draw comes from the start of a low bow and the kirioroshi begins the most quickly of the three.

EISHIN RYU

辰谷川英信流ー中伝

The tools of the warrior are claws and teeth. When one looks into the heart of things, one sees that those with teeth bite, those with claws grab, and those with stingers, sting. This is not taught, it is the way of nature. The birds and the bees are like this; what then do they who travel the path of man use? Teeth and claws—the sword.

—Karl F. Friday and Seki Humitake, Legacies of the Sword

When in this world's unpleasing youth
Our godlike race began,
The longest arm, the sharpest tooth,
Gave man control of man;

'Til, bruised and bitten to the bone
And taught by pain and fear,
He learned to deal the far-off stone,
And poke the long, safe spear.

So tooth and nail were obsolete
as means against a foe,
'til, bored by uniform defeat,
Some genius built the bow.
—Rudyard Kipling

Eishin ryu in muso shinden ryu iaido comprises the chuden, or middle set, of 10 kata all originating from the tatehiza posture. Both offensive and defensive in nature, this group deals with the court setting in which rows of samurai are sitting fairly close together. This set was added to the original "hidden" standing techniques of Jinsuke Shigenobu by Hasegawa Eishin, seventh headmaster, at the beginning of the Tokugawa shogunate.

The method of assuming tatehiza is similar to that of assuming seiza in Omori ryu, sliding the left foot to the rear first and then dropping the left knee to the floor before bringing the right foot up to it. All chiburi in this ryu are of the yoko variety. The noto of this group also is like that of Omori ryu except it is even shorter, bringing the mune to the koiguchi one-half to two-thirds of the way toward the kissaki. Another characteristic of the group as a whole is that during the noto one side of the body is rotated away from the fallen enemy, gaining distance from him in the process. This is similar to the noto of seitei—yonhon me (tsuka ate), which is taken in part from the Eishin Jikiden ryu.

The pattern of the starting direction of the series of kata is easy to remember: three to the front, two to the left, two to the right, two to the rear, and finally the last one to the front. Unlike the other four groups of kata in muso shinden ryu, the Eishin ryu can be performed sequentially, without leaving the floor. Minor changes in the starting direction are made to facilitate this. Whether the Kamimoto-ha way of doing this is in any way similar to Oe Masamichi's original *haya nuki* is conjecture. At any rate, our ryu-ha use both hands for the kirioroshi rather than making one-handed cuts.

IPPON ME – YOKOGUMO (CLOUD COVER)

横雲

Bunkai

You are seated in tatehiza and perceive a threat from in front by a seated opponent. You rise into kiza and cut across his neck and force him back. You slide forward and finish him off with a sho-men kirioroshi, toss the blood off your blade, and sheathe it while rotating away from his body.

Technique

This is the Eishin equivalent of seitei ippon me.

- Assume tatehiza by sliding your left leg to the rear and then kneeling on the left knee up on the left toe while doing a left-leg hakamabiki with your right hand. Then bring your right foot alongside your left knee, do a right-leg hakamabiki with the right hand and sit on your left foot. Place your hands, fingers curled, palms down, on each mid-thigh.
- Acknowledge the threat from the front with your eyes.
- Place the straightened fingers of your right hand on the top of the tsuka, keeping them together and angled 45 degrees forward.
- Begin to push the blade out of the saya as you pull your knees toward one another. This starts to elevate your body.
- Move the tsuka to your left as it continues to move out of the saya.
- When the kissaki clears the koiguchi, step out with your right leg slightly past 90 degrees, swing your right leg and foot behind your right knee, and launch the nukitsuke, tipping first to your left of the enemy and then dragging it across his throat with your right arm. Do a simultaneous sayabiki, rotating the shoulders slightly but not the hips. Pause.
- Perform furikaburi and kirioroshi as in seitei – ippon me.

Figure 97: Yokogumo is the Eishin equivalent of shohato. The swordsman comes out of tatehiza to make the nukitsuke.

- Perform yoko chiburi, and then do a noto that brings the tip half of the blade to the koiguchi first. Then extend the tsuka to your right in order to drop the kissaki into it.
- The first half of the blade length goes into the saya rapidly. At the same time rotate your shoulders and hips toward the right and bring your right foot in to the side of your left knee.
- The rest of the blade is passed into the saya in a slow, thoughtful fashion during which time you rotate it to vertical with the left hand via the saya, and settle back onto your left foot, which remains up on its toes. Pause.
- Move your body back to the front by stepping out with your right foot and rotating the left leg behind the left knee, if necessary. Pause.
- Stand up, pulling your left foot forward with your right leg.
- Drop your right hand unobtrusively to your right side.
- Step back with your left foot to position yourself for the next motion.

Technical Notes

- In assuming tatehiza, the buttocks should be on the flattened inside of the left foot. The right foot should be against the inside of the left knee and not extending out past it.
- It takes some time to learn to get into tatehiza while maintaining control over your hakama. A gentle tap with the right hand on the hakama, left leg first then right, should suffice. If this is not accomplished, the hakama may get fouled by your foot motion with disastrous results.
- When rising to do nukitsuke, pull the left and right knees and thighs toward each other. This will start your trunk upward. Shift your weigh to your left knee. Do not lean forward.
- Be sure to accompany the yoko chiburi with a brisk sayabiki and then do it again with the start of the noto.
- Rotating the body while doing the noto consists of pulling your right foot in to the inside of your left knee, keeping your hips over your left foot (which is up on its toes), and turning your shoulders slightly to your right.
- This body turning, unique to Eishin, means that to maintain metsuke you must turn your head slightly to the left as your body turns to the right in order to keep your eyes pointed straight at your enemy on the floor in front of you.

NIHON ME – TORAISOKU (ONE LEG OF A TIGER)

虎一足

Bunkai

You are seated in tatehiza when threatened from the front by a low, horizontal cut aimed at your right knee. You slide your left leg back and block the cut with the side of your blade, slide forward, and strike your attacker with a sho-men kirioroshi. You then toss the blood off your blade and sheathe it.

Technique

- Assume tatehiza in the Eishin manner.
- Lock your eyes on your adversary to the front and firmly grip the tsuka with your right hand pushed up against the tsuba as you grip the koiguchi with your left hand.
- Tighten your abdominal muscles and pull your knees toward the midline in order to allow your body to rise partly on your right leg.
- Using the same timing, both draw the blade and slide your left foot back behind you without lowering your left knee to the ground.
- Your back foot should stop moving as the kissaki comes out of the koiguchi. Swing the blade forward and down, with the ha upward into a low block in front of your right ankle.
- Drop your left knee to ground and perform furikaburi, sliding the koiguchi to your hara with your left hand and sliding your left knee forward to your right foot just as in ippon me.

Figure 98: Toraisoku. The block is just like inyoshintai kaewaza

- Finish your enemy with a sho-men kirioroshi. Pause.
- Perform a chiburi and noto just as in ippon me. Stand.

Technical Notes

- When the right hand initially reaches the tsuka it is grasped firmly right at the tsuba rather than with the usual finger technique. As the left foot slides to the rear, the hand actually pulls the blade out of the saya.
- When the kissaki is close to the koiguchi pull the saya back with the left hand, releasing the blade.
- At that point swing the blade down as far in front of your right foot as you can and still stay upright. This should be accompanied by a concomitant sayabiki. Pause.
- Finish as in ippon me.
- The grip is changed in this kata to provide strength. As the block starts in earnest, the thumb may be placed to the side of the tsuka for greater stability
- The strongest mechanical advantage is sought when blocking the enemy's cut. Block just in front of his habaki, not near the tip of his sword
- The blade of a katana is easily chipped so block with the side of the blade, or even with a little of the mune leading.

SANBON ME – INAZUMA (LIGHTNING)

稲妻

Bunkai

You are seated in tatehiza when threatened from the front. You force the attacker back with a diagonal nukitsuke while sliding your left foot back to gain striking distance and then finish

Figure 99: Inazuma. The swordsman comes out of tatehiza and pushes the opponent back with a diagonal nukitsuke.

him with a sho-men kirioroshi. Then you shake the blood from your blade and sheathe it.

Technique

- Assume tatehiza in the Eishin manner.
- Lock your eyes on your adversary to the front and place your right hand upon the tsuba as you grip the koiguchi with your left hand. Break the seal of the koiguchi on the habaki.
- Tighten your abdominal muscles and pull your knees toward the midline in order to allow your body to rise partly on your right leg as you push the blade out of the saya.
- Using the same timing, both draw the blade and slide your left foot back behind you without lowering your left knee to the ground. Keep your upper body vertical; don't bend forward at the waist.
- As the blade advances, you rotate the saya with your left hand so that it winds up at a 30-degree angle to the vertical.
- Your back foot should stop moving as the kissaki comes out of the koiguchi. Make a diagonal cut across your enemy starting with wrist action and ending with your arm. The cut should go from his right neck and stop at his left chest wall.
- Drop your left knee to ground and perform furikaburi, sliding the koiguchi to your hara with your left hand and sliding your left knee forward to your right foot just as in ippon me.
- Finish your enemy with a sho-men kirioroshi. Pause.
- Perform a chiburi and noto just as in ippon me. Stand.

Technical Notes

- The nukitsuke is to drive your opponent backward. Do not take the sword too far past his chest or you will invite midline retaliation.

- Sliding the left foot back provides you with enough space to cut a near enemy. Your head should not bob or lean forward. Keep your back straight.

YONHON ME – UKIGUMO (FLOATING CLOUDS)

浮雲

Bunkai

You are sitting in tatehiza with two others seated to your right. The one closest to you reaches behind you and grabs your saya. You stand, twisting your saya and throwing him off balance. You strike him on the head and then cut over him to the one next to him. You make a supported horizontal cut over both their heads, kick the nearest enemy's support out from under him and finish him off with a kirioroshi at 90 degrees to your body. You then throw the blood off your blade and sheathe it.

Technique

This is done to the first of the pair.

- Turn toward your left using your left foot first.
- Assume tatehiza using Eishin technique.
- Stand, stepping to the left with the left foot and weighting it. Swing the tsuka way to the left, pulling it about 6 inches from your obi. This levers the tip of the saya toward your front to the right of your right thigh, pushing forward the enemy that is holding your saya.
- Step your left foot back and across your right foot, standing on its instep and bend your knees for stability.
- Draw and cut with your blade with your right hand in a short, curved line to your right and power it with a twisting sayabiki.
- Without moving the sword, spin to the right on your left foot, do a sayabiki and slide your right foot behind you with your body 180 degrees from your last direction.
- While kneeling, place the palm of your left hand on the mune of your blade about a foot from the kissaki; swing the blade in a 90-degree arc horizontally until it is in front of you. As the cut is made, the left hand slips back along the mune to the tsuba. At the end of the cut the blade is slightly to your right, your left hand is at the habaki, and your head and eyes are to the left, looking at your opponent.
- Simultaneously flip the kissaki from left to right by rotating your right wrist toward the right, move your left hand to the tsuka, and pull your body forward with your left leg until your right knee touches your left heel.
- Step out to a 90-degree angle with your left leg. You may choose to stamp with this step as you are pinning your opponent with your foot.
- Turn your trunk and shoulders to the left as you perform furikaburi.
- Strike with a vertical kirioroshi, 90 degrees to your left from a forward angle. Pause.
- Perform yoko chiburi and straighten your trunk and shoulders at the same time. Pause.
- Perform an Eishin-style noto and rotate your body to the left, sitting on your right heel with the left knee at 45 degrees to your body. Pause.
- Slide your left foot forward and rotate your right foot and leg directly behind your right knee. Your right hand is still on the tsuka.
- Stand and draw your right foot up to the left. Drop your right hand to your side.

Technical Notes

- After you step to the left, lean a little in that direction. Keep your eyes behind you on the opponent hanging on to the tip of your saya that you have just levered forward alongside your right ankle.
- When bringing the tsuka to the right, do so in an arc. What you are doing is hitting the nearest opponent on the back of his neck, further throwing him forward on his face in front of you.
- When your left foot steps over the right, the ankle should be turned as far as it will go to point the sole of the foot upward and the instep downward. This facilitates the 180-degree step turn that follows.
- When the feet are crossed, the knees should both be bent with at least a 90-degree angle

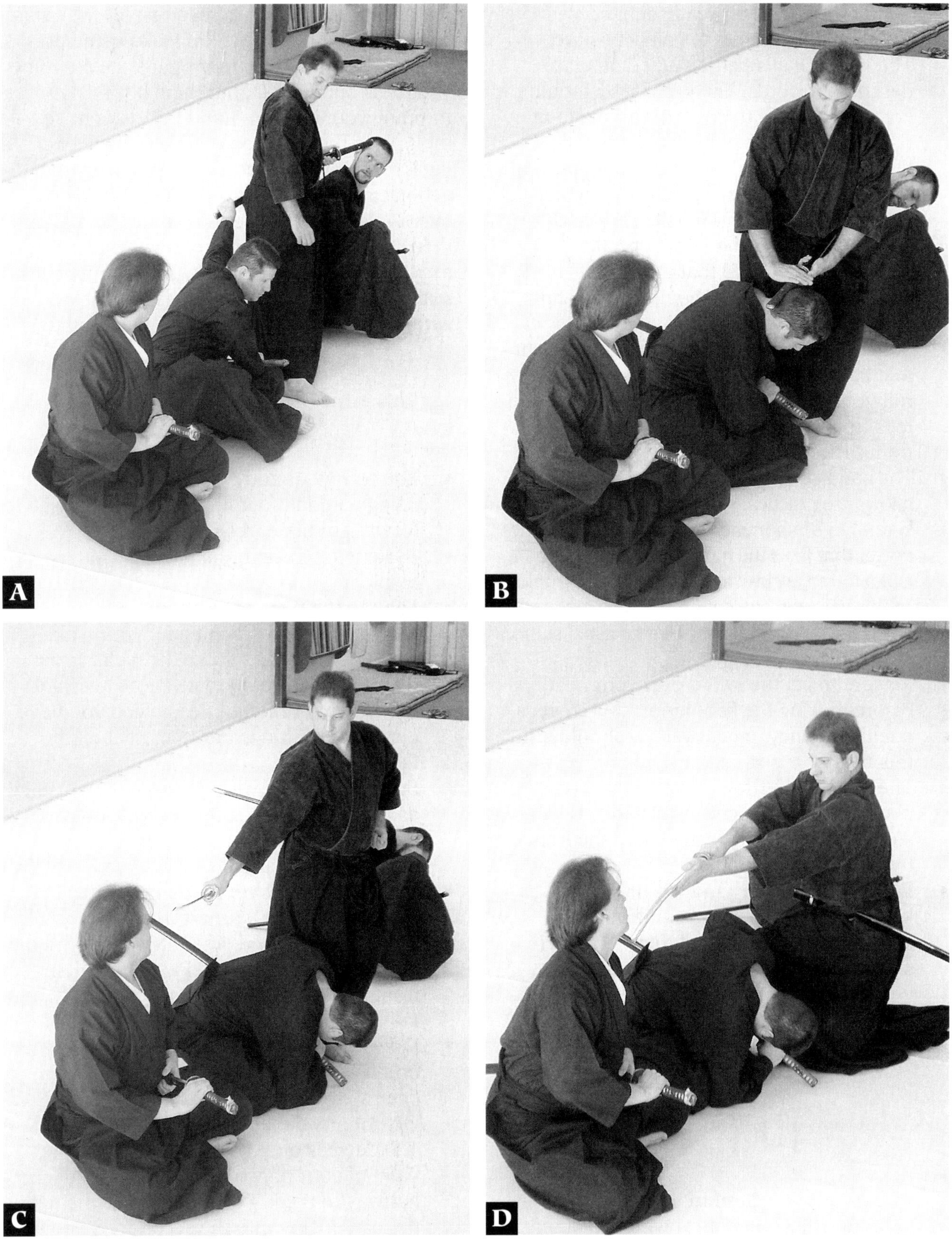

Figures 100A – D: Ukigumo is a defense against a grab to the saya occurring within a line of swordsmen sitting in tatehiza.

between them. This greatly enhances stability in this rather ungainly posture.

- The nukitsuke is particularly difficult to describe in words. The right hand should be kept close to the thigh, with the sword at right angles to the arm. The arc of the kissaki has as small a radius as is practical. Power comes from the sayabiki. The net effect is a movement of both arms and hands around the body in opposite directions in a move that would be expected to push the shoulders back and the chest out.
- Start the spinning step by moving the right foot around in an arc behind you as you roll your left foot over onto its sole with the toes in new forward position, 180 degrees from the old one.
- The hand-supported cut is a technique that allows the practical working length of the katana to be shortened. The left hand provides power that frees the right hand holding the tsuka to move close to and around the trunk. In this way you can cut an enemy a foot away when the working distance in the usual stance is closer to a meter.
- Be sure to get the sword over your head before making the final kirioroshi. There is a real tendency to cut over the shoulder in this move.
- The yoko chiburi winds up a large arc because the usual cutting distance is supplemented by the rotation to the front by the hips and shoulders.
- Despite the turning and twisting in this kata, you must picture your enemy and keep your eyes and head toward him. He starts out on your right and winds up on your left.

GOHON ME – YAMASHITA OROSHI (MOUNTAIN STORM)

山下嵐

Bunkai

You are sitting in tatehiza with two other samurai in a line to your right. You notice that the one closest to you is reaching for the tsuka of your sword. You raise the tsuka with your left hand as you raise your right knee by lifting your heel and then stomp them both down, trapping your enemy's hand in between. You then place the tsuka on the back of the enemy's neck, pushing his head down and using the action to pull youself closer to him. You cut over top of the first enemy into the second and then spin around to your rear. You slide forward and then turn backward, gaining striking distance, and finish the first enemy with kirioroshi as he is lying on the ground.

Technique

This is the second of a pair that start to the left.

- You turn your body 90 degrees to your left using your left foot first. Keep your metsuke forward until nearly turned.
- Assume tatehiza in the usual Eishin fashion.
- Look to the right as you spot your neighbor's hand reaching for your tsuka. Rise into full kiza. Grasp the tsuka in with your left hand rotating it 180 degrees and lift it over your right knee, which you have elevated by lifting your right heel off the floor.
- Strike your knee with the back of the tsuka as you drop your right heel back down on the floor, smashing the enemy's hand between tsuka and knee.
- Lift the tsuka off your right knee (the opponent's hand), turn it over 180 degrees with your left hand, and place it behind the neck of your opponent. Push it down in front and to the right of you, causing him to fall forward on his face.
- Draw the sword, keeping it as close to your body as practical and cut the second enemy over the sprawled body of the first.
- Do not move the sword, but spin around 180 degrees on your left knee. Place the palm of your hand on the mune about halfway to the kissaki. Cut across the top of the first enemy into the second. As you spin around, your left hand slides toward the

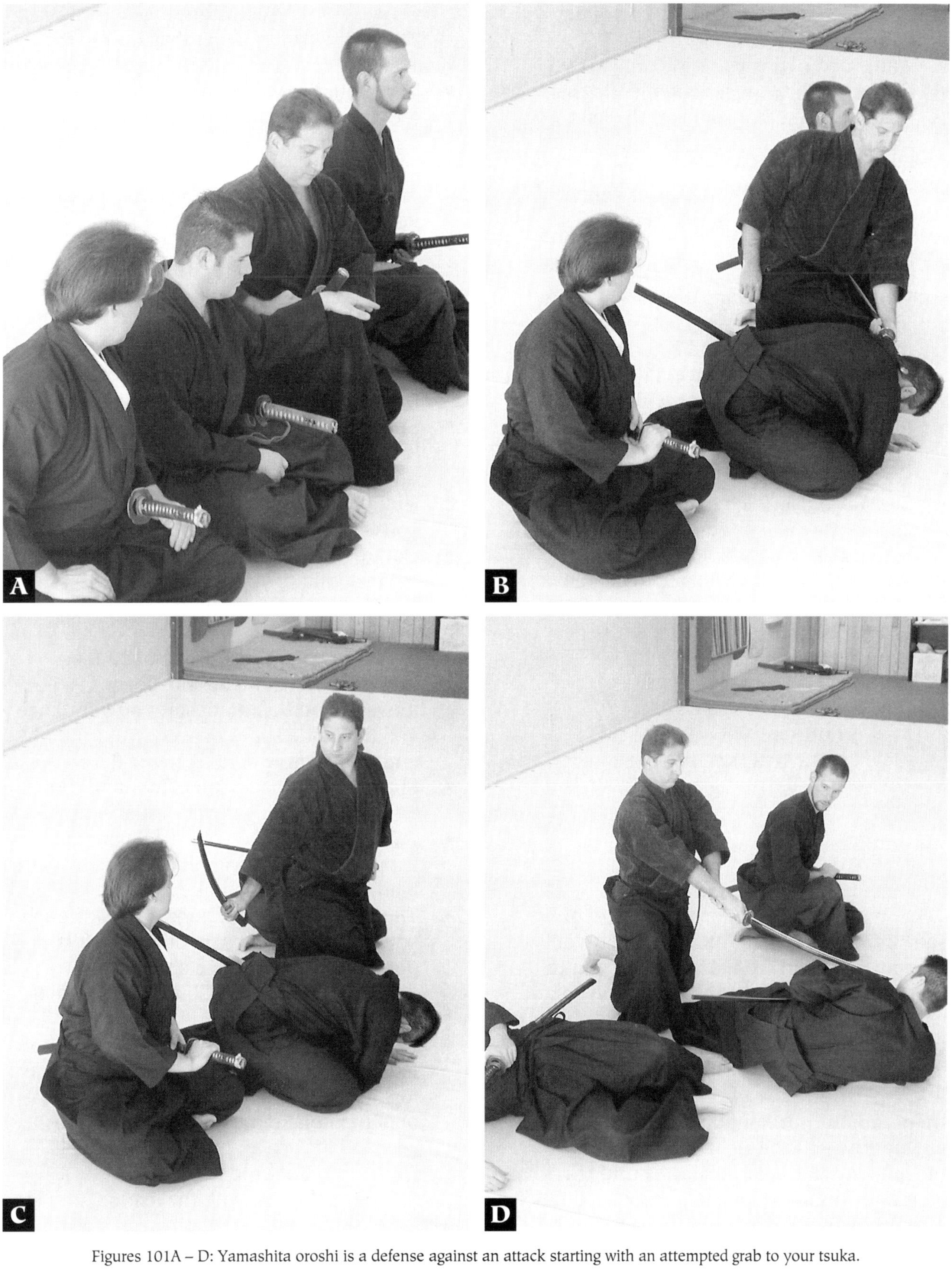

Figures 101A – D: Yamashita oroshi is a defense against an attack starting with an attempted grab to your tsuka.

habaki and you step out at 90 degrees with your right leg.

- At the end of this cut, slide out past 90 degrees with the right foot and flip the blade from the horizontal to the left to leaning right of vertical and assume a normal cutting grip on the tsuka.
- Drag your left knee up to your right heel using your right leg and keeping the sword motionless.
- Turn about 135 degrees to the left around your left knee as you perform furikaburi. Step out with your right foot past 90 degrees in the new direction and cut in kirioroshi as you pull up your left knee. Pause.
- Perform yoko chiburi in the Eishin manner.
- As the sword is returned to the saya, rotate your body to the right and bring the right knee up to a 45-degree angle.
- Sit back on your left foot, which is still on its toes, as the tsuba approaches and reaches the koiguchi. Pause.
- Rotate around the left knee to the left, setting both knees at a 90-degree angle. Stand. Pull your left foot up to the right one using your right leg. Drop your right hand to your side.

ROPPON ME – IWANAMI (BREAKING WAVES)

岩浪

Bunkai

You are in a long horizontal line of samurai all sitting in tatehiza when you perceive a threat from another seated to your left. You draw the saya off your blade as you slide your left foot back and then pivot to the left, thrusting into your enemy. You bounce your sword with your knee to allow its withdrawal from the body, and then you cut horizontally across the enemy as you pivot to the right 180 degrees. You move forward to gain distance and then turn and finish off your enemy with a kirioroshi. You shake the blood off your blade and sheathe it.

Technique

This is the first of a pair that start to the right.

- Turn your body to your right using your left foot first and using zanshin.
- Assume tatehiza using Eishin technique.
- Place the fingers of your right hand on top of the tsuka and break the habaki from the koiguchi as your look to your left.
- Slide your left foot and leg way behind you as you continue to draw the saya off the blade. Keep your back straight.
- When the kissaki comes free of the koiguchi, drop your left knee to the floor. Pinch the thumb and index finger of your left hand on either side of the kissaki.
- Spin 90 degrees to your left on your left knee. At the same time move your right leg up with the knee at 90 degrees, pull the tsuka behind you to your right, and put your left palm on your left knee.
- Control the blade between your thumb and the last joint of your index finger, keeping the blade alongside and parallel to your right thigh.
- Thrust the blade forward about a foot, keeping it horizontal to the floor. As it goes forward, your left hand stays on your knee and the blade slides between your thumb and index finger parallel to the floor.
- Lift your right heel off the floor and drop it back, withdrawing the sword as you do.
- Swing both arms to your right, continuing to support the mune with your left hand as the blade passes horizontally in front of you.
- Then cut left to right, horizontally through your enemy as you spin on your left knee pivoting your trunk and shoulders 90 degrees to your right. Continue to look at your fallen enemy.
- Finish the kata exactly like Eishin – gohon me by flipping the blade over as you slide forward and then turn back to strike the opponent one more time with a kirioroshi.

Technical Notes

Sliding to the rear with the left foot and leg while holding the sword motionless with the right fingers accomplishes the draw. This takes

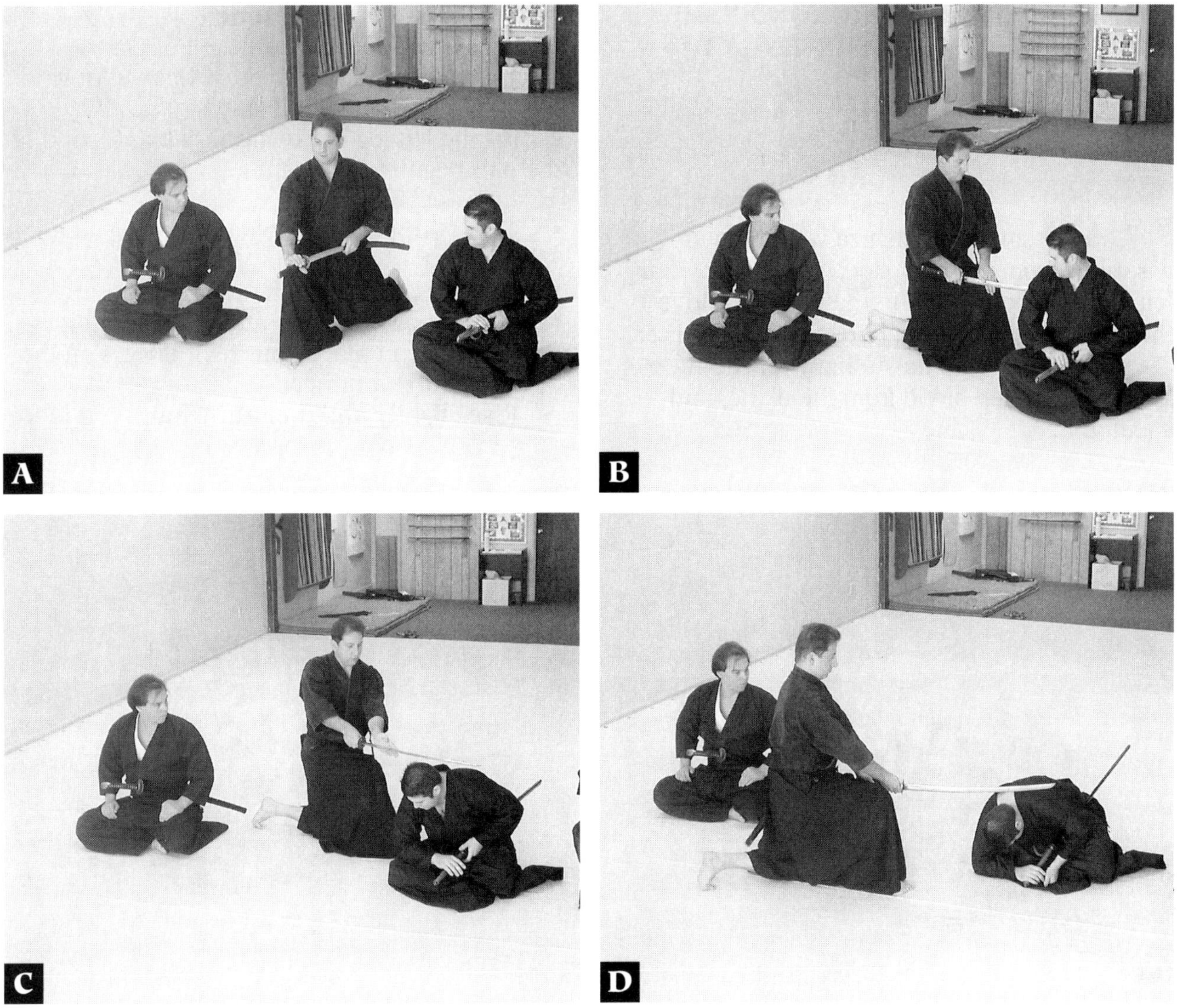

Figures 102A through D: The thrust and two cuts in the kata iwanami.

some coordination and balance. You must not lean forward or pull out the sword by the tsuka.

- Getting the blade to the right of your right knee is accomplished through the guiding action of your left fingers as you flip the blade end for end. At the same time, the right hand turns the blade over and takes the tsuka and blade horizontally along your right side against your obi.
- The thrust is short and straight, forward of your lead (right) knee.
- Bouncing the sword blade with your knee also bounces the body, allowing the easy withdrawal of the blade from the enemy's body.
- The momentum of the supported cut that occurs at the same time aids spinning to the right on the left knee.
- Make an attempt to slide the right foot out as far as it will go during the next two steps to get the required working distance for the finishing kirioroshi.
- Don't forget to keep looking at the enemy on the ground no matter which way the body is pivoting.
- Be sure to keep your back straight during the final cut.

NANAHON ME – UROKO GAESHI (FISH SCALING RETURNING/CUT)

鱗返

Bunkai

You are sitting in tatehiza when you are assaulted from your left side. You spin to your left, sliding the left foot to the rear, and drive the attacker back with a horizontal nukitsuke. You slide forward to finish him with sho-men kirioroshi, sweep blood from the blade, and sheathe it.

Technique

This is the Eishin equivalent of Omori nihon me, except that you don't move forward during the nukitsuke but stay in place by sliding the left leg backward. It is the second of the pair begun to the right.

- Turn your body to the right moving your left foot first.
- Assume tatehiza in the Eishin fashion.
- Become aware of the attack to your left side. As you place your right fingers on the tsuka turn your head.
- Rise slightly and then turn your right foot

Figures103A and B: Uroko gaeshi. You are threatened from your left while sitting in tatehiza. (B) is in midturn.

90 degrees to the left, weight it, and then spin around it 90 degrees.
- As soon as your body has turned, during which the sword is partly drawn, the left foot slides to the rear. The saya is pulled from the kissaki and the nukitsuke is launched. Augment its force with a sayabiki.
- Pull your left knee forward with your right leg as you pull the koiguchi to your hara. Perform furikaburi.
- Slide your right foot out past 90 degrees, and as your left knee slides forward cut down with a vertical kirioroshi. The blade should be 6 inches from the floor with the hands at midline at the hara. Pause.
- Close with the chiburi and noto used with the other Eishin kata described above.

Technical Notes
- When spinning to the left stay as low as possible but don't bend over. It should be made to look effortless.
- When doing nukitsuke keep the back straight and the shoulders relaxed. The sayabiki should look like the conclusion of a single continuous sweep of sword and body.

HACHIHON ME – NAMI GAESHI (RETURNING WAVES)

浪返

Bunkai

This is just like the last kata except the attack is from your rear so you turn 180 degrees, not just 90.

Technique

This is kind of a cross between the Eishin equivalent of seitei–nihon me and the previous kata. It is the first of the pair of rearward-directed kata. Since this is essentially the previous kata done with a 180-degree turn, only that aspect will be discussed.

- To get all the way around to make the cut, an alternating combination of foot movements is necessary.
- First put your weight on your left foot as you rotate your right one as far to your left as it will go. Then put your weight on your right foot as you twist your body around it. (It also helps to kind of sweep the left foot in an arc to carry the body around before stepping back with it.)
- As in the previous kata, keep as low as possible and your back straight.

A

B

C

Figure 104A – C Nami gaeshi. In this kata you are sitting in tatehiza when attacked from the rear. Note that during the nukitsuke, as in the previous kata the left knee is off the ground.

KYUHON ME – TAIKOTOSHI (WATERFALL)

滝落

Bunkai

You are seated in tatehiza when an opponent behind you grabs your saya. You stand up, sweeping your saya out so that the enemy falls first behind and then in front of you. You then make two staggering steps away from him, appearing drunk or at least off balance. You suddenly lean over thrusting into his head and then dropping to your left knee, finishing him off with kirioroshi. You toss the blood off your blade and sheathe it.

Technique

This is the second of the pair to your rear.

- Turn to your rear using your left foot and first exhibiting zanshin.
- Assume tatehiza using Eishin technique.
- As you feel your opponent grab your saya, stand and step out behind yourself with your left foot, turning your trunk 90 degrees to your left. At the same time, sweep the tsuka up through your obi about 14 inches and way to your left. This levers the end of the saya (and your opponent's hand) behind you.
- You then take a step back to the right, with your left foot crossing in front of your left foot and keeping the step high. At the same time sweep the koiguchi with your left hand up in front of your face.
- As your left foot hits the ground grasp the tsuka and start to draw the blade.
- As the sword arcs over your head, tsuka going to the right and slightly down, kissaki still to your left but rising, step your right foot out to right.
- Rotate the saya to facilitate the draw.
- As you step, your body leans first toward the step but then back toward the opponent as your reweight your left foot in a somewhat stiff-legged, toppling fashion.
- Bend sideways at the waist and thrust the kissaki into your opponent's head, sending him to the floor.
- Spin 90 degrees to the left and, as you come down on your left knee, finish the opponent off on the ground with a kirioroshi. Pause.
- End with a standard Eishin chiburi and noto.

Technical Notes

- When you initially step to your left, move the sword as if there were a person attached to the tip of the saya (kojiri).
- When you sweep the sword back you twist it so that the ha is pointed to your left. Your sword and your left foot move together, the latter staying high for a moment.
- The timing of the steps is at first hesitant and then with a little overshoot, making it look as if you are wobbling off balance because of drink.
- The thrust should come suddenly out of your wobbling toward your enemy, and then the kirioroshi out of nowhere as you drop. Be sure to cut over your head.
- Be careful not to make any noise with your knee or to strike the floor with your blade.

JIPPON ME – NUKIUCHI (DRAW AND STRIKE)

抜打

Bunkai

Called makko in Eishin ryu, this kata is essentially the same as that done in Omori ryu, but the sword is handled a little differently. The draw is more vertical, in front of your chest, before you move the sword over your head for the cut. The block is much less well developed.

Figures 105A – F: Taikotoshi. A stiff-legged, rocking kind of step is used that gives the impression of being intoxicated.

Figures 106A – C: The Eishin style of nukiuchi.

OKUDEN – SUWARI

奥伝ー立膝の部

Without doubt, the greatest danger the bugei face in the West (a danger shared precisely by other Japanese arts and for precisely the same reason) is the celebration of their omote and the concomitant ignorance surrounding their ura. The observable in a culture travels easily. The underlying spirit is most difficult to export.

—*Dave Lowry,* Sword and Brush

In trying to change or adapt the traditional techniques of the martial arts, we are viewing the techniques as ends in themselves. Formalized techniques preserve an "inner teaching" which the student is required to dig out and absorb if he is to gain deeper understanding. In the case of the martial arts, the issue is not how we change the techniques as much as it is in how we change ourselves by understanding these techniques.

—*Kensho Furuya,* Kodo: Ancient Ways

The okuden suwari waza are the highest or hidden or secret level of training. As a group they use the quickest of the noto. The kissaki is brought to the koiguchi directly without any sliding of the mune over the left hand at all. The sliding of the blade into the saya is done very rapidly until only about 8 inches of the blade remain exposed. At that point the noto becomes slower and progressively more pensive. There should, however, be no actual pause in the sword movement. Obviously this takes a lot of careful practice; the technique is quite likely to cause you to cut your left hand with the very tip of the blade. Also, the movement toward the saya should be done with very decisive wrist movement or the kissaki will drop below the level of the koiguchi during its rearward travel.

Eishin added the suwari waza, or seated set, to the original jinsuke techniques. Eight in number, they represent techniques used from the tatehiza position when your movements are limited in one way or another by doorways, ladders, walls, or porches. In several you are taking out sentries. Like Eishin ryu waza, many of the okuden waza are said to have been renamed by Oe Masamichi. In this case however, the Muso Shinden ryu adopted the newer names.

IPPON ME – KASUMI
(MIST)

霞

Bunkai

You are sitting in tatehiza when you are threatened from the front. You rise to kiza and cut horizontally, back and forth, driving the enemy back by the action. You then slide forward and finish off the opponent with sho-men kirioroshi. You then throw off the blood from your blade and sheathe it.

Technique

This is the okuden version of all the other ippon me kata and was originally called mukobarai. It differs from the Omori version in that the nukitsuke turns and comes back (kirigaeshi) before beginning the furikaburi. Other differences are the yoko chiburi and the okuden-style noto.

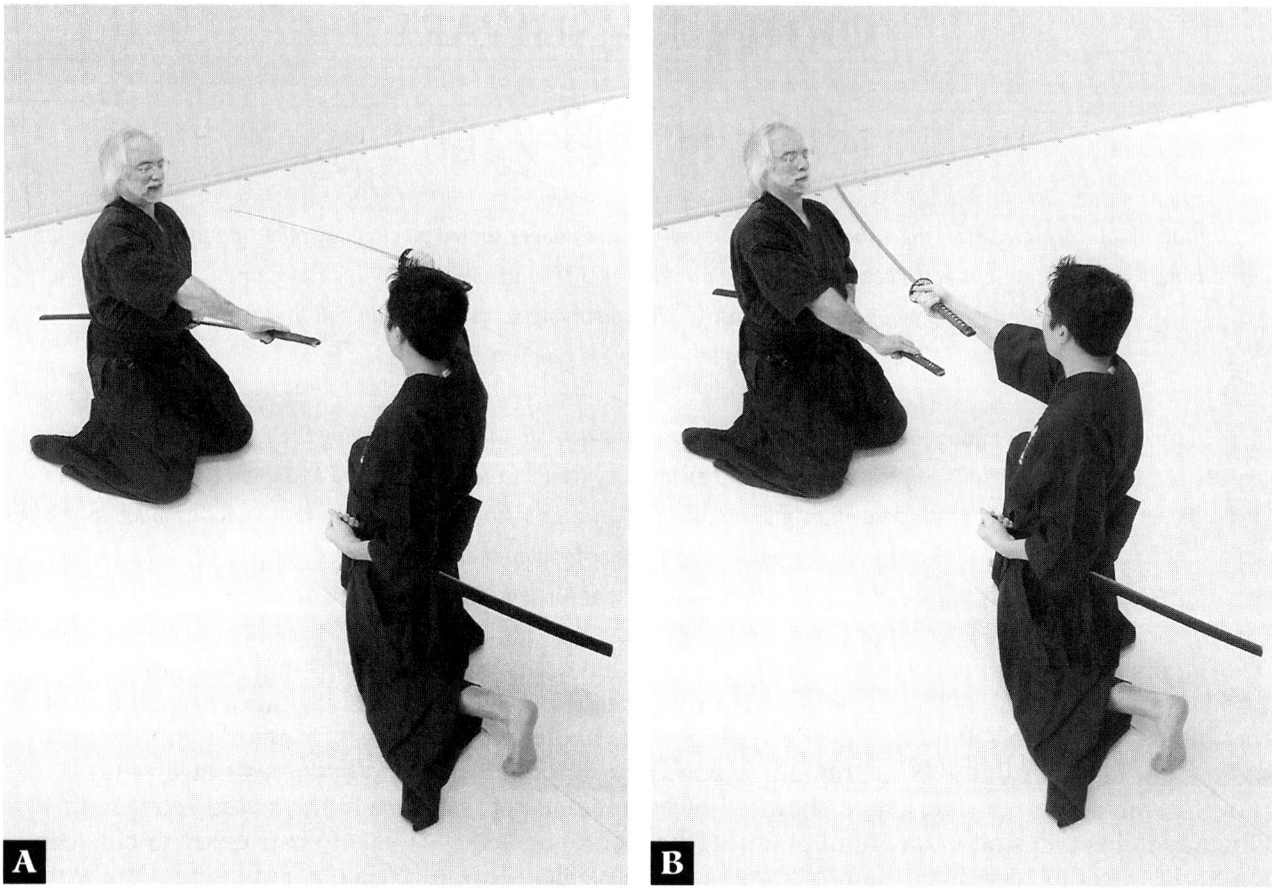

Figures 107A and B: Kasume. This kata is like yokogumo except that the kissaki goes back and forth across the opponent.

- Assume tatehiza by stepping back with the left foot and dropping down on the left knee. Perform left hakamabiki with your right hand and sit back on the medial aspect of your left foot. Perform right hakamabiki with your right hand and slide your right foot toward your left knee, keeping the right toe only an inch or so forward of the knee toward the front (just as done in the Eishin group).
- As you perceive frontal danger, your right fingers rise to the top of the tsuka staying parallel to each other and pointed 45 degrees to the left of front.
- Begin to pull your knees together and rise toward kiza as you push the sword from the saya.
- As the draw continues, the tsuka drifts toward your left.
- When the kissaki is near the koiguchi, the saya is pulled off the rest of the blade by the beginning of a sayabiki.
- At the same time your right foot slides forward with your knee past 90 degrees and your left leg rotates on your left knee, putting your foot directly behind your left knee.
- Your right wrist drives the kissaki toward the left of your opponent. The arm follows it.
- You augment the power of the cut by completing the sayabiki.
- As the nukitsuke begins, your right leg drags your body and left knee forward slightly.
- When you reach the normal extent of a horizontal nukitsuke, you rotate your right wrist clockwise, and with palm upward, bring the sword back along the same path it just took.
- Near the end of the return nukitsuke you convert the motion into furikaburi.

- The sayabiki reverses, and the koiguchi is brought around to your hara as your right leg drags your left knee forward. Your head slides under the tsuka as it is elevated.
- Slide your right foot out forward so that the knee is bent more than 90 degrees as your left hand approaches the tsuka.
- As your left knee is pulled forward you perform a sho-men kirioroshi. The sword should stop with the kissaki 6 inches above the floor, the hands in the midline at hara height. Pause.
- Perform a yoko chiburi by rotating the blade counterclockwise and moving it as a unit down and out toward the right. It ends with the right hand at obi level, top of hand straight, kissaki pointed at a point 10 feet in front of you. Pause.
- As the blade moves to the right, your left hand simultaneously slides to the saya, with your thumb on the top and fingers vertical and parallel.
- You begin noto by turning your wrist toward your left. This directs the kissaki exactly at the koiguchi. Unlike other noto techniques, your right arm remains extended and motionless until the blade enters the saya. Only your wrist moves the blade. Your grip is converted to the "horseshoe" during this motion, that is, holding the tsuka by your finger and thumb tips only.
- The kissaki should engage either the koiguchi directly, or your index finger that is extended below it.
- Sayabiki is performed to further control the kissaki but your right arm does not move out or sideways.
- The sword is quickly swept into the saya by your right hand until there are about 8 inches still exposed. At the same time your right leg is brought back into essentially a tatehiza position with your right foot near your left knee and your right knee out at 45 degrees.
- The noto is not interrupted at this point but the motion is slowed considerably. The saya is rotated by the left hand, turning the blade. All the settling of your spirit and body must occur during this short, slow segment.
- Your right leg and left foot are then straightened with both knees held at right angles and you stand up with your hand still on the tsuka.
- Pull your left leg up to your right with your right leg. Raise your eyes and drop your right hand unobtrusively to your side.

Technical Notes

- This begins and ends like Eishin ippon me. The main difference is the back-and-forth motion of the kissaki. This is a real cut, but the idea is more to startle the opponent into moving backward by putting the moving blade "in his face."
- When reversing the blade during its horizontal travel, it helps to make a little rollover so that the sword turns around a tight curve rather than simply reversing direction in the same plane. This should be very subtle, however. In the shinkage ryu, most sword motions are parts of spirals, which are believed to make the sword more responsive to sudden changes dictated by the opponent.

NIHON ME – SUNEGAKO (ENCIRCLED LEG)

脛囲

Bunkai

You are attacked from the front while you sit in tatehiza. You do not beat your opponent to the draw, and your left leg is restrained so that you must use your nukitsuke to block his strike toward your forward ankle while stepping back with your left leg to gain purchase. Thereafter you drop to your left knee, slide forward during a furikaburi, and cut down your enemy with a sho-men kirioroshi. You throw the blood off your blade and sheathe it using okuden technique.

In fact, this technique is essentially that of Eishin nippon me, except the block comes quicker and somewhat more directly from the saya and the chiburi and noto are those of the omori series. It was originally knonw at tsukadome.

SANBON ME – SHIHOGIRI (FOUR-WAY CUT)

四方切

Bunkai

You are sitting in tatehiza when four opponents threaten you: three in front, one from behind. You rise into kiza and advance, suddenly thrusting back behind you. You then perform kirioroshi in the original direction first, and then to the left and to the right, advancing on your knees during each cut. You toss the blood off your blade and sheathe it. This was originally known at shisumi. *Note:* In some schools the first cut (thrust) is to the immediate rear, not to the left rear.

Technique

- You settle into tatehiza pointing forward, using the same technique as in Eishin kata.
- Your right fingers approach and sit on top of the tsuka as you identify the threat.
- You rise to kiza by pulling your knees together.
- You then slide your right foot out 45 degrees to the right and then you pull your left knee toward your right knee with your right leg. At the same time you draw the sword from the saya, keeping the mune against your chest and do a complete sayabiki.
- You keep your upper body straight and thrust back with the sword along your chest 45 degrees forward of where you stepped out from. At the same time, rotate the koiguchi to your hara so that your hands cross at the midline, with your left hand below your right.
- You then perform furikaburi as you rotate toward the direction of the original draw.
- You slide your right foot out to the front so that your knee is more than a 90-degree angle.

Figures108A – C: Characteristic movements of shihogiri of suwari waza.

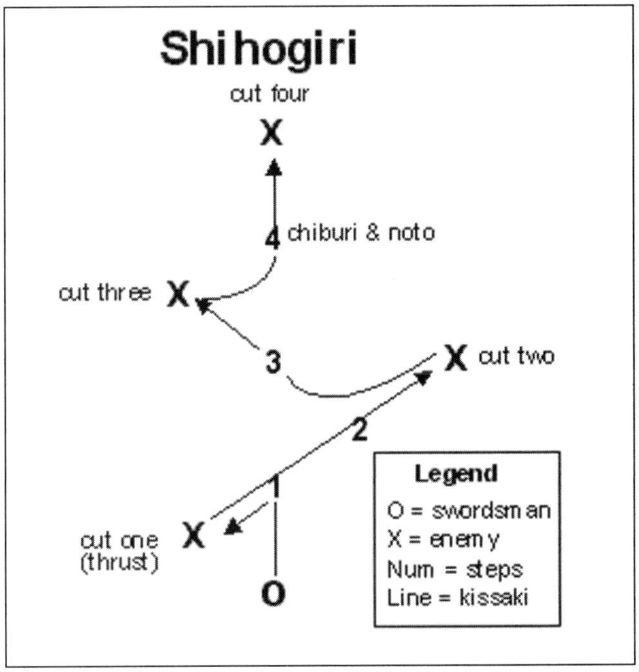

Figure 109: Diagram of suwari waza shihogiri.

- As you pull your left knee toward your right foot, you perform kirioroshi. Briefly pause.
- You turn on your left knee, stepping out with your right foot 90 degrees toward your left so that your right knee is at more than 90 degrees. Simultaneously perform furikaburi.
- Pull your left knee up using your right leg and perform kirioroshi. Pause briefly.
- Spin on your left knee 45 degrees your right (toward the original "forward").
- Slide your right foot out so that your knee is at more than 90 degrees and perform kirioroshi.
- Pull your left knee toward your right foot as you perform kirioroshi. Pause.
- Perform chiburi and noto as in suwari waza ippon me, pulling your right foot to your left knee and twisting your body and shoulders somewhat to the right. The saya should be perpendicular to the front direction.
- Come up on your left knee and straighten your left foot out behind it. Simultaneously slide your right leg straight out in front of you, with your left knee and at 90 degrees rotating your hips and shoulders perpendicular to the forward direction. Pull the tsuka back to your hara.
- Stand and bring your back foot up to the other one. Drop your right hand to your side.

Technical Notes

- Your thrust stops with the mune tight against your left biceps and the tsuka tucked in under your right wrist.
- All your cuts are made as the forward leg pulls the back leg forward.
- Your left leg streams behind your left knee as you change directions. It should always be pointed straight with regard to the direction of cut.
- You use the okuden noto in which the kissaki goes directly into the koiguchi without sliding along the web of your left hand first.

YONHON ME – TOZUMI (BLOCKED DOOR)

戸詰

Bunkai

You are sitting in a doorway, unable to see to either side. As you slide out of the doorway, you are confronted with an enemy on either side. You make a quick vertical nukitsuke to your right, spin and finish off the enemy to the left. You toss the blood off your blade and sheathe it. This was originally called misumi.

Technique

- Assume a forward tatehiza in an Eishin fashion.
- Slide your right foot out in front of you. At the same time you start to draw rotate the saya counterclockwise about 45 degrees as the sword comes out.
- Rise to your left knee.
- Pull your body forward with your right leg. (The kissaki should be at the koiguchi by the end of the slide.)
- As your body stops, a one-handed vertical strike is made to your right, parallel to the wall supposedly on either side of the door you emerged from.
- Turn 180 degrees to the left by pivoting on

Figures 110A and B: The two cuts of tozumi.

your right knee and strike with a sho-men kirioroshi. Pause.

- Perform standard okuden chiburi and noto.
- Push your right foot out with the leg at a right angle and straighten the left foot behind the knee.
- Stand and drag your left foot up to the right.

Technical Notes

- You are deep in a doorway. You have to slide far enough forward to clear the frame and you must cut as soon as you are free of the doorway, first to the right then the left.
- Be sure to orient the left foot directly behind the left knee before the second cut.

- The okuden noto allows you to replace the sword following the second cut despite the presence of the wall immediately to your left.

GOHON ME – TOWAKI (BENEATH DOORWAY)

戸脇

Bunkai

You are sitting in tatehiza and then exit a doorway. You are threatened from each side, just as in the previous kata. Here you choose to thrust into the enemy to your left first, before finishing the one on the right with a sho-men kirioroshi. This was originally called mukozume.

Technique

- You sit in tatehiza using Eishin technique.
- Slide your right foot out straight in front as far as it can practically go and stay soles-down on the floor.
- Place your right fingers on top of the tsuka as you grasp the saya with your left hand.
- As you begin to push the sword out of the saya, allow your right leg to put your body up onto your left knee and then pull it out of the imagined doorway until it gets to your right foot. While this is occurring, continue to draw your blade horizontally across your chest.
- As your body stops moving forward, pull the saya into a sayabiki and lay the mune of the sword blade horizontally along your chest at nipple height.
- Immediately thrust the blade horizontally to your left. At the same time rotate the koiguchi around the top of your obi with your left hand, bringing your biceps up to stop the tsuba from going out too far.
- Rotate around your left knee keeping the leg behind it, step out with your right foot, and perform a vertical sho-men kirioroshi 180 degrees to the right of your original thrust. Pause.
- While remaining in kiza, perform a vertical chiburi and noto as described in the beginning sections of this book. Take care that the kojiri of the saya does not strike the floor during the noto, for it will be very close because you are on your knees.
- Rotate 90 degrees to the left around your left knee then stand and bring your left foot up to your right one.

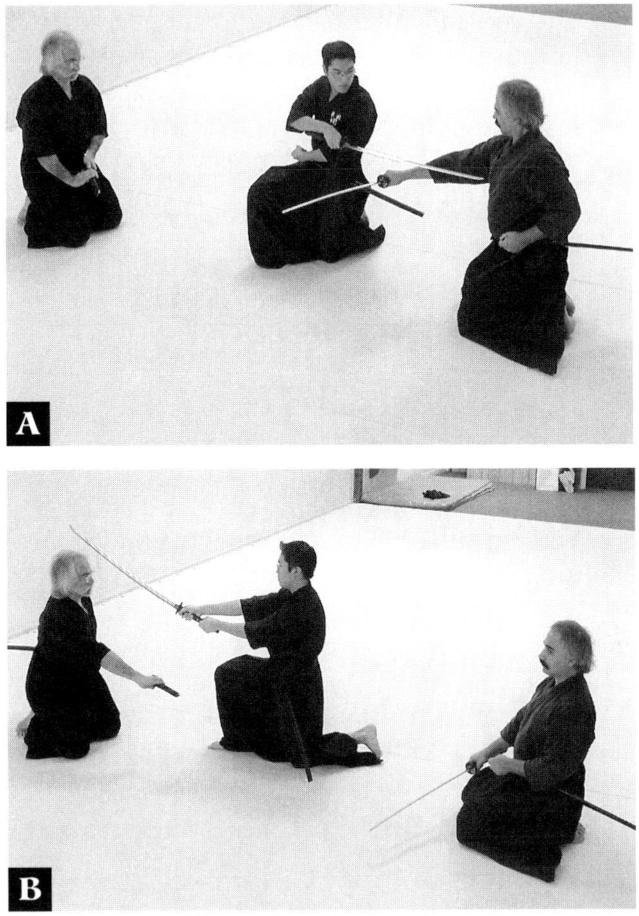

Figures 111A and B: The two cuts of towaki.

Technical Notes

- As with the previous kata, you are pulling yourself out of a doorway, probably out onto a porch.
- You must thrust as soon as you are free of the door or you will be cut first.
- The thrust is parallel to the wall to your left out of the doorway.
- The cut to the right is parallel to the wall on that side of the door.

- The vertical chiburi and noto are necessary because there is not enough room between you and the wall to do classic ones.
- A variation of the last two kata is to pull yourself back into the doorway using your left leg and remaining in tatehiza instead of standing.

ROPPON ME – TANASHITA (BENEATH LEDGE)

棚下

Bunkai

You are sitting in tatehiza looking under a stairway or ramp at an enemy. You attack by drawing your sword, placing it over your back and sliding under the ramp until you are free to perform an overhead strike. You then shake the blood from your blade and sheathe it.

Technique

- Assume tatehiza in the Eishin fashion.
- Bring your right fingers up to the tsuka; bend your body, shoulders, and head forward as you push your blade out of the saya in front of you.
- While continuing to bend forward perform a very close furikaburi, placing the mune of the blade on the back of your head and neck.
- Continue to support the koiguchi with your left hand.
- Keeping as low as possible, slide your right

Figure 112: Tanashita. The swordsman must come out from under an overhang to be able to strike his opponent.

foot out as far in front of you as it will go.
- Pull yourself forward with your right leg, keeping to the ground in front of you.
- Rise up into the standard kneeling position with your left knee down and your right leg forward, then raise your blade over your head.
- Slide your right foot out again, past 90 degrees, and as your pull yourself forward and performing a sho-men kirioroshi. Pause.
- Perform a yoko chiburi and okuden noto, pulling your right leg back with your knee up as you do in Eishin.
- Assume the kiza and then stand, pulling your back (left) leg forward.
- Drop your hand.

Technical Notes

- Try to keep as near to the ground as possible. During the first furikaburi, the blade should stay near, first, your left ear and then the top of your head.
- When you stretch out and make your first sliding step, keep the blade from bouncing or twisting as you slide.
- You straighten up, raise your sword, and step with the right foot all at the same time.
- Cut on motion of the back knee sliding forward.

NANAHON ME – RYOZUME (BOTH SIDES BLOCKED)

両詰

Bunkai

You are sitting in tatehiza under an overhanging ledge when someone crawls in to attack you from your front. You draw your blade, keeping it close, and then thrust at your opponent, pushing him back out from under the overhang. Keeping the kissaki pointed at the enemy, you slide out from under the overhang yourself and then finish him off with the overhead sho-men kirioroshi you could not complete in the tight quarters. You then shake off the blood and sheathe your sword.

Technique

- Assume tatehiza as in the previous kata.

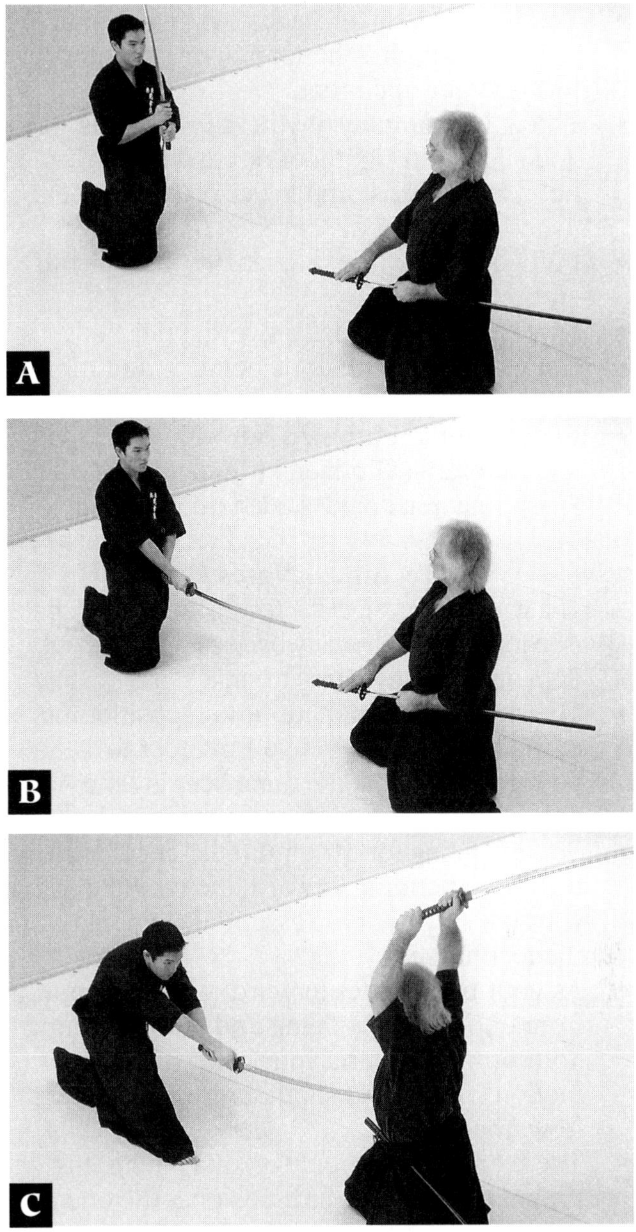

Figures 113A – C: Ryozume. This is also an attack out from under an overhang.

- Place your right fingers on the tsuka and push your sword from your saya, keeping it flat and somewhat to the right (exactly the opposite of a noto).
- Perform a furikaburi keeping the sword horizontal and close to your head. Then bring the tsuka down close in front of your face until it reaches your hara. This should look like a very slow, very tight sho-men cut with no extension whatsoever.

- Rotate the blade as it goes over your head and face until it is horizontal and pointed toward your opponent.
- Thrust horizontally at your opponent as you slide your right foot out toward him. Bend at the waist and lower your shoulders to get maximum distance.
- Pull your body forward, leaving your sword motionless.
- As you get closer to the sword, your body comes upright with arms bending and hips under shoulders and head.
- Perform furikaburi, step out with your right foot, and do a sho-men kirioroshi. Pause.
- Finish with a standard okuden chiburi and noto.

Technical Notes

- The whole purpose of the technique of this kata is to force your adversary back as you slide out from under the overhang to strike him.
- The combined furikaburi and repositioning of the blade in front of you in order to perform the thrust are done keeping the sword as close to your body as possible.
- You are going for maximum distance in the thrust, so bending forward and pushing with your left foot are essential elements of the technique.
- As your body slides forward, you come out from under the overhang and straighten up. Your arms bend and your head stays motionless as your shoulders and hips slide forward under it.
- There are only a couple of kata where it is proper to bend forward: this one, the one following, and the two inyoshintai kata of the Omori ryu (Kamimoto-ha also bends forward during the thrust of seitei morotezuki).

HACHIHON ME – TORABASHIRI (CHARGING TIGER)

虎走

Bunkai

You are sitting in tatehiza observing a sentry in the dark or with his back turned to you. You silently run toward him drawing, dropping to a knee, slashing, and then finishing him off. You then are chased back by another sentry and you finish him off in the same fashion while you retreat.

Technique

- Assume tatehiza in the okuden manner.
- Bring your right fingers to the tsuka and your left hand to the saya as you start to pinch your knees together in expectation of rising up.
- Rise past kiza and assume a low crouch on both feet. Bend somewhat at the waist but don't overdo it.
- Take four short, sliding steps forward, starting with your right foot. The timing of these steps is increasingly fast as you approach the sentry.
- The fifth step consists of sliding your right foot forward and dropping to your left knee. As you do this you draw your sword for a horizontal cut.
- You perform a nukitsuke with a good sayabiki, which ends as your left knee contacts the ground.
- You immediately perform furikaburi and kirioroshi in the usual fashion. Pause.
- Perform an okuden chiburi and start an okuden noto.
- When the sword is halfway into the saya start a series of four sliding steps with your left (back) leg back toward whence you came. The rhythm is the same as the forward action, but the steps get progressively quicker. Continue to finish the noto but leave your hands on the tsuka and saya.
- The fifth step consists of sliding your left leg back and dropping to your left knee.
- You do the same nukitsuke, furikaburi, and kirioroshi you did the first time. Pause.
- Then do an okuden chiburi and noto while in kiza.
- Stand, bring your left foot up to your right one, and drop your right hand.

Technical Notes

- The sliding steps should look effortless. You

Figures 114A and B: Torabashiri. This is an exercise in silent running in a hakama. Notice that the left knee is off the ground at the time of the nukitsuke.

must do this in a way that does not cause your head to bounce.

- The posture makes you look diminutive until you strike.
- You speed up as you get to your target. In a way, all the timing of this part is like a simple nukitsuke. You start slowly and cautiously, reading your adversary and gradually speeding up, gaining confidence until you are committed to a cut.
- When you drop to your knee for the nukitsuke, you should try to slide a little using the momentum of your forward motion to augment the power of your cut.
- In order to start the rearward movement, coordinate a slide of your left foot with the backward movement of your blade sliding into the saya.
- On the fifth step backward plant your right foot and slide your left back as you draw. This gives your opponent the appearance that your body is still moving backward when in fact, it is not. In this fashion you draw him into your cut.

OKUDEN – TACHI

奥伝ー立業の部

In training don't think about martial arts with your head; put your head in your locker with your clothes. Put on your uniform, enter the training area, bow humbly, and throw yourself completely into your training. What more is there?
—Kensho Furuya, Kodo: Ancient Ways

The ryu do not exist as autonomous entities. Without loving and strict ministration, they will soon stagnate and evaporate. To keep them alive and fresh and flowing is the responsibility of those bugeisha entrusted with their care.
—Dave Lowry, Sword and Brush

All the rivers run into the sea, yet the sea is not full, unto the place from whence the rivers come, thither they return again.
—Ecclesiastes 1:7

The okuden tachi waza (or secret standing set) is the most advanced of the levels and presumably represents the remnants of the original techniques developed and taught by Hayashizaki Jinsuke Shigenobu. To what extent they resemble the original is a matter of conjecture: they have undergone the interpretation of 21 generations of headmasters since his time. In general they represent either large, crowd-controlling kata, or smaller specialized situations such as striking over a balcony or when exiting a doorway. These use the fastest, shortest of the noto, just like the okuden suwari waza.

IPPON ME – YUKIZURI (PULL TOGETHER)

行連

Bunkai

You are walking through a doorway with a wall on each side. Upon exiting you find yourself threatened by adversaries on either side. You step to the left avoiding a cut from the right, draw and perform a right vertical nukitsuke. You then quickly turn in the opposite direction and finish off the opponent on the left with a kirioroshi. You flick the blood from your blade and return it to its saya.

Technique

This is pretty much the tachi waza version of suwari yonhon me, except that this is probably the original and the suwari waza is the more recent addition.

- Begin walking forward, starting with your right foot.
- Following the third step (right) you react to a threat from both your right and left by first stepping sideways toward your left, placing your right fingers on the tsuka and rocking back on the left foot while at the same time beginning a near vertical nukitsuke.
- When the kissaki reaches the koiguchi step to your right with your right foot, and on your back-foot motion cut the right-hand challenger.
- Immediately turn 180 degrees while performing furikaburi and cut the left enemy with a sho-

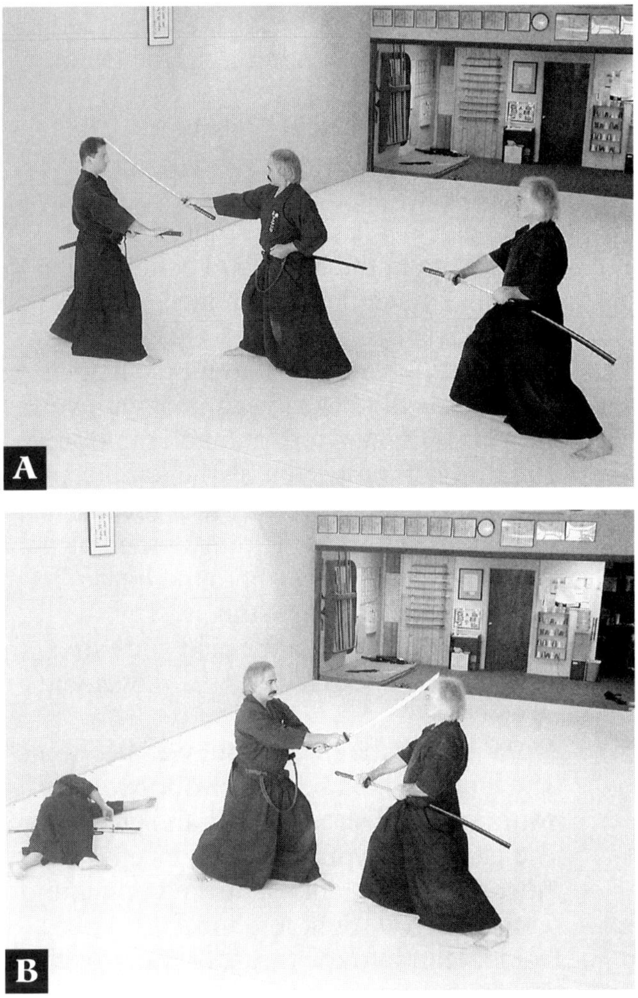

Figures 115A and B: Yukizuri.
The swordsman quickly cuts right, then left.

men kirioroshi without stepping out with the right foot (i.e., cut with left foot forward). Pause.

- Perform a yoko chiburi and then an okuden noto.
- Bring your right foot up to your left, and as you turn 90 degrees to your right you drop your right hand to your side.

Technical Notes

- You must respond with your eyes and head before you step to your left.
- You don't so much pull your blade out but pull the saya off the motionless blade while shifting your body sideways. When the blade is completely exposed, your body moves back to the right and you cut in that direction.
- The nukitsuke should be at about a 30-degree angle off vertical, and the blade should cover your body from left shoulder to right waist. Do not let the kissaki go farther sideways than the line of your right shoulder.
- Do not hesitate after the nukitsuke, but immediately pivot on the balls of your feet to your rear.
- Be sure the kirioroshi starts from midline above your head, not over a shoulder.
- The cut is begun with a contraction of the abdominal muscles, rotating the hips under the spine, and pulling the back (left) foot forward. This, rather than the arms, provides the power for the cut.

NIHON ME – TSUKEDACHI (SUCCESSFUL COMBINATION)

連達

Bunkai

As in the last kata, you are exiting a doorway and find opponents in the same positions as in the first kata. This time you shift toward the right, drawing your sword, and thrust sideways into the left-side enemy. You then turn 180 degrees and cut the other man with a sho-men cut, shake off the blood, and sheathe your blade.

Technique

This is the standing equivalent of suwari gohon me, but developmentally older.

- You begin by walking forward, starting with the right foot.
- As you step out of the imaginary doorway you notice a threat on each side of you and respond with your eyes.
- After your second step forward, you grip the tsuka with your right hand and step with your right foot to the right, avoiding the attack from your left.
- As you shift to the right, you draw your

Figures 116A and B: Tsukedachi. The swordsman quickly thrusts to the left then cuts to the right.

sword, keeping it as close to your body as you can. At the end you put your weight on the right foot with your blade horizontal, the mune against your chest at nipple height, and your left hand in sayabiki.

- You step horizontally to the left with your left foot first, and when your back foot moves up you thrust into your first opponent. As you thrust you rotate the koiguchi along the top of your obi to your hara with your left hand.
- Immediately swivel on the balls of your feet 180 degrees to the right while performing furikaburi.
- Strike the second opponent with a sho-men kirioroshi. Pause.
- Perform an okuden chiburi and noto. Move your left foot up to your right one.
- Turn 90 degrees to the left with your left foot and drop your hand from the tsuka.

Technical Notes

- As you draw for the thrust to the first enemy, keep the blade against your body at all times. As it first comes out of the koiguchi from the backward action of the sayabiki, the entire sword, including the kissaki, will be at obi level. Quickly slide the mune up your chest to nipple height without the blade losing contact with your body or losing its horizontal orientation.
- The thrust is supported by the left biceps that is brought forward by the "reverse sayabiki:" that is, the sliding of the koiguchi around the top of the obi to the hara. The biceps keep the thrust straight. The movement of both hands also adds strength to the thrust and balances the movement in-yo.
- At the end of the thrust your weight should be evenly divided between your two feet. Your right heel should be off the ground. The tsuba is beyond your left biceps muscle, and the tsuka is tucked under and parallel to your right forearm.
- Do not lean into the thrust or thrust behind the line of your shoulders.
- There is no pause between thrust and cut, left and right. Pivot on ball of your left foot and on the right heel as you do furikaburi and be sure to cut from over your head.

SANBON ME – SOMAKURI (ALL WHIRLWIND)

惣捲

Bunkai

You are walking forward and are confronted from the front. You draw your sword and perform a series of progressively lower yoko cuts, sweep across your enemy's belly, and then finish him off with a sho-men cut. You clean your blade and sheathe it. This was originally called gohogiri.

Figure 117: The horizontal cut in somakuri is delivered with a left step.

Technique

- This kata is the origin of the seitei kata sougiri. Two differences are the fourth step and the type of noto used.
- Begin walking forward with your right foot first.
- As you take your third step (with your right foot), place your fingers upon the tsuka.
- Reweight your left foot and pull your right foot backward as you pull the saya off your stationary blade and perform furikaburi.
- Step forward again with your right foot and make a right yoko-men strike to the midline of the neck on back-foot motion.
- Make another right-foot shuffle step and make a lower yoko strike to the enemy's left neck on the back-foot motion to the midline of his chest.
- Make another sliding right-foot step as you make a lower diagonal cut to the enemy's right shoulder to the middle of his abdomen.
- Step forward deeply with your left foot as you bring your sword down to obi level and cut horizontally across your enemy's hara.
- Step with your right foot as you finish him off with a sho-men kirioroshi.
- Perform okuden chiburi and noto.

Technical Notes

- The draw of the sword should be done so that the sword does not appear to move but the body and saya step back away from it, and then as it rises up, the body moves back underneath it. The forward-backward rhythm should be like the ebb and flow of the surf.
- Each successive vertical cut is made at a greater angle, but they all start from directly overhead. This prevents telegraphing your move to your enemy, as well as leaving open more options in response to your enemy's potential actions.
- The horizontal cut also starts from straight above your head, and then drops down to belt level before moving clockwise from your left. Keep your hands in your center.
- The transition from the end of the horizontal slash to the final kirioroshi is not a formal furikaburi but a rapid flipping up of the blade with a lot of wrist action. This change in timing throws your opponent's timing off as the cut comes more quickly that expected.

YONHON ME – SODOME (COMPLETE RESOLUTION)

総留

Bunkai

You are walking in an alley and are confronted head-on by a crowd. You pressure them to retreat by performing a series of yoko nukitsuke as you advance until they are out of the alley. Then you complete your chiburi and noto. An optional kata is to do the same thing while retreating through the alley. This was originally known at hanashiuchi.

Technique

- Start walking forward, starting with your right foot.

- On the end of the first step put your right fingers on the tsuka.
- During the second (left foot) step draw the blade with it rotated off vertical by about 20 degrees. Hold the tsuka high enough so that you can see your enemy under it.
- On the back-foot motion of the third step perform a diagonal nukitsuke, covering your left shoulder to your right hip. At the same time do a sayabiki.
- Your stance during the cut should be slightly rotated toward your left so that you are offering a smaller target. Your knees should be bent and your feet evenly weighted. Pause.
- Begin a seitei-type noto. As the blade slides into the saya you step with your left (back) foot across the front of your right foot. At the end of the step the blade should be no farther in the saya than half.
- Step forward with your right foot and make another diagonal nukitsuke just like the first.
- Repeat the fifth and sixth steps one more time (total of three nukitsuke).
- After the pause following the third nukitsuke, pivot on the balls of your feet toward the front and at the same time do a yoko chiburi. Pause.

To continue backward:

- Begin a seitei-type noto. As the blade slides in you step with your right foot back behind your left, keeping your knees bent. At the end of this step, no more than half the blade should be within the saya.
- As you step back with your left foot make another diagonal nukitsuke.
- Repeat the ninth and 10th steps nine twice more.
- Do a yoko chiburi as in step eight.
- Do a seitei noto, bring up the left foot, and drop your right hand to your side.

Technical Notes

- As you move forward, you make a series of sideways shuffles with your feet. When your left foot advances over your right you are sheathing the blade at the same rate. You are cutting with each right-foot advance.

Figure 118: Sodome is an exercise in crowd control.

- When you are retreating you are sheathing during the right-foot backward step and cutting on the left foot's retreat.
- No matter which direction you are going in, the shuffle step requires your knees to be bent.
- At the time of each nukitsuke your weight should be evenly divided between your feet.
- Forward and backward, you body faces the left to present a smaller target. The only time you are pointed forward is when you do a chiburi and the final noto.
- Be sure your nukitsuke are high and crisp and accompanied by a strong sayabiki. Each should be identical.

GOHON ME – SHINOBU (STEALTHILY)

信夫

Bunkai

You are confronted by a crowd arrayed in front of you whose ringleader is in the center toward the rear. As you walk forward you scatter the crowd with a wide horizontal nukitsuke and then make a surprise kirioroshi, throwing off the enemies' timing and striking the leader with a sho-men cut while you lead with the "wrong" (left) foot. This was originally called yoru no tachi (literally, faithful husband).

Technique

- Begin walking forward with your right foot.
- On the second step place your hands on the tsuka.
- On the third step (right foot) do a wide, relatively slow, horizontal nukitsuke.
- At the end of the nukitsuke, way to your right, rotate your wrist to do a very quick furikaburi.
- On the fourth step (left foot) do a sho-men kirioroshi.
- Do a yoko chiburi and an okuden noto.

Technical Notes

- This is pretty straightforward except for the timing of the kirioroshi. Ordinarily you would take one step to do a furikaburi and cut on the next right footstep. Doing the kirioroshi on the left foot throws your enemy's timing off.

Figure 119: Controlling the crowd with a sweeping nukitsuke in the kata shinobu.

Figure 120: Tapping on the ground to "draw the fire" of your opponent in the alternate version of shinobu.

- The wide horizontal nukitsuke is to scatter the retainers in front of the ringleader to get to him quickly.

Author's note: The above description is of the kata as taught by Dach Sensei. It seems likely to the author based on the study of old films and the literature that this version evolved from a technique also called *shinobu* (stealthily) or *yodachi* (night sword). In this version, the bunkai is that of finding an opponent in the dark by tapping the tip of the sword on the ground and then cutting based on the noise of the enemy attacking that place. One method of doing this is nicely described and illustrated by K. Taylor (1993).

ROPPON ME – YUKICHIGAI (DISAGREEMENT)

伝違

Bunkai

Two opponents approach you from the front and rear. You move forward, striking the first one in the face with the kashira, pushing him back. You turn and block the strike coming at you from the opponent that was following your back and finish him with a vertical kirioroshi. You then turn back around and kill the original opponent with a vertical strike. You clean your blade and place it back in its saya.

Technique

- This is similar to seitei hachihon me except that the strike is higher and closer and you use a block as you turn rather than preparing for a thrust.
- Begin walking forward with your right foot first.
- On the third step place your right fingers on the tsuka.
- On the back-foot motion of the third step you drive the kashira into the face of your opponent.
- Step around behind with your right foot, simultaneously holding the tsuka up and pulling the saya off the blade as you turn, forming a block.
- Step through with your right foot while

doing furikaburi and on the back (left) foot motion you perform a sho-men kirioroshi.

- Step back again and cut to the front with a sho-men kirioroshi.
- Perform a yoko chiburi and an okuden noto.

Technical Notes

- When performing the strike, it is very easy to pull the saya up too high. It may come out of your obi or, more commonly, stay in the obi, but on the draw get pushed down inside your hakama, which pretty much limits your motion.
- The furikaburi that goes from the block and to the kirioroshi is very quick and requires a flexible wrist.
- After each sho-men strike, as you turn, do not allow the kissaki to drift right or left but leave them embedded in the enemies until they are pulled out by your forward motion.
- This kata is performed fairly close in, not with the ranging kind of reversal steps used in morotezuki.

Figures 121A – D: Sequence of events during yukichigai.

NANAHON ME – SODE SURIGAESHI (SLEEVE REPLY)

袖摺返

Bunkai

You approach a hostile crowd with the leader behind its center. You draw your sword and, holding it vertically in your right hand, sweep the crowd away from in front of the leader. You finish him off with a vertical cut, then clean and replace your blade.

Technique

This is one of those kata (such as Omori kyuhon) in which once you start walking, you keep walking.

- Begin to walk forward starting with your right foot.
- On the third (right-foot) step place your

Figure 122: Spreading the crowd away in order to cut the ring leader standing behind them in sode surigaeshi.

right fingers on the tsuka.

- Rock back on your left foot as you pull the saya from the stationary blade and then cross your forearms, right in front of left, holding the sword vertical, ha pointed to your left. Your left hand is open, fingers pointed up, palm toward the right.
- Step forward with your right foot again and as you do so sweep both arms across your front, essentially pushing the crowd away to either side. To facilitate that, as you sweep the sword from left to right twist your wrist so that the ha leads the blade.
- As you take your next (left-foot) step, simultaneously perform furikaburi.
- As you take the next step (right foot) on the back-foot motion perform a sho-men kirioroshi. Pause.
- Do a yoko chiburi and an okuden noto.

Technical Notes

- This draw is another in which the sword appears not to move and the body pulls the saya off with its reverse motion.
- You must complete the crossing of your arms before starting to step forward again.
- You make your sweeping move on the forward motion of your front (right) foot, not the back foot. The same goes for the furikaburi on the next (left) step.
- The backward/forward motion of your body during the third and fourth steps should be like the ebb and flow of the surf.
- In sweeping the arms the hand does what the sword does; the front, either the palm or the ha, turns 180 degrees during the sweep, allowing each to threaten the crowd you are trying to disperse.
- Your steps dictate the timing of this kata; the upper body motion must be adjusted to match the steady motion of the stepping.
- Slide your feet and don't bob up and down while doing this kata.
- The final cut, kirioroshi, is made on the back foot movement. The cut should be delayed until the last moment—it is important not to get the sword over your head too fast or it will have to hang there awhile, telegraphing your intent.

HACHIHON ME – MON IRI (GATE PERSON)

門人

Bunkai

You are standing under a gate when you are threatened from the front and back simultaneously. You step forward, drawing your blade close into your hara, bring it alongside your right hip and immediately thrust it into the front enemy. You then turn and strike the enemy behind you and then turn again and finish the first one before tossing off the blood and sheathing your sword. This was originally called kakuresute.

Technique

- Start walking forward with your right foot first.
- By the end of this step your right fingers should be on the top of your tsuka.
- As start your second (left-foot) step you draw your sword, swinging the tsuka toward the right and then behind you, keeping the mune on your obi at all times.
- By the time you finish this step, the tsuka should be tucked in along your right hip with the sword horizontal and pointing forward.
- Take your third step (right foot), and on the rear-foot action thrust the blade into your front opponent's solar plexus. Do this with a simultaneous sayabiki.
- Turn to your left exactly as you do in the second half of seitei hachihon me, stepping off to your rear with your left foot as you bring your head and saya around, and then stepping through with your right foot while doing a furikaburi.
- On the motion of the back foot ending this step, finish the challenger in back with a sho-men kirioroshi.
- Reverse directions again and strike the enemy in front with a sho-men cut.
- Perform a yoko chiburi and an okuden noto.

Technical Notes

- This has elements of other, earlier kata. The

Figures 123A – D: Parts of the sequence of mon iri.

main difference is the speed with which you must get your sword positioned and then perform the thrust.

- Control your sword near the end of this draw by resting the mune on your obi and grasping the kissaki with the index finger and thumb of your right hand in an unobtrusive manner.
- Keeping the blade close in and getting it parallel to your direction of travel robs your opponent of the ability to judge the working distance of your blade (maai).
- Be sure to do a good sayabiki with the thrust.
- The first reversal (gaeshi) is like that in gamman ate (one-handed), the second, is like that in morotezuki (two-handed).

KYUHON ME – KABEZOE (WALL COMPANION)

壁添え

Bunkai

You are walking out of a second-story doorway onto a balcony with a railing. As you walk up to it you draw and then cut over the top of the railing down onto the head of your rival below. You must get up on your toes to do this. You then throw the blood off your blade and sheathe it, settling back down onto the soles of your feet as you do. This was originally known as hito naka.

Technique

- You start walking forward with your right foot.
- By the end of the second step, you have placed your right fingers upon the tsuka.
- As you begin the third step you draw the blade vertically and perform furikaburi.
- As your back (left) foot comes up to level with your right one, you cut, bending somewhat at the waist and standing up on your toes. Pause.
- Perform a vertical chiburi and noto while keeping your heels off the floor.
- As the blade slides into the saya, drop your heels to the floor.
- Drop your right hand to your side.

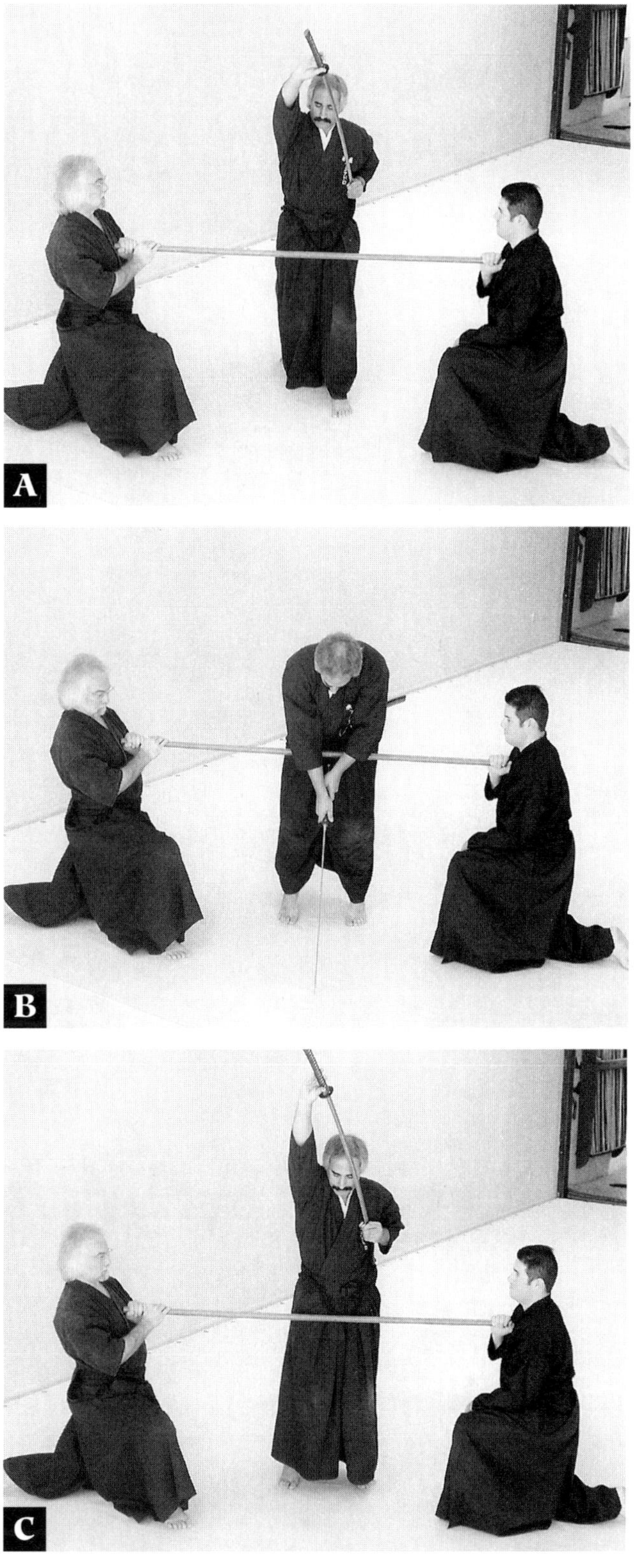

Figures 124A – C: The draw, cut, and sheathing for kabezoe. The pole represents a balcony rail. The enemy is on the floor below, and the strike is going to the top of his head. Note how the sword comes out and goes in the same direction.

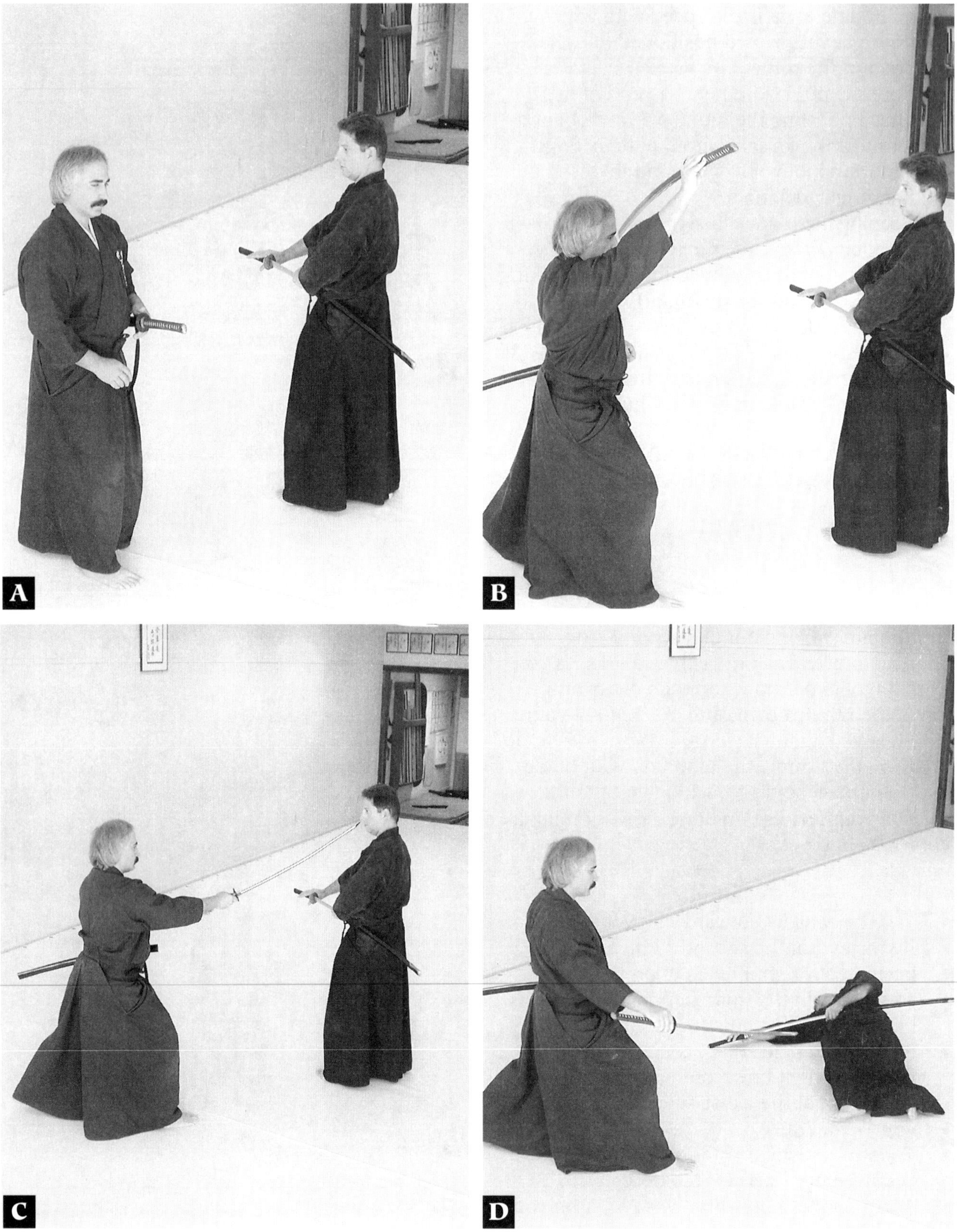

Figures 125A through D: Some of the steps of ukenagashi.

Technical Notes

- The kirioroshi, bending at the waist, and getting up on toes should all be simultaneous and smooth enough not to throw you off balance.
- The kissaki should end up only inches from the floor at the end of the cut (in actuality it's below your feet).
- When you do your chiburi, you're still leaning over the railing.
- Straighten up as you do your noto and come down from your toes during the time that the last third of the blade is sheathed.
- The blade is drawn and replaced at the same vertical angle in front of the left shoulder.

Author's note: An alternate interpretation and performance of this kata is with the action occuring in an extremely narrow alley, which requires the tight approach to both the cut and the chiburi noto, but without any railing.

JIPPON ME – UKENAGASHI (FLOWING BLOCK)

流受

Bunkai

You are approaching another samurai, and about to pass on the street, when he starts to draw as he gets opposite you. You draw and block his cut and then hop back a step as you finish him off with a vertical kirioroshi. You step back as you throw off the blood and sheathe your sword and continue on your way. This was originally known as yurumi nuki.

Technique

- You start walking forward with your right foot first.
- On the third step place your right fingers on the tsuka.
- Weight your back (left) foot without stepping back and raise your sword into an overhead block, such as in the other ukenagashi, while looking 45 degrees to your left.
- Perform furikaburi.
- As you prepare for kirioroshi, you hop backward with the back (left) foot and at the same time turn about 45 degrees to your left.
- Your feet land, front first, closely followed by the rear as the sword cuts your opponent with a sho-men kirioroshi. Pause.
- Perform a yoko-chiburi as you step rearward a half step, left foot first, then the right trailing. Pause.
- Perform okuden noto. Step up with your left foot, rotating to your right to point in the original starting direction. Step to the rear as you drop your right hand unobtrusively to your side.

Technical Notes

- The essence of this kata is that your challenger has gotten too close to you before he starts to draw. You cannot draw and thrust as in tsukedachi.
- You use the block to gain time to step back and then cut quickly, ruining his timing. You have to jump backward to gain proper spacing (maai) during the cut, and then you use the stamping of your feet to gain power in the cut, much as in kendo.
- As in all ukenagashi, be sure your block is in front as well as above your left shoulder.
- After the cut you're still close enough that you must step backward to do your chiburi and noto.

JUIPPON ME – ITOMAGOI (FAREWELL VISIT)

暇し

Bunkai

You are seated in seiza facing another samurai your lord has ordered you to kill. As you begin bowing to each other you suddenly draw and instantly cut him with a vertical kirioroshi strengthened by a lateral motion of your knees. Remaining seated, you perform a chiburi and noto and then assume a quiet seiza.

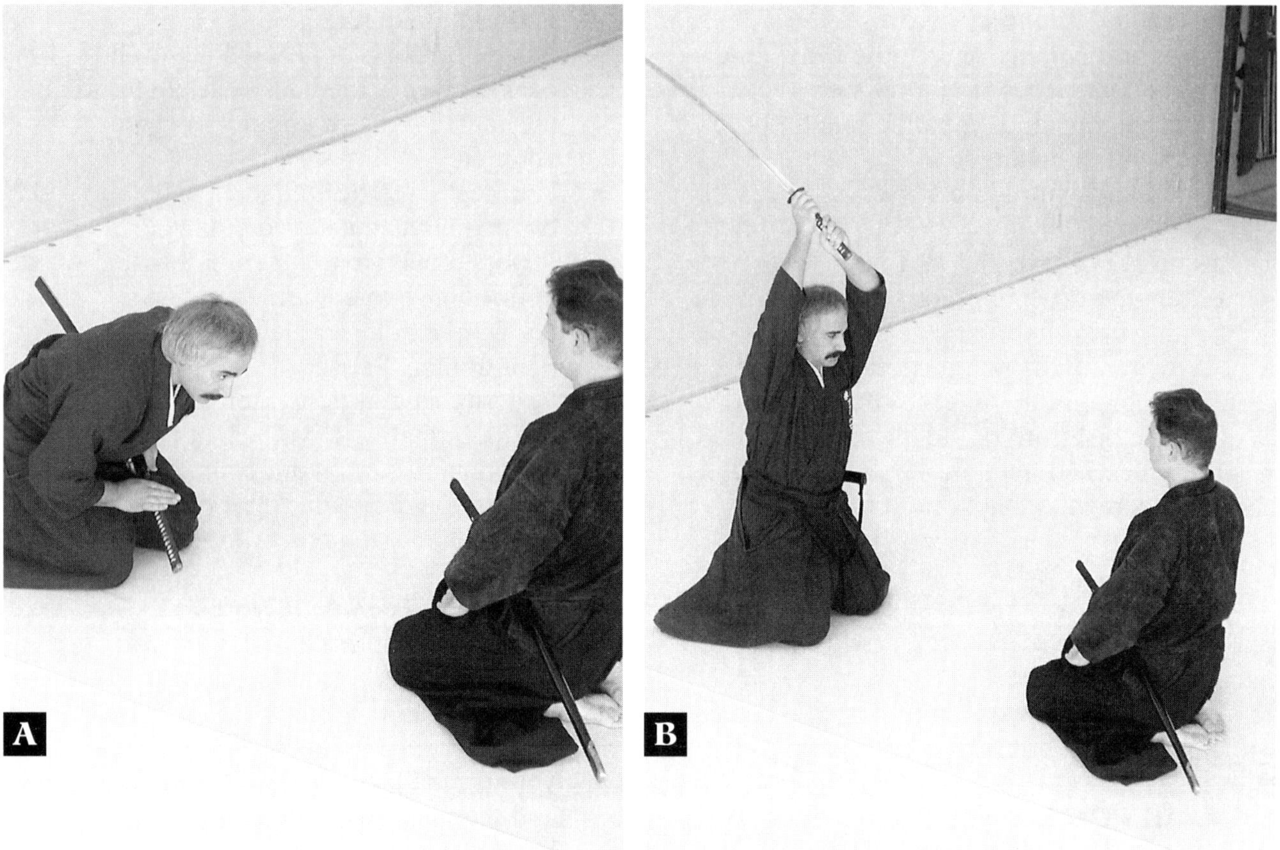

Figures 126A and B: Two of the steps of itomagoi. Notice that the draw comes from much more of a bow than occurs with the other variations of nukiuchi.

Technique

- This is similar to the other varieties of nukiuchi except for the following:
  - An actual bow is begun.
  - The tsuka with your right hand on it goes nearly to the floor before the draw starts.
  - There is little block, and the cut is initiated quicker with a minimum of movement.

TACTICS

Kendo students face each other in standing position to determine victory or defeat. Iai is the art of cutting, thrusting, and defense, with great diversity of application. While sitting, standing, or walking, and attacked from all sides, the swordsman must anticipate, defend and retaliate. Iai is concerned with attack and defense in terms of ma-ai, hasuji, te-no-uchi: distance, the center of the sword stroke, and grasping the tsuka. In unity with the same is the spirit of entering into the opponent's attack with harmonious sword and body action, to defeat the enemy though his psychological weakness. This is true self-defense.

Yet greater than technique is spiritual training. Iai does not necessarily mean to cut an enemy, but rather to cut the enemy within yourself. Victory in Iai is the non-revengeful heart and the cessation of conflict though not drawing the sword. Thus, you may understand why the Iai of old was called saya-no-uchi, invincibility without drawing the sword.

In other words, Iai is a training process toward human perfection, never of murderous intent, but peaceful-minded. The modern significance of Iai is peace and tranquility for human life. In the larger sense Iai means the Way of Dwelling in Harmony: through endless practice seeking harmony with the Universe.

—Kazuo Oya

Victories often have hidden causes. ... Muhammad (PBUH) said, "War is trickery." An Arab proverb says, "Many a trick is worth more than a tribe."

—Ibn Kaldoun, Muqaddimah

As clearly demonstrated in foregoing sections, the kata we practice today were derived during different historical periods. They were purposely modified by numerous headmasters and have gradually evolved and are evolving today as they are transmitted to each generation of students. To draw generalities about Japanese swordsmanship from a knowledge of iaido kata is speculative at best. On the other hand, taken as a whole, certain patterns appear from these kata.

It is known that the typical one-on-one sword fight lasted but a few seconds. With two adversaries unafraid to die and confident in their skill and their honor, one of three outcomes would quickly occur. One or another of the swordsman would die, or they both would die (*aiuchi*). There was little time for speculation or planning. Once either of the swordsmen committed himself the die was cast and the outcome a matter of reflex. Survival or not depended to a great extent on a swordsman's ability to mislead his opponent as to his intentions, his reach, or his physical presence.

One of the tactics that permeates these kata is the nature of the one-handed cut. While it certainly would cause damage if successful in striking the adversary, it seems much more important as a means of throwing the opponent off his stride. The assumption is that it takes a certain amount of time to set up a killing cut. The one-handed cut is much less likely to finish the opponent, but can be made more quickly. This throws the opponent's timing off and forces him to restart the process of attack or, indeed, to go into a defensive posture.

Often following up the one-handed cut is a quick two-handed kirioroshi. In many kata, tricks are used to make the second cut more quickly than would be expected. This is graphically illustrated by the many versions of ukenagashi, but also evident in as basic a kata as seitei ippon me. A variation on this theme is the use of a one-handed cut or tsuka strike toward one opponent as a diversion to enable you to quickly finish off the second opponent coming from another direction, such as in seitei yonhon me. Attention is then redirected toward the original opponent.

The basic kirioroshi is made following a step with the right foot, when the back (left) foot moves up. Another way of confusing your opponent and throwing off his timing is to cut on a left step, as in okuden yonhon me.

In all martial arts, especially those using weapons, controlling the distance between you and your opponent is essential. "Choking up" on a weapon such as a jo, as you would with a baseball bat, can easily shorten its working distance. This is more difficult with a katana, but it can be done. The techniques in which the left hand is placed on the mune of the blade to control it in close demonstrate this. They include Eishin yonhon and gohan me, as well as the thrust (tsuki) of seitei kyuhon me. In fact, all the thrusts are used when you have stepped well inside of your opponent's "defensive circle." Other examples of cutting in close are the kata Omori kyuhon me, in which you stand your ground and come off the floor as you cut without stepping, and seitei kyuhon me, where you make your nukitsuke as you step backward. In fact, in all the Eishin ryu kata you slide back away from your opponent to gain working space as you do your chiburi.

Another technique that facilitates getting your strike in early is the conversion of a block to a cut. In seitei sanbon me, for example, the initial block turns the power of your opponent's strike back onto him as you use it to quickly flip your blade up before its downward plunge into a kirioroshi.

The choice of which chiburi to use appears to have been influenced by the position of possible second attacks from the original opponent or others. In the case of an opponent on the floor close to you while you stand above, the reverse chiburi allows simply dropping the kissaki to block a low strike. The yoko chiburi used in conjunction with a rotation of the hips in Eishin ryu provides the same protection when the iaidoka is kneeling. You can mount a defense by pulling the mune close to your abdomen and using your left hand to push a slash of the monouchi into your opponent on the ground. The Omori chiburi with the right arm extended and the kissaki to the rear provides great visibility, and combined

with swiveling of your hips allows a counterattack to almost all cardinal points. Finally, the vertical chiburi is used in tight corners or when it is dark.

Another tactic common to this school of iaido is moving different parts of the body simultaneously. Motion at a single point is easily spotted, even in peripheral vision, and can be dealt with directly. When two or more actions are undertaken at the same time, it is much more likely that the significance of one of them will be missed. An example is that of seitei hachihon me. As the body turns after the forward kashira strike the saya is surreptitiously removed from the blade, baring it for the subsequent thrust. This action is hidden in the blur of the spinning body and further de-emphasized by there really being no separate arm movement to attract attention.

Perhaps the most pervasive, if not universal, technique of all in these kata is to not take a course of action until the last moment. If, for example, you have made the first kirioroshi in seitei roppon me and are reversing your direction to finish the second opponent, you do not commit yourself to a shomen cut until you can see your target and know what he is doing. If you bring your blade up above your head too quickly, not only are you telegraphing your intent but you are precluding a horizontal or other cut that you might wish to employ. Seitei hachihon me is another great example. The thrust is a one-handed action, so the turnaround is also one-handed. If you bring the left hand up to the tsuka, not only are you telegraphing but your left arm physically blocks your view of your opponent. This is the reason that head movement always precedes foot and sword movement when you are changing the direction of attack. Seeing what your opponent is doing before committing the rest of your body and your blade is critical to survival.

APPENDIX A

All-Japan Kendo Federation Judging Guide

Translation of the Judging Guide from New Edition All Japan Kendo Federation Iai, *1990. Distributed at the Third Annual AUSKF Iaido Summer Camp in Memphis, Tennessee, September 5, 1999.*

Points to watch as described in the ZNKR Iai and further checks considering technical principles.

IPPON ME - MAE

Is the player imagining a front opponent as he sits down?
Is the nukitsuke executed at the same time the sword leaves the saya?
Is sufficient sayabiki shown during nukitsuke?
Are the positions of the kissaki, right hand, elbow, and shoulder correct?
Is the furikaburi made with a backward thrusting movement past the left ear?
Does the kissaki drop below the horizontal when the sword is above the head?
Does the left knee pass the right heel as it is slid forward?
Is the cut executed without pause?
Does the cut finish a little lower than horizontal?
When initiating the chiburi action, is the right palm turned upwards and is the cutting edge of the sword pointing to the left?
Is the posture correct during chiburi?
Is the noto executed correctly?

NIHON ME – USHIRO

Is the player imagining a back opponent as he sits down?
Is the head turning with the body?
Is the player drawing the sword as he is turning and is the left foot being placed a little to the left on the nukitsuke?
Are the positions of the kissaki, right hand, elbow, and shoulder correct?

Is the player cutting correctly to the temple of the opponent?

Does the right knee pass the left heel as it is slid forward?

SANBON ME – UKENAGASHI

Is the player imagining a left opponent as he sits down?

Is the ukenagashi movement expressed clearly?

Is the upper half of body covered by the sword in the ukenagashi position?

Is the left foot drawn back behind the right and is the cut diagonal?

Are the ukenagashi action and the cut executed as one continuous movement?

Is the right hand above the shoulder as the cut begins?

Is the kissaki upright over the shoulder as the cut begins?

Is the left fist in front of the navel and is the kissaki slightly down on completion of the cut?

YONHON ME – TSUKAATE

Is the player imagining the opponents as he sits down?

Is the player aiming the tsuka correctly at the solar plexus of the opponent?

Is the first opponent still being pressured by the tsukagashira as the sayabiki is performed?

Is the ridge of the sword near the monouchi touching the left chest and is the edge turned outwards?

On the thrust to the rear, is the left hand holding the saya turned inwards in front of the navel and is the right elbow extended on making the thrust?

When turning again to the front, is the head turning before the body?

As the body is again turned to the front, is there a pulling movement as the sword is raised above the head, and is the cut itself vertical?

When sitting, is zanshin shown as the left knee is placed on the floor to the sankyo position?

GOHAN ME – KESAGIRI

Is the right hand above the shoulder as the sword is turned on the initial cut?

Is the kissaki pointing upwards and is the blade vertical as the initial cut is completed? Attention: the angle of the upwards cut and the angle of the downwards cut were not the same (March 1997) — but are the same now.

Does the monouchi reach out of the body side as the downward cut is completed?

Is the left hand gripping the saya as the left foot is moved back on the chiburi action?

ROPPON ME – MOROTETSUKI

On the initial diagonal cut, does the cut stop at chin height?

Does the height of the kissaki in chudan correctly express the intent to thrust at the solar plexus?

Is the thrust executed with the correct body movement?

Is the rear foot tsugiasi as the chudan kamae is adopted and is the thrust made accurately to the opponent solar plexus?

As the sword is drawn out, is there a feeling of ukenagashi as the sword is raised above the head?

Is the foot on which the body turns pointing forward, and is the heel foot being lifted a little off the floor?

NANAHON ME – SANPOGIRI

Is the opponent to the front intimidated with the spirit?

Is the right foot placed a little forward with the left pivoting foot on the initial cut?

When making the first cut to the right, does the cut stop at chin height?

Is the player conscious of the opponent in front as he turns to the left?

After turning to the opponent on the left, is the vertical cut made without pausing?

Is the sword raised above the head with the feeling of ukenagashi before the final cut?

Is the head turning toward the opponent before the rest of the body?

When making the second cut perpendicular to the left is on the left foot sufficient vigor?

Is the head turning toward the front opponent before the rest of the body?

Is enough concentration shown after the noto?

HACHIHON ME – GANMANATE

Is that tsukagashira aimed correctly at the point between the eyes?

Is there a feeling of pushing with the tsukagashira against the opponent in front as the saya is pulled back to make the turn to the rear?

Is the right fist placed correctly on the top of the ilium when facing the opponent to the rear?

In this position, does the body turn round perfectly, and is the rear heel held a little off the floor?

Is the thrust made with the feet pointing forward?

Is the right fist a little lower than the kissaki and in line with the right hip when making the thrust, and is sufficient sayabiki shown during the thrust?

Is the sword pulled out and raised above the head in a ukenagaahi movement?

Is sufficient concentration shown after the noto?

KYUHON ME – SOETETSUKI

When making the initial diagonal cut is the right fist at navel height and is the kissaki slightly higher than the fist?

Does the monouchi reach out of the body side on the initial cut?

Is the blade gripped between the thumb and index finger of left hand at around its center point, and is the right fist on the right hip?

Is the kissaki pointing at the abdomen of the opponent when making the preparation for the thrust?

When making the thrust, does the right fist stop in front of the navel?

When showing zanshin is the right arm straight and is the right fist no higher than the nipple?

Does the kissaki remain still when starting the chiburi?

Is sufficient concentration shown after the noto?

JIPPON ME – SHIHOGIRI

Is the tsukaate made strongly and with the side of the tsuka?

Is there the feeling of pushing the first opponent with the tsukagashira as the sayabiki is made on the initial turn?

When doing the sayabiki, is the ridge of the sword near the monouchi touching the left chest and is the right hand held away from the body?

Is the thrust to the solar plexus made without pause?

When making the thrust, is the saya pulled in front of the navel, and are the left and right hands moved toward each other?

Is there the feeling of pulling the sword out as the sword is raised above the head?

Is the sword raised above the head for the final cut as part of the wakigamae action and not after wakigamae?

Is there the feeling of ukenagashi as the sword is raised above the head when pivoting on the left foot to turn to the right rear? Is the cut made on the right foot?

Is sufficient concentration shown after noto?

APPENDIX B

Training Strategies

Use the longest sword appropriate for your size right from the start. This will prevent sloppy habits like ineffectual sayabiki or poor right-hand control during the noto. Youngsters who are still growing might have to use a blade initially slightly long, but they will grow into and through it soon enough.

You can practice the proper path for the sword during a chiburi from hasso no kamae or during a Omori chiburi by placing a vertical sheet of cardboard at the proper distance so that it is scratched or just barely cut by the kissaki at the point of its farthest travel, when the elbow joint locks in extension. This will help you eliminate twisting the blade with your wrist as you make this motion. It also has the added benefit of helping you get a feel for the proper cutting distance (maai) for your sword. The latter can also be appreciated by striking at the leaves of trees or bushes.

In the performance of a chiburi either from hasso or jodan no kamae, or during Omori chiburi, the flat plane through which the blade travels is fixed by the starting position of the blade before the movement even begins. If the blade is at the wrong angle, then the only way the blade will end up in the right place is if you twist your wrist and tsuka during the cut, as noted. One trick to fix the correct starting position in your mind is to start at the ending position of the chiburi and then move the blade backward through a flat plane until it is near your face. Since, in the starting position, either hasso or jodan, the ha of the blade is pointed directly ahead, this must be readjusted just prior to the start of the cutting part of the chiburi.

You can practice and perfect the motion and timing of kesagiri by making the up-down motions continuously using your right hand only. A trick that can be used comes from the philosophy of shinkage ryu, which states that all motions should be spiral. An imperceptible circle with the kissaki at the point of direction change will increase power, smoothing and speeding the motion. If it can be detected, however, it's too much. To understand where the power should come from in a kesagiri-type cut, do it two-handed but one hand at a time, cutting up with the right hand and changing hands to the left hand for the downward part. Then do the same thing, but keep both hands in contact with the tsuka during the downward half. Be sure to use a small amount of hip rotation with the sword motion.

The same technique can be applied to the motion of the first okuden kata, kasume, in which a back-and-forth horizontal cut is performed in front of your opponent's face.

Practicing drawing from seiza horizontally in all four directions and going back into seiza after each nukitsuke facilitates learning to rise and cut from seiza and, especially, develop the necessary timing. This is sort of like doing the first part of each of the first four Omori kata without finishing them. You will find that the back foot streams around behind the hips, as though it is under tow, when you do this smoothly. One of the aims is to keep the back foot straight during each cut (parallel to the cut), no matter which direction the cut is in. When doing this, you will find that it is easy to incorporate the power of your turning body into your nukitsuke when rotating clockwise. More difficult is getting power into your nukitsuke when you are turning counterclockwise. The power should come from the movement of your right foot and leg swinging behind you as well as the snap of your sayabiki.

The eight-way cutting exercise (*happogiri*) is a good way to practice cutting in conjunction with the footwork necessary to change directions, as well as to practice using hip rotation to power the cuts. It is most easily described as relative to a compass on the floor.

You start by drawing a diagonal nukitsuke toward north, then bring your feet together as you go into chudan no kamae. Step forward with the right foot as you perform furikaburi and make a sho-men cut as the back foot comes forward in okuriashi. Turn counterclockwise on your right foot and then step out with your left, cutting to the southwest. Turn clockwise on your left foot, and step out with the right, and cut to the northwest. Turn counterclockwise 180 degrees and step out with your left foot cutting to the southeast. Turn clockwise on your left foot, step out with your right foot and cut to the west. Turn 180 degrees counterclockwise on your right foot, step with your left, and cut to the east. Turn clockwise to the southeast in a similar fashion and then finish by turning counterclockwise and cutting back toward the north. Bring your left foot up to your right and do a vertical chiburi and noto. In summary, you alternate the direction of each cut, always rotating on the forward foot, which also alternates, but you make an overall progression counterclockwise. There are two 180-degree turns in the middle of the routine. You never step through to make an ayumiashi. With modification, this exercise can also be done kneeling. Be sure to use your hips to initiate each cut.

Practicing yoko chiburi and noto while in seiza is a good way of learning to keep your saya and sword horizontal to the floor. (The blade and/or the saya hitting the floor only emphasizes any loss of control.) Then make vertical cuts in seiza to further hone the same control. Keep your back straight.

Developing proper timing for the various parts of a kata can be difficult. It should be directed from the actions of the imaginary opponent, but this is difficult for a beginner. After learning the steps of a kata well, practice it at different speeds: normal, then too fast, and, finally, too slowly. Pay attention to what feels appropriate when fast and what feels better when slow, what throws you off balance and what feels clumsy. When moving slowly, if you are off balance you will not be able to gloss over it, because you will fall. Finally, try to put it all back into the kata again, going at the appropriate speed for each section.

Practicing kata very slowly also provides real insight into where the power should be and how to relax during the rest of the kata. For example, in seitei ippon me everything is soft until the end of nukitsuke, then soft again until the end of the kirioroshi, then soft again until the end of chiburi, and finally until the kissaki drops into the koiguchi. So, there are only four instances of tightness or muscle power in that particular kata. These four places also are where exhalation should occur to be consistent with Taoist principles.

It is good training with very little time expended to practice 25 cuts a day. Doing 100 to 200 consecutively will teach you movement while conserving your energy between cuts. Remember that when the sword moves back over your head, the tip should move first from wrist action and the arms should be relaxed. The blade does not pause over your head, but the cut is made immediately upon the blade's reaching its highest point above your head. Power comes from the hips, which move slightly ahead of the sword; it does not come from the back or the elbows.

Practitioners of aikido practice with bokken and jo in order to understand what those weapons can do and how to defend against them. As a swordsman, learning a modicum of jo, sai, or jujutsu will provide you with an invaluable perspective on the strengths and weaknesses of the sword. Likewise, learning to do the kendo kata with a partner will provide insight into aspects of closing with an enemy, effective distance, economy of motion, timing, and balance that will add immeasurably to the realism of your iaido. Iaidoka really miss something by not routinely performing two-person kata unless they also do kendo or their dojo performs some kind of *kumitachi* (practice fencing).

The noto is a very important part of each kata. Don't anticipate your next kata before you complete your noto. As you start to sheathe the sword, start thinking about whether you are being attacked from the side or back. Be prepared to draw and cut to your left, your right, or behind you. Actually do this sometimes before your noto is complete. Then think of this every time you do a noto. This is very important in learning to develop zanshin. Once, during a concerted effort by our class to really consider an imminent attack during noto practice, a student to my left volunteered the fact that he could actually feel my presence during a particular noto. Without a doubt that was my least ambiguous experience with projecting ki.

To correct the error of bending forward during a cut, bend your front knee more and increase the power with the left hand. Tuck your hips under your waist more (rotate your pelvis) and initially aim your cut higher. Push your rear heel backward. Relax during the downward movement of your arms.

To deal with too much right-hand power, make some yoko-men cuts using your left hand only. Be sure the fleshy part of the base of your left thumb is on top of the tsuba, or you will hit the floor with the blade. That action will also prevent the sword from bobbling when it is stopped. Proper tension with the fourth and fifth fingers, relaxing the shoulders and arms during the cut and the "wringing" of the hands around the tsuka (shibori) are also important in this control.

To force yourself to do an effective sayabiki during noto, draw the sword with the right hand near the kashira end of the tsuka and do several noto in succession without turning your hips. Then go back to the normal hand position near the tsuka and do several more noto.

Besides cutting pigskin to get a proper appreciation for slicing there is another even more realistic method. If you have access to a shinken and are also in a part of the country where deer hunting is popular, it should not be difficult to get permission from a successful hunter to cut the inedible parts (such as the limbs and neck) of an already harvested deer. This is more likely to happen if you make your case for a legal doe, rather than some trophy buck.

Many kata involve rotation around an axis that runs though a knee and the top of your head. To learn to keep that axis straight, balance a Styrofoam cup on your head during the action.

All cuts should begin as an acceleration of the monouchi caused by the action of your wrists. To test your technique, have an assistant carefully drape a rag loosely over the monouchi of your blade while it is behind your head before a cut. When you cut, if the rag falls behind you, you're moving your arms first. If the rag is thrown way ahead of you, your cut was begun properly. You can also do this alone by putting a cardboard or plastic tumbler over the kissaki and cutting. This trick also works well for practicing chiburi from hasso and jodan no kamae.

APPENDIX C

Peculiarities of the Individual Kata

The numbers refer to those used in the Table of Contents.

Kata in which you bend forward: 6, 17, 23, 40, and 41.
Kata that are offensive in nature: 12, 24, 34, 40, 42, 50, and 53.
Kata in which you do a vertical chiburi and noto: 39 and 50.
Kata in which you do a reverse chiburi and noto: 3, 5, 18, 19, and 20.
Kata in which you draw your enemy into a cut by feigning withdrawal: 9.
Kata in which you receive a cut with a block and rapidly return the cut: 3, 11, 12, 18, 20, and 52.
Kata with forward thrusts: 6, 8, 9, 31, 33, and 50.
Kata with sideways (left) or backward thrusts: 4, 10, 37, 39, and 44.
Kata where you do a kirioroshi with the left foot forward: 2, 10, 14, 16, 28, 37, 43, and 47.
Kata in which you make an aggressive move after starting a noto: 17, 23, and 46.
Kata in which you hold the sword still and move the saya off of it: 4, 8, 11, 30, 45, 48, and 49.
Kata in which you put your feet parallel together: 6, 20, and 21.
Kata in which you push or pull your opponent with your saya: 4, 28, 33 37, 39, and 44.
Kata that contain or threaten a strike with the kashira: 4, 8, 9, 10, 29, and 48.
Kata in which you cross your legs: 28, 33, and 46.
Kata in which it is acceptable to perform kirioroshi starting with the kissaki lower than the tsuka: 4 and 12.
Kata in which you place your left hand on the mune: 9, 20, 28, 29, and 30.
Kata that contain a low right block: 17, 23, 26, and 36.

APPENDIX D

Swords, Parts, and Repair Resources

Sources of iaito, shinken, repairs, replacement parts, and clothing.

All U.S. Kendo Federation (AUSKF)
List of member dojo (kendo and iaido), upcoming events
www.kendo-usa.org

Aoi Arts
Antique blades, fittings, and armor
www.aoi-art.ab.psiweb.com

Aquastone
P.O. Box 315
El Cerrito, CA 94530
Polishing stones, burnishing and woodworking tools, paint

Axt, Russell
1646 Hopper St.
Santa Rosa, CA 95403
Custom Tsuka and saya, wrapping, sword stands

Babin, Richard—Gakeshi Fusa
http://rbabinmd.com
Saya and habaki

Benson, Robert
Bushido: Japanese sword polishing and restoration, antique fittings, accessories, polishing, restoration, appraisal
www.togishi.com

Bugei Trading Company
Modern blades, accessories, art, and all things samurai.
www.bugei.com

Bujin Design
Clothing, equipment bags
www.bujindesign.com

Christianson, Mike
Masamune Sword Shop
25025 Redland Boulevard
Loma Linda, CA 92354
Antique blades and fittings
www.masamuneswordshop.com/index.html

Condell, Cary—Ikkyudo
Antique blades and fittings, research, and appraisals
www.ikkyudo.com

Elder, Bob—East Coast Martial Arts Supply
Modern blades, cutting supplies, clothing
www.ecmas.com

Gaijin's Guide
Series of very practical tapes on the non-traditional restoration of blades and koshirae
www.islandnet.com/~gaijin/guide.htm

Hughes, Robert—Keichodo
Antique blades, fittings, armor, restoration
www.keichodo.com

Konno, Tatsuhiko—Token Konno
Sword restoration, polishing, research, and appraisal
www.tokenkonnoart.com

Lohman, Fred
Fittings of modern manufacture, handles, saya, and supplies
www.wnstar.com/katana or
www.japanese-swords.com

Majestic Fantasy
Modern blades, fittings
www.majestic-n.com

Mantis Swords
Modern blades.
www.mantisswords.com

Mugendo Budogu
Books, tapes, weapons, clothing (including formal attire)
www.budogu.com

Nishijin Sword Shop
Modern blades, fittings, supplies, some antiques
http://japanesesword.net

Pepin, Tim
Antique fittings
www.samuraisword.com

Pollard, Rick—Nosyuiaido—Cutting Edge Technologies
Modern blades, iaito, clothing, accessories, embroidery
www.nosyuiaido.com

Satcho Japanese Sword Books Supplies
Books, antique and modern, supplies
www.satcho.com

Sho-Shin
Antique blades, fittings, smith information
www.sho-shin.com

Tokugawa Art
Antique blades, fittings, armor
www.sanmei.com/shop_e/enter.html

Tozando
Iaito, modern blades, clothing, accessories
www.tozando.com/eng/index.html

Tan, Alfred
Antique and modern blades, fittings
www.japanesesword.com

Weissberg, Fred
Antique blades, fittings, books
www.nihonto.com

GLOSSARY

47 Ronin – The tale of the *Loyal 47 Ronin* or *Chushingura* is one of the most famous samurai stories and a metaphor for bushido. In 1701, Asano, the Lord of Ako, is deceitfully forced to commit seppuku. Instead of following him immediately in death, his retainers dishonor themselves in the eyes of their contemporaries to avenge their Lord Asano some 3 years later. They then commit seppuku. Many books and movies address this story, including the classic film directed by Kenji Mizoguchi.

Adams, William (1560-1616 approx.) – An English pilot, shipbuilder, and navigator who fought under Drake during the rout of the Spanish Armada. He reached Japan with a few other survivors at the end of an ill-fated trading voyage for the Dutch. He became a confidant of Tokugawa Ieyasu and rose to high social status despite being European. He was the protagonist of James Clavell's novel *Shogun* and Robert Lund's novel *Daishi-San*.

Aikido – "Way of Harmony with Spirit," it is a defensive martial art based on love developed in part from daito ryu aikijutsu by Morihei Ueshiba. It is more closely related to the Chinese internal arts (*nei-dan*) such as *taiji* and *baqua* than most Japanese arts and is very concerned with breath control, blending with the attacker, and redirecting *ki* (inner energy).

Aikuchi – A sword, usually a tanto, with no tsuba in which the fuchi is fitted to and abuts the koiguchi directly.

Amateratsu – The Sun Goddess, the first issue of Izanagi and Izanami, who in Japanese mythology created the Japanese Islands, Gods, and people. The emperors are believed to be her direct descendents. The Great Shrine at Ise is dedicated to her and her order.

Amakuni (c. 800 A.D.) – Believed to be the original Japanese sword smith who changed the mainland blade to the typical curved, one-edged tachi. His most famous sword is Kogarasu-maru (Little Crow).

Amida Buddhism – A popular and rather undemanding Buddhist order that believe that all that is necessary to reach heaven is to once in your life bring the Amida Buddha into it. The mantra, *namu amida butsu* is used for this purpose.

Ainu – Indigenous peoples of the islands of Japan prior to the arrival of the people of Yamato (Yayoi). They are also called *emishi* in Japanese. They remain as a group only in the northern island of Hokkaido.

Ashigaru – Literally "fleet feet." The foot soldier conscripted from the lower classes to fight in the large pitched battles of the period of the country at war and the successors to the harquebusiers.

Ashikaga – A daimyo family that served as shogun in Kyoto to the imperial court after the Kamakura (Hojo) Shogunate collapsed.

Aiuchi –Mutual cut. The result of each swordsman simultaneously striking a killing blow.

Ayumiashi – A form of walking whereby the lead foot alternates left-right with each stride (essentially, a normal Western stride). It is used for covering ground but seldom associated with a sword cut.

Bakufu – The military government bureaucracy of some historical periods that reached its ascendancy during the Tokugawa Shogunate.

Battojutsu – The techniques of cutting with a katana.

Bokken – A wooden practice sword, synonymous with bokuto. They were used in some challenges and were/are potentially lethal, though not to the extent as a katana.

Bokuto – Same as bokken.

Bon Festival (Obon) – A Japanese festival celebrated on the 15th day of the 7th lunar month (August 15 in the modern calendar). The ancestors are believed to return to their villages to mingle with the living during this time. Bonfires, or *mukaebi,* are lit to aid the spirits in finding the way to their home villages.

Brook, Ray (born 1949) – A product of the 1960s, he grew dissatisfied with his English existence and moved to Japan. Becoming enamored with the shakuhachi, he became a virtuoso. He now teaches and performs from his headquarters in British Columbia.

Bu – A Japanese measure of length equal to 3 mm or around 1/10 of an inch.

Budo – The "martial way," implying a more modern and spiritual interpretation of martial arts than that of medieval Japan.

Budoka – A practitioner of the martial way.

Bugeisha – A connoisseur of the martial way

Bunkai – The practical application of a kata.

Bushido – The totality of the ethical basis of samurai beliefs and behavior. The original documents and concepts were collected, translated, and explained in 1899 by Inazo Nitobe.

Chambara – "B" samurai movies, like the low-budget Western movies of the 1930s through the 1950s.

Chi Kung (qi qung) – Chinese exercises designed to gain control over the flow of chi (ki) through the body for either health or martial purposes. The movements are like simplified repetitive ta'i chi chu'an movements.

Chiburi – The act of throwing off the blood on the blade before sheathing it.

Choji – A very fine oil scented with clove for use on forged blades.

Choshu – A domain on the China Sea entrance to the Inland Sea on the southern end of Honshu that controlled shipping into the sea. It was particularly active in the overthrow of the Tokugawa bakufu and one of the few domains whose daimyo supported such activities.

Chosokabe – The clan of the original lord of Tosa, a domain on the Pacific side of the island of Shikoku. Members were replaced by the Yamanouchi clan under the orders of Ieyasu Tokugawa after the Battle of Sekigahara. Reduced to the status of lower samurai, many were supportive of the imperial loyalists such as Sakamoto Ryoma.

Chudan – The middle skill level of muso shinden ryu iaido and jikiden Eishin ryu.

Compton, Dr. Walter A. (1911 – 1990) – A physician with service in the Pacific War and chairman of the board of Miles Laboratory, he was a serious collector and devoted student of Japanese blades. He was personally responsible for the return to Japan of many blades of artistic and historic significance following the war, including a *kunimune* National Treasure.

Confucianism – Following the directives of Confucius (551 – 479 B.C.), the most influential philosopher in all of China's history and greatly influencing all oriental societies. He used the relationships within the family rather than the individual to define humanity and stressed that man's purposes were attained though harmonious social interactions. He defined the vertical social structure of oriental father/teacher and children/student relationships adopted by the dojo as well as most other oriental social structure.

Cooper, Jeff – Retired U.S. Marine, author, philosopher, critic, champion of the two-handed combat handgun stance, and founder of Gunsite, a school for the use of firearms and other weapons in the art of practical self-defense.

Dai Nippon Butokukai – Greater Japan Martial Arts Association. The supervising body for many of Japan's martial arts during the Taisho Period before World War II.

Daimyo – Hereditary landowners and warlords of the various domains during the feudal period of Japanese history, to whom samurai swore allegiance.

Daisho – Matched set of two swords, usually a katana (large, or daito) and a wakizashi (small, or shoto). This pair of swords was only carried by the samurai class.

Dan – Senior ranks of many martial arts ryu generally described as "black belts."

Dan tien – The center of balance in Chinese martial arts that exists several centimeters below the navel, inside the abdomen. Chi is lowered into this area by proper breathing before circulating through the vessels and meridians of the body. The hara is a Japanese equivalent (also called the tanden).

Dannoura, Battle of (April 25, 1185) – The decisive battle of the Gempei War that took place in the narrows of the inland sea between Honshu and Kyushu. Many of the Taira ships were driven onto the shore by Yoshitsune, who had the weather position. Most of the rest were swept out to sea. Yoshitsune was said to have told his archers to concentrate on the Taira steersmen exclusively. There are numerous tales of restless ghosts of the warriors, and of the child Emperor Antoku and his mother and attendants who perished off Dannoura that day, among them, the story called *Hoichi, the Earless*.

Daruma – The semilegendary Indian prince (Bodhidharma) turned monk who founded Buddhism in China in 520. After rebuking the monarch of Nanking for his worldliness, he retired to the Shaolin monastery in Hunan Province. It is said that he meditated night and day for nine years in a cave and thereafter introduced martial techniques to the temple to strengthen the monk's bodies as well as provide a means of self-defense.

Daibutsu – The giant cast bronze Buddha at Nara, commissioned by Emperor Shomu, constituting the largest casting up to that date. Completed in 768 A.D., it weighs 250 tons and stands 45 feet tall.

Do – Way, road, or path. Used in the sense of a way to travel through life.

Do – The breastplate of medieval Japanese armor and of modern kendo gear.

Dogen (1200 – 1253) – Born near Kyoto of high-ranking parents, he took vows in the Tendai school but became disillusioned by the corruption of his temple and traveled to China where he became an adherent to the Tsao-tung sect of Chu'an. After several years he returned to spread this path to enlightenment in Japan as Soto Zen. Its major teachings were that all acts are holy and that the only way to enlightenment is seated meditation (zazen) with both body (yo) and mind (in) in balance.

Dojo – Place of the way. A place where the way is practiced (e.g., practice hall).

Do-maru – Circular breastplate. The newer style of armor adopted when infantry-based pitched battles came into vogue.

Donahue, John J. – A contemporary anthropologist specializing in Japanese history language and culture, and a longtime martial artist including the practice of kendo in Buffalo, New York. He is an associate editor for the *Journal of Asian Martial Arts* and author of the book, *Complete Kendo*.

Draeger, Donn (1922 – 1982) – A U.S. Marine veteran of World War II and the Korean War, he became the first Western master of Japanese budo in Japan and, among other accomplishments, a teacher at the Kodokan. He was a prolific writer and is responsible for introducing much that is known about budo and its history in the West today, as well as organizing the martial arts societies in the United States.

Edo (Yedo) – Early name for Tokyo and the seat of the Tokugawa shogunate.

Eisai (1141 – 1215) – Myoan Eisai formed the Rinzai sect of Zen that reintroduced the concept of meditation to the Japanese in a form readily embraced by royalty and warriors alike.

Embu – Demonstration of one or more techniques.

Enzan no metsuke – Distant mountain viewing. A method of watching an opponent without sacrificing the rest of your peripheral vision so that you remain ready for any sudden change.

Friday, Karl – Associate professor of Japanese history at University of Georgia and martial artist whose publications include *Legacies of the Sword* and *Hired Swords: The Rise of Private Warrior Power in Early Japan*.

Fudoshin – Maintaining a calm demeanor, similar to hi jyu shin.

Fujiwara – An aristocratic feudal clan that became regents to the emperors in Kyoto during the Heian Period. They gradually increased their power by marrying their daughters to the emperors, assuming all posts of influence and eventually forcing emperors to abdicate in favor of Fujiwara grandsons.

Funejima – The island on which Musashi Miyamoto defeated Sasaki Kojiro of the Ganryu style using a bokken carved from an oar during the boat ride. Later referred to as Ganryu Island.

Furikaburi – The act of bringing the sword over the head in anticipation of a vertical sword strike.

Furuya, Kensho (b. 1948) – Author of *Kodo: Ancient Ways* and master of aikido and iaido as well as an ordained Soto Zen Buddhist priest who lives and teaches in Los Angeles.

Fuchi – The metal cap on the pommel (tsuka) of a sword at the tsuba end through which the blade passes. It strengthens the handle and prevents the wood from splitting.

Futsunushi no kami – The kami enshrined at kashima-ji who has great significance to martial arts and was reportedly the inspiration for the development of the first school of swordsmanship, tenshin shoden katori Shinto ryu.

Gaijin ashi – Literally "foreign feet." An insult regarding the Western habit of placing the heel down on the ground first and then slapping down the toes.

Gempei War – The 5-year effort (1180 – 1185) that ended the Taira bid for control of the empire at the hands of the victorious Minamoto.

Gendai – Current or contemporary.

Gendaito – Traditional swords made during the Taisho and later periods—also used is "shinsakuto," newly made swords.

Genji – Alternate reading of the Minamoto clan name.

Go – A board game of strategy, in which one player attempts to surround the opponent's pieces.

Go-Daigo – Emperor at the end of the Kamakura Period who attempted to recombine the two courts (imperial and shogun). He was driven into exile, and his followers continued to harass the bakufu from the mountains as guerilla warriors.

Goshi – The landed gentry of feudal Japanese society just below samurai rank and variably influential, depending on how important commerce was to the individual domain.

Gunto – Military sword. Usually refers to a mass produced military blade of the Pacific War often around 2 shaku 2 sun in length, made of nontraditional steel. Many were tempered in oil, not water, which is cooler and does not allow the proper crystallization to take place. Some were made of stainless steel.

Habaki – The soft metal wedge that fits over the blade at the tsuba end of a sword and holds the blade tightly in the saya.

Hachimanbara – The fourth battle of the struggle between the Uesugi and Takeda

Shingen in which Takeda's chief of staff, Yamamoto Kansuke, makes a monumental error and sacrifices himself in battle. Takeda is overrun and almost lost defending himself with only a war fan. The details are described in the 1969 film, *Samurai Banners,* starring Toshiro Mifune.

Hairei – Kneeling bow to the instructor or competitor.

Hakama – Skirt-like pants worn over belt and jacket by samurai and practitioners of aikido, iaido, and kendo.

Hakamabiki – To sweep the hakama out from behind the knees with the hand before assuming seiza or tatehiza.

Hakudo Nakayama (1869-1958) – Sixteenth headmaster of the shimomura-ha of Jinsuke Eishin ryu. He subsequently was instrumental in the conversion of this iaijutsu into modern iaido.

Han – The name given the previous feudal domains (*koku*) by the Meiji government following the restoration. The name, from the Chinese, was an attempt to reduce the significance of the domain in the new scheme of things.

Hara – The center of emotion and intuition as well as the physical center of balance in martial arts. There is some hint of this in the English expressions "having a gut feeling" or "not having the stomach for it."

Harquebusiers – The handlers of matchlock muskets, or hand cannons, introduced into Japan by the Portuguese in the 16th century.

Hasegawa Mondonosuke Eishin (c. 1700) – Seventh headmaster of Jinsuke Eishin ryu, which was presumably named for him. He was instrumental in adapting the original techniques to the newly popular katana adding suwari waza to the school.

Haya nuki – The name of a method of performing the chuden waza (Eishin ryu kata) one after another without pause. It is thought to have been developed by the 17th headmaster of the tanimura-ha, Oe Masamichi (1853 – 1927).

Hayashi Rokudayu Morimasa (1661 – 1732) – The ninth headmaster of the Jinsuke Eishin ryu, he served Yamanouchi Toyomasa of Tosa during a time that the Han was splitting into factions. He was trained in shinkage ryu that was part of the technique of the Mito domain where he grew up. He also trained with Omori Rokurozaemon Masamitsu in Edo and was responsible for bringing Omori ryu with him when he moved to Tosa and incorporating it into Tosa swordsmanship.

Hayashizaki Jinsuke Shigenobu (1546 – 1621) – Popularly considered to be the father of iaijutsu, creating a system of sword drawing and striking he referred to as battojutsu, which he claimed was divinely inspired and based on the Chinese concept of yin and yang (Japanese in and yo).

Heian Period (794 – 1156 A.D.) – The era of Japanese history following by the move of the imperial capitol from Nara to Kyoto. A time of classic arts and the formation of a court on the Chinese model.

Heiho – Technique. Dave Lowry points out the meaning of "heiho is heiho." The hei represents two different kanji, ironically "war" and "peace," so that the phrase means the principles of conflict and of domestic peace are the same.

Heiji War – One of the wars during the Heian period in which the Taira gained influence at the expense of the Minamoto.

Heike – Alternate reading of the Taira clan name.

Hi – A grove running along each side of a blade that lightens it.

Hito-rei edict (1876) – The edict of the Meiji government banning the wearing of swords.

Hogan War – A militarily insignificant uprising with massive political significance. The forces of Heian regent Fujiwara Yorinaga and Taira and Minamoto supporters of the Emperor Go-Shirakawa clash in Kyoto. The regent's forces defending the status quo are defeated. This represented the first demonstrable move toward the future feudal social system.

Hojo – A nonwarrior feudal clan that became shoguns during the Kamakura period following the third Minamoto shogun.

Hoki Ryu – A school of iaido whose style includes a kiai (shout) at the time of cuts.

Hyoshi – Timing. In budo, the adjustment of the bugeisha to the activity of his opponent

Iaidoka – A practitioner of iaido.

Iaijutsu – Techniques of drawing and cutting as opposed to the way of drawing and cutting.

Iaito – A nonferrous practice sword for use in iaido.

Ibn Ikbal – An Arabic Sufi philosopher of the Middle Ages.

Ibn Khaldoun, Abd ar Rahman abu Zayd ibn Muhammad (1332 – 1402) – An Arabic scholar of an Andalusian family (Spanish Moors). Near the end of the 14th century he wrote the *Muqaddimah*, the first known scholarly treatise attempting to describe the cyclic pattern in man's political and social organization, emphasizing human cooperation and the influence of geography and religion.

Ikebana – The art of flower arranging.

Inazu Nitobe – An author of Japanese descent who, while living in Victorian Europe, undertook to research and catalogue in English what he had been taught as a child about morality in feudal Japan. It was first published in 1899 and explained bushido to the world for the first time.

Ise Grand Shrine – Arguably the most important Shinto shrine. Here is enshrined the spirit of the Sun Goddess, Amateratsu. The high priestess of this shrine was politically powerful during much of Japanese history. The shrine was regularly visited by the imperial family and members of the court. Following the Meiji Restoration this shrine and its order played a big role in the reinvigoration of Shinto as an instrument of nationalism.

Jalaludin Rumi (d. 1273) – An Afghan Sufi master who published the book *Couplets of Inner Meaning*, considered part of the world's great literature.

Jidaigaki – High-class samurai movies made after World War II, usually at Toho Studio by such directors as Akira Kurosawa, Masaki Kobayashi, and Kenji Mizoguchi.

Jimmu – The first human emperor of Japan (believed to be mythical).

Jo – A short staff of about four shaku in length, conceived of by Muso Gonnosuke, who used it in the only recorded successful challenge to Musashi Miyamoto. Slightly longer than a katana, it exploits this difference as well as its double-ended nature.

Jo ha kyu – The variation in tempo and timing of the various parts of a single kata.

Jutsu – A technique or method as opposed to a way (do).

Kamae – A body stance or position. While iaido claims not to have stances, kamae form basic parts of the continuum of a kata.

Kamakura – A seaside town surrounded by hills west of Tokyo that served as capital for the Minamoto and Hojo shoguns. It has many shrines, including a large one to Hachiman, the god of war who was patron to the Minamoto clan, as well as a giant bronze Buddha.

Kami – Shinto gods or spirits.

Kami no ashi – In the dojo, the foot closest to the kamiza.

Kamiza – The resting place for the kami in a dojo that follows Shinto tradition. It is the first place to be bowed to at the beginning of practice. In most dojo, it is the same as the shinza.

Kaishaku – The second, who during ritual suicide (seppuku) finishes the condemned man by severing his head. It is the jikiden Eishin ryu name for Omori nanahon me.

Kamikaze – Divine wind. Originally referred to the sudden storm that dispersed the Mongol's ships during their second attempted invasion of the Japanese islands in 1181. Subsequently the term was taken as a name for several ultranationalist endeavors, notably the suicide bombers during the defense of Japan in the Pacific War.

Kanji – The Chinese characters used in written Japanese.

Kano, Jijoro (1860 – 1938) – Founder of the modern art of Judo and father of modern sports in general in Japan. He opened the Kodokan dojo in 1884.

Kanto – The lowland, rich plains in central Honshu, draining into Tokyo Bay. An early and perpetual center of political and economic power.

Kashima Grand Shrine – Where man was taught the martial arts by the god Takemikazuchi. An important site for martial study, the ritual there today includes sword motion very much like the seitei kata, Kasagiri.

Kata – A choreographed martial activity that is repeated by a student for the purpose of perfecting a skill.

Katakana – The phonetic alphabet used by the Japanese to spell foreign words. The other two alphabets are hiragana, which is used for native Japanese words, and Romanji, which are our Latin characters sometimes used for English words.

Katana – A sword of 2 shaku or greater worn thrust through the obi, sharp edge upward.

Katori Grand Shrine – Where Futsunushi-no-Mikoyo, the companion of the god Takemikazuchi who was sent by Amaterasu to pacify the Earth (Japan) is enshrined. He is also believed to have taught martial arts to man.

Keller, Helen (1880 – 1968) – Born in Florence, Alabama, both blind and deaf from a fever at age 19 months, she overcame obviously tremendous obstacles to become a woman of letters and an inspiring public speaker. A Japanese woman said of her, "For many generations, more than we can count, we bowed our heads and submitted to blindness and beggary. This blind and deaf woman lifts her head high and teaches us to win our way by work and laughter. She brings light and hope to the heart."

Kemmu Restoration (1334 AD) – The attempt by Emperor Go-Daigo to reestablish the court's primary role in the administration of land management and tax collection. It was unsuccessful because while the military clans were feuding among themselves, they still retained the power to prevent a return to the court's "golden years" of the Heian Period. Small and large land owners and tenants retained more faith in the ability of the warrior class to protect their interests than to turn them over to the care of a frivolous court in Kyoto.

Ken – Sword. One of two common symbols for sword, the other is "to."

Kendo – Way of the sword. An art in which bamboo swords and rudimentary armor are used in actual combat.

Kenjutsu – Sword techniques, the precursor of kendo.

Ki (Chinese chi) – The life force that circulates within all living things, heaven and earth, which can be mobilized by special breathing techniques. It defines health in Taoist medicine.

Kiai – Joined to spirit. An expression of having your act all together during a strike, the cry at the time of a cut or strike in the martial arts.

Kimono – A robe-like outer garment, often of silk, worn by the Japanese. It usually has full Chinese sleeves and is overlapped left over right in front and secured by an obi. Kimono for men are usually somber, but women's can be quite colorful. One made of cotton for light wear or after a bath is a yakuta.

Kinai – The fertile plain at the southern end of Honshu Island draining into the Inland Sea. This was the first area to be settled when the original Japanese of Kyushu expanded their culture north to Honshu seeking better quality land on which to grow their crops. This is the location of the original capitals, Nara and Kyoto, as well as Osaka and Nagoya.

Kipling, Rudyard (1865 – 1936) – An English correspondent, novelist, and poet born in India whose works include *Gunga Din, The Jungle Book, Kim, Captains Courageous,* and *Just So Stories*. His iconoclastic approach and pro-imperial sentiment were and are particularly thought provoking.

Kirioroshi – Storm cut. The finishing cut of a kata.

Kiza – Kneeling.

Koan – An illogical riddle used by Zen teachers to force their disciples into thinking in terms of paradoxes. Two of the most famous involve the sound of one hand clapping and the appearance of your face prior to the birth of your parents.

Kojiki – Chronicle of old facts. The first official history of Japan known to exist completed in 712 A.D. Most historians agree that anything recorded to have happened before 550 A.D. is mythic or imaginary.

Koku – Country. Originally referred to domains (the archipelago was referred to as everything under heaven), and only to the Japanese nation as a whole after the Meiji restoration.

Kokutai – The entire gestalt of "Japaneseness" consciously invented following the Meiji restoration.

Kokyu – Breathing, breath control.

Konfu – The royal burial mounds of Japan, which date from the period of the same name just before those of recorded history (200 – 300 A.D.).

Koryu – Old stream. The original or traditional techniques of a modern ryu. The techniques other than seitei.

Koshirae – The fittings that allow a blade to be worn and used in battle. Many are works of art and collectable in their own right.

Kristofferson, Kris – A contemporary songwriter and actor associated with the Texas school of country music epitomized by *The Outlaws*.

Kurigata – The ring on the omote of the saya to which the sageo is affixed.

Kusunoki Musashige (d. 1336) – A general who supported the cause of the Emperor Go-Daigo and the junior division of the imperial family during the period of the northern and southern courts. He fought a series of guerilla wars and defensive actions on mounts Hiei and Kasagi, and later in Akasaka and Chihaya, until defeat at Minatogawa drove him to seppuku.

Kyoto – A city south of Lake Biwa in southern Honshu in the Kanai, which served as the capitol during the Heian Period and the home of the emperor and his court during most of the rest of the following periods of Japanese history. It is one of the few Japanese cities that did not have to be rebuilt after the Pacific War. Thus Kyoto continues to reflect more strongly than most cities the feeling of feudal Japan.

Kyu – A student rank from sixth to first kyu, which is just under shodan (first black belt). Students holding these ranks are termed *mudansha* (without dan rank).

Li I-Yu – A Chinese martial artist and Taoist who contributed *Essentials of Form and Push-Hands* to the Taiji classics in the mid-19th century.

Lowry, Dave – A contemporary freelance writer who regularly contributes to martial arts and woman's health issues literature. He has monthly columns in *Black Belt, Inside Karate, Furyu,* and *Fighting Arts International*. His books include *Autumn Lightning, Persimmon Wind,* and *Sword and Brush*.

Maai – The distance between two opponents in battle, important in any martial art, it is critical in iaido in order to be able to reach the opponent without being cut in the process. To some extent it is a method of subterfuge, of trying to seem closer than you really are to encourage an attack or, conversely, trying to seem too far away to be able to strike successfully while you set up your own offensive move.

Majime – "Sincerity," but within the concept of a person's omote and ura in complete accord. In other words, acting in no way misleading in intention.

Manyoshu (late 8th century) – A compilation of nearly contemporary poetry providing a picture of the court life of the Asuka Period. The poem included here is reported to have been written by Prince Shika upon the movement of the court to Fujiwara no Miya in 672 A.D.

Masamune, Goro (1264 – 1343) – Son of Kunimitsu, the founder of the Segami (Soshu) school of sword making, Masamune was of great influence on the development of the *uchigatana* in the early Muromachi Period. One of his students founded the Mino school of sword making, the last of the gokaden of Koto swords.

Mei – The signature of the smith carved on the tang of a sword

Meiji Restoration (1868-1912) – Enlightened rule. The name adapted for his reign by the 122nd emperor, Mutsuhito, following the restoration of imperial rule in 1868. It was characterized by a great reorganization of the nation around a new constitution based largely on a German model.

Mekugi – The peg that holds the tsuka securely on the nakago.

Mekugi ana – The hole in the nakago for the mekugi to go through.

Mengu – Certificate of competence awarded for a given level of a martial art.

Menuki – The metal talismans on either side of the tsuka, under the tsuka-ito that provide a more secure grip. Originals are highly collectable.

Metsuke – "Sight." In iaido, it is the eye position of the iaidoka that demonstrates his observation of his imaginary enemy. Historically, the term also refers to the spies employed by the Tokugawa shoguns, such as the komuso, shakuhachi-playing wandering monks.

Minamoto – A feudal clan from the Kanto Pplain of Honshu also known as the Genji. They were in bitter conflict with the Taira clan (also known as the Heike) for control over the empire in the late Heian Period.

Minamoto Yoritomo – Hero of the Gempei War who swept away the Taira hopes of leadership and became the first military dictator of Japan (shogun). He moved his headquarters to Kamakura in 1180 and clinched his claim as shogun by his victory at Ichinotani largely by the efforts of his half-brother Yoshitsune. A brutal dictator, he was killed in 1190 by a fall from a horse. Yoritomo was well matched to his wife, Masako, who had a similar personality and was ultimately responsible for her own family (Hojo) replacing the Minamoto clan as shoguns.

Minamoto Yoshitsune – Yoritomo's half-brother. When he tried to ride into Kamakura with Taira prisoners from the battle of Ichinotani he was denied entrance. Despite pleading letters assuring his allegiance to his brother, he was hunted down and forced to kill himself. The plight of Yoshitsune and his wanderings with his retainer, Benkei, has been immortalized in the No drama *Ataka*, its Kabuki theater counterpart *Kanjincho*, and in several movies including Akira Kurosawa's *The Men Who Tread on the Tiger's Tail*.

Minowa Castle, the Battle of (1565) – The final of five battles between the Uesugi and Takeda clans in which the Uesugi are defeated and their last heir slain.

Mishima, Yukio (1925 – 1970) – A Japanese novelist and playwright who came to prominence after the Pacific War, whose complex works had themes including eroticism, homosexuality, purity through death, the search for real existence, and the conflict between traditional and newer Japanese values. Originally a small, sickly looking young man, he became obsessed with weight lifting and, later, kendo and judo. Toward the end of his roman-candle-like life he championed an almost fascist nationalism. His novels include *Confessions of a Mask, The Sound of Waves, The Temple of the Golden Pavilion,* and *The Sailor Who Fell from Grace with the Sea*. The day following completion of his masterpiece tetralogy, *The Sea of Fertility,* he committed a very public seppuku on the roof of the Self-Defense Forces Ministry in Tokyo.

Monouchi – The first 12 inches or so of the blade behind the kissaki; the part intended for cutting.

Monsuke – A formal jacket of silk with the family crest (*mon*) on the lapels, sleeves, and back.

Morris, Glenn – Contemporary author, psychologist, and martial artist. His books include *Path Notes of an American Ninja Master*, *Shadow Strategies of an American Ninja Master,* and *Martial Arts Madness*.

Mudansha – A student without a dan rank (of no or kyu rank).

Murphy, Michael – Contemporary author who has written two best sellers on the mysticism of golf, *Golf in the Kingdom* and *The Kingdom of Shivas Irons*.

Musashi Miyamoto (1584 – 1645) – Probably the most famous Japanese swordsman of all time. Much mystery surrounds him, but he must have been unique as he was described as fearsome in appearance and never taking a bath. He fought 60 successful duels, winning many with a bokken. His most famous was with Sasaki Kojiro in 1612. He is credited with inventing the two-sword technique but is not conclusively known to have used it. He was also an artist of some note with brush and ink. Toward the end of his life he adopted a solitary lifestyle and wrote the philosophical *Book of Five Rings* (*Go Rin Sho*), still very popular today as a battle plan for life.

Musha shugyo – In general, shugyo is any significant activity that is particularly challenging with a potential for personal growth. In martial arts, the wandering a medieval swordsman would take following his formal training to gain experience and wisdom from challenges.

Mushin – Literally "no mind." The state in which conscious effort is not necessary to accomplish the task at hand. The Chinese term is wu wei, without effort. A modern but less deep concept is "muscle memory."

Muto – Literally "no sword." It refers to unarmed techniques against a sword as well as the use of a sword under the conditions of mushin (not conscious of the sword).

Nagashima, Battle of (1574) – The Ikko (single-minded) were an Ameda Buddhist sect with great influence in the general rural population that opposed both competing Buddhist sects and the feudal system in general. They constituted a significant opposing power to unification. Nobunaga slaughtered 20,000 Ikko men, women, and children by fire, ending the siege at Nagashima castle.

Naginata – A polearm consisting of a curved blade at the end of an armored staff. It was effectively used by samurai women in defense of the home as well as against horsemen in pitched battle.

Nakago ana – The hole in the center of a tsuba that allows the tang of the blade to pass through it.

Nakao, Yajin (b. 1887, Miyagi Prefecture) – A Japanese-American resident of California from 1907 and a charter member the Delta Haiku Club. He was held in the Stockton Assembly Camp and later moved to the Rohwer Concentration Camp in Arkansas for the duration of World War II. After the war he returned to Modesto, California.

Nambokucho Period (1336 – 1392) – Synonymous with Ashikaga Period – the period of warring courts, or of the northern and southern courts just before the unification by Oda Nobunaga.

Nasu no Yoichi – A famous Minamoto warrior who rose to the challenge and shot a fan off the mast of a Taira ship from a swimming horse during the Battle of Yashima during the Gempei War.

Nirvana – The state of selflessness in which a person has true knowledge of himself and the universe.

Nihon Shoki – *Record Book of Japan*. An early official history of Japan completed in 720 A.D.

Nihonto – Literally, "Japanese sword." A true Japanese sword blade made of native steel by a licensed smith with the blessing of the Japanese government as a work of art. The term includes both swords of antiquity and those of contemporary sword smiths (gendaito). A nihonto must be forged steel, sharp, greater than 6 inches in length, and have a peg-hole in its tang.

Nikko – A community in the Japanese Alps several hours north of Tokyo of important early Shinto significance because of the mountains and hot springs. A large shrine complex (Tosho-gu) was constructed here to honor Ieyasu Tokugawa. It is here that the "hear, see, speak no evil" monkeys originated, carved on a stable building.

Noda Castle – In the siege of Noda Castle (1574) defended by the forces of Nobunaga and Ieyasu, Takada Shingen is reportedly shot by sniper fire forcing his brother, Nobukudo to withdraw their forces back to Kai just before a probable success. The story forms the basis of the Kurosawa movie *Kagemusha.*

Noto – Replacing the sword in the saya, sheathing the blade as well as personal aggression at the end of a kata.

Nugui – Finely ground ferrous oxide suspended in oil used for finish polishing a blade.

Nukitsuke – Drawing and cutting in a single move.

Obi – Belt.

Oda Nobunaga (1534 – 1582) – A warlord not of martial origins. He overthrew the Ashikaga shoguns and went a long way toward the unification of Japan under his military dictatorship. He is known to have been particularly ruthless, and demonstrated the anachronistic nature of the budo war ethic by defeating the traditional budo army of Takeda at Nagashino (1575) by using conscript *ashigaru* armed with yari and muskets hiding behind bulwarks. He disappeared when he was betrayed by a turncoat general, Akechi Mitsuhide, who attacked him at the Honno-ji.

Oe Masamichi (1853 – 1927) – The 17th headmaster of the Tanimura-ha. He reorganized Tosa iai, combining techniques of both lineages, particularly the Omori influence of the seated kata. He is believed to have coined the name muso jukiden Eishin ryu, as well as renaming many of the kata in the Omori and okuden sets.

Okehazama (1560) – A battle in which Oda Nobunaga's greatly outnumbered troops defeated the superior force lead by Yoshimoto Imagawa.

Okudan – The highest level of waza in the muso shinden and jikiden Eishin ryu, consisting of both sitting and standing sets. (*Oku* means hidden or secret.)

Okuriashi – A type of stepping in which the lead foot, whether going forward or backward, moves first, followed by the opposite foot. In this way the feet always maintain the same relationship to one another. It is always used when taking action with the sword. It is dramatically demonstrated in kendo and in seitei juippon me.

Omote – The outer or obvious aspect of an object or action. The side of the sword worn away from the swordsman to which the sageo is attached.

Omori Rokurozaemon Masamitsu (c.1770) – A sword master of the Tokyo region, he had been a student of Eishin. He later studied ogasawara ryu etiquette and shinkage ryu swordsmanship. He developed 12 kata of seated waza that were eventually incorporated into Jinsuke Eishin ryu as the beginning or shoden kata and continue as such in modern muso shinden ryu iaido.

Onin War (1467 – 1477) – A series of civil wars fought during the end of the Ashikaga shogunate at a time when social conventions had deteriorated to abysmal extent. Ostensibly over imperial succession, it resulted from a struggle for land and power by the daimyo families and shattered the central government as well as the city of Kyoto, ushering in the *sengoku jidai.*

Oshigata – A tracing on tissue paper of the tang and kissaki of a blade used for documentation, identification, and study.

Osaka Castle – The remaining stronghold of Hideyori Toyatoma after the death of his father Hidiyoshi. It fell to Ieyasu in 1615, cementing his hold on the shogunate.

Oya, Kazuo – President of the All Japan Kendo Federation (ZNKR) at the time of the World Championships held in Los Angeles in 1971.

Prince Yamato – The legendary budoka of early Japanese history who embodies the characteristics of the ideal Japanese warrior hero: bravery, martial prowess, sensitivity, a noble struggle against avarice, and an early death.

Red Beard – An Akira Kurasawa film starring

Toshiro Mifune as a country doctor whose humanity softens the lofty plans of an attending intern.

Rei – Bow.

Reiho – Etiquette.

Reishiki – Etiquette.

Ronin – "Wave person." A masterless samurai. Forced to forage for himself, a ronin might become a farmer, brigand, teacher of martial arts, or bodyguard (*yojimbo*). Some became folk heroes.

Ryu no Maki – *Dragon Scroll*, a treatise on technique from the Kashima Shinkage lineage probably dating back to at least the late 17th century.

Ryu – Stream. A traditional teaching or curriculum.

Ryu-ha – A traditional school or branch thereof.

Sageo – The cord attached to the kuragata of the saya that is made fast to the obi.

Sageto – The carry position for the sword, in which the left arm is straight and the sword is held below the level of the obi.

Saho – Preparation.

Sai – A trident-like one-handed pitchfork used in Okinawan kobudo, often in pairs.

Saigyo (1118 – 1190) – A member of the Fujiwara clan. He renounced his duties and became a wandering monk-poet contributing to the meditative travel diary tradition. Legends of and references to his life and poetry are found in much of Japanese arts including painting, poetry, and theater.

Samé – The ray skin used to wrap the tsuka that strengthens it and gives it a non-slip surface.

Samurai – A high social class of medieval Japan composed of warriors dedicated to the service their liege lord.

Sasaki Kojiro – The most famous of Musashi's dueling casualties. He was killed by Musashi using a bokken carved from an oar on Funejima later to be known as Ganryujima after Sasaki's style. The story is told in the third part of Hiroshi Inogaki's samurai trilogy, *Duel at Ganryu Island*, starring Toshiro Mifune and Koji Tsuruta.

Satori – A sudden attainment of enlightenment.

Satsuma – A maritime domain on the southernmost tip of the southernmost island, Kyushu, whose capital was Kagoshima. Satsuma was a powerful and independent domain with intentions toward replacing the Tokugawa with its ruling clan, the Shimazu. Satsuma joined the other anti-bakufu domain but lost out when the emperor replaced the shogunate. Satsuma warriors later attempted to replace the Meiji government with a shogun but were soundly trounced by the imperial army.

Saya – Scabbard, or sword sheath.

Saya ate – Striking someone's saya with your saya (by accident). This is a social taboo that at the least causes you loss of face.

Saya no uchi – Winning by so dominating your opponent that you impose your will without drawing your blade.

Sayabiki – The action whereby the saya is pulled back and around the obi with the left hand as a countermove to a sword strike to the front.

Seiza – Proper sitting. The formal sitting position whereby you kneel on both knees about a fist apart with your feet touching behind you and sit back on your ankles, keeping your back straight and your hands on your thighs.

Semé – Pressure. The technique of controlling an opponent by constantly threatening and pressuring him.

Sengoku jidai – The period of the "country at war" starting with the Onin War and ending with Oda Nobunaga's triumph. It was during this time that classic warriors and budo both reached their zenith.

Seppuku – Ritual suicide accomplished by self-disemboweling. It was often used as a death sentence by a daimyo, but it also was used as an alternative to either being taken prisoner or to regain the honor of the family of someone disgraced. The concept is thoroughly explored in Kobayashi's movie, *Harakiri*, a tale of revenge starring Tatsuya Nakadai.

Shaku – A measurement of length. One shaku is 11.93 inches or nearly 1 foot. It is composed of 10 sun which in turn are made up of 10 bu.

Shakuhachi – One foot, 8 inches. The traditional five-hole Japanese bamboo flute often of this length used extensively as a means of meditation. It was originally borrowed from China in the 8th century and became famous when adopted by *komuso*, wandering Buddhist monks "of nothingness and emptiness," who often served as spies for the Tokugawa bakufu.

Shibori – The motion of the hands, one to the other, during a vertical sword cut. They rotate toward each other, the left clockwise, and the right counterclockwise as if wringing out a wet towel. This gets each wrist further over the tsuka as the cut progresses adding to the strength and stability of the cut.

Shimabara, Battle of (1637) – An uprising of Christians rebelling against the shogun's edict that banned their religion. They held their castle against the Tokugawa bakufu for a year but were defeated after many of the defenders starved to death.

Shimo no ashi – In the dojo, the foot farthest from the kamiza

Shimomura-ha – The branch of Jinsuke Eishin ryu tradition championed by Shimomura Sadama, a classic Japanese warrior of high social rank.

Shimpan – A senior student of budo, usually with some teaching responsibility.

Shinai – The compound bamboo sword used in modern kendo.

Shinkage ryu – School of swordsmanship founded by the Yagyu clan.

Shinken – A forged iron blade of modern manufacture, usually of less than art-sword quality designed for iaido or cutting practice or contests.

Shinsa – A contest or judging.

Shinsakuto – Newly made sword. A tempered steel sword of modern Japanese manufacture by a registered swordsmith using traditional techniques. This term is coming to mean blades designed to be used in competition as opposed to modern art swords (gendaito).

Shinto – Way of the kami. The indigenous religion of Japan. It is more of an amalgam of the attitudes, ideas, ways, and spirituality of being Japanese. It offers no messiah or enlightened one, nor does it have a scripture or much in the way of moral teachings.

Shinza – "Place of the gods," like a kamiza in a dojo.

Shirasaya – "Resting saya." The unfinished, continuous softwood saya and tsuka used to store a valuable blade when unused for any length of time.

Shirei – Less formal seated bow to instructor or opponent.

Shishi – "Men of high purpose." The name adopted by the pro-imperialists bent on the destruction of the Tokugawa bakufu and the return of the emperor to power. Also, "lion."

Shodan – The first-degree dan (black belt) rank.

Shoden – The beginning set of kata in muso shinden and jikiden Eishin ryu koryu iaido (not seitei).

Shoen – The manor houses of the aristocracy that served briefly as a transition between imperial (central) and warrior (decentralized) control of Japanese land during the Kamakura and Muromachi periods.

Shogunate – Military dictatorship

Sho-men – An overhead strike to the top of the head.

Showa (1926 – 1994) – The reign of Emperor Hirohito characterized by intensive ultra-nationalism and military adventurism, as well as conflicts between extremes of the political right and the left. Blades of this era have had, until recently, a poor reputation. It is clear now that despite the disruption caused by the Pacific War, some excellent blades of traditional manufacture were produced during this period. One example is that of the Yasukuni smiths.

Silla – One of the three kingdoms of medieval Korea that became powerful enough to oust the Japanese from the peninsula.

Sohei – During the Heian Period, the temples

became large and rich and of increasing political importance. Militant warrior monks called sohei were trained in budo to protect the lands and from time to time to come down out of the hills to coerce the emperor or regent.

Sudo, Phillip Toshio – Japanese-American musician and writer whose book, *Zen Guitar*, a concise treatise on the relationship between Zen and guitar playing, really serves as a manual on Zen philosophy in general.

Suigetsu – "Water moon." Referring to the reflection of the moon in a pool of water. A metaphor for being more, and less, than what is apparent.

Suihei – "Water carrying." Holding the sword so that the tip is slightly higher than the blade or tsuka.

Suino, Nicklaus – A contemporary martial artist and author who studied and successfully competed at iaido in Japan under Katsuo Yamaguchi. His books include the *Art of Japanese Swordsmanship: A Manual of Eishin-Ryu Iaido, Practice Drills for Japanese Swordsmanship*, and *Arts of Strength, Arts of Serenity*. He teaches martial arts in Michigan.

Suki – A break in concentration that may serve as an opening for an attack by your opponent. It should be avoided.

Sun – A traditional measure of length equal to about 1.2 inches. Ten sun equal a shaku.

Suwari waza – Seated techniques.

Tachi – The first of the classic Japanese swords, preceding the katana. It developed during the time that samurai fought on horseback. It was worn suspended from the obi, ha downward. Compared with the katana it was longer, heavier, and often had a greater curvature and a curled tsuka. Many existing tachi were cut back to katana dimensions by creating a new nakago further up the blade. This often obliterated the signature. Tachi also refers to a standing position.

Tachi rei – Standing bow.

Taiho – The basic set of iaido waza supported by the All Japan Iaido Federation (ZNIR).

Taira – An independent and powerful clan that vied with the Minamoto clan for control over the Kyoto court. Also known as the Heike. While initially successful and exerting great power in the Rokuhara Period, it was vanquished by the Minamoto clan in the Gempei War (1180-1185).

Taisho (1912 – 1926) – Great justice. The name of the reign of Emperor Yoshihito. The period was characterized by a general democratization and of the emperor becoming increasingly symbolic.

Takeda Shingen (1521 – 1573) – One of the most famous daimyo of the age of warring states, he ruled the Kai domain and struggled for power over the Kanto Plain with the Uesugi clan. He was instrumental in establishing the technique of massed spearmen and harquebusiers. He was nearly killed in the fourth of five battles with the Uesugi in 1561 but prevailed at the end. He is the subject of several movies, including Kurosawa's *Samurai Banners* (*Fuurin Kazan*) and Kadokawa's *Heaven and Earth*.

Tales of the Heike (Heike Monogatori) – A long series of tales of intrigue and deception as well as a stirring description of warfare written during the Heian Period. A popular, though incomplete, novel based on it is *The Heike Story* by Eiji Yoshikawa. The *Tales* are one of the most significant examples of classical Japanese literature.

Tamahagane – The impure, heterogeneous, native steel produced in an open-pit smelter (*tatara*) from iron sand that is used to produce a nihonto.

Tamishigiri – Practice cutting using a nihonto and a rolled bamboo mat soaked in water.

Tanegeshima – A small island where the Portuguese first introduced firearms and where the Japanese became proficient in its quality manufacture. Tanegeshima became synonymous with hand cannon.

Tanimura-Ha – The line of Jinsuke-Eishin swordsmanship that was championed by the goshi of Tosa under Tanimura Kame no Jo Yorikatsu who developed a style of iaijutsu at his Chidokan training hall.

Tanto – A short blade, a shaku or less, used as a dagger and often hidden in the clothing instead of through the obi. It also sometimes replaced the wakizashi in a pair of swords and was popular as a weapon of the samurai wife.

Taoism – A Chinese philosophy that stresses the unity of all things, the cyclic nature of all events and processes, and the dual nature inherent in all things (yang and yin). This philosophy permeated every aspect of Chinese culture and was more popular with the average Chinese than Confucianism, which was rather elitist. In Japan, Taoist concepts merged comfortably with both Shinto and Buddhist beliefs. The precepts of Taoism are a major influence in many, if not all, oriental martial arts as well as Traditional Chinese Medicine.

Tatehiza – The half-sitting position with the right knee elevated and the left foot under the left buttock. It was easier to sit this way in yoroi and to move into a battle position in a hurry.

Te no uchi – The hand position necessary for proper cutting.

Teito – The "ready" position of carrying the sword in which the left arm is bent and the sword is at the obi.

Tenka – "All below heaven." The term used to describe the Japanese "nation" during feudal times.

Tenka taihei – The "great national peace" imposed by the Tokugawa Shogunate.

To – Sword.

Togarashi – A sword polisher. Much more is implied than just that. The togarashi shapes, sharpens, and polishes the blade, thus revealing the artistry within the steel. He also serves as historian and appraiser of swords. It requires a 15-year apprenticeship, and only a few are trusted with the national treasures.

Tokugawa – A feudal clan from the Kanto region that made up the shogunate based in Edo that lasted from 1603 to 1868 and resulted in an enforced peace. It restructured the society and the place of the samurai with a resultant loss of martial prowess. The clan was unable to repel the surge of Europeans into Japan, which lead to the Tokugawa downfall and the reinstatement of the emperor as ruler of Japan.

Tokugawa Ieyasu (1542 – 1616) – One of several daimyo who fought to forcibly unify Japan and overthrow the Ashikaga shogunate in the process. Following Nobunaga and Hideyoshi's successes, Ieyasu completed the job with decisive victories at Sekigahara and Osaka Castle. He became the first Tokugawa shogun in 1603, starting the 250 years of the Edo era. He is enshrined at Nikko.

Tokaido – Most famous of the roads between Kyoto and Tokyo by which passed communications between the two courts and daimyo and their entourage, fulfilling their residency requirements during the Edo period. It was the subject of woodcut prints by Hiroshige, among others. The western route through the mountains was called the Tozando.

Torei – A bow to the sword, either independently or as part of the etiquette before or after practice or a demonstration of iaido *(embu)*.

Tosa – A domain on the Pacific side of Shikoku in western Japan whose capital was Kochi. Because of its harbor, Tosa was an important and wealthy center of commerce. While its daimyo clan, Yamanouchi, was loyal to the Tokugawa bakufu many of its lower ranking samurai were zealous imperial loyalists who eventually accomplished the Meiji restoration. The master swordsmen of Tosa played a pivotal role in the development of both jikiden Eishin and Muso Shinden ryu iaido.

Toyotomi Hideyoshi (1536-1598) – From humble origins, he succeeded his lord, Oda Nobunaga, nearly unifying Japan under one command. He is famous for establishing a rigid class structure and disarming the Japanese population. He also initiated two unsuccessful attempts to invade Korea. He set his son up as successor, but the son was killed by Ieyasu

Tokugawa at the siege of Osaka Castle in 1615.

Tsuba – The hand guard between the tsuka and blade. It was made of iron, brass, or other copper alloys. Artworks in their own right, originals are very collectable and command a pretty price.

Tsuka – The handle of a Japanese sword. It was made of wood, covered by ray skin (samé) over which a ribbon of silk, cotton, or leather is laced.

Tsukahara Bokuden (1490 – 1571) – One of the best known of the early 16th century wandering swordsmen. He was born in Kashima, where a kami important to martial arts is enshrined. He was schooled early in Shinto ryu school swordsmanship. He successfully completed three musha shugyo and served as sword instructor to the Ashikaga shoguns.

Tsuka-ito – The ribbon lacing over the samé of the tsuka. It is usually cotton on an iaito, but is often silk or leather on a nihonto.

Tsunetomo Yamamoto (1659 – 1719) – He was a samurai and vassal to Nabeshima Mitsushige of Hizen domain, now modern Saga. When his lord died, he retired to a monastery, and his recollections were collected into *Hidden Leaves* (*Hagakure*). While he seems not to have contributed much of historical importance in his own lifetime, he provided one of the most graphic pictures of 17th century samurai philosophy available to us today.

Tsuneo, Nishioka – Student of shinto muso ryu under Shimizu Takaji, from whom he received mengyo of complete transmission, he currently holds hanshi hachidan by the All Japan Kendo Federation. He is the author of several books and is dedicated to the preservation of the teachings of Shimizu Sensei.

Uchigatana – Early name for katana.

Uchiko – A mild abrasive powder used to remove old oil from a nihonto during cleaning.

Ueshiba Morihei (1883 – 1969) – Founder of aikido, the way of harmony of the spirit. Born a sickly child and later suffering from beriberi, he was encouraged toward athletics. He performed a distinguished service in the Russo-Japanese War where he was found to excel at bayonet. He continued to study martial arts, and at the age of 43 he received an enlightenment concerning love as the foundation of budo. He spent the rest of his life in Iwama farming and developing the techniques of Aikido.

Uesugi Kenshin (1530 – 1578) – Originally Nageo Kagetora, daimyo of the Echigo domain, he offered support to the ill-fated constable of the Kanto region under Ashikaga Takauji, Uesugi Norimasa. After being named Norimasa's heir, he persuaded him to step down as constable and assumed the title himself using the name Uesugi Kenshin. He fought five major battles in Kawanakajima between 1553 and 1564 against Takeda Shingen, who was bent on carving a path to the ocean from his landlocked Kai province.

Uji – Feudal clan.

Ukiyo – Fugitive. A term used in conjunction with the subject of the popular arts of the genroku period at the beginning of the 18th century. It refers to the actors, musicians, singers, and "ladies" of that period.

Ura – "Hidden side." In reference to a katana, the side toward the body of the iaidoka; with reference to a kata, the hidden meaning within the obvious technique.

Wakizashi – The "helper sword," of between 1 and 2 shaku that was the smaller (shoto) of the daisho pair. It could be worn alone by classes other than the samurai.

Waza –Technique.

Yagyu – A family of minor nobles from around Nara who developed a style of swordsmanship called shikage-ryu. The elder Muneyoshi and his son Muninori gave a demonstration of their technique to Tokugawa Ieyasu in 1594, including a barehanded defense called "no sword" (muto). He so impressed Ieyasu that his son was made sword instructor to the Tokugawa clan. Later members of the clan, notably Munenori's son, Jubei Mitsuyoshi, are the source of many tales of subterfuge on behalf of the Tokugawa bakufu. They serve as the villains in the fiction story *Lone Wolf*.

Yagyu Munenori (1571-1646) – The inheritor of Muneyoshi's yagyu shinkage-ryu, he served as a sword instructor to three Tokugawa shogun and compiled the philosophy of the school in the manuscript *The Sword and the Mind* (*Heiho Kadensho*).

Yamabushi – Members of a mystical sect of Buddhism who went (and still go) on austere mountain pilgrimages or marathons. Minamoto Yoshitsune and his entourage are disguised as yamabushi in the tale of *The Men Who Tread on the Tiger's Tail*, an adaptation of a No and later, Kabuki favorite.

Yamamoto Kansuke (1492-1561) – The chief of staff and the crafty strategist of Takeda Shingen. He was reportedly handicapped in some way. When he made a fatal error of judgment in the fourth battle with the Uesugi at Hachimanbara, he avenged himself by falling in battle. His story is immortalized in the film, *Samurai Banners*.

Yamanouchi – The clan that served as daimyos for Tosa after the battle of Sekigahara ousting the Chosokabe clan. They remained loyal to the Tokugawa bakufu. Yamanouchi Yodo was a direct antagonist of Sakamoto Ryoma and the other shishi during the birth of the Meiji Restoration, and yet he was instrumental in convincing the last Tokugawa shogun to retire peacefully.

Yamato – An early name for Japan. The domain established in the Kinai Plain during the original spread of Japanese from Kyushu in an attempt to find more fertile farmland. Also, one of the five koto sword styles.

Yari – Spear. The yari came in to its own as a battle weapon with the massed troops of ashigaru assembled by Takeda Shingen.

Yasukuni – A Shinto shrine and national memorial dedicated all Japan's domestic and foreign war dead. It was originally designed to house the spirits of those who died overthrowing the Tokugawa regime. It was subsequently co-opted by the ultranationalists. Among those enshrined there are 14 World War II war criminals executed by the Allies, including Hideki Tojo, along with more than 2 million other Japanese war dead. The shrine sponsored smiths who made traditional blades styled after koto. Each used a name starting with Yasu (e.g., Yasushige, Yasuoki). Yasukuni blades are some of the few of the Showa Period considered as gendaito by collectors.

Yokohama – A seaport on Tokyo Bay between Tokyo and Yakusuka in which foreigners were allowed to remain in strongholds during the Edo Period. It is where Commodore Perry landed.

Yoko-men – An overhead strike to the side of the head.

***Yojimbo* –** A 1961 film directed by Akira Kurosawa, and starring Toshiro Mifune as a ronin who confronts two warring gangs in a village.

Yoroi – The boxy armor used by samurai in battle during the period when they were on horseback and the favored weapon was the bow.

Yoshimoto Imagawa – He lost his head to the greatly outnumbered troops of Oda Nobunaga at the battle of Okehazama in 1560.

Yoshikawa, Eiji – A contemporary Japanese novelist whose techniques have been influenced entirely by Japanese classics. His books include *The Heike Story*, *Musashi*, and *Taiko*.

Zanshin – Literally, "continuing mind." The constant awareness of an iaidoka to new challenges from his environment.

Zazen – The act of sitting meditation. Zazen is a critical feature of most Zen Buddhist sects. It is performed in seiza or one of the lotus postures with one of several hand positions and often begins with a regulation of breathing to facilitate smooth ki flow throughout the body.

Zen – A branch of Buddhism adopted by the Japanese from the Chinese. It generally considers the here-and-now to be all that is important. Enlightenment comes from truly experiencing common tasks. Some branches use koan (cryptic riddles) to break the initiates from logical thought. It generally discourages intellectualism, acknowledges fate as a given, supports monasticism, and considers death a part of life.

Zen Nihon Iaido Renmei (ZNIR) – All Japan Iaido Federation, another governing body of Iaido in Japan besides the ZNKR.

Zen Nihon Kendo Renmei (ZNKR) – All Japan Kendo Federation. The major governing body of kendo and iaido in Japan since the end of World War II. It was this organization that developed seitei waza.

SELECT BIBLIOGRAPHY

Babin, Richard W. "Amateur Sayacraft: Scabbards in the Making." *Journal of Asian Martial Arts* 9 (2000).

Brooks, Ray. *Blowing Zen: Finding an Authentic Life*. Tiburon, Calif.: H. J. Kramer, 2000.

Cooper, Jeff. *To Ride, Shoot Straight, and Speak the Truth*. Boulder, Colo.: Paladin Press, 1998.

Craig, Darrell. *Iai: The Art of Drawing the Sword*. Boston: Charles E. Tuttle Co., 1988.

De Cristoforo, V. K. *May Sky: There Is Always Tomorrow*. Los Angeles: Sun & Moon Press, 1997.

Friday, Karl F., and Seki Humitake. *Legacies of the Sword*. Honolulu: University of Hawaii Press, 1997.

Fujitani, T. *Splendid Monarchy: Power and Pageantry in Modern Japan*. Berkeley: University of California Press, 1984.

Fuller, Richard, and Ron Gregory. *Military Swords of Japan 1868 to 1945*. London: Arms and Armour Press, 1993.

Hillsborough, Romulus. *Ryoma: Life of a Renaissance Samurai*. San Francisco: Ridgeback Press, 1999.

Hunter, Janet E. *Concise History of Modern Japanese History*. Berkeley: University of California Press, 1984.

Ibn Khaldoun. *Muqaddimah*. Translated by Franz Rosenthal. Princeton: Princeton University Press, 1967.

Kishida, Tom. *Yasukuni-to: Tradition and Ideal Beauty*. Translated by Kenji Mishina. Tokyo: Yuzankaku Publishing Co., 2002.

Kornfield, Jack. *After the Ecstasy, the Laundry*. New York: Bantam Books, 2000.

Lo, Benjamin P. J., Martin Inn, Susan Foe, and Robert Amacker. *The Essence of T'ai Chi Ch'uan: The Literary Tradition*. Berkeley, Calif.: North Atlantic Books, 1979.

Lowry, Dave. *Persimmon Wind*. Boston: Charles E. Tuttle Co., 1997.

__________. *Sword and Brush: The Spirit of the Martial Arts*. Boston: Shambhala, 1995.

__________. *Bokken: Art of the Japanese Sword*. Santa Clara, Calif.: Ohara Publications, 1986.

Mishima, Yukio. *Runaway Horses*. New York: Vintage Books, 1973.

Morris, G. *Martial Arts Madness: A User's Guide to the Esoteric Martial Arts*. Berkeley, Calif.: Frog, Ltd., 1998.

Murphy, Michael. *The Kingdom of the Shivas Irons*. New York: Broadway Books, 1997.

Musashi, Miyamoto. *A Book of Five Rings*. Woodstock, N.Y.: Overlook Press, 1982.

Nagayama, Kokan. *The Connoisseur's Book of Japanese Swords*. Translated by Kenji Mishina. Tokyo: Kodansha International, 1998.

One Hundred Masterpieces from the Collection of Walter A. Compton. Catalog edited by Sarah Izzard. New York: Christie, Manson & Woods, 1992.

Pressfield, Steven. *Gates of Fire: An Epic Novel of the Battle of Thermopylae.* New York: Bantam Books, 1998.

Ratti, Oscar, and Adele Westbrook. *Secrets of the Samurai.* Boston: Charles E. Tuttle Co., 1973.

Reed, William. *Ki: A Practical Guide for Westerners.* New York: Japan Publications, 1986.

Sato, Hiroaki, and Burton Watson. *From the Country of Eight Islands.* New York: Columbia University Press, 1986.

Sato, Kanzan Earle Joe. *The Japanese Sword.* Tokyo: Kodansha International, 1983.

Shah, Idries. *The Way of the Sufi.* New York, Dutton, 1970.

Shimabukuro, Masayuki, and Leonard J. Pellman. *Flashing Steel: Mastering Eishin-Ryu.* Berkeley, Calif.: Frog, Ltd., 1995.

Sudo, Phillip Toshio. *Zen Guitar.* New York: Fireside Books, 1998.

Suino, Nicklaus. *The Art of Japanese Swordsmanship.* New York: Weatherhill, 1994.

Taylor, Kimberley. "The History of Iaido: A Japanese Sword Art." *Journal of Asian Martial Arts* 2 (1993).

Taylor, Kimberley, and Goyo Ohmi. "The Omori Ryu: A History and Explanation." *Journal of Asian Martial Arts* 6 (1997).

Tsuneo, Nishioka. "Uchidachi and Shidachi," *Sword & Spirit: Classical Warrior Traditions of Japan, Vol. 2.* Edited by Diane Skoss. Berkeley Heights, N.J.: Koryu Books, 1999.

Turnbull, Steven R. *The Lone Samurai and the Martial Arts.* New York: Sterling Publications, 1992.

Wagner, Gordon, and Donn Draeger. *Japanese Swordsmanship: Technique and Practice.* New York, Weatherhill, 1991.

Yagyu, Munimori. *The Sword and the Mind.* Woodstock, N.Y.: Overlook Press, 1985.

Yamamoto, Tsunetomo. *Hagakure: The Book of the Samurai.* Translated by William S. Wilson. Tokyo: Kodansha International, 1979.

Yoshikawa, Eiji. *The Heike Story.* Boston: Charles E. Tuttle Co., 1956.

Yumoto, John M. *The Samurai Sword: A Handbook.* Boston: Charles E. Tuttle Co., 1958.

All Japan Kendo Federation Iai - New Edition
(0nly covers first ten Seitei Waza)
新版　　全日本剣道連盟居合
平成７年１１月１０日　第４刷発伝
監　修（財）全全日本剣道連盟
編　纂　　　　剣道日本編集部
発行者　　　　森　田　親　男
印刷製本　抹式会社東京印書館
発伝所スキーツヤーナル抹式会社
ISBN4-7899-2035-6c0075

Nakayama Hakudo Muso Shinden Ryu Iai by Kamimoto Eiichi
Five Volume set
帥　中山はくど先生口述
夢想神伝流居合
平成元年十一月二十八日　第二刷発行
編者著　紙本榮一
印刷製本　抹式会社東京印書館

Muso Shinden Ryu Iaido by Yamatsuta Jukichi
夢想神伝流　居合道
平成１１年８月２０日　甫版発行
者著　　山蔦重吉
発行者　今堀信明
発行所　抹式会社　愛隆堂 (Airyudo)
印刷　モリモト印刷抹式会社
製本　抹式会社右毛製本所
ISBN4-7502-0160-X

ABOUT THE AUTHOR

Richard W. Babin is a practicing head and neck surgeon specializing in cancers of the mouth, throat, and neck, extensive sinus disease, and reconstruction of the face, jaw, neck, and aero digestive tract. Born, raised, and trained on the West Coast, he has expressed a lifelong interest in things oriental. His father was a wooden-boat builder, his mother an accomplished artist in the classical Chinese style.

After completing his residency at UCLA he served two years active duty in the U.S. Air Force as chief of head and neck surgery at Maxwell Field during the Vietnam conflict. He then joined the faculty of medicine at the University of Iowa and later became professor and chairman of the department at the University of Tennessee. He authored 65 professional articles in refereed journals including original vestibular research, contributed to 8 textbooks of medicine, trained 40 surgical residents, and served as sponsor and research advisor for 5 visiting Egyptian resident surgeons. He left academic medicine in 1990 for a rural private practice but remains on the university clinical faculty, teaching family practice residents in his office and hospital.

Upon arriving in Memphis in 1983 he joined the U.S. Navy Reserve, serving as officer in charge of a reserve detachment and later as executive officer of a 500-bed reserve fleet hospital, rising to the rank of navy captain. He also trained with and provided medical support for Golf Company of the 3/23 Marines, accompanying them on landing exercises in the Philippines and desert warfare training at Twentynine Palms, California. During the Gulf War, he singlehandedly medically cleared the entire company for mobilization, for which he was awarded the Navy Commendation Medal. He also qualified as expert in pistol and rifle and served as a relief surgeon at Yokusuka, Japan, for 5 weeks. He taught numerous classes of Advanced Trauma Life Support at both Fort Sam Houston and Bethesda Naval Hospital.

His interest in the martial arts began with several years of judo in the 1960s in San Francisco. Upon entering private practice he began studying yang-style taiji, which he still pursues. He has practiced muso shinden ryu iaido for eight years and has been awarded the rank of Sandan by the All U.S. Kendo Federation. He is a regular competitor in the annual National Iaido Championship. Despite his busy practice he currently practices aikido, iaido, and taiji roughly 10 hours a week. He is a collector and restorer of Japanese swords and has published an article on the manufacture of sheaths (saya) in the *Journal of Asian Martial Arts*. He has submitted two others on the manufacture of blade-collars (habaki) and one entitled "Balance and the Martial Arts." He has been invited to lecture the public on the latter topic locally on several occasions.

Babin lives with Nancy, his wife of 36 years, and three Birman cats in Memphis. His other interests include bluegrass and Western guitar, which he has played for 40 years, the Japanese flute (shakuhachi), fishing, and firearms of all types. He has been a life member of the National Rifle Association since 1975.